The Failure of America's Foreign Wars

Edited by
Richard M. Ebeling
and
Jacob G. Hornberger

THE FUTURE
OF FREEDOM
FOUNDATION

Fairfax, Virginia

ISBN 0-9640447-5-7 (hb.)— ISBN 0-9640447-6-5 (pbk.)
Copyright © 1996

The Future of Freedom Foundation
11350 Random Hills Road, Suite 800
Fairfax, Virginia 22030

Library of Congress
Catalog Card Number: 96-083955

Printed in the United States of America

Contents

Founded in 1989, *The Future of Freedom Foundation is a tax-exempt educational foundation that presents an uncompromising moral, philosophical, and economic case for individual freedom, private property, and limited government. The Foundation aims to influence a shift in thinking away from the welfare-state, managed-economy philosophy toward the private-property, free-market philosophy.*

Most of the essays in this volume appeared in the monthly publication of The Foundation, Freedom Daily. *Subscribers come from thirty countries. The price for a one-year subscription to* Freedom Daily *is $15 ($20 foreign).*

Preface

For over one hundred years, the American way of life was unique: no income taxation, welfare, Social Security, Medicare, Medicaid, public schooling, economic regulations, or welfare. Except for allowing slavery, government's role was primarily limited to protecting people from the violence of others, both foreign and domestic, and providing a judiciary by which people could peacefully resolve their disputes. People were free to live their lives the way they chose, as long as they did so peacefully. They could accumulate unlimited amounts of wealth and decide for themselves what to do with it. The result was the most prosperous, healthy, and charitable period in history.

But perhaps the most important aspect of the American philosophy during the nineteenth century was the American people's refusal to permit their government officials to engage in foreign wars. Our ancestors had learned the lessons of history—that war is the greatest enemy of liberty and the best friend to omnipotent government.

They also understood that people throughout the world had been fighting for centuries. The best contribution Americans could make to the world would be to stay out of the conflicts and instead be a model that other nations could emulate. Thus, Americans limited their government to protecting them from invasion and prohibited their president from engaging in war without a congressionally approved declaration of war.

Unfortunately, with the advent of the welfare state, twentieth-century Americans abandoned the ideals and principles of their ancestors. The welfare state brought us paternalistic government that takes care of us, watches over us, plans and directs our lives, and plunders and redistributes our wealth. The welfare state brought all of the things our ancestors warned us about: loss of liberty, exorbitant taxes, and swarms of bureaucrats who harass us and eat out our substance.

The abandonment also took place in foreign affairs. If the government could plan and provide welfare for millions of Americans, why stop there? Why not do the same for Europeans as well as for people all over the world?

It began with the Spanish-American War in 1898. But the truly fateful step took place with America's intervention into World War I. The American government decided that it was time to end the endless series of European wars, once and for all. So Americans were conscripted and sent overseas to ensure that that would be the last European war anyone would ever see. Through American intervention, the world would finally be made safe for democracy. It would be the war to end all future wars.

Alas, it would not be. Instead, American intervention so dramatically altered the balance of power in Europe that a decimated Germany became fertile ground for the rise of Adolf Hitler a little over a decade later. Before long, U.S. government officials were clamoring for entry into World War II. This time, they said, they would get it right.

As in World War I, Germany was again decimated. But the aftermath was not exactly what the global planners had envisioned: East Germany and Eastern Europe, including Poland, Czechoslovakia, and Hungary, suffered under totalitarian, communist dictatorship (as distinct from totalitarian, Nazi dictatorship)—and continued to do so for over fifty years. Americans who had lost loved ones on the European battlefields were consoled by American public officials with: "At least they died so that Eastern Europe could be under the domination of our communist allies rather than the Nazis."

Then came decades of a Cold War against America's World War II allies—the communists—with the attendant rise in the modern military-industrial complex. There were also hot wars in Korea and Vietnam, in which tens of thousands of American men and women were killed or injured. And, of course, there have been the hundreds of other smaller interventions and wars throughout the world. Each time, Americans were assured this war or this intervention would help bring a peaceful and harmonious world.

The result was the exact opposite. Perpetual war brought death, destruction, and a loss of liberty for the American people. It never brought a lasting peace in the world.

On the eve of the twenty-first century, Americans are faced with competing visions of where we want our nation to go. On the one hand, we have the vision of America's Founders: individual liberty, private property, and limited government, in which there is no welfare, Social Security, income taxation, Medicare, Medicaid, regulations, subsidies, and the like. Equally important, no foreign wars.

On the other hand, we have the vision of the twentieth-century public officials: ever-increasing taxation, regulations, and political plunder. And, of course, body bags and caskets as part of their attempt to remake the world into one gigantic welfare state.

The stakes are too high for any American to ignore. For with foreign wars, not only do we have taxation and regulation, we also have the specter of funerals and wheelchairs for husbands, fathers, sons, wives, mothers, and daughters.

It is time for the American people to recognize that our ancestors were right and that twentieth-century public officials were wrong. It is time to recapture the principles of our Founders. It is time to lead the world out of the welfare-state darkness in which it has plunged during most of our lifetime. And the time to do so is now.

—Jacob G. Hornberger
Founder and President
The Future of Freedom Foundation

Introduction

The twentieth century has been the era of the social engineer. Regardless of the labels the social engineer has chosen to use at various times and in different places—communism, socialism, fascism, Nazism, social liberalism, welfare statism, interventionism, one-worldism—they all have added up to the same thing: individuals and society are to be reshaped and designed according to the specifications of the social engineer.

The presumption is that individuals—left to themselves, in peaceful and free interaction with their fellow men—will create social outcomes less desirable and more harmful than if society is made to conform to the pattern the social engineer has constructed for it. The social engineer claims to know the "real needs" of the people far better than those people themselves. He is confident that he understands the "real causes" of human problems and conflicts much better than most people because those people are misguided by ignorance or blinded by their own narrow, selfish interests.

And the social engineer is positive that he knows the "real" or "better" solutions to the difficulties and tragedies of the human condition, in comparison with the solutions individuals might find within themselves and in voluntary agreement, compromise, and association with their fellow men.

Since men in society often choose to act and associate in ways different from how the social engineer thinks they should, the engineer turns to the state as the vehicle to make people conform to his plan for them. Through the power of the state, the social engineer tries to remake the institutions of society, redirect human behavior into channels he thinks are better, and redistribute the social outcomes into the patterns that he considers to be superior.

In its more brutal and comprehensive form, social engineering has led to the concentration camps of Nazi Germany and the Gulag in the Soviet Union. In both these societies, the individual was stripped of all human autonomy and personal dignity. In the Western countries, it has led to extensive economic regulation, income redistribution, the undermining of the traditional institutions of civil society (the family, freedom of association, community-oriented self-help), and moral paternalism by the state. Here, too, the individual's sense of personal independence and moral responsibility have been weakened, as the state and its bureaucracies have asserted authority over increasing corners of everyone's life.

In a century dominated by the vision of the social engineer, it should have come as no surprise that international relations and global conflicts would be influenced by the same ideas that guided the domestic affairs of the nations of the world. Both the Russian revolutionary vanguards of the bright, new, communist future and the German racial purist of the National Socialist new order in Europe could not stop themselves at their own borders. Marxian ideology required the reshaping of the class relationships in every society around the world. Nazi doctrine required the hierarchical subordination of inferior peoples to a master race.

America, too, had its global calling, according to the social engineers. America should not merely be a "beacon of freedom" that would be, through its allegiance to its traditional principles of individual liberty and a free, self-governing society, an example and a model for multitudes of others in other lands living in tyranny and yearning to breathe free. No, this older, nineteenth-century conception of America's contribution to the betterment of the world was discarded in the twentieth century. According to Woodrow Wilson, it was to make the world safe for democracy; according to Franklin D. Roosevelt, it was to give the world a New Deal; according to every president since World War II, it was to supply "leadership" and to be a global policeman in the name of the "free world" against totalitarian tyranny.

The social engineers thrust America into the global bonfires of the insanities. Hundreds of thousands of Americans were sacrificed on the altar of two world wars and several regional conflicts in the name of world peace. Traditional American freedoms were restricted or sometimes lost in the name of national security. The honest, hard-earned wealth of millions of Americans was taxed away and consumed in military combat, war preparedness, and foreign-aid give-aways to socialist and interventionist governments and to third-world despots willing to declare their loyalty to the West for the right price.

In the name of "freedom," the U.S. government trained the secret police of other countries in the fine art of surveillance and interrogation—techniques that many governments in those countries then used against their own citizens and in matters having nothing to do with "fighting communism." The U.S. government overthrew other governments and gave moral sanction to the assassination of foreign leaders and the execution of the "politically unreliable." In the name of "free enterprise," the U.S. government subsidized public works projects, financed nationalized industries in various parts of the world, and participated in compulsory land redistributions.

In the eyes of the social engineers, all of these policies were necessary at the time and essential for the fulfillment of America's active participation in the world. Peoples in other lands did not realize that their backward traditions and institutions were breeding grounds for the enemies of global freedom. They had to be coerced into new ways for their own good and that of the rest of the world. Foreign governments would not follow American global leadership and had to be threatened or bribed to do so. Many Americans were too ignorant to understand that the only way to fight communism was to foster mild socialism and welfare redistributivism—and that their incomes would have to be taxed to pay for these farseeing, progressive policies.

Even now, with the end of the Cold War and the collapse of communism, the American social engineers continue with their calls for American globalism. Before, America had to be actively involved politically and militarily in the world because, it was argued, there was no other major power to stand up to the Soviet threat. Now, when the Soviet Union is gone, it is argued that America is the only "superpower" left on the face of the earth and that the world needs the United States to provide political and military leadership to prevent regional conflicts and global chaos. It seems that no matter how much the world may change, the social engineers can always unearth new rationales for their continuing desire to meddle in other people's affairs, whether at home or abroad.

It is time to commit the social engineer and his meddling mentality to the dustbin of history. Social engineering at home has long shown its moral and practical bankruptcy. Woodrow Wilson's New Freedoms, Franklin Roosevelt's New Deal, Harry Truman's Fair

Deal, John F. Kennedy's New Frontier, and Lyndon Johnson's Great Society did not make America a freer country, a more just society, or a more prosperous nation. Their planning schemes and intervention-ist programs politicized American society, diminished the freedoms of the American people, perpetuated poverty, and created new political favoritisms.

Nor have America's global meddling and foreign intervention-ist adventures made the world free or secure. Woodrow Wilson's intervention in World War I helped to create the conditions for the old order in Europe to be replaced with communism in Russia, fascism in Italy, and eventually Hitler and Nazism in Germany. Franklin Roosevelt's intervention in World War II replaced Nazi tyranny with Soviet domination and terror in half of Europe; and it substituted Japanese imperialism in East Asia with the communist conquest of China as well as Marxist regimes in half of Korea and Vietnam. Having helped create the conditions for communist victory in those lands, the United States then found itself fighting two bloody wars in Asia in the post–World War II era—against the very tyrannies its earlier intervention had helped to bring to power. In both the Korean and Vietnam wars, the communists prevailed against the American social engineers and their sophisticated "fine-tuning" conceptions of "limited war" and "controlled escalation."

And so far in the new post–Cold War era, the social engineers continue to try to make the world over in their own image through military intervention in Panama, the Middle East, Somalia, Haiti, and the former Yugoslavia. In Panama, one corrupt regime was merely substituted for another, although one more to the liking of the people in Washington; in the Middle East, an undemocratic govern-ment was reestablished in Kuwait, and the same tyrant continued to rule in Baghdad after American airpower successfully killed thou-sands of unfortunate Iraqi soldiers and civilians; Somalia has re-turned to the same clan conflict that prevailed before U.N. interven-tion under U.S. military leadership; in Haiti, a brutal regime has been replaced by another, headed by a mentally unstable closet Marxist; and in the former Yugoslavia, the United States and its European allies bomb those they label aggressors and send tens of thousands of their military forces to Bosnia as "peacemakers" in a conflict that is grounded in centuries-old animosities between ethnic and religious groups who possess no refined notion of individual liberty, private property rights, or the Western idea of the rule of law.

The social engineer's typical response is to argue that the outcomes were better than if America had remained in its archaic isolation of the past and that the social engineers have always meant well—that they had "good intentions." It's just that things got out of hand—or that other peoples and governments would not go along with the peace plan—or that the wrong people were in charge—or that they had not had enough of other people's money to make it turn out all right—or . . .

Of course, we can never know for certain what would have happened if the United States had not undertaken the foreign interventionist path it followed in the twentieth century. That always must remain speculative "what if" history. But it is no different from any retrospective evaluation that any of us makes in deciding, as best we can, whether we have made the right choices and followed the best courses of action—when we take stock of the things we've done and try to decide whether there are things we can learn from our past actions so as to not make the same types of mistakes in the future.

If the British had not been convinced that Woodrow Wilson would finally bring America into the First World War, isn't it possible that the belligerents might have settled for some type of compromise peace in 1916 or early 1917? Perhaps, then, we would have been saved from the scourge that followed from the successful Bolshevik Revolution in Russia at the end of 1917. Perhaps the post-war conditions in Germany would have been significantly different, possibly preventing Hitler from coming to power.

If Churchill had not worked so hard for American intervention in the Second World War, and if Franklin Roosevelt had not been so driven to bring America into the war, isn't it possible that there might have been a compromise peace signed in the summer of 1940? Yes, it would have left Hitler in power in the center of Europe for the time being, but, maybe, the Nazis would have then been able to avail themselves of their original "final solution" to the "Jewish problem," which was to expel the Jews in Europe to Madagascar. Even as barbaric as that would have been, would it not have been a better "solution" than the reality of the death camps? And if Hitler still had then turned east against his partner-in-crime—Stalin—and attacked the Soviet Union, might not, maybe, the two totalitarian giants have exhausted and destroyed themselves, leaving the door open for the peoples occupied by both the Nazis and the Soviets to eventually free themselves?

If Roosevelt had been more willing to find a compromise with Japan in 1941, isn't it possible that the attack on Pearl Harbor might never have occurred? Yes, any such compromise in East Asia prob-ably would have left Japan in a strong position, but such a compro-mise might have ended the Japanese war in China; and, maybe,

China, not reduced to that state of political and economic chaos as actually existed in the period right after 1945, might not have been conquered by the Chinese communists under Mao Zedong.

Who can say with any high degree of certainty that this "alternative history" would have been impossible or worse than the one actually experienced? The fundamental delusion of the social engineer is his unswerving confidence that he knows how to set the world right, regardless of the expense to others or the consequences for society as a whole. The twentieth century has demonstrated what a fantasy his belief really is.

This century of the social engineer is coming to an end. Another century is right before us. It is time to change course. It is time to find our way back to the path of individual liberty, limited government, and nonintervention in both domestic and foreign affairs. The Future of Freedom Foundation exists to help in this endeavor to return America back to its original noninterventionist roots.

The essays in the present volume, *The Failure of America's Foreign Wars*, critically evaluate the path the United States has followed over the last century. They explain the ideas that have drawn America into numerous wars and conflicts around the world and analyze the disastrous consequences that have resulted from these foreign adventures. And they articulate an alternative vision of a foreign policy more consistent with the premises of a free society. Most of the essays originally appeared in the pages of The Future of Freedom Foundation's monthly publication, *Freedom Daily*. They have been brought together in the hope that they can assist in bringing about that freer and better world that can be ours in the twenty-first century.

—*Richard M. Ebeling*
Vice President of Academic Affairs
The Future of Freedom Foundation

1

Dismantling America's Military Empire

by Jacob G. Hornberger

As President Dwight D. Eisenhower warned us thirty years ago, the military-industrial complex is a menace and a threat to the freedom and well-being of the American people. The time has come to dismantle America's military empire.

Since the end of World War II, the proponents of conscription, taxation, military spending, and war repeatedly told us, "The only reason we favor these deprivations of liberty is to stop the communist threat. If there were no communist threat, America's warfare state could be ended."

The Soviet Union is now dismantled. The communist threat to America has ended. Yet, what are the proponents of the warfare state now saying? "The military budget must be reduced somewhat, but it is necessary for the United States to maintain its military predominance in the world to combat the new enemies of 'uncertainty and unpredictability.' Moreover, those who have become dependent on military spending have a right to continue receiving it."

With the fall of communism, Americans have a unique opportunity: not simply to *reduce* their government's military budget but to *fully and completely dismantle their nation's military-industrial complex.*

From the time our nation was founded until the Franklin D. Roosevelt administration, the American people, by and large, favored a policy of nonintervention in the affairs of other nations. In fact, until 1941, the party platforms of both the Republicans and Democrats opposed United States governmental involvement in foreign wars.

After World War II, those who had benefited from the military largess—in both the public and private sectors—were panicked. They knew that after all previous wars, the American people had demanded a dismantling of the military complex that the wars had produced.

But the communist threat gave new life to the military-industrial complex at the end of World War II. For in order to avoid conquest by the communists, they said, it was necessary to use their same tactics—including the continual and constant buildup of military forces.

Today, at the end of the Cold War, those within the military-industrial complex are as panicked as they were at the end of previous wars. For they know that the possibility looms that the American people are going to discover the nonmilitaristic heritage of their ancestors—and demand not simply a reduction in American military might, but instead the dismantling of it.

Is the primary threat to the American people one of taxation, conscription, and foreign wars? These are certainly a large part of the problem. Governmental spending for military purposes constitutes just about the largest percentage of total governmental expenditures. Moreover, the hundreds of thousands of people who benefit, directly and indirectly, from the military largess have the fiercest and most effective special-interest lobbyists in Washington. And periodic foreign wars waged by our government against new official enemies are now accepted as part of the everyday lives of the American people.

But taxation, conscription, and foreign wars are not the biggest threats arising from a huge, standing military force. The real threat—as our American and British ancestors understood so well—is that, at some point, the guns might be pointed not at foreigners, but at us—the American people.

I realize that some of you already are saying to yourselves, "There is no way that those in our government, and especially those in the Pentagon, would ever use their military force against the American people."

But let us consider a scenario. Assume the American people decide to end America's welfare-warfare state, regulated-economy way of life. Pursuant to the Constitution, they persuade two-thirds of their state legislatures to call a constitutional convention to consider amendments to the Constitution which abolish: income taxation and the Internal Revenue Service, all welfare and regulatory laws, all immigration and trade restrictions, all foreign troops and foreign aid, conscription, the standing army (including the Pentagon), and virtually every bureaucracy of the U.S. government.

Most Americans innocently believe that the Congress would meekly obey and call the constitutional convention, as required by the Constitution. But Americans might well discover what foreigners have discovered: that when politicians, bureaucrats and bureaucracies are attacked, they fight back.

How could they retaliate? Imagine the following pronouncement by the president of the United States:

> My fellow Americans—as a result of the constitutional convention which the state legislatures have recently called for, our nation is in deep crisis. National security has never been more at stake. Abolishing America's welfare state, regulated economy, and standing army would result in conflict, chaos, and unemployment, both here and abroad. Therefore, pursuant to the authority granted to me by the Congress, I hereby declare a national emergency. The government shall continue as is throughout this emergency. The constitutional convention will not be called, and the Constitution will not be amended. Income taxes will continue to be collected and strictly enforced by the IRS. All citizens will immediately surrender their gold and their weapons. Domestic order will be preserved by the FBI, the CIA, the BATF, the DEA, and the armed forces of the United States and the United Nations. These agencies are hereby vested with the authority, upheld many years ago by the Supreme Court, to round up potential dissidents, place them and their families in internment camps, and seize their properties. Acting together, our nation will survive the extreme acts of the state legislatures. Acting together, we shall preserve our freedom.

Unlikely? Has the U.S. government ever declared "national emergencies" and jailed potential dissidents during those "emergencies"? Has it ever ordered troops into America's cities to maintain "order"? Has it ever fired on and killed domestic dissenters? Has it ever incarcerated large groups of people who had not been accused of any crimes? Has it ever confiscated private property?

3

One of these days, the American people might very well discover that American politicians and bureaucrats will violently resist losing their parasitic grip on the citizenry. And one can only wonder where the proponents of gun control will be standing (or hiding) then.

But would you have us turn toward isolationism? it is asked. The goal is to isolate the U.S. government, not the American people. For the latter, not the former, are our nation's greatest diplomats of peace and friendship. If trade and immigration restrictions were abolished, the American people would not be isolated from the rest of the world—on the contrary, they would be interacting with people all over the globe.

But wouldn't this cause Americans to become more dependent on people in other nations? Absolutely—just as foreigners would become more dependent on us. And it is these interdependencies that we should value and cherish, for they are the greatest deterrents to the mother's milk of the military-industrial complex—conflict and war.

But what about foreign tyrants? Shouldn't our government act as judge, jury, and executioner to put them down? No! If Americans are upset over foreign tyranny, they can risk their own lives and fortunes to help oppose the tyrants. No government has any legitimate role in interfering with the affairs of other nations.

Today, the Pentagon sees America as a new Roman Empire—with American politicians and bureaucrats ruling the world through military might. For the military-industrial complex, the empire means bigger budgets and more power. But for us—the citizenry, the empire holds a darker destiny: death, destruction, taxation, enslavement, impoverishment, and collapse.

Our government was founded to protect the United States from attack, not to rule the world through force of arms. The possibility of any nation attacking our country in the foreseeable future is virtually nonexistent. Windows of opportunity do not often repeat themselves. Americans should "seize the day" by dismantling not only their welfare state but their military empire as well.

This essay originally appeared in the July 1992 issue of Freedom Daily, *published by The Future of Freedom Foundation.*

2

Foreign Policy and Foreign Wars

by Richard M. Ebeling

W hen the Founding Fathers wrote and then defended the case for passage of the Constitution in 1787–1788, they did so with a strong belief in the natural rights of man—rights that Thomas Jefferson had so eloquently expressed in the Declaration of Independence in 1776. But their idealism was tempered with stark realism, based on historical knowledge and personal experience about both human nature and the nature of governments.

The separation of legislative, executive, and judicial powers was considered essential if the human inclination toward political abuse of power was to be prevented. "No political truth is certainly of greater intrinsic value, or is stamped with the authority of more enlightened patrons of liberty," stated James Madison in *The Federalist Papers*, "than that . . . the accumulation of all power, legislative, executive and judiciary, in the same hands, whether of one, a few, or many, and whether hereditary, self-appointed, or elective, may justly be pronounced the very definition of tyranny."

Division of power and responsibilities, therefore, was seen as an essential—though neither a perfect nor guaranteed—tool to assure that the freedom and property of individuals would not become political plunder to be devoured by either majorities or minorities.

Issues concerning war and peace and individual liberty were of deep concern to the Founding Fathers for the same reason. When the matter came up at the convention as to which branch of government would have the authority to "make war," disagreement arose. Pierce Butler of South Carolina wanted that power to reside in the president, who, he said, "will have all the requisite qualities." James Madison and Elbridge Gerry of Massachusetts were for "leaving to the Executive the power to repel sudden attacks" but proposed changing the wording to "declare" rather than "make war," and then only with the approval of both Houses of Congress. Oliver Ellsworth of Connecticut agreed, saying that "it should be more easy to get out of war than into it." George Mason of Virginia also was "against giving the power of war to the Executive, because [he was] not safely to be trusted with it." Mason "was for clogging rather than facilitating war."

Thus, in the final, ratified Constitution, the Congress, in Article 1, Section 8, was given the sole authority, "to Declare War," while the President, in Article II, Section 2, was made "Commander in Chief of the Army and Navy of the United States, and the Militia of the several States, when called into the actual service of the United States." Civilian authority over the military was established, with constitutionally divided power over its application in war: Congress declared war, and the president oversaw its execution.

The Founding Fathers possessed no misconceptions about the potentially aggressive nature of governments toward their neighbors. John Jay, in *The Federalist Papers*, insightfully enumerated the various motives, rationales, and passions that had led nations down the road to war through the ages.

But neither did they have any illusions that Americans could be any less susceptible to similar motives and passions. The Constitution, through a division of powers, was meant to put procedural hurdles and delays in the way before the passions of the moment could result in declarations of war and the initiation of hostilities against other nations.

Yet, in spite of these constitutional restraints, the United States has participated in four foreign wars in the twentieth century—two world wars, the Korean "police action," and the Vietnam conflict— and in three of these, the United States was neither directly attacked nor threatened by a foreign enemy. Why, then, did we intervene?

The answer lies in the ideology of the welfare state. First, in the years preceding World War I, and then again in the 1930s, American intellectuals and politicians undertook grand experiments in social engineering. The Progressive Era of Theodore Roosevelt and Woodrow Wilson and the New Deal days of Franklin D. Roosevelt were the crucial decades for the implementation of the politics of government intervention and economic regulation. It was the duty and responsibility of the state to manage, oversee, and control the social and economic affairs of the citizenry.

The social engineers believed that people left alone to manage their own affairs invariably went astray, with the result being poverty, economic exploitation, and social decay. Enlightened leadership, under wise government, would provide the population with the economic prosperity and social harmony that the governmental policymakers knew, in their hearts, that they had the knowledge and expertise to provide. The good wanted state power so they could benefit their fellow men.

And what was good for Americans at home surely would be no less beneficial for the masses of people across the oceans. Was not Europe a caldron of political intrigue and corruption? Were not the people of Asia, Africa, and Latin America suffering in squalor and ignorance—the victims of tribal despots and imperialist exploiters— easy prey to that even greater threat of communist propaganda and revolution?

America's first crusade was in 1917, when Woodrow Wilson, insisting that the United States had the moral duty to take the lead and "make the world safe for democracy," asked for, and got, a declaration of war from Congress. Americans, however, were repulsed in the years following World War I, when instead of democracy, they saw that all that came out of our participation in that noble crusade was communism in Russia, fascism in Italy, Nazism in Germany, and imperialist spoils for the victorious European allies.

But World War II seemed to offer the opportunity for a second chance. The American "arsenal of democracy" would free the world of Hitler and Imperial Japan and then pursue an international course of permanent foreign intervention to create "a better world." What the world got was the Cold War, with the Soviet Union gaining an Eastern European empire, and with China being lost behind what became known as the communist "Bamboo Curtain."

America's rewards were global commitments that required hundreds of thousands of American soldiers permanently stationed in Europe; two bloody wars in Asia that cost the lives of over a hundred thousand Americans; a huge defense budget that siphoned off hundreds of billions of dollars from the private sector for four decades; and even more tens of billions of dollars in military and foreign aid to any government in any part of the world, no matter how corrupt, just as long as it declared itself "anticommunist." And as one of the founders of *Human Events*, Felix Morley, pointed out in his book, *Freedom and Federalism*, in the heyday of Keynesian economics in the 1950s and 1960s, defense spending became a tool for "priming the pump" and guaranteeing "full employment" through government expenditures.

But communism is now dying under the weight of its own political corruption and economic failures. And the European and Asian countries that benefited from decades of being on the American defense and foreign aid dole have decided they want to grow up and manage their own affairs.

But rather than be delighted that the Cold War welfare state can finally be ended, American political and foreign policymakers are petrified. The global social engineers in Washington are suddenly faced with a world that does not want to be under the tutelage of American paternalism and dominance. They are busy scrambling for some way to "keep America in Europe," maintain Washington's political control and influence over international affairs, and guarantee that America will remain "in harm's way," potentially drawn into numerous controversies and conflicts around the world.

If it is undesirable for the United States government to intervene in the economic and social affairs of its citizenry—as the advocate of individual freedom steadfastly believes—then it is equally undesirable for the United States government to intervene in the internal affairs of other nations or the conflicts that sometimes arise among nations.

The first duty of the American government is to protect the life, liberty, and property of the citizens of the United States from foreign aggressors. Once a government sets itself the task of trying to rectify the errors and choices of its own citizens, it soon begins sliding down a slippery slope in which the end result is state supervision and regulation of all of its citizens' activities—and all in the name of a higher "social good."

Just as our neighbors often do things of which we do not approve, or which we do not consider good or wise, so do other nations. But to follow the path of attempting to set the world straight can lead to nothing but perpetual intervention and war in the name of world peace and global welfare. And these have been precisely the results of America's global crusade to save the world since 1945.

The end of communism and the economic growth of Europe and Asia give us a new opportunity to forswear the global Welfare State, free ourselves from foreign political and military entanglements, and follow George Washington's wise advice of free commercial relationships with all, but foreign alliances and intrigues with none.

This essay originally appeared in the November 1990 issue of Freedom Daily, *published by The Future of Freedom Foundation.*

3

The Power to Declare War— Who Speaks for the Constitution?

by Doug Bandow

When presidents lose domestic support, they invariably look overseas for crises to solve. President Clinton is no different. After the Republicans swept Congress, he immediately flew off to the Pacific for a series of meetings with foreign leaders. Aides predict that he will continue to pay greater attention to foreign policy, where he is able to operate with fewer restrictions from a hostile Congress.

But foreign policy means more than just international summits. It also means war, as is evident from the Clinton administration's continuing attempt to push America, through the NATO alliance, into a larger role in the Balkans imbroglio. So far, President Bill Clinton has undertaken or considered military action in Bosnia, Haiti, Korea, and Somalia. At no point has he indicated a willingness to seriously involve Congress in the decision-making process. To the contrary, in late 1993 he stated: "I would strenuously oppose attempts to encroach on the President's foreign policy powers."

In this way, at least, he is acting like many of his predecessors. Bill Clinton emphasizes that he is the commander-in-chief, and, he claims, "The Constitution leaves the President, for good and sufficient reasons, the ultimate decision-making authority." As such, he argues, he is entitled to do whatever he pleases with the military: "The President must make the ultimate decision."

In fact, such an attitude has been broadly held by chief executives around the world. A decade ago, then-Defense Secretary Caspar Weinberger observed of America's great Cold War adversary:

> Now who among the Soviets voted that they should invade Afghanistan? Maybe one, maybe five men in the Kremlin. Who has the ability to change that and bring them home? Maybe one, maybe five men in the Kremlin. Nobody else. And that is, I think, the height of immorality.

Yet, the president served by Secretary Weinberger, Ronald Reagan, made not the slightest pretense of consulting Congress before invading Grenada and overthrowing its government. George Bush attacked Panama and deposed its military dictator, Manuel Noriega, with merely a nod to Congress and only reluctantly accepted a legislative vote before going to war against Iraq. And President Clinton ended up only a Carter-brokered agreement away from forcibly invading Haiti. (Of course, even congressional assent would not mean that these or other military actions would be morally or practically justifiable.)

Alas, this executive presumption goes back to Richard Nixon and Harry Truman, and, indeed, much further. It was also shared by the various potentates who once ruled Europe. Observed Abraham Lincoln, a "strong" president who faced perhaps America's greatest crisis: "Kings had always been involving and impoverishing their people in wars, pretending generally, if not always, that the good of the people was the object." He rejected the contention that presidents have expansive war-making powers independent of Congress: "This, our Convention, understood to be the most oppressive of all Kingly oppressions; and they naturally resolved to so frame the Constitution that no one man should hold the power of bringing this oppression upon us." The opposing view, he concluded, "destroys the whole matter, and places our President where kings have always stood."

It was for this reason that many early Americans opposed the proposed Constitution, fearing that it gave to the president powers too similar to those of Britain's king. Not so, nationalist Alexander Hamilton reassured his countrymen. In fact, the president's authority was

> in substance much inferior to it. It would amount to nothing more than the supreme command and direction of the land and

naval forces . . . while that of the British King extends to the declaring of war and to the raising and regulating of fleets and armies; all of which by the Constitution would appertain of the legislature.

Perhaps part of the problem is that modern chief executives, who increasingly style themselves after their monarchical forebears, making war around the globe on their own initiative, do not understand which legislature Hamilton was referring to. Bill Clinton moved up by twenty-four hours his planned invasion of Haiti to forestall an adverse congressional vote, but did press for legislative blessing from the United Nations American diplomats successfully lobbied members of the Security Council: the enlightened nations of Nigeria, Oman, Pakistan, for instance, along with China, whose rulers' commitment to democracy is well known; Djibouti, with a total population less than that of a single congressional district; and Rwanda, then still represented by a diplomat from the defeated Hutu regime. Thus, President Clinton was granted permission by a smattering of foreign autocrats to take the United States to war.

But the U.S. Constitution, to which the president swears allegiance, refers not to the United Nations but rather to the American Congress. Article 1, Sec. 8 (11) states that "Congress shall have the power . . . to declare war." As Alexander Hamilton indicated, the president is commander-in-chief, but he is to fulfill his responsibilities only within the framework established by the Constitution and subject to the control of Congress.

Of this, there simply is no doubt. Wrote James Madison in 1793, it is necessary to adhere to the "fundamental doctrine of the Constitution that the power to declare war is fully and exclusively vested in the legislature." Modern supporters of the doctrine of president-as-Caesar make much of the fact that convention delegates changed Congress' authority from "make" to "declare" war, but they did so, explained Madison, only to allow the president the authority to respond to a sudden attack. When Pierce Butler of South Carolina formally proposed giving the president the power to start war, Elbridge Gerry of Massachusetts said that he "never expected to hear in a republic a motion to empower the executive to declare war." Butler's motion was quickly rejected.

The reasoning of the conferees in opposing Butler's measure was simple. Explained Virginia's George Mason, the president "is not safely to be entrusted with" the power to decide on war. Mason therefore favored "clogging rather than facilitating war." James Wilson, though an advocate of a strong presidency, approvingly

13

observed that the new constitutional system "will not hurry us into war." Instead, "it is calculated to guard against it. It will not be in the power of a single man, or a single body of men, to involve us in such distress." Similarly, Thomas Jefferson wrote: "We have already given . . . one effectual check to the dog of war by transferring the power of letting him loose."

Even Hamilton agreed with his long-time adversary on this point, pointing out that the war powers of the president were "in substance much inferior to" that of the British king. And Hamilton supported this result even while backing strong executive power. As he wrote in the *Federalist* No. 75:

> The history of human conduct does not warrant that exalted opinion of human virtue which would make it wise in a nation to commit interests of so delicate and momentous a kind, as those which concern its intercourse with the rest of the world, to the sole disposal of a magistrate created and circumstanced as would be a President of the United States.

This fundamental concern of the Constitution's framers—an unwillingness to trust "a single man . . . to involve us in such distress," in Wilson's words—has certainly been validated by American history. The manifold dishonest and secret machinations of this century's presidents, especially the "strong" ones so highly rated by historians, prove how dangerous it is to trust chief executives with minor grants of authority, let alone the power to take the nation into war. If requiring a legislative vote is no guarantee that the public will be protected from unnecessary and bloody national crusades, it does at least force a debate and more easily allow voters to ultimately hold someone responsible for their decisions.

Against this abundant historical record there is no serious rebuttal. George Bush, for instance, stated that "I don't think I need it" when asked if congressional approval was necessary before attacking Iraq. Why? "Many attorneys," he said, had "so advised me." He apparently did not bother to read the Constitution himself. Onetime law professor Bill Clinton offered no better justification. When it came to both Bosnia and Haiti in late 1993, Clinton said that he opposed "any attempts to encroach on" his prerogatives. He did, however, echo George Bush in saying that he would "encourage congressional authorization of any military involvement in Bosnia." As for Haiti, he stated in August 1994: "I would welcome the support of the Congress and I hope that I will have that. But like my predecessors in both parties, I have not agreed that I was constitution-

14

ally mandated to get it." In short, the president desired a guaranteed affirmative vote. The Constitution, however, does not limit Congress to voting yes.

The fact that the Constitution gives Congress the final decision as to war and peace does not mean that there are no gray areas. But the existence of some unclear cases does not mean that there are no unambiguous instances where congressional approval is required, such as defending South Korea from North Korea, spending a decade warring in Indochina, invading Panama and Haiti, transporting a half-million soldiers to the Middle East to attack Iraq, conquering Haiti, and intervening on Bosnia's side in the Balkan civil war.

Part II

What conceivable justification is there for ignoring the Constitution's straightforward requirement regarding the power to declare war? Advocates of expansive executive war power—oddly enough, including some conservatives who claim to believe in a jurisprudence of "original intent"—have come up with a number of reasons to give the president virtually unrestrained authority to act.

One is that the president has some undefined "foreign-affairs power" that apparently overrides the war-powers provision. Yet the Constitution carefully circumscribes the president's authority in foreign affairs in a number of ways—the Senate must approve treaties and ambassadors, for instance. Both the House and Senate regulate commerce with other countries; establish the military; organize the militia; make decisions covering the use of these forces; and oversee the rules of war (by authorizing letters of marquis and reprisal, defining and punishing piracy, and so forth). All told, writes Jack Rakove, historian and director of the American studies program at Stanford University, the constitutional provisions

> that laid the strongest foundation for a major executive role in foreign policy are more safely explained as a cautious reaction against the defects of exclusive senatorial control of foreign relations than as a bold attempt to convert the noble office of a republican presidency into a vigorous national leader in world affairs.

One Supreme Court decision, *United States v. Curtiss-Wright Exporting Corp.*, propagates the notion that the presidency is the "sole organ" for the conduct of international affairs, but modern courts treat the majority's rambling opinion, filled with nonbinding dicta, with great caution. And for good reason: Justice Sutherland's peculiarly expansive notions of executive power were not shared by his colleagues and cannot supersede the text of the Constitution. As Rakove points out:

> The expansive notions of executive power that Hamilton and his allies espoused after 1789—smacking as they did of monarchical prerogatives—would probably have doomed the Constitution to rejection had they been advanced in 1787–1788 and were for that very reason illegitimate and incorrect.

Even more so, had the Constitution's advocates advanced the far greater pretensions espoused by Justice Sutherland and today's chief executives, the proposed new government would have been rejected with little debate.

If there is no countervailing presidential power, are there exceptions to the congressional war power? For instance, presidents argue that they must be able to use the military for "defensive" purposes. True enough—in fact, no one would disagree. But defensive means *defensive*. At the constitutional convention, Roger Sherman of Connecticut stated that "the executive should be able to repel and not to commence war."

There was nothing defensive about overthrowing ruling regimes in Panama and Haiti, for instance. Nor was there anything defensive about joining the conflict between Kuwait and Iraq, as contended by Robert Tucker of the Center for National Security Law. Back in 1990, he argued:

> When the president seeks to respond defensively against Saddam Hussein's aggressive war (a crime against all nations under international law), he no more becomes the aggressor than did Franklin D. Roosevelt through the Normandy landing.

What Tucker missed, of course, was that President Roosevelt did not send off an American expeditionary force until securing a declaration of war against Germany from Congress. The Founders' fundamental objective remains no less valid today: to prevent the president—any president—from getting America into war without congressional consent. They did not care whether his action would start a new war or merely join an existing one; their goal was to prevent America's promiscuous participation in irrelevant overseas conflicts.

Similar is the contention that presidents must be able to instantly respond to foreign crises, most of which do not even involve direct attacks on the United States. In practice, instantaneous intervention overseas—perhaps to save American lives or prevent irreversible damage to serious U.S. interests—is rarely even arguably necessary. There was obviously no rush to occupy Haiti to restore Jean-Bertrand Aristide to power after three years in exile. Nothing prevented President Bush from requesting a declaration of war against Panama before sending in the troops even if there was a compelling case to invade. Nor could he argue that the exigencies of time prevented a congressional vote on his plans to attack Iraq.

In fact, so desirous were the Founders in circumscribing the authority of the president that they did not even intend to grant him power to unilaterally undertake reprisals against other nations for committing acts of war (in contrast to commencing war) against the United States. While serving as secretary of state, Thomas Jefferson wrote:

> The making of a reprisal on a nation is a very serious thing. Remonstrance and refusal of satisfaction ought to precede; and when reprisal follows, it is considered an act of war, and never failed to produce it in the case of a nation able to make war; besides, if the case were important and ripe for that step, Congress must be called upon to take it; the right of reprisal being expressly lodged with them by the Constitution, and not with the executive.

Alexander Hamilton, too, opposed giving the executive other than the most narrow authority to undertake military action. In *Federalist* No. 69 he stated that the president would possess "nothing more than the supreme command and direction of the military and naval forces, as first General and Admiral." This was no mere propaganda stance designed to win approval of the Constitution. To the contrary, in 1798 he advised James McHenry, secretary of war under John Adams, that the president as commander-in-chief can at most "repel *force* by *force.* . . . Any thing beyond this must fall under the idea of *reprisals* and requires the sanction of that Department [i.e., the Congress] which is to declare or make war." Notably, Hamilton makes no distinction between the terms "declare" and "make."

Another argument is that it is impractical to involve the legislative branch in foreign affairs. Congressional war votes in 1812, 1846, 1898, 1917, 1941, 1964, and 1991 prove the contrary, however. While 535 legislators cannot direct the course of an attack on Britain, Mexico, Spain, Germany, Vietnam, Iraq, Haiti, or anywhere else, that is not their job. That is why the Constitution has made the president commander-in-chief. What Congress is to do is decide whether or not the nation should go to war.

Such congressional debates need not even tip off adversaries as to the imminence of military action. Congress has four times approved conditional declarations of war, authorizing the president to use force if certain objectives were not achieved. In three instances, the executive branch peacefully resolved the disputes; in the fourth case war ensued, after Spain refused Congress's demand that it withdraw its forces from Cuba. Following these precedents, the president could ask Congress to allow the use of force against another nation—Haiti, Serbia, North Korea, or whatever—if certain conditions were not met after a certain amount of time. Legislators could then answer yes or no.

Part III

The favorite justification for presidents unilaterally wandering off to war around the globe seems to be: everyone else does it. Proponents of executive war making contend that ample precedents—two hundred or more troop deployments without congressional approval—exist for the president to act without a congressional declaration. Yet, this list chiefly consists of, as constitutional scholar Edward Corwin put it, "fights with pirates, landings of small naval contingents on barbarous or semi-barbarous coasts, the dispatch of small bodies of troops to chase bandits or cattle rustlers across the Mexican border, and the like." These are dubious justifications for, say, ousting an existing government and occupying an entire nation. Anyway, *et tu* remains an unpersuasive reason to ignore the nation's fundamental law; the fact that past chief executives acted lawlessly does not empower the current one to do likewise.

Successive presidents have been able to ignore the Constitution's clear strictures only because successive congresses have allowed them to do so. A Democratically controlled Congress let Harry Truman treat a major land war in Asia as a "police action." From Vietnam to Iraq, Republican congressmen steadfastly defended the right of Republican presidents to levy war on foreign nations. When George Bush introduced troops into Somalia, Republican congressmen opposed invoking the War Powers Resolution which, they complained, unconstitutionally limited the chief executive's power. Then a Democrat was elected president: Republicans suddenly reread the Constitution. In late 1993, Senate Republican Leader Robert Dole proposed legislation requiring congressional approval for American deployments in Bosnia or Haiti. Congress should be heard "before the body bags are counted, before the caskets come home," he argued.

Democratic legislators, in contrast, spent years attempting to constrain Republican presidents. But when some Republicans questioned Bill Clinton's authority in Somalia early in his presidency, Senate Democrats, led by then-majority leader George Mitchell, rallied to the president's defense. And many of the same Democrats backed President Clinton on his claimed authority to occupy Haiti. Indeed, numerous past Democratic skeptics of military adventurism encouraged the president to unilaterally invade the island nation. Particularly striking was the about-face of many members of the Black Caucus, such as Gulf War opponents Nita Lowey, Major Owens, and Maxine Waters.

Many other legislators simply prefer to avoid taking any responsibility on the usually volatile issue of military intervention. Complained Rep. Lee Hamilton, chairman of the House Foreign Affairs Committee, "Congress basically wants to let the president make the decision" to deploy troops overseas. Then legislators can carp if the adventure goes awry or applaud if it succeeds.

For the last four decades, the war power has been a political football. Former Democratic congressman Bill Gray was right last year when he complained that the partisan pirouettes on executive war making are "kind of confusing and perplexing." When Republicans hold the presidency, they assert that the executive can do as he pleases; Democratic legislators eloquently appeal to the Constitution.

Now, a Democratic president believes it is more important to win a vote in the United Nations than in Congress. GOP legislators warn of the risks of an overbearing executive, while many Democrats stand silent.

In short, both sides deserve censure. As Sen. Joseph Biden, an opponent of the Gulf War but enthusiastic proponent of intervention in Bosnia, has cracked, "The Republicans have found God." But the Democrats have proved to be no more consistent, and at least it is better to have found God, as have the Republicans, than whatever partisan idol the Democrats are now worshipping.

Partisan wrangling aside, it is time for all sides to reexamine their commitment to the Constitution. At the very least, presidents should take their oath of allegiance to the Constitution seriously. And legislators should want to protect their own institutional authority. If all else fails, the stakes are so high that the American people should consider an amendment to the Constitution expressly prohibiting the president from going to war without congressional approval. As James Madison warned, "War is, in fact, the true source of

19

executive aggrandizement." But much more is at stake than merely a theoretical dispute between the different branches of the federal government.

The point is, the Founders vested the power to declare in Congress because they feared presidents would do precisely what they are doing today—regularly taking the nation into overseas conflicts that have only the most tangential interest to the security of the United States. The result has been hundreds of thousands of soldiers killed, hundreds of billions of dollars squandered, numerous civil liberties lost, and a host of government bureaucracies spawned. In short, even if the Constitution was not clear, the issue of war and peace is too important to leave to the president. "International support is fine," observed Senate Majority Leader Robert Dole in 1993, "but it is no substitute for the support of Congress and the American people."

The Constitution *is* clear, however. Congress needs to be willing, even eager, to say no when presidents propose overseas military adventures. And Congress needs to sanction presidents who exceed their authority—cutting White House budgets, restricting executive authority, and even impeachment, if necessary.

And presidents need to respect the law. The latter might seem to be the impossible dream, but it was not that long ago when a president acknowledged the limits of his authority. If anyone could have legitimately staked a claim to being an aggressive commander-in-chief, it was former Army general and military hero Dwight Eisenhower. Yet in January 1956, he stated: "When it comes to the matter of war, there is only one place that I would go, and that is to the Congress of the United States." A few months later, he explained: "I am not going to order any troops into anything that can be interpreted as war, until Congress directs it."

If President Clinton and his successors want to risk the lives of young Americans for sundry purposes—whether to restore a demagogue to power in the name of Haitian democracy or something else—let them follow Eisenhower's lead and go to Congress for permission. Then we can have the serious national debate intended by the nation's Founders.

This essay originally appeared in the June, July, and August 1995 issues of Freedom Daily, *published by The Future of Freedom Foundation.*

4

The Case for an America First Foreign Policy

by Ralph Raico

Rethinking the Foundations

The distinguished speakers at this conference of The Future of Freedom Foundation have demonstrated the urgent need for drastic change in America: the need to slash taxing and spending, to free money from government manipulation, to privatize education, to rein in the bureaucrats, and to restore constitutional government. But such a revolutionary program of reform will never be possible unless we institute a radical change in the area that conditions and shapes all the others—the area of foreign affairs.

With the end of the Cold War, the time has come to rethink the foundations of American foreign policy. What is the purpose of our foreign policy? What is the mission of our armed forces?

Should we, as many today are urging, embark on yet another global crusade, this time to make—and forever keep—the whole world "democratic"? Should the American military, as others propose, act as a kind of super Red Cross, ready to send relief to victims of famine, earthquakes, etc., around the world—or at least the victims the media decide are worthy of notice? Without any conscious choice on the part of the people, we are in danger of slipping into the roles of both global enforcer of "democracy" and global social worker. Meanwhile, American sovereignty over our own armed forces is compromised, as precedents are set for the United Nations to become the de facto director of American power in combat areas overseas.

What I propose in the place of this democratic and humanitarian globalism is a return to our traditional policy of avoiding foreign wars and *defending America*. This may be called the policy of nonintervention in the affairs of other countries; or neutrality; or—as its enemies dubbed it, and as it is known to everyone who has passed through the public schools, "isolationism." In homage to the courageous men and women who opposed Franklin Roosevelt's drive to war—Charles Lindbergh, Robert Taft, John T. Flynn, Colonel McCormick, and the others—I will call it the policy of America First.

The Traditional American Course

For most of our history, America First *was* the foreign policy of the United States. The record is laid out by the great historian Charles A. Beard in *A Foreign Policy for America*, published in 1940. In our dealings overseas, we followed the guidelines laid down by George Washington in his Farewell Address to the American people:

> The great rule of conduct for us in regard to foreign nations is— in extending our commercial relations—to have with them as little *political* connection as possible.

Significantly, it is these lines that Richard Cobden—the greatest libertarian theorist of international relations—placed as the motto of his first published work.

George Washington's outlook thus involved three main principles. First, we would engage in mutually beneficial, peaceful commerce with the rest of the world, but "forcing nothing," as Washington made a point of adding. Second, while trading with them, we would avoid entanglements in their political affairs and their quarrels with other nations. Finally, we would always remain strong enough to defend ourselves from attack.

That this system was endorsed by John Adams, Thomas Jefferson, James Madison, and the other Founders as well was no accident. America First was the natural counterpart to the form of government—the Republic—which they had instituted. The monarchies of the Old World were massive war machines, exploiting the people to fund their never-ending conflicts and the military and civilian bureaucracies those conflicts necessitated. Those nations were dedicated to pomp and glory and the power of the state. America would be different—*Novus Ordo Seclorum*, "The New Order of the Ages," as it still states on the back of dollar bills. Here the rights of the people were to be all-important. Government power was to be strictly limited and mainly exercised by the localities and the states (hence, the Tenth Amendment). Low taxes and the anticipated liquidation of the public debt would ensure that the citizens would not be systemically plundered, as was the way in Europe.

But, in order to forestall high taxes, debt, and the centralization of power, we had to steer clear of war. That is why the advice of the Founders was: if you want to preserve the system we have established, keep out of wars except when required to defend the United States, and avoid political entanglements overseas, since these are likely to lead us into war.

The principle was reiterated by American leaders throughout the first century of our history—by James Monroe, John Quincy Adams, Daniel Webster, Henry Clay, William Seward, and others.

The policy of America First in no way meant "isolation" from the world. No one was ever more of a cosmopolitan than Jefferson. America, following Jefferson, welcomed trade and cultural exchange with all nations, while steadfastly rejecting political connections. American civilization and the American economy flourished, as we abstained from meddling overseas.

This noninterventionist America, devoted to solving our own problems and developing our own civilization, soon became *stupor mundi*—the wonder of the world. Everywhere peoples struggling for their liberty looked for inspiration to the Great Republic of the West. America served the cause of freedom in foreign lands, not by sending troops, or bombers, or foreign aid, but by being—in the words of Henry Clay—"a light to all nations": the shining example of a happy and prosperous people enjoying their God-given rights in peace.

Traditional American policy did not consider it our business to distinguish among foreign regimes as to their morality, ideology, or provenance. If a regime had the attributes of a state, we recognized it and dealt with it. There were no "outlaw" states. We carried on business with governments ranging from Tsarist Russia to republican France.

And Americans were generous towards the unfortunates of the world as no people had ever been in history. Americans—the people themselves, through their voluntary efforts, not the government through taxation—poured out immense sums to relieve the sufferings of victims of floods, famines, wars, and religious persecutions everywhere. This—not today's international income transfers at the point of a gun—was *true* compassion.

The Rise of Empire

Beginning at the end of the nineteenth century, however, a great transformation took place in the official American attitude towards the rest of the world. The political elite of the country was won over

23

to a policy of "global responsibility"—which meant, more and more, intrusion into other nations' affairs, backed up by growing American military strength.

The landmarks along this road are the Spanish-American War and the conquest of the Philippines under William McKinley; Theodore Roosevelt's noisy promotion of the United States as a world power; and—most fateful of all—Woodrow Wilson's embroiling us in the First World War.

Establishment historians like to give the impression that all these steps were inevitable—just as they claim that the cancerous growth of government at home has been preordained and unavoidable. But, in fact, each move away from America First and towards globalism was the result of political choice and struggle. It didn't have to happen that way. At the turn of the century, for instance, the new imperialism was fought tooth and nail by the classical liberals of the time: men like Edward Atkinson, Carl Schurz, E. L. Godkin, Andrew Carnegie, and, above all, William Graham Sumner. They lost out, because the forces arrayed against them proved more powerful. The libertarians of the day were no match for the civilian and military bureaucrats in Washington, the capitalist interests anxious for government backing for their export trade and investments abroad, and, above all, the political class, with its new vision of America as a world power.

The decisive turn came with Woodrow Wilson and World War I. Wilson presented the nation with the starkest possible alternative to our traditional policy. For more than a century, the American attitude was the one expressed by John Quincy Adams, who, as secretary of state to James Monroe, was the real author of the Monroe Doctrine. Adams declared:

> Wherever the standard of freedom and independence has been or shall be unfurled, there will be America's heart, her benedictions, and her prayers. But she does not go abroad in search of monsters to destroy. She is the well-wisher to the freedom and independence of all. She is the champion and vindicator only of her own.

Instead of acting as "a light to all nations," America, in Wilson's conception, would scour the earth in search of antidemocratic monsters to destroy. The enlightened leaders in Washington would continually tap the immense power created by our free institutions in an endless crusade to export "democracy" to all the rest of mankind.

This first experiment in democracy-exporting, however, turned out badly. By pushing our way into Europe's bloody quarrel, we ensured that there would be no compromise peace, but total triumph for one side. The result was the vindictive Treaty of Versailles, virtually guaranteeing another world war. We forced the Germans to give up their Kaiser, which made it possible, fourteen years later, for a demagogue like Hitler to seize power.

Mr. Wilson's War, as it was called, also demonstrated the high costs at home of "exporting democracy" abroad. In every area of life, Americans lost liberties to Washington as taxes and the public debt skyrocketed, government controls pervaded the economy, and the authority of federal agents and censors reached into every city and town. While the people longed for a return to "normalcy," the transformation of law, institutions, and, most of all, attitudes, could never be undone.

Franklin Roosevelt and the "Last Good War"

Advocates of globalism prefer to ignore the disastrous outcome of our intervention in the First World War. Instead, the case they constantly hold up to us is World War II and the "lessons" supposedly taught by this "last good war."

The era of the Second World War has been so mythologized by propagandists that it is easy to lose sight of some fundamental truths. The fact is that, regardless of how evil Hitler and the Japanese leaders were, the people of the United States were manipulated and maneuvered into a war which the great majority of them did not want. The war party comprised Franklin Roosevelt and his administration, in Washington, and the political elite of the country, residing mainly on the eastern seaboard. They were aided and abetted by the tone-setting mass media and by the British government, which, of course, had its own reasons to involve us in war.

The quality New York City papers and Henry Luce's publishing empire of *Time*, *Life*, and *Fortune* were relentless in their push for war. In Luce's conception, participating in the conflict would usher in an "American Century" of power and glory. As we look around the United States at the end of "our" century, we can perhaps judge how much good all the power and glory has done us.

Even more influential than the press was Hollywood. Gore Vidal, in his little book, *Screening History*, has written of the Hollywood of the 1930s: how one movie after another, with the best actors and the most lavish productions, hailed the greatness and goodness of the British Empire. Vidal writes:

For those who find disagreeable today's Zionist propaganda, I can only say that gallant little Israel of today must have learned a great deal from the gallant little Englanders of the 1930s. The English kept up a propaganda campaign that was to permeate our entire culture.

Hollywood gave us not a single film on Washington, Jefferson, Madison, the presidential Lincoln, or Jefferson Davis. Instead, British propaganda films "were making us all weirdly English." This was no accident; the director Alexander Korda became the center of a colony of British expatriates who promoted their government's line. A little later, still in the period before Pearl Harbor, Hollywood turned out a flood of anti-Nazi films. There were no films, however, on Stalin's mass murders, which were being committed at that very time. Soon the movie studios would give us films like *Mission to Moscow* and Lillian Hellman's *North Star*, glorifying life in Stalin's Russia.

As was finally revealed in *A Man Called Intrepid*, Winston Churchill commissioned the agent William Stephenson (code-named "Intrepid") to work for American entry into the war. From his headquarters in Rockefeller Center, and with Roosevelt's knowledge and support, Stephenson collaborated with the FBI and other federal agencies, spreading disinformation and systematically breaking American law—all with the aim of discrediting the America First movement and bringing us into the war. Harry Hopkins, Roosevelt's close advisor and confidant, was a go-between to Winston Churchill. Hopkins went to England, in January 1941, to report to Churchill on Roosevelt's plans. This is how Churchill recounted the meeting, in his memoirs:

> Here was an envoy from the President of supreme importance to our life. With gleaming eye and quiet, constrained passion he said: "The President is determined that we shall win the war together. Make no mistake about it. He has sent me here to tell you that at all costs and by all means he will carry you through, no matter what happens to him—there is nothing that he will not do so far as he has human power." There he sat, slim, frail, ill, but absolutely glowing with refined comprehension of the Cause. It was to the defeat, ruin, and slaughter of Hitler, to the exclusion of all other purposes, loyalties and aims.

All this time, Roosevelt was telling the American people that he was striving tirelessly for peace. Despite the fact that each step on the road to war—the destroyer deal, Lend-Lease, using the U.S. Navy to convoy ships to Britain—was illegal under international law, Roosevelt protested that it was all on behalf of peace. To his friend Churchill, however, he told a different story. Many years later, some of the relevant documents were declassified. Here is the report in the *New York Times* for January 2, 1972:

> War-Entry Plans Laid to Roosevelt. Britain releases Her Data on Talks with Churchill. London. AP. Formerly top-secret British government papers made public today said that President Franklin D. Roosevelt told Prime Minister Churchill in August, 1941, that he was looking for an incident to justify opening hostilities against Nazi Germany. Churchill reported to the War Cabinet [that] "he [Roosevelt] was obviously determined that they should come in.... The President had said that he would become more and more provocative. If the Germans did not like it, they could attack American forces. Everything was to be done to force an incident."

Such an "incident" occurred in September 1941, with the USS *Greer*. In a radio address, Roosevelt declared: "I tell you the blunt fact that the German submarine fired first upon this American destroyer, without warning, and with deliberate design to sink the ship." He then issued the shoot-on-sight order: American warships were to shoot German vessels "on sight" in the North Atlantic.

Afterwards the truth—known to Roosevelt at the time—came out: a British warplane had informed the *Greer* that a German submarine was in the area. The *Greer* located the submarine and kept tracking it, meanwhile broadcasting its location to any and all British planes and ships in the area. One British plane dropped depth charges, but missed; finally, after hours of being tracked by the *Greer*, the submarine turned and fired a torpedo, which also missed. The *Greer* answered with eight depth charges, then, a few hours later, more depth charges. Finally, both ships broke off the engagement.

These facts are not in question. That Roosevelt lied about the *Greer* is conceded by all pro-Roosevelt historians. For instance, Robert Dallek, of UCLA, in his major work, *Franklin D. Roosevelt and American Foreign, 1932–1945*, states:

> In light of the national unwillingness to face up fully to the international dangers facing the country, it is difficult to fault Roosevelt for building a consensus by devious means. Yet for all the need to mislead the country in its own interest, the President's

deviousness also injured the national well-being in the long run. His action in the *Greer* incident created a precedent for manipulation of public opinion which would be repeated by later Presidents in less justifiable circumstances.

Dallek notes some of Roosevelt's maneuvers to bring America into the war:

> Roosevelt's use of the FBI also formed an important precedent for arbitrary action by subsequent Presidents. Roosevelt sanctioned FBI actions and the establishment of an agency for "special operations" which undermined democratic institutions. He not only allowed FBI investigations of political opponents and unlawful wiretappings and mail-openings, he also used the Bureau to gather information on "the attitude of Congressional groups toward the President's foreign policy."

There is no dispute over whether Roosevelt lied in order to drive America into war. The only issue is: was he justified? His admirers, right and left, believe he was. They agree with Thomas A. Bailey, of Stanford, who wrote in his book *The Man in the Street: The Impact of American Public Opinion on Foreign Policy*:

> Franklin Roosevelt repeatedly deceived the American people during the period before Pearl Harbor. He was like the physician who must tell the patient lies for the patient's own good. Because the masses are notoriously short-sighted and generally cannot see the danger until it is at their throats, our statesmen are forced to deceive them into an awareness of their own long-term interests. This is clearly what Roosevelt had to do, and who shall say that posterity will not thank him for it?

Sometimes Roosevelt's lies were laughably transparent. Thus, to quote Dallek, "Roosevelt told a press conference on September 30 [1941] that Article 124 of the Russian Constitution guaranteed freedom of conscience: 'Freedom equally to use propaganda against religion,' he said, 'which is essentially what is the rule in this country, only we don't put it quite the same way.'"

As Dallek comments: "Roosevelt knew full well that there was no freedom of religion in the Soviet Union."

Now imagine for a moment that Herbert Hoover or Robert Taft or another conservative leader had said, in 1941, that the Jews enjoyed full freedom in Nazi Germany. Do you think that we might have heard of such a ridiculous and shameful statement? Is it not likely, in fact, that it would have been drummed into our heads from the time we were in high school? Yet here is Roosevelt making a precisely analogous defense of Stalinist Russia, and his outrageous statement has disappeared down an Orwellian memory hole.

Franklin Roosevelt was, above all else, a liar. His name should be linked in the history books to lying as the name of Genghis Khan is to cruelty and Romeo's to romance. And it was at Roosevelt's school that all of our leaders have studied. Republican or Democrat, liberal or "conservative," they all love and revere Franklin Roosevelt. From Roosevelt they all learned to lie to us for our own good: to lie about the Soviet "threat" in 1947, about Arbenz in Guatemala, Mossadegh in Iran, and Bosch in the Dominican Republic; to lie about those Navy ships in the Gulf of Tonkin attacked "without provocation" in 1964 and about the Israeli attack on the USS *Liberty* in 1967; to lie about our support of death squads in El Salvador and Guatemala, about the Korean jet liner, about the airstrip in Grenada, about Noriega in Panama; to lie about Iran and Iraq and more "unprovoked aggression," and about "restoring democracy" in Haiti— just as they lie today about the murders in Waco and at Ruby Ridge. Ever since Roosevelt, it has been lying as a way of government in what was once the Great Republic of the West.

Whether you think that going to war against Hitler—and in the process allying with Stalin, who killed more people and killed them earlier than Hitler did—was justified or not, you must have qualms as to *how* it was done. Our economic strangling of the Japanese led them to conclude that there was no alternative to attacking the United States. Our de facto alliance with Britain led Hitler to declare formal war on America after Pearl Harbor, since we were virtually at war with Germany anyway. While reassuring the people that he was working day and night for peace, Roosevelt pursued a course guaranteed to get us into war. Yet, if a nation can be maneuvered into war through such systematic deception by its leader, in what sense is there still government by the people?

War Crimes in the "Last Good War"

A never-ending stream of propaganda depicts World War II as a crusade of pristine virtue. While enemy war crimes of a half-century ago continue to be paraded before us on practically a daily basis, we are never informed of the crimes committed by the Allies.

Anyone concerned with the truth can still read it in William Henry Chamberlin's great revisionist work, *America's Second Crusade.*

The terror-bombing of the German cities deliberately targeted the civilian population; it resulted in about 600,000 civilian deaths, culminating in the destruction of Dresden, the "Florence of the North." Roosevelt's fatuous policy of unconditional surrender demoralized the heroic German anti-Nazi resistance and caused the Germans to fight on to the bitter end. The insane Morgenthau Plan, aimed at reducing Germany to an agricultural and pastoral nation, was signed by Roosevelt and Churchill, but, thankfully, never wholly carried out, although it influenced Allied policy after the war. The atom bombing of the Japanese cities, it is true, is sometimes highlighted—much to the consternation of so-called conservatives—but most Americans seem to take it in stride: as if the annihilation of close to 200,000 civilians—including the incineration of 40,000 or so schoolchildren—could be sloughed off with the comment that, after all, war is hell.

In 1995, as the anniversary of the end of World War II was celebrated, there were certain inconvenient facts that our leaders and the compliant media left out of the story. They did not mention that fifty years ago much of Europe was turned into a communist killing field: that around 20,000 right-wingers were killed in France (more victims than during the Reign of Terror), not all of whom were "collaborators," to use that silly word—after all, the greatest "collaborators" were Roosevelt and Churchill, who "collaborated" with Stalin. They did not mention how Churchill's protégé, Marshal Tito, went on a killing spree, murdering tens of thousands of Slovene and Croat prisoners of war, and murdering some 5,000 people in *Trieste*, in Italy, when the Reds gained temporary control of the city. They did not mention the expulsion of over 15,000,000 Germans from their ancestral homelands in the eastern territories, in the course of which close to 2,000,000 of them died. Now, 2,000,000 is not 6,000,000— but it's not nothing. They did not mention the massacre of tens of thousands of German civilians in camps the Reds set up in Poland, or the death by starvation and exposure of more tens of thousands of German POWs in Allied camps. They did not mention how Britain and America sent back hundreds of thousands of anti-Communist fighters—Soviet subjects who had sided with the Germans against Stalin—to the tender mercies of the NKVD and the amenities of the Gulag.

None of this was mentioned during the 1995 commemorations because their purpose was to enshrine the Second World War as an immaculate crusade and the model and justification for an endless number of crusades in the years and generations to come. This is precisely what happened with the American Civil War. The horrors attendant on the Yankee conquest of the South and the shamefulness of the era of Reconstruction—as well as the despotism Lincoln imposed on the whole country—these are never referred to anymore, lest doubt be cast on the sempiternal justice of that first and proto-typical crusade for virtue.

The Cold War: "Scaring the Hell Out of the American People"

With World War II the precedent was established: it is the job of the president of the United States to identify foreign foes the people are too "short-sighted" to recognize, and it is his right to deceive and manipulate the people into waging war against them.

Starting in 1947, with the Truman Doctrine, the public was again and again misled about the dangers facing America. At the time, Sen. Arthur Vandenberg advised Truman that if he wanted to get his "Truman Doctrine"—the recipe for endless foreign involvement—passed, he would have to "scare the hell out of the American people." That is what successive administrations have done. For close to fifty years, as Dr. Robert Higgs, of the Independent Institute, has written, we have had "a state of continuous national emergency and sustained military readiness without precedent in American history." What is politely called "information management"—the lies and half-truths spread by the thousands of hired propagandists in every agency in Washington—has served to keep the people quiet.

Probably the least of the injuries inflicted on us by a half-century of the Cold War is the monetary cost: Higgs has estimated that, even leaving out veterans' benefits and foreign aid, the cost of military expenditures for the period 1948–1989 has been the equivalent of $10 trillion in 1993 dollars.

But much worse has been the harm done to our constitutional system. In 1950, Harry Truman—who has become another great hero to the bipartisan globalist cabal—involved us in war in Korea. In doing so, Truman surpassed even Roosevelt: he asked Congress for no declaration of war, relying, instead, on the UN Security Council's condemnation of North Korea as an aggressor. In fact, Truman expressed the wish that the Russians had vetoed that UN declaration—so that it would have been crystal clear that, as president, he needed no authority beyond his own will to plunge the nation into war.

31

Now, the Constitution is very specific on this point: Article I, Section 8, states: "The Congress shall have power to declare war, grant letters of marque and reprisal, and make rules concerning capture on land and water."

The Founding Fathers were unmistakably clear on this point. As commander-in-chief, the president has the authority to deploy American forces to repel attack or *once war is declared by Congress*. The reason for this division of powers, according to James Madison was that "the executive is the department most distinguished by its propensity to war; hence it is the practice of all states, in proportion as they are free, to disarm this propensity." So unequivocal was the American principle that, as the constitutional scholars, Francis D. Wormuth and Edwin B. Firmage, have written: "Not until 1950 was it asserted by any officer or organ of the United States government that the President had a constitutional right to initiate war."

Truman's contempt for the traditional liberties of Americans went even further. The record is set forth in Wormuth and Firmage's book, *To Chain the Dog of War*. In 1952, in the face of a threatened strike in the steel industry, Truman ordered the steel mills of the country seized. By a vote of 6–3, the Supreme Court rejected this brazen grab for power. Yet Chief Justice Vinson, an old Truman crony, justified his action:

> A review of executive action demonstrates that our Presidents have on many occasions exhibited the leadership contemplated by the Framers. . . . With or without statutory authorization, Presidents have at such times dealt with national emergencies by acting promptly and resolutely. . . .

So, according to the chief justice, the president could declare a "national emergency" and then do anything he wished. There seemed to be no limit to Truman's claims of arbitrary power under cover of war. On April 8, Truman held a press conference, at which, according to the *New York Times*, he was asked:

> If it is proper under your inherent powers to seize the steel mills, can you, in your opinion, seize the newspapers and the radio stations? Mr. Truman replied that under similar circumstances the President had to do whatever he believed was best for the country. The President refused to elaborate. But White House sources said the President's point was that he had the

power in an emergency, to take over "any portion of the business community acting to jeopardize all the people."

This is the Harry Truman who is today acclaimed and honored by all American politicians, from Bill Clinton to Newt Gingrich.

It is sobering to realize that in 1952 only two votes on the Supreme Court stood in the way of unrestrained presidential control over the liberties and properties of American citizens. And it is frightening to see how far the hysteria created by war and warlike emergencies can drive us towards real dictatorship.

The Imperial Presidency

By now the Constitution has become a dead letter on the question of war and peace. What the Founding Fathers feared—that the president would be able, on his own, to ensnare us in war—has become a reality. A particularly saddening aspect of this is the eagerness of so-called conservatives to rush to vindicate the president's alleged right to start wars. Barry Goldwater spoke up for it at the time of the Vietnam War; Judge Bork has gone on record to the same effect; and recently Sen. John McCain, of Arizona, a Republican "expert" on foreign affairs, has stated that, while he advised against sending troops to Haiti, there was no doubt that the president had the authority to send American forces anywhere in the world—including into battle—at any time he wished.

Conservatives often speak of restoring the Constitution. A test of their honesty will be how hard they fight to restore to Congress the sole authority to engage America in war.

The Cold War created an Imperial Presidency. During these decades, by simple presidential decree, the United States waged full-scale war, lasting for years; overthrew foreign governments; arranged political assassinations; trained and equipped terrorists for action on foreign soil; mined the harbors of countries with which we were at peace; and performed innumerable other acts of war. Often the government operated through "covert action." In this way, various presidents carried on paramilitary actions in Tibet for close to twenty years; waged war in Laos for decades; engaged in a secret war in Vietnam under Kennedy and in Cambodia under Nixon; and raised the Kurds against Iraq—a state with which we were then at peace—and then abandoned them to be slaughtered. None of this was known to the American public—let alone approved by them—nor was it known even to Congress. Edwin B. Firmage, who has detailed these transgressions, writes that all this was done "in violation of the Constitution, in disregard of the laws and prerogatives of Congress, and in open defiance of international law and morality."

This is not even to mention the "covert actions" *against the American people themselves*: the secret testing of nuclear materials and other weapons on our civilian population and the secret radioactive contamination of land and water in various areas of the United States.

Through government "information management," as Robert Higgs notes, the American people have been kept in a state of constant anxiety over the existence of potentially fatal "gaps"—beginning with the "infantry gap" right after the Second World War, which Truman proposed to fill with Universal Military Training. There were, we were told, 175 Soviet divisions poised to invade Western Europe. In actuality, a third of those divisions were severely undermanned and another third badly equipped. Moreover, Stalin, preoccupied with trying to digest Eastern Europe and rebuild Russia, had not the slightest intention of undertaking another war. Then came the "bomber gap" in the 1950s, then the famous "missile gap" that John Kennedy tried to frighten us with, then an "anti-missile gap" and a "first-strike missile gap." "All," writes Higgs, "were revealed in due course to have been false alarms." Finally, it was left to conservative hawks to discover a nonexistent "window of vulnerability" after an imaginary "decade of neglect"—and to begin spending the country into bankruptcy under Ronald Reagan.

What has been the result of all this war and preparation for war, extending now uninterruptedly for more than half a century? As Jonathan Hughes, of Northwestern, put it:

> National emergency became the catch-all justification for extension of federal power into the private economy. The legitimacy of federal control became an accepted part of economic life. What was once considered an extraordinary imposition of federal power—say, automatic payroll deduction of the income tax—became normal.

With each war and its aftermath, the federal government shows a "ratchet-effect"—two steps forward and one step back:

> The experience after World War I was repeated after the Korean War, as it had been after World War II. Once expanded by the fiscal force of war expenditures, the size of government—as

measured by spending outlays—did not then contract back to prewar levels. Another zero was added to the federal numbers.

General Objections to Interventionism

Thus, the history of our departure from an America First foreign policy has been anything but auspicious. In addition, a number of theoretical considerations weigh heavily against permitting our politicians to go poking around the world, miring us in foreign problems that are none of our concern.

There is no reason to suppose that our leaders are any more competent in international affairs than they are in domestic affairs. The process by which they are selected—now absurdly and almost surrealistically reduced to mindless thirty-second television commercials—is practically guaranteed to produce political leaders who are liars or fools or both.

Foreign intervention will often be dictated by purely partisan-political considerations. It is well known that the president receives "a shot in the arm" in the opinion polls when he "gets tough" with some foreign devil or other. Thus, it often pays to invent foreign devils—new "Hitlers" at every turn—Saddam Hussein, Colonel Kadafi, Aidid in Somalia, General Cedras in Haiti, and who knows who else in the future.

The decision to intervene is subject, like all political decisions, to the influence of pressure groups. Just as with domestic policy, foreign policy will be shaped by pressures exerted by various constituencies with their own axes to grind. Meanwhile, the interests of the public at large are lost in the shuffle. This is the basic teaching of the school of public choice. Consider a particular domestic statute, say, the law restricting the importation of sugar. Less than 1 percent of the American people have an interest in a high price for sugar; everyone else has an interest in a low price. How is it then that we have a policy of keeping the price of sugar high? The reason is that the benefits of a high price policy are concentrated, while the costs are diffused. So the interest group spends time and money and votes to make sure it gets what it wants.

Similarly in foreign policy: it cannot be emphasized enough that the American people, by and large, have virtually no interest in foreign affairs. They know nothing about foreign countries, their histories, and their problems, and they care nothing about them. In truth, no people was ever less suited to be an imperial nation than the Americans. Inevitably, therefore, a globalist foreign policy will be determined, not by the American people themselves, but by small groups and cliques which do care—and care a lot.

That such groups and cliques exist is beyond doubt. There are, first of all, those powerful individuals and corporations with foreign financial interests, who wish to use the agencies of the American government—the State Department, CIA, Defense Department, and so on—to protect their interests, thus socializing the costs of doing business abroad. The American Zionists are, of course, another classic case. George Ball was a certified member of the establishment, but one with a lingering affection for the old notion of an independent American foreign policy. In his last book (with his son Douglas), *The Passionate Attachment*, Ball set down in detail how we have become the docile accomplice of Israel in its quarrel with the Arab peoples.

But there are other cases, as well: the Greek community in America, for instance, with its concern for the Greek-Turkish conflict. Recently, we have seen a good example of this principle at work in regard to Haiti. The immense majority of Americans had not the slightest interest in involvement in Haiti. Why, then, did we threaten and bully and finally land troops in Haiti to return "Father" Aristide to power? What moved Clinton to act—besides the prospect of a "shot-in-the-arm" in the polls—was the clout of the Black Caucus in Congress. It will be interesting to observe, as black "consciousness" grows, and American blacks come to feel a greater attachment to Africa, how Democratic presidents will embroil us more and more in the intractable messes of that seemingly doomed continent.

But even supposing that an activist foreign policy were formulated by competent leaders, who never exploited it for personal political advantage, and who were invulnerable to pressures from special interests: still, the world is such a complicated place that, inevitably, there will be unintended consequences of American interventions. We went to war in 1917 to make the world safe for democracy. The result was the Versailles Treaty, Hitler's coming to power, and World War II. The result of American support of Israel has been to turn hundreds of millions of people in the Islamic world into enemies of the United States—people who otherwise would have no reason to hate us. And the result of *that* is terrorism against Americans, abroad and on the soil of the United States itself. Already some are beginning to speak of the coming "inevitable" war with Islam.

A globalist policy leads, as William Graham Sumner warned a century ago, to an abandonment of our traditional republican form of government. It perverts our constitutional system, concentrating power in the presidency, rather than Congress, and in Washington, instead of the states and localities. Thus, power is situated in the places (the executive branch, Washington) furthest from popular oversight, and activity centered in the area of policy most distant from the interests and concerns of the people.

Finally, focusing on foreign affairs diverts our attention from the desperate need for reforms at home. These imperative reforms go far beyond anything that has been suggested—sincerely or not—by any Republican leader. We will never be able to undertake them if— at any moment—the politicians can choose to distract us by concocting some foreign crisis or other.

Do we have problems at home that cry out for our attention? Here is a small sample: we have law enforcement agencies that are, literally, out of control—the Drug Enforcement Agency, of course, but also the BATF, the FBI, and others—agencies that have besieged and massacred American citizens in their homes. We have an unprecedented campaign by politicians and the mass media to deprive Americans of their right to bear arms. We have an educational system that is being transformed at every level into an apparatus for indoctrinating American children in the dogmas of political correctness. We have the continuing erosion of the most basic rights to private property, in the name of a lunatic "environmentalism." We have a situation of racial conflict that is worsening all the time, as whites become second-class citizens in America, and young blacks are brainwashed into blaming whites for all their ills. We have the creation, through welfare, of a vast underclass that is turning our cities, one after the other, into jungles. We have an elite class of self-appointed social engineers—in the universities, the media, and the major foundations—intent on reshaping our culture, our values, even our national identity—and using the full power of government to do it. The elite's initiatives in the Clinton administration have been the boldest so far. The social engineers may have been temporarily blocked, but we can be sure that, after a strategic retreat, they will return to the attack.

On a deeper level, we have the continuing metamorphosis of the mentality of the American people—the government-sponsored diffusion of a rotten egalitarian, antiproperty, antibusiness mind-set. If you doubt this, try to talk to the average intelligent college student about the "sacred right of private property."

A New Beginning for America

With the end of the Cold War, it is time for Americans to begin enjoying the "peace dividend" they so richly deserve. The last thing we need now is yet another global crusade, to right every wrong and wipe away every tear. It may be that—in some sense—Americans are a "chosen" people, something special in the history of mankind. But, if so, it was not to take up and forever carry the cross of "global responsibility" that we were chosen. Rather, because of our origin in the universal ideals of reason, freedom, and individual rights, America's mission is to stand as a light to all nations: "This is what a society of free men and women looks like—this is how it works."

Ironically, as we have become a world power, America has less and less appeal to peoples around the world. Of course, the miserably poor and the appallingly tyrannized still flock here. But the model of America has fewer and fewer admirers in advanced countries. What is there to admire, after all, in our crime-ridden streets, our Third-World cities, our society plagued by racial strife? We can send planes and ships and armies everywhere on earth—we are the greatest military power that ever existed—and at home our civilization is crumbling. The governments of Britain and Germany have, in recent memory, felt compelled to issue warnings to their citizens against traveling to the United States—as if America were another Baja California. The more we have been able to project force around the globe, the more the beacon light of America has dimmed.

What does a foreign policy of America First imply? We must have defense forces and intelligence agencies adequate to meet any and every threat to the life, liberty, and property of Americans in the United States. Investors should be free to place their capital overseas *at their own risk*: there are plenty of countries that welcome American investment with open arms. The U.S. State Department and the Navy and Marines should not be placed at the disposal of the international corporations to act as their marketing agents and Pinkerton guards abroad.

One thing America First does *not* imply is protectionism. Rather, our rule should be free trade between America and the world—*unilateral* free trade, not *government-managed* trade, which our leaders are currently promoting.

It goes without saying that, culturally, we should be open to the world and the world to us—as we were for over a century, as we followed the principle of America First. In years and generations to come, technology will enhance the ease of communication and transportation beyond our dreams, and commerce among peoples will continue its phenomenal growth. In that sense, the peoples of the world will grow closer than ever before. But none of this entails—as the interventionists like to pretend—that we must surrender our national sovereignty, that the United States of America must cease to exist. *We are cosmopolitans, but we are not citizens of the world. We are citizens of the United States.* This is our land; this is our home. Technology will never erase that fact. To put it simply: when the EPA, or the Civil Rights Commission, or the BATF comes for you, you will not be able to vanish into cyberspace.

The decline of American sovereignty must be stopped. Naturally, we should negotiate international agreements for the rational protection of the global environment, as well as for other purposes. But the worst the future could hold for us is a world government, annulling our existence as a nation, and substituting the bogus UN "rights" to welfare and racial integration for our American Bill of Rights—beginning, of course, with the right of Americans to keep and bear arms, which the federal and international bureaucrats hate with such a strange passion.

We are citizens of the United States, and it is we who will have to decide whether it will be Empire or the Republic.

This paper was delivered at The Future of Freedom Foundation's fifth anniversary conference in October 1994.

5

Conscription

by Daniel Webster

This bill [for conscription] indeed is less undisguised in its object, and less direct in its means, than some of the measures proposed. It is an attempt to exercise the power of forcing the free men of this country into the ranks of an army, for the general purposes of war, under color of a military service. It is a distinct system, introduced for new purposes, and not connected with any power, which the Constitution has conferred on Congress. . . .

The question is nothing less, than whether the most essential rights of personal liberty shall be surrendered, and despotism embraced in its worst form. . . . I am anxious, above all things, to stand acquitted before GOD, and my conscience, and in the public judgments, of all participations in the Counsels, which have brought us to our present condition, and which now threaten the dissolution of the Government. When the present generation of men shall be swept away, and that this Government ever existed shall be a matter of history only, I desire that it may then be known, that you have not proceeded in your course unadmonished and unforewarned. Let it then be known, that there were those, who would have stopped you, in the career of your measures, and held you back, as by the skirts of your garments, from the precipice, over which you are plunging, and drawing after you the Government of your Country. . . .

Conscription is chosen as the most promising instrument, both of overcoming reluctance to the Service, and of subduing the difficulties which arise from the deficiencies of the Exchequer. The administration asserts the right to fill the ranks of the regular army by compulsion. . . .

Is this, Sir, consistent with the character of a free Government? Is this civil liberty? Is this the real character of our Constitution? No, Sir, indeed it is not. The Constitution is libelled, foully libelled. The people of this country have not established for themselves such a fabric of despotism. They have not purchased at a vast expense of their own treasure and their own blood a Magna Charta to be slaves. Where is it written in the Constitution, in what article or section is it contained, that you may take children from their parents, and parents from their children, and compel them to fight the battles of any war, in which the folly or the wickedness of Government may engage it? Under what concealment has this power lain hidden, which now for the first time comes forth, with a tremendous and baleful aspect, to trample down and destroy the dearest rights of personal liberty? Who will show me any constitutional injunction, which makes it the duty of the American people to surrender every thing valuable in life, and even life itself, not when the safety of their country and its liberties may demand the sacrifice, but whenever the purposes of an ambitious and mischievous Government may require it? Sir, I almost disdain to go to quotations and references to prove that such an abominable doctrine has no foundation in the Constitution of the country. It is enough to know that the instrument was intended as the basis of a free Government, and that the power contended for is incompatible with any notion of personal liberty. An attempt to maintain this doctrine upon the provisions of the Constitution is an exercise of perverse ingenuity to extract slavery from the substance of a free Government. It is an attempt to show, by proof and argument, that we ourselves are subjects of despotism, and that we have a right to chains and bondage, firmly secured to us and our children, by the provisions of our Government.

The supporters of the measures before us act on the principle that it is their task to raise arbitrary powers, by construction, out of a plain written charter of National Liberty. It is their pleasing duty to free us of the delusion, which we have fondly cherished, that we are the subjects of a mild, free and limited Government, and to demonstrate by a regular chain of premises and conclusions, that Government possesses over us a power more tyrannical, more arbitrary, more dangerous, more allied to blood and murder, more full of every form of mischief, more productive of every sort and degree of misery, than has been exercised by any civilized Government, with a single exception, in modern times. . . .

Sir, in granting Congress the power to raise armies, the People have granted all the means which are ordinary and usual, and which are consistent with the liberties and security of the People themselves; and they have granted no others. To talk about the unlimited power of the Government over the means to execute its authority, is to hold a language which is true only in regard to despotism. The tyranny of Arbitrary Government consists as much in its means as in its end; and it would be a ridiculous and absurd constitution which should be less cautious to guard against abuses in the one case than in the other. All the means and instruments which a free Government exercises, as well as the ends and objects which it pursues, are to partake of its own essential character, and to be conformed to its genuine spirit. A free Government with arbitrary means to administer it is a contradiction; a free Government without adequate provision for personal security is an absurdity; a free Government, with an uncontrolled power of military conscription, is a solecism, at once the most ridiculous and abominable that ever entered into the head of man. . . .

Nor is it, Sir, for the defense of his own house and home, that he who is the subject of military draft is to perform the task allotted to him. You will put him upon a service equally foreign to his interests and abhorrent to his feelings. With his aid you are to push your purposes of conquest. The battles which he is to fight are the battles of invasion; battles which he detests perhaps and abhors, less from the danger and the death that gather over them, and the blood with which they drench the plain, than from the principles in which they have their origin. If, Sir, in this strife he fall—if, while ready to obey every rightful command of Government, he is forced from home against right, not to contend for the defense of his country, but to prosecute a miserable and detestable project of invasion, and in that strife he fall, 'tis murder. It may stalk above the cognizance of human law, but in the sight of Heaven it is murder; and though millions of years may roll away, while his ashes and yours lie mingled together in the earth, the day will yet come, when his spirit and the spirits of his children must be met at the bar of omnipotent justice. May God, in his compassion, shield me from any participation in the enormity of this guilt. . . .

A military force cannot be raised, in this manner, but by the means of a military force. If the administration has found that it can not form an army without conscription, it will find, if it venture on these experiments, that it can not enforce conscription without an army. The Government was not constituted for such purposes. Framed in the spirit of liberty, and in the love of peace, it has no powers which render it able to enforce such laws. The attempt, if we rashly make it, will fail; and having already thrown away our peace, we may thereby throw away our Government.

This is an excerpt of a speech delivered by Daniel Webster (1782–1852) before the U.S. House of Representatives on December 9, 1814. A conscription bill was then before Congress, backed by the secretary of war, in order to further the conflict for the conquest of Canada. This excerpt is taken from Volume II of Ideas on Liberty, *published in 1954 by The Foundation for Economic Education, Irvington, New York. It was reprinted in the November 1990 issue of* Freedom Daily, *published by The Future of Freedom Foundation.*

6

Patriotism

by Herbert Spencer

Were any one to call me dishonest or untruthful he would touch me to the quick. Were he to say that I am unpatriotic, he would leave me unmoved. "What, then, have you no love of country?" That is a question not to be answered in a breath.

The early abolition of serfdom in England, the early growth of relatively free institutions, and the greater recognition of popular claims after the decay of feudalism had divorced the masses from the soil, were traits of English life which may be looked back upon with pride. When it was decided that any slave who set foot in England became free; when the importation of slaves into the Colonies was stopped; when twenty millions were paid for the emancipation of slaves in the West Indies; and when, however unadvisedly, a fleet was maintained to stop the slave-trade; our countrymen did things worthy to be admired. And when England gave a home to political refugees and took up the causes of small states struggling for freedom, it again exhibited noble traits which excite affection. But there are traits, unhappily of late more frequently displayed, which do the reverse. Contemplation of the acts by which England has acquired over eighty possessions—settlements, colonies, protectorates, etc.— does not arouse feelings of satisfaction. The transitions from missionaries to resident agents, then to officials having armed forces, then to punishments of those who resist their rule, ending in so-called "pacification"—these processes of annexation, now gradual and now sudden. . . . If because my love of country does not survive these and many other adverse experiences I am called unpatriotic—well, I am content to be so called.

To me the cry "Our country, right or wrong!" seems detestable. By association with love of country the sentiment it expresses gains a certain justification. Do but pull off the cloak, however, and the contained sentiment is seen to be of the lowest. Let us observe the alternative cases.

Suppose our country is in the right—suppose it is resisting invasion. Then the idea and feeling embodied in the cry are righteous. It may be effectively contended that self-defense is not only justified but is a duty. Now suppose, contrariwise, that our country is the aggressor—has taken possession of others' territory, or is forcing by arms certain commodities on a nation which does not want them, or is backing up some of its agents in "punishing" those who have retaliated. Suppose it is doing something which, by the hypothesis, is admitted to be wrong. What is then the implication of the cry? The right is on the side of those who oppose us; the wrong is on our side. How in that case is to be expressed the so-called patriotic wish? Evidently the words must stand—"Down with the right, up with the wrong!" Now in other relations this combination of aims implies the acme of wickedness. In the minds of past men there existed, and there still exists in many minds, a belief in a personalized principle of evil—a Being going up and down in the world everywhere fighting against the good and helping the bad to triumph. Can there be more briefly expressed the aim of that Being than in the words—"Up with the wrong and down with the right"? Do the so-called patriots like the endorsement?

Some years ago I gave expression to my own feeling—antipatriotic feeling, it will doubtless be called—in a somewhat startling way. It was at the time of the second Afghan war, when, in pursuance of what were thought to be "our interests," we were invading Afghanistan. News had come that some of our troops were in danger. At the Athenaeum Club a well-known military man—then a captain but now a general—drew my attention to a telegram containing this news, and read it to me in a manner implying the belief that I should share his anxiety. I astounded him by replying—"When men hire themselves out to shoot other men to order, asking nothing about the justice of their cause, I don't care if they are shot themselves."

I foresee the exclamation which will be called forth. Such a principle, it will be said, if accepted, would make an army impossible and a government powerless. It would never do to have each soldier use his judgment about the purpose for which a battle is waged.

Military organization would be paralyzed and our country would be a prey to the first invader.

Not so fast, is the reply. For one war an army would remain just as available as now—a war of national defense. In such a war every soldier would be conscious of the justice of his cause. He would not be engaged in dealing death among men about whose doings, good or ill, he knew nothing, but among men who were manifest transgressors against himself and his compatriots. Only aggressive war would be negatived, not defensive war.

Of course it may be said, and said truly, that if there is no aggressive war there can be no defensive war. It is clear, however, that one nation may limit itself to defensive war when other nations do not. So that the principle remains operative.

But those whose cry is—"Our country, right or wrong!" and who would add to our eighty-odd possessions others to be similarly obtained, will contemplate with disgust such a restriction upon military action. To them no folly seems greater than that of practicing on Monday the principles they profess on Sunday.

Herbert Spencer (1820–1903), an Englishman, ranks as one of the foremost individualist philosophers in history. This essay appeared in his Facts and Comments, *published in 1902. It was reprinted in the May 1990 issue of* Freedom Daily, *published by The Future of Freedom Foundation.*

7

The Conquest of
the United States by Spain
(1898)

by William Graham Sumner

Spain was the first, for a long time the greatest, of the modern imperialistic states. The United States, by its historical origin, its traditions, and its principles, is the chief representative of the revolt and reaction against that kind of a state. I intend to show that, by the line of action now proposed to us, which we call expansion and imperialism, we are throwing away some of the most important elements of the American symbol and are adopting some of the most important elements of the Spanish symbol. We have beaten Spain in a military conflict, but we are submitting to be conquered by her on the field of ideas and policies. Expansionism and imperialism are nothing but the old philosophies of national prosperity which have brought Spain to where she now is. Those philosophies appeal to national vanity and national cupidity. They are seductive, especially upon the first view and the most superficial judgment, and therefore it cannot be denied that they are very strong for popular effect. They are delusions, and they will lead us to ruin unless we are hard-headed enough to resist them. In any case the year 1898 is a great landmark in the history of the United States. . . .

Spanish mistakes arose, in part, from confusing the public treasury with the national wealth. They thought that, when gold flowed into the public treasury, that was the same as an increase of wealth of the people. It really meant that the people were bearing the burdens of the imperial system and that the profits of it went into the public treasury; that is, into the hands of the king. It was no wonder, then, that as the burdens grew greater the people grew poorer. . . .

Now what will hasten the day when our present advantages will wear out and when we shall come down to the conditions of the older and densely populated nations? The answer is: war, debt, taxation, diplomacy, a grand governmental system, pomp, glory, a big army and navy, lavish expenditures, political jobbery—in a word, imperialism. In the old days the democratic masses of this country, who knew little about our modern doctrines of social philosophy, had a sound instinct on these matters, and it is no small ground of political disquietude to see it decline. They resisted every appeal to their vanity in the way of pomp and glory which they knew must be paid for. They dreaded a public debt and a standing army. They were narrow-minded and went too far with these notions, but they were, at least, right, if they wanted to strengthen democracy. . . .

Expansion and imperialism are at war with the best traditions, principles, and interests of the American people, and . . . they will plunge us into a network of difficult problems and political perils, which we might have avoided, while they offer us no corresponding advantage in return. . . .

And yet this scheme of a republic which our fathers formed was a glorious dream which demands more than a word of respect and affection before it passes away. Indeed, it is not fair to call it a dream or even an ideal; it was a possibility which was within our reach if we had been wise enough to grasp and hold it. . . . There were to be no armies except a militia, which would have no functions but those of police. . . . They would have no public debt. They repudiated with scorn the notion that a public debt is a public blessing; if debt was incurred in war it was to be paid in peace and not entailed on posterity. There was to be no grand diplomacy, because they intended to mind their own business and not be involved in any of the intrigues to which European statesmen were accustomed. . . . Our fathers would have an economical government, even if grand people called it a parsimonious one, and taxes should be no greater than were absolutely necessary to pay for such a government. The citizen was to keep all the rest of his earnings and use them as he thought best for the happiness of himself and his family; he was, above all, to be insured peace and quiet while he pursued his honest industry and obeyed the laws. No adventurous policies of conquest or ambition, such as, in the belief of our fathers, kings and nobles had forced, for their own advantage, on European states, would ever be undertaken by a free democratic republic. Therefore the citizen here would never be forced to leave his family or to give his sons to shed blood for glory and to leave widows and orphans in misery for nothing. Justice and law were to reign in the midst of simplicity, and a government which had little to do was to offer little field for ambition. In a society where industry, frugality, and prudence were honored, it was believed that the vices of wealth would never flourish. . . .

There are people who are boasting of their patriotism, because they say that we have taken our place now amongst the nations of the earth by virtue of this war [the Spanish-American War]. My patriotism is of the kind which is outraged by the notion that the United States never was a great nation until in a petty three months' campaign it knocked to pieces a poor, decrepit, bankrupt old state like Spain. To hold such an opinion as that is to abandon all American standards, to put shame and scorn on all that our ancestors tried to build up here, and to go over to the standards of which Spain is a representative.

William Graham Sumner (1840–1910), an American sociologist and econo-mist, was one of the most ardent proponents of individual freedom. This essay is from his War and Other Essays, *published by Yale University Press, New Haven. It was reprinted in the May 1990 issue of* Freedom Daily, *published by The Future of Freedom Foundation.*

8

American Foreign Policy— The Turning Point, 1898–1919

by Ralph Raico

Part I

With the end of the twentieth century rapidly approaching, this is a time to look back and gain some perspective on where we stand as a nation. Were the Founding Fathers somehow to return, they would find it impossible to recognize our political system. The major cause of this transformation has been America's involvement in war and preparation for war over the past hundred years. War has warped our constitutional order, the course of our national development, and the very mentality of our people.

The process of distortion started about a century ago, when certain fateful steps were taken that in time altered fundamentally the character of our republic. One idea of America was abandoned and another took its place, although no conscious, deliberate decision was ever made. Eventually, this change affected all areas of American life, so that today our nation is radically different from the original ideal, and, indeed, from the ideal probably still cherished by most Americans.

The turning point was signaled by a series of military adventures: the war with Spain, the war for the conquest of the Philippines, and, finally, our entry into the First World War. Together, they represented a profound break with American traditions of government.

Until the end of the nineteenth century, American foreign policy essentially followed the guidelines laid down by George

Washington, in his Farewell Address to the American people: "The great rule of conduct for us in regard to foreign nations is—in extending our commercial relations—to have with them as little *political* connection as possible."

The purpose of Washington's admonition against entanglements with foreign powers was to minimize the chance of war. James Madison, the father of the Constitution, expressed this understanding when he wrote:

> Of all enemies to public liberty, war is, perhaps, the most to be dreaded, because it comprises and develops the germ of every other. War is the parent of armies; from these proceed debts and taxes; and armies, and debts, and taxes are the known instruments for bringing the many under the domination of the few.

History taught that republics that engaged in frequent wars eventually lost their character as free states. Hence, war was to be undertaken only in defense of our nation against attack. The system of government that the Founders were bequeathing to us—with its division of powers, checks and balances, and power concentrated in the states rather than the federal government—depended on peace as the normal condition of our society.

This was the position not only of Washington and Madison, but of John Adams, Thomas Jefferson, and the other men who presided over the birth of the United States. For over a century, it was adhered to and elaborated by our leading statesmen. It could be called neutrality, or nonintervention, or America First, or, as its modern enemies dubbed it, isolationism. The great revisionist historian Charles A. Beard called it Continental Americanism. This is how Beard defined it in *A Foreign Policy for America*, published in 1940:

> [It is] a concentration of interest on the continental domain and on building here a civilization in many respects peculiar to American life and the potentials of the American heritage. In concrete terms, the words mean non-intervention in the controversies and wars of Europe and Asia and resistance to the intrusion of European or Asiatic powers, systems, and imperial ambitions into the western hemisphere [as threatening to our security].

An important implication of this principle was that, while we honored the struggle for freedom of other peoples, we would not become a knight-errant, spreading our ideals throughout the world

54

by force of arms. John Quincy Adams, secretary of state to James Monroe and later himself president of the United States, declared, in 1821:

> Wherever the standard of freedom and independence has been or shall be unfurled, there will be America's heart, her benedictions, and her prayers. But she does not go abroad in search of monsters to destroy. She is the well-wisher to the freedom and independence of all. She is the champion and vindicator only of her own.

John Quincy Adams was the real architect of what became known as the Monroe Doctrine. In order to ensure our security, we advised European powers to refrain from interfering in the Western Hemisphere. In return, however, we promised not to interfere in the affairs of Europe. The implied contract was broken and the Monroe Doctrine annulled in the early twentieth century by Theodore Roosevelt and, above all, Woodrow Wilson.

This noninterventionist America, devoted to solving its own problems and developing its own civilization, became the wonder of the world. The eyes and hopes of freedom-loving peoples were turned to the Great Republic of the West.

But sometimes the leaders of peoples fighting for their independence misunderstood the American point of view. This was the case with the Hungarians, who had fought a losing battle against the Habsburg monarchy and its Russian allies. Their cause was championed by many sectors of American public opinion. When the Hungarian patriot Louis Kossuth came to America, he was wildly cheered. He was presented to the president and Congress and hailed by the secretary of state, Daniel Webster. But they all refused to help in any concrete way. No public money, no arms, aid, or troops were forthcoming for the Hungarian cause. Kossuth grew bitter and disillusioned. He sought the help of Henry Clay, by then the grand old man of American politics. Clay explained to Kossuth why the American leaders had acted as they did: By giving official support to the Hungarian cause, we would have abandoned "our ancient policy of amity and non-intervention." Clay explained:

> By the policy to which we have adhered since the days of Washington . . . we have done more for the cause of liberty in the world than arms could effect; we have shown to other nations the way to greatness and happiness. . . . Far better is it for ourselves, for Hungary, and the cause of liberty, that, adhering

to our pacific system and avoiding the distant wars of Europe, we should keep our lamp burning brightly on this western shore, as a light to all nations, than to hazard its utter extinction amid the ruins of fallen and falling republics in Europe.

Similarly, in 1863, when Russia crushed a Polish revolt with great brutality, the French Emperor invited us to join in a protest to the Tsar. Lincoln's secretary of state, William Seward, replied, defending "our policy of non-intervention—straight, absolute, and peculiar as it may seem to other nations":

The American people must be content to recommend the cause of human progress by the wisdom with which they should exercise the powers of self-government, forbearing at all times, and in every way, from foreign alliances, intervention, and interference.

This policy by no means entailed the "isolation" of the United States. Throughout these decades, trade and cultural exchange flourished, as American civilization progressed and we became an economic powerhouse. The only thing that was prohibited was the kind of intervention in foreign affairs that was likely to embroil us in war.

Towards the end of the nineteenth century, however, a different philosophy began to emerge. In Europe, the free-trade and noninterventionist ideas of the classical liberals were fading; more and more, the European states went in for imperialism. The establishment of colonies and coaling stations around the globe—and the creation of vast armies and navies to occupy and garrison them—became the order of the day.

In the United States, this imperialism found an echo in the political class. In 1890, Admiral Alfred Thayer Mahan, of the Naval War College, published *The Influence of Sea Power Upon History*. Soon translated into many foreign languages, it was used by imperialists in Britain, Germany, Japan, and elsewhere to intensify the naval arms race and the scramble for colonies. In America, a young politician named Theodore Roosevelt made it his Bible.

The great Democratic president Grover Cleveland—strict constitutionalist and champion of the gold standard, free trade, and laissez-faire—held out against the rising tide. But ideas of a "manifest destiny" for America transcending the continent and stretching out to the whole world were taking over the Republican Party. Roosevelt, Mahan, Sen. Henry Cabot Lodge, John Hay, and others formed a cabal imbued with the new, proudly imperialist vision. They called their program "the large policy."

To them, America up until then had been too small. As Roosevelt declared, "The trouble with our nation is that we incline to fall into mere animal sloth and ease." Americans lacked the will to plunge into the bracing current of world politics, to court great dangers, and do great deeds. Instead, they were mired in their own petty and parochial affairs—their families, their work, their communities, their churches, and schools. In spite of themselves, the American people would have to be dragged to greatness by their leaders.

Often, the imperialists put their case in terms of the allegedly urgent need to find foreign markets and capital outlets for American business. But this was a propaganda ploy, and American business itself was largely skeptical of this appeal. Charles Beard, no great friend of capitalists, wrote, "Loyalty to the facts of the historical record must ascribe the idea of imperial expansion mainly to naval officers and politicians rather than to businessmen." For instance, as the imperialist frenzy spread and began to converge on hostility to Spain and Spanish policy in Cuba, a Boston stockbroker voiced the views of many of his class when he complained to Senator Lodge that what businessmen really wanted was "peace and quiet." He added, with amazing prescience, "If we attempt to regulate the affairs of the whole world we will be in hot water from now until the end of time."

In 1896, the imperialists got their chance, when William McKinley replaced Grover Cleveland as president. McKinley has the reputation of an "archconservative." In reality, as Walter Karp wrote in his brilliant work *The Politics of War*, "What McKinley envisioned for the American Republic was a genuine new order of things, a modern centralized order, elitist in every way, and profoundly alien to the spirit of the Republic." The key to McKinley's transformation of America would be the "large policy." McKinley made Hay his secretary of state and brought Theodore Roosevelt into the Navy Department. And a golden opportunity presented itself: the plight of Spain in its rebellious colony Cuba.

Part II

The year 1898 was a landmark in American history. It was the year America went to war with Spain—our first engagement with a foreign enemy in the dawning age of modern warfare. Aside from a few scant periods of retrenchment, we have been embroiled in foreign politics ever since.

Starting in the 1880s, a group of Cubans agitated for independence from Spain. Like many revolutionaries before and after, they had little real support among the mass of the population. Thus they resorted to terrorist tactics— devastating the countryside, dynamiting railroads, and killing those who stood in their way. The Spanish authorities responded with harsh countermeasures.

Some American investors in Cuba grew restive, but the real forces pushing America towards intervention were not a handful of sugarcane planters. The slogans the rebels used—"freedom" and "independence"—resonated with many Americans, who knew nothing of the real circumstances in Cuba. Also playing a part was the "black legend"—the stereotype of the Spaniards as blood-thirsty despots that Americans had inherited from their English forebears. It was easy for Americans to believe the stories peddled by the insurgents, especially when the "yellow" press discovered that whipping up hysteria over largely concocted Spanish "atrocities"— while keeping quiet about those committed by the rebels—sold papers.

Politicians on the lookout for publicity and popular favor saw a gold mine in the Cuban issue. Soon the American government was directing notes to Spain expressing its "concern" over "events" in Cuba. In fact, the "events" were merely the tactics colonial powers typically used in fighting a guerrilla war. As bad or worse was being done by Britain, France, Germany, and others all over the globe in that age of imperialism. Spain, aware of the immense superiority of American forces, responded to the interference from Washington by attempts at appeasement, while trying to preserve the shreds of its dignity as an ancient imperial power.

When William McKinley became president in 1897, he was already planning to expand America's role in the world. Spain's Cuban troubles provided the perfect opportunity. Publicly, McKinley declared: "We want no wars of conquest; we must avoid the temptation of territorial aggression." But within the U. S. government, the influential cabal that was seeking war and expansion knew they had found their man. Sen. Henry Cabot Lodge wrote to Theodore Roosevelt, now at the Navy Department, "Unless I am profoundly mistaken, the Administration is now committed to the large policy we both desire." This "large policy," also supported by Secretary of State John Hay and other key figures, aimed at breaking decisively with our tradition of nonintervention and neutrality in foreign affairs. The United States would at last assume its "global responsibilities," and join the other great powers in the scramble for territory around the world.

The leaders of the war party camouflaged their plans by speaking of the need to procure markets for American industry and were even able to convince a few business leaders to parrot their line. But in reality none of this clique of haughty patricians— "old money," for the most part—had any strong interest in business, or even much respect for it, except as the source of national strength. Like similar cliques in Britain, Germany, Russia, and elsewhere at the time, their aim was the enhancement of the power and glory of their state.

In order to escalate the pressure on Spain, the battleship USS *Maine* was dispatched to Havana harbor. On the night of February 15, 1898, the *Maine* exploded, killing 252 men. Suspicion immediately focused on the Spaniards— although they had the least to gain from the destruction of the *Maine*. It was much more likely that the boilers had blown up—or even that the rebels themselves had mined the ship, to draw America into a war the rebels could not win on their own. The press screamed for vengeance against perfidious Spain, and interventionist politicians believed their hour had come.

McKinley, anxious to preserve his image as a cautious statesman, bided his time. He pressed Spain to stop fighting the rebels and start negotiating with them for Cuban independence, hinting broadly that the alternative was war. The Spaniards, averse to simply handing the island over to a terrorist junta, were willing to grant autonomy. Finally, desperate to avoid war with America, Madrid did proclaim an armistice—a stunning concession for one sovereign state to make at the bidding of another.

But this was not enough for McKinley, who had his eyes set on bagging a few of Spain's remaining possessions. On April 11, he delivered his war message to Congress, carefully omitting to mention the concession of an armistice. A week later, Congress passed the war resolution McKinley wanted.

In the Far East, Commodore George Dewey was given the go-ahead to carry out a prearranged plan: proceed to the Philippines and secure control of Manila harbor. This he did, bringing along Emilio Aguinaldo and his Filipino independence fighters. In the Caribbean, American forces quickly subdued the Spaniards in Cuba, and then, after Spain sued for peace, went on to take over Puerto Rico, as well. In three months, the fighting was over. It had been, as Secretary of State John Hay famously put it, "a splendid little war."

The quick U.S. trouncing of decrepit Spain filled the American public with euphoria. It was a victory, people believed, for American ideals and the American way of life against an Old World tyranny. Our triumphant arms would guarantee Cuba a free and democratic future.

Against this tidal wave of public elation, one man spoke out. He was William Graham Sumner—Yale professor, famed social scientist, and tireless fighter for private enterprise, free trade, and the gold standard. Now he was about to enter his hardest fight of all.

On January 16, 1899, Sumner addressed an overflow crowd of the Yale chapter of Phi Beta Kappa. He knew that the assembled Yalies and the rest of the audience were brimming with patriotic pride. With studied irony, Sumner titled his talk "The Conquest of the United States by Spain." (It is contained in the Liberty Press edition of *On Liberty, Society, and Politics: The Essential Essays of William Graham Sumner.*)

Sumner threw down the gauntlet:

> We have beaten Spain in a military conflict, but we are submitting to be conquered by her on the field of ideas and policies. Expansionism and imperialism are nothing but the old philosophies of national prosperity which have brought Spain to where she is now.

Sumner proceeded to outline the original vision of America cherished by the Founding Fathers, radically different from what prevailed among the nations of Europe:

> They would have no court and no pomp; nor orders, or ribbons, or decorations, or titles. They would have no public debt. . . . There was to be no grand diplomacy, because they intended to mind their own business, and not be involved in any of the intrigues to which European statesmen were accustomed. There was to be no balance of power and no "reason of state" to cost the life and happiness of citizens.

This had been the American idea, our signature as a nation: "It is by virtue of this conception of a commonwealth that the United States has stood for something unique and grand in the history of mankind and that its people have been happy."

The system the Founders bequeathed to us, Sumner held, was a delicate one, providing for the division and balance of powers and aimed at keeping government small and local. It was no accident that Washington, Jefferson, and the others who created the republic issued clear warnings against "foreign entanglements." A policy of foreign adventurism would, in the nature of things, bend and twist and ultimately shatter our original system. As foreign affairs became more important, power would shift from communities and states to the federal government, and, within that, from Congress to the president. An ever busy foreign policy could only be carried out by the president, often without the knowledge of the people. Thus, the American system, based on local government, states' rights, and Congress as the voice of the people on the national level, would more and more give way to a bloated bureaucracy headed by an imperial presidency.

But now, with the war against Spain and the philosophy behind it, we were letting ourselves in for the old European way, Sumner declared—"war, debt, taxation, diplomacy, a grand governmental system, pomp, glory, a big army and navy, lavish expenditures, political jobbery—in a word, imperialism."

Already, it seems, the global meddlers had come up with what was to be their favorite smear word: "isolationist." And already Sumner had the appropriate retort. The imperialists "warn us against the terrors of 'isolation,' " he said, but "our ancestors all came here to isolate themselves" from the burdens of the Old World. "When the others are all struggling under debt and taxes, who would not be isolated in the enjoyment of his own earnings for the benefit of his own family?"

In abandoning our own system, there would be, Sumner freely admitted, compensations. Immortal glory is not nothing, as the Spaniards well knew. To be a part, even a pawn, in a mighty enterprise of armies and navies, to identify with great imperial power projected around the world, to see the flag raised on victorious battlefields—many peoples in history thought that game well worth the candle. Only . . . only, it was not the *American* way. That way had been more modest, more prosaic, parochial, and, yes, middle class. It was based on the idea that we were here to live out our lives, minding our own business, enjoying our liberty and pursuing our happiness in our work, families, churches, and communities. It had been the "small policy."

There is a logic in human affairs, Sumner the social scientist cautioned—once you make a certain decision, some paths that were open to you before are closed, and you are led, step by step, in a certain direction. America was choosing the path of world power, and Sumner had little hope that his words could change that. Why was he speaking out then? Simply because "this scheme of a republic which our fathers formed was a glorious dream which demands more than a word of respect and affection before it passes away."

Sumner had to endure a storm of abuse for spoiling the national victory party. But suddenly the imperialists had problems of their own: before they could take control of the Philippines, they had to defeat Aguinaldo and his Filipino insurgents, now fighting for independence from America.

Part III

By 1899, the United States was involved in its first war in Asia. Three others were to follow in the course of the next century: against Japan, North Korea and China, and, finally, Vietnam. But our first Asian war was against the Filipinos.

At the end of the Spanish-American War, we collected Puerto Rico as a colony, set up a protectorate over Cuba, and annexed the Hawaiian Islands. President McKinley also forced Spain to cede the Philippine Islands. To the American people, McKinley explained that, almost against his will, he had been led to make the decision to annex: "There was nothing left for us to do but to take them all, and educate the Filipinos, and uplift and civilize and christianize them as our fellow-men for whom Christ also died." McKinley was either unaware or simply chose not to inform the people that, except for some Muslim tribesmen in the south, the Filipinos were Roman Catholics, and, therefore, by most accounts, already Christians. In reality, the annexation of the Philippines was the centerpiece of the "large policy" pushed by the imperialist cabal to enlist the United States in the ranks of the great powers. To encourage the Americans in their new role, Rudyard Kipling, the British imperialist writer, composed a poem urging them to "take up the White Man's Burden."

There was a problem, however. When the war with Spain started, Emilio Aguinaldo, the leader of the Philippine independence movement, had been brought to the islands by Commodore Dewey himself. Aguinaldo had raised an army of Filipino troops who had acquitted themselves well against the Spanish forces. But they had fought side by side with the Americans to gain their independence from Spain, not to change imperial masters. With the Spaniards gone, the Filipinos prepared a constitution for their new country—while McKinley prepared to conquer it. Hostilities broke out in February 1899, and an American army of 60,000 men was sent halfway across the globe to subdue a native people.

Probably a majority of Americans joined in the fun of the faraway war. But thoughtful citizens wondered what this strange adventure would mean for the Republic.

To protest the war with Spain, the Anti-Imperialist League had been formed. It included some of the most distinguished figures in politics, business, journalism, and education. Most were also, not by accident, believers in the classical-liberal, laissez-faire vision of American society and staunch advocates of free enterprise, small government, low taxes, and the gold standard. Now the League turned its efforts to ending the war against the Philippines and stopping the annexation of the islands. What was occurring, they warned, was a revolution. While most Americans remained seemingly unaware or unconcerned, the United States was entering onto the road of imperialism, which, the League declared, "is hostile to liberty and tends towards militarism, an evil from which it is our glory to be free." The "large policy" of global expansion would mean never-ending war and preparation for war; and that would mean ever increasing government control and ever higher taxes.

Carl Schurz, leader of the German-American community, had come here to escape militarism and arbitrary government in his native country. He pointed out the consequences of the new dispensation: "Every American farmer and workingman, when going to his toil, will, like his European brother, have to carry a fully-armed soldier on his back." Edward Atkinson, who was head of a Boston insurance company and a radical libertarian, produced a series of pamphlets, including "The Cost of a National Crime," detailing the U.S. military oppression of the Filipinos as well as the burgeoning cost of the war to peaceful American taxpayers. E. L. Godkin, editor of *The Nation*, at the time the country's leading classical-liberal magazine, accused the imperialists of wanting to make America into "a great nation" in the European style and thus prove that Washington and Jefferson had been a pair of "old fools." Andrew Carnegie critiqued the doctrine that annexation of the Philippines was somehow required for American prosperity. And Mark Twain weighed in with sardonic blasts at a marauding American government that was betraying the principles it allegedly upheld. For their pains, the opponents of the war were smeared as contemptible "traitors" by the establishment press, led by the *New York Times*.

The anti-imperialists gained powerful ammunition for their attacks when letters from American soldiers to their families at home detailed—often with naive pride—the atrocities being committed by U.S. troops. Prisoners were routinely shot, whole villages burned down, civilians, including children, killed in batches of hundreds— all with the knowledge of—and usually under the direction of— commanding officers. Soon the Filipino victims were in the tens of thousands, and the number of American casualties far outnumbered those of the Spanish-American War itself. Americans in the Philippines were conducting themselves worse than the Spaniards ever had in Cuba. People wondered: How did we ever get ourselves into such a mess? The anti-imperialists pointed out that this was how the British were acting in the Sudan, the Italians in Abyssinia, the Germans in Southwest Africa. It was part of the price of empire.

The dirty war went on until, in March 1901, Aguinaldo was captured and the Filipino fighters surrendered. But now America was an Asiatic power, plunged into the maelstrom of the imperialist struggle in the Far East. Secretary of State John Hay proclaimed the "Open Door" policy in China: American diplomatic, political, and, if necessary, military power would be applied to *force* free trade throughout China. Our advance base in the Philippines and our wide-ranging Chinese policy would obviously entail conflict with powers already there. Already, at the Navy Department, they were beginning to talk of the coming "inevitable" war with Japan.

We began to meddle in world affairs—or, as the imperialists put it, to assume our "global responsibilities"—in ways our leaders had studiously avoided before. We took part in international conferences; we dispatched troops to China to join those of the other powers in putting down the Boxer Rebellion of Chinese patriots; we sailed our shining new navy around the world to show that we too had become a world power; and our government became a promoter of overseas investment and foreign trade on a grand scale and at taxpayers' expense. In Washington, the bureaucracies expanded at the State Department, the Navy Department, and elsewhere, filled with bright young men steeped in the new vision of America's global destiny. More and more, the American wealth machine was diverted to furnishing the underpinnings of world power.

When McKinley was assassinated in 1901, he was succeeded as president by one of the country's prime imperialists. Theodore Roosevelt was a politician of the new breed through and through. With great insight, H. L. Mencken later compared him with Kaiser Wilhelm of Germany. Both loved big armies and, especially, navies, Mencken wrote, and both believed in strong government both at home and abroad; no one ever heard either of them ever speak of the rights of man, only of the duties of citizens to the state. Interestingly, Teddy Roosevelt was a boyhood hero of a later American president— Lyndon Johnson—who admired his "toughness."

A good deal of that reputation for "toughness" derived from the Perdicaris affair in 1904. This episode showed for the first time how an instant "success" overseas could be used by a president for his own political advantage. A Republican convention was meeting in Chicago, without much enthusiasm, to renominate Roosevelt for president. Ion Perdicaris was a wealthy merchant living in Morocco. Allegedly an American citizen, he had been seized by a Moroccan chieftain named Raisuli and held for ransom. Roosevelt rushed American warships to Tangiers, and the famous, curt message was telegraphed to the Sultan: "Perdicaris alive or Raisuli dead."

When the Republican convention heard the news, it went wild with patriotic fervor. The only problem was that the State Department had already informed Roosevelt that Perdicaris was no longer an American citizen, having registered as a Greek subject in Athens for business reasons. Moreover, arrangements had already been made to free him. Roosevelt was aware of all of this; but the political gain from deceiving the public was too tempting. In time, other presidents would learn the same trick of projecting American power overseas simply to give their personal popularity a much-needed boost.

In 1912, Woodrow Wilson was elected president in a three-way election. Wilson was a "progressive," a leader in the movement that advocated using the full power of government to create "real democracy" at home. But Wilson's horizons were much broader than the United States. Preaching the gospel of "making the world safe for democracy," he aimed to extend the progressive creed to the ends of the earth. More than Franklin Roosevelt himself, Woodrow Wilson is the patron saint of the "exporting democracy" clique in America today.

Even before the crisis came, Wilson announced his new revelation:

> It is America's duty and privilege to stand shoulder to shoulder to lift the burdens of mankind in the future and show the paths of freedom to all the world. America is henceforth to stand for the assertion of the right of one nation to serve the other nations of the world.

Soon America had its chance to serve. In 1914, Europe went to war, the bloodiest and costliest war in history up to that time.

The First World War was triggered by the assassination of the Archduke Francis Ferdinand, heir to the throne of Austria-Hungary, in Sarajevo, by a Bosnian Serb. But the war's twisted roots went back for decades in the dark and complex diplomacy of the great powers. By 1914, Europe was an armed camp, divided into two great opposing blocks: the Triple Entente of France, Russia, and England, and the Triple Alliance of Germany, Austria-Hungary, and a less-than-reliable Italy. All the powers had vast armies and navies, equipped with the latest, most expensive weapons modern technology could produce.

When they heard of the murder of the Archduke (and of his wife Sophie), the Austrians decided to put an end, once and for all, to the Serbian threat to their tottering empire. They felt secure in the support of a powerful Germany. But Serbia was the protégé of Russia and the key to Russia's designs in the Balkans. And Russia was allied with France, which in turn was linked to Britain by a "cordial understanding," or Entente Cordiale. In the last weeks of July, halfhearted peace proposals were swept aside, as mutual fear gripped the European leaders and the orders were issued to mobilize the great armies. Ultimatums and declarations of war followed each other in rapid succession. By August 4, 1914, the European powers were at war and their armies were on the march.

Part IV

Once war broke out in 1914, each of the European powers felt that its very existence was at stake, and rules of international law were rapidly abandoned.

The Germans violated Belgian neutrality because their war plan called for the quick defeat of France, and that could best be accomplished if the German army cut through Belgium. Britain declared a blockade of Germany that was illegal according to the accepted rules, since it was effected simply by laying mines, rather than by closing off German harbors with the use of surface ships. The Germans protested that the aim of the blockade—to starve them into submission by denying food to the civilian population—was also illegal. The British, who held undisputed command of the seas, ignored the German protests.

In the United States, public opinion was sharply divided, although into unequal segments. The great majority of Americans saw no reason for us to become involved in what was rapidly becoming a bloodbath. They felt that the European powers, having indulged themselves in rampant imperialism and militarism for a generation, were now reaping the whirlwind of their own political vices. For most Americans, the wisdom of the Founding Fathers' advice—steer clear of foreign entanglements—was being demonstrated as never before.

But these tens of millions of Americans who wished for peace were mostly content to go about their business, trusting their government to keep the nation out of war. Meanwhile, a much smaller segment of the population harbored very different feelings. Concentrated on the eastern seaboard, and centered in New York, its members included most of the country's social elite, which was by inclination and family tradition strongly pro-English. Prominent among the supporters of the Allied cause were the major New York banks. After it was over, Thomas W. Lamont, senior partner of the House of Morgan, referred to the first weeks of the European war:

Those were the days when American citizens were being urged to remain neutral in action, in word, and even in thought. But our firm had never for one moment been neutral. We didn't know how to be. From the very start, we did everything we could to contribute to the cause of the Allies.

It was Woodrow Wilson himself, the president of the United States, who had cautioned his countrymen to remain neutral, even in thought. Yet in Washington, Wilson was surrounded by supporters of the English cause, the most important being Col. Edward M. House, his advisor and intimate friend. The American ambassador to Britain, Walter Hines Page, was so pro-British he sometimes even astonished his English hosts. The only man in government who seemed to reflect the people's desire for peace was the secretary of state, William Jennings Bryan. For, despite his protestations of neutrality, Woodrow Wilson, deep down, was as much a partisan of England as most of his advisors. In private, Wilson confided to his press secretary:

> England is fighting our fight, and you may well understand that I shall not, in the present state of the world's affairs, place obstacles in her way when she is fighting for her life—and the life of the world.

What Wilson was referring to were the violations of neutral rights being committed on the seas by the British in implementing their hunger blockade. American ships could not enter vast areas, on pain of being blown up by mines. Ships carrying goods that no one except the British considered to be contraband were prohibited from sailing to Germany and even to neutral ports. Mail bound for the continent was seized and searched. Occasionally, Washington chided the British government in a mild protest. But Walter Hines Page, our ambassador, was always ready to explain to his English friends that we did not really mean it.

The Germans announced that they were responding to the British blockade with submarine warfare, while admitting that they could not guarantee that neutral interests would be safeguarded. Now Washington came down hard. A note was sent to Berlin:

> If the commanders of German vessels should destroy on the high seas an American vessel or the lives of American citizens, it would be difficult for the Government of the United States to

view the act in any other light than as an indefensible violation of neutral rights.

The United States, the note warned, would hold Germany "strictly accountable" for the loss of American ships or lives through the actions of German submarines. The Germans replied that they would cease submarine warfare if the British lifted their illegal blockade.

On May 7, 1915, cruising off the southern coast of Ireland, Capt. Walter Schwieger, of U-boat 20, found a target. Schwieger suspected the truth: that although a passenger liner, the British ship was carrying large amounts of explosives. From captured documents, Schwieger knew that many British merchant ships had been outfitted with guns and were under instructions to ram any surfacing submarine. He took no chances and fired a torpedo. An explosion aboard the ship caused it to start sinking at once. Schwieger had sunk the *Lusitania*, star of the British Cunard Line. Around 1,200 persons were killed, including 128 Americans.

Just as with the *Maine* in Havana in 1898 and the battleships at Pearl Harbor in 1941, mystery still surrounds the sinking of the *Lusitania*. Why was it sailing without destroyer escort through a notorious submarine zone? The first lord of the admiralty, Winston Churchill, had declared that there was nothing he would not do for his country, including "embroiling" neutrals in the war on England's side. A number of students of the case have concluded that the sinking of the *Lusitania* had been arranged, in order to bring America into the war.

This was exactly what many influential Americans now demanded, including Theodore Roosevelt and Henry Cabot Lodge. Colonel House noted in his diary: "I have concluded that war with Germany is inevitable," and advised Wilson accordingly. Secretary of State Bryan tried to stem the hysteria. He pointed to what an investigation had revealed—that the *Lusitania* was carrying 5,500 cases of ammunition—and declared that Americans should not book passage on British ships with mixed cargoes of "bullets and babies." Bryan told Wilson:

> We unsparingly denounce the retaliatory methods employed by Germany, without condemning the announced purpose of the Allies to starve the non-combatants of Germany and without complaining of the conduct of Great Britain in relying on passengers, including men, women, and children of the United States, to give immunity to a vessel carrying munitions of war.

Wilson hesitated. Finally, he decided to give the Germans one last warning, again holding them "strictly accountable," but not admonishing the British in any way. Bryan, realizing that this policy sooner or later meant war, resigned.

Meanwhile, public opinion was starting to shift. There is no doubt that outside of the corridor that ran from Boston to Washington, the majority of Americans still demanded peace. Yet the influential newspapers were more and more urging "action" against Germany, and British propaganda was taking its toll. Many Americans were startled to read about the horrendous atrocities committed by German troops in Belgium: nuns raped and murdered; prisoners crucified on barn doors; babies maimed and slaughtered for amusement. Perhaps England was not just defending its own political and strategic interests, but really fighting for civilization itself? And wasn't the cause of civilization an American cause as well? After the war was over, investigations by various commissions revealed the truth: though the Germans were harsh in punishing civilians who chose to engage in combat, the "atrocities" were a hoax. Later, Joseph Goebbels, Nazi minister of propaganda, admired the British propaganda in World War I so much that he modeled his own campaigns on the "big lie" of the "Belgian atrocities."

In Berlin, the Kaiser's government decided to discontinue attacks on enemy passenger liners, even if armed and carrying munitions of war. But they insisted that the British should be compelled to "observe the rules of international law universally recognized before the War," and terminate their blockade. This condition, however, Wilson chose to ignore. The diplomatic controversy between Germany and the United States dragged on for months.

A noisy campaign for "preparedness" began in the United States, led by Theodore Roosevelt and Gen. Leonard Wood. The aim was to instill in the public an awareness of alleged threats to our national security. Summer camps, financed by security-minded bankers and industrialists, were held to train college students and even businessmen in the military arts. To familiarize Americans with the threat from overseas, the National Security League was launched, funded by U.S. Steel, the Rockefeller oil companies, and others concerned with national defense.

In 1916, Wilson was up for reelection. The Republicans had nominated the Supreme Court justice, Charles Evans Hughes, who called for a stronger stand against Germany. When the Democrats met in St. Louis, Wilson and his friends were in for a surprise. They had become used to the pro-Allied attitudes prevalent in Washington and the Eastern press. Now, they witnessed an assembly where every mention of peace was greeted with wild cheers. When one speaker used the phrase, "Wilson kept us out of war," it was taken up by the whole convention. "He kept us out of war!" became the slogan of the campaign and won Wilson the votes of the Midwest, the mountain states, and California. Wilson had been reelected on a peace platform.

On the Western Front, the year 1916 brought inconceivable horrors. In the battles at Verdun and on the Somme, hundreds of thousands were killed on both sides. And still, despite all the carnage and the introduction of weapons like the tank and poison gas, neither side could crack the front.

But the British hunger blockade was slowly starving the enemy, and in the winter of 1916–17, the German potato crop failed. The military chiefs urged the Kaiser to order unrestricted submarine warfare, to force Britain to its knees before Germany collapsed. They conceded that, given Wilson's policy, America would enter the war, but they promised that Britain would sue for peace before the U.S. forces could arrive. On January 31, 1917, Germany declared that any ship found in the waters around the British Isles would be sunk. To Wilson, Germany was breaking its pledge. He continued to abide by his position: Americans have the sacred right—which will, under all circumstances, be backed up the their government—to travel on armed belligerent merchant ships carrying munitions of war through submarine zones. On February 2, the United States severed diplomatic relations with Germany.

Part V

When the United States broke off diplomatic relations with Germany in February 1917, war did not immediately follow. President Wilson hesitated to take that final, fateful step, first asking Congress for authority to arm U.S. merchant ships. Since such a transformation of merchant ships into warships was a belligerent act under international law, the pro-peace forces in the Senate, led by Robert M. LaFollette of Wisconsin, fought back. For daring to oppose him, Wilson reviled them as "a little group of willful men, representing no opinion but their own" who "have rendered the great Government of the United States helpless and contemptible." For the moment, however, Wilson was stymied.

Then British intelligence produced a bombshell. They intercepted and passed on to Wilson a secret telegram from a foreign-office official in Berlin named Zimmermann to the German ambassador in Mexico City. The note stated that though efforts would be made to keep the United States neutral, if America *should* enter the war, Germany would seek an alliance with Mexico. For its help,

Mexico would regain its lost territories in Texas, New Mexico, and Arizona.

When the Zimmermann telegram was made public, Americans were outraged. Wilson exploited the turnaround in public opinion and issued an executive order stationing units of the United States Navy on board U.S. merchant ships. Soon, German submarines began sinking American ships in the declared war zones. Wilson, satisfied in his own mind that the responsibility for aggression lay solely with Germany, went to Congress for a declaration of war.

Wilson's war speech showed off his great rhetorical skills at their most brilliant. At the same time, it revealed his conception of what our entry in the war meant, as well as the full measure of Wilson's deviation from traditional American foreign policy:

> We shall fight for the things which we have always carried nearest our hearts—for democracy, for the rights and liberties of small nations, for a universal dominion of right by such a concert of free peoples as shall bring peace and safety to all nations and make the world itself at last free. America is privileged to spend her blood for the principles that gave her birth and happiness and the peace which she has treasured. God helping her, she can do no other.

No longer would the aim and purpose of our foreign policy be to keep our nation safe from attack. Now it was our "privilege" to pour out our blood—and hard-earned wealth—until the whole world was forever free. If that meant that we would be involved in never-ending war and preparation for war, then it was well worth the price, because *someday, somehow,* the outcome would be freedom and peace for all mankind.

Senator LaFollette rose to reply to Wilson, in a last, desperate try at averting war. He punctured Wilson's hypocritical plea to help free "small nations": Were we going to war to free Ireland, Egypt, Cyprus, French Indo-China? He challenged Wilson to put the war declaration to a vote of the people. Finally, he ripped the mask off the movement that, in his view, was pushing the country into war against the popular will: the Eastern money interests.

Congress voted the declaration of war, by 82 to 6 in the Senate, and 373 to 50 in the House of Representatives. One of the antiwar votes in the House was cast by Jeannette Rankin of Idaho, the first woman ever to sit in the Congress of the United States. On December 8, 1941, Rankin would be the only member of Congress to vote against the declaration of war with Japan.

71

The progressive intellectuals signed on to the war with a vengeance. They realized that war would offer them opportunities unavailable in sober peacetime to fulfill their goal: the extension of the power of government over all of American society.

In all the belligerent countries, this greatest of wars up to this time required the total mobilization of the nation's resources. Governments were granted powers beyond any they had enjoyed before. The economy was placed under state direction; manpower was directed either into war production or the military services; and public opinion was controlled and manipulated by the state. In this socialization of society, Germany led the way, but Britain, France, and the other warring states were not far behind. Once America entered the war, the same process began over here.

The Lever Act of 1917 gave the federal government jurisdiction over the food and fuel supplies of the nation. Communication lines and the merchant marine were likewise placed under government control. The War Labor Administration was set up to oversee wages and conditions of work throughout the country. Legislation was passed enabling Washington to take over the railway network of the United States, which occurred in December 1917. The War Industries Board, headed by Bernard Baruch, had the power to intervene in any economic transaction anywhere in the land that it considered might affect the war effort. Loans were granted to America's "co-belligerents," mainly Britain and France. After the war, our sister-democracies reneged on the loans—calling us "Uncle Shylock" for even asking for the money back—so this amounted to our first foreign aid program. In the greatest of the countless affronts to individual liberty, American men were drafted by the millions to fight in a foreign war.

The frenzy of interventionism in the economy broke the mold of old habits and traditions of limited government in America. Bernard Baruch, virtually the incarnation of the new class of politically connected businessmen, was convinced that a new chapter in our history had begun:

> The War Industries Board experience had a great influence upon the thinking of business and government. We helped bury the dogmas of laissez-faire, which had for so long molded American economic and political thought. Our experience taught that government direction of the economy need not be inefficient or undemocratic, and suggested that in time of danger it was imperative.

Socialists—many of them by now called themselves by the old name "liberal"—were gleeful. They had felt frustrated in their attempt to push their ideas and programs through in peacetime America: the ingrained resistance of the people to giving up their liberties had worked against them. Now John Dewey, the socialist philosopher and educator, looked on with satisfaction as the United States went the way of Germany, Britain, and the other belligerents:

> In every warring country there has been the same demand that in the time of great national stress production for profit be subordinated to production for use. Legal possession and individual property rights have had to give way before social requirements. The old conception of the absoluteness of private property the world over has received a blow from which it will never wholly recover. Conscription has brought home to countries which have been the home of the individualistic tradition the supremacy of public need over private possession. No matter how many among the special agencies for public control decay with the disappearance of the war stress, the movement will never go backward.

Like economic freedoms, civil liberties, too, were sacrificed. The Espionage Act was used to stifle any criticism of the war; Eugene Debs, for instance, the leader of the Socialist Party, was sentenced to ten years in federal prison for stating at a convention of his party that it was the bankers who had gotten us into the war. The first government agency for propaganda in our history was set up, known popularly as the Creel Committee, with a staff of hundreds of employees. It sent books, pamphlets, and speakers into every corner of the country, rousing the war spirit and reviling the enemy. The public school system, of course, proved to be a pliant tool of the government. The state's propaganda line was spread to tens of millions of school children and their families. Teachers who were insufficiently ardent for war were dismissed. After the war, a national commission on education boasted:

> Upon the declaration of war, the school machinery of every State was placed at the disposal of the Federal Government, which found in it a valuable means for the quick dissemination of the information and instruction needed to develop an enlightened and unified public opinion.

President Wilson took up the crusade begun by Theodore Roosevelt against "hyphenated Americans," warning the "men and women of German birth who live among us" that "if there should be any disloyalty, it will be dealt with with the firm hand of stern repression." In fact, Americans of German descent, including Lutheran ministers, as well as Irish-Americans, were mercilessly hounded by federal agents, local authorities, and state-sponsored groups of "patriotic" citizens. Hatred of everything German was fanned to absurd lengths, with symphony orchestras, for instance, pledging not to perform works by German composers for the duration of the war.

In Europe, the casualties mounted to staggering heights, especially on the Western Front. Battles like those at Verdun, the Somme, and Passchendaele claimed hundreds of thousands of dead on both sides. Yet the stalemate continued, as America raised a vast conscript army of fresh recruits to add to the butchery. Thrones were toppled: in Russia, the Tsarist monarchy came to an end; after a brief interim government under Alexander Kerensky, who refused to withdraw Russia from the war, V. I. Lenin and his Bolsheviks were able to seize power and establish the first communist state.

In January 1918, Wilson addressed Congress once more to lay down the principles of a new world order that would guarantee eternal peace. The speech set forth fourteen points. There would be no more "secret diplomacy"; and freedom of the seas, free trade, and disarmament of all nations would be the order of the day. In Europe, state boundaries would be redrawn according to the principle of the self-determination of national groups. Finally, dearest to Wilson's heart, there would be established a League of Nations, "a general association of nations . . . under specific covenants for the purpose of affording mutual guarantees of political independence and territorial integrity to great and small states alike." A few weeks later, Wilson stressed that the peace conference would see to it that "there shall be no annexations, no contributions, no punitive damages."

Wilson was promising the peoples of the warring nations, including the American people, a just world order that would "make the world itself at last free" and assure peace for all time. This was the vision he had cherished deep in his heart from the beginning, and it was the real reason for our entry into the First World War. But first Wilson would have to sell it to the canny politicians of Europe.

Part VI

The vast changes that the First World War was to bring about began to occur even while the war was still going on. In February 1917, the Tsarist Russian state collapsed, and a provisional government was established. But in October, it gave way to the Bolsheviks, led by V. I. Lenin, who promised the Russian masses what they yearned for—peace. In January 1918, Lenin concluded a peace treaty with the Central Powers. The eastern front had ceased to exist.

Now, with Russia out of the war, German divisions in the east were shipped to the western front in a race with time. The Germans calculated that they had reserves and resources for one last offensive before the Americans began arriving in large enough numbers to decide the outcome of the war. In March 1918, they threw everything they had left into a final attempt to crack the western front.

For the first few weeks, it looked as if they might succeed. But those years of fighting the whole world had sapped Germany's strength, and there were already over a million fresh American troops in France, with thousands more arriving every day. The offensive was halted, the Allied counteroffensive launched, and, in September, the German high command advised the Kaiser to seek an armistice. As Germany's few allies—Bulgaria, Turkey, and, finally, Austria-Hungary—were knocked out of the war, Berlin announced it was ready to discuss peace terms on the basis of Wilson's Fourteen Points. On November 11, 1918, Germany signed the armistice agreement, and the guns fell silent.

America had won the war for the Allies. Instead of letting the European nations find their own way to a compromise peace, American power had swung the balance decisively in favor of Britain and France. Among the consequences was the fall of the Kaiser and the old Germany, which Wilson, believing his own propaganda, considered the epitome of evil. Yet George Kennan, the diplomat and historian, wrote wryly after the Second World War:

> Today if one were offered the chance of having back again the Germany of 1913—a Germany run by conservative but relatively moderate people, no Nazis and no Communists—a vigorous Germany, full of energy and confidence, able to play a part again in the balancing-off of Russian power in Europe, in many ways it would not sound so bad.

The novel regime that Wilson insisted on as a condition of negotiating peace—the Weimar Republic—was to career from one crisis to another until, finally, in 1933, it succumbed to Adolf Hitler.

In 1919, when Wilson appeared at the Paris Peace Conference, his popularity and prestige eclipsed that of any world leader before him. Now he was ready to create his new world order, his real aim in steering America into war. But, like virtually all American leaders who have dabbled in international politics, he knew practically nothing of the problems of other countries and peoples. What Wilson did possess was a little bundle of abstract principles: democracy, self-determination of nations, and, above all, his cherished dream, the League of Nations. By applying these few principles, he fully intended to solve, once and for all, the colossally complex, age-old problems of Europe, if not of the whole world.

That the Germans had not been invited to participate in framing the treaties already augured ill for any lasting peace. Historically, peace conferences had included, as a matter of course, both the victors *and* the vanquished—as the Congress of Vienna had included representatives of defeated France after the Napoleonic wars. The purpose of such a conference, it had always been assumed, was to make peace with the defeated nation, with which one would, after all, have to live. But vengeance was the order of the day at Paris in 1919. The treaty would be written by the victors and then imposed on the Germans when the time came.

Very soon it became obvious that the Princeton professor was out of his depth among the seasoned European politicians: Clemenceau of France, Lloyd George of Britain, and the surprisingly greedy Orlando of Italy. During the war the Allies had concluded a series of secret treaties among themselves to divide the spoils once the fighting was over. Wilson had chosen to ignore these agreements, as he pretended to the American people and to himself that the war was being fought for pure and righteous reasons. Now, at Paris, each of the Allies claimed its share of the territorial plunder, mainly in the form of the Arab parts of the Turkish Empire and the German colonies. These—including Palestine, Syria, Iraq, Southwest Africa, Tanganyika, Samoa, etc.—were accordingly parceled out, the victors preserving their pose of virtue by calling them *mandates* instead of *colonies*.

To serve the security and economic interests of the victors and their clients, the principle of self-determination was shamelessly flouted. Germans in the Sudetenland, Danzig, the Polish Corridor, the Saar, and Austria were prohibited from joining their fatherland. One quarter of the Hungarians were divided among neighboring countries. Germany itself was reduced to a fifth-rate military power, allowed no tanks, planes, or submarines, and permitted an army of only 100,000 men, in a Europe that remained armed to the teeth. Reparations were not fixed—they were to commence immediately and continue for decades. And in Article 231 of the Treaty of Versailles, the Germans were forced to confess that they and their allies were alone responsible for starting the war.

Wilson soon realized that the promise he had held out—of a peace with "no annexations, no contributions, no punitive damages"—had been betrayed. Occasionally, he raised a feeble voice of protest. But Clemenceau and the others quickly whipped him into line by simply hinting that they might not go along with his beloved League of Nations. Finally, it was too much for Wilson. He had an emotional and physical breakdown and left the conference.

By the time he returned, Wilson had convinced himself that as long as the League came into being, it did not matter what injustices he agreed to. When presented with the Treaty of Versailles, the German delegates at first refused to sign. They were threatened with a resumption of the war. Since they were now totally disarmed, having put their faith in Wilson's promises, the Germans had no choice but to acquiesce. They insisted that this was no true peace treaty but a *Diktat*—a dictated peace. Many of the veteran diplomats present understood and were filled with foreboding: Germany would abide by the treaty until the day it became strong enough to tear it up.

Wilson signed the Treaty of Versailles, including the Covenant of the League of Nations, and the treaties with the other defeated nations, on behalf of the United States. Now he had to submit them to the U.S. Senate, controlled by the Republicans. Led by Henry Cabot Lodge of Massachusetts, they were even more interventionist than Wilson, well aware that Wall Street strongly favored the League. But they attached a few innocuous amendments to the treaty, to make political hay. Wilson was outraged at such presumption and ordered Senate Democrats to vote against the Republican version, which they did. Republicans voted against Wilson's unadulterated treaty, so neither version could gain the two-thirds majority needed. Thus, the United States never signed the Treaty of Versailles—a few years later, under President Harding, we simply declared the war with Germany ended—and never joined the League.

Generations of schoolchildren have been taught that it was the dreadful "isolationists" who torpedoed Wilson's project of a league to outlaw war and who thus paved the road to World War II. In fact, it was Wilson himself who started the world on the road to another war by helping to cobble together a vindictive and unworkable peace. As for the League, its real purpose was to lock in the borders of 1919— to preserve forever the balance of power at the point where Germany and Russia did not count and British and French imperialism were triumphant across the globe. It is not surprising that most patriotic Americans wanted their country to have nothing to do with the League of Nations.

In 1920, the American people showed their hatred for the whole rotten Wilsonian system of economic control, the military draft, the Espionage Act, and war and meddling abroad. A pleasant nonentity named Warren Harding achieved the greatest landslide in any presidential election to that time by simply promising a return to "normalcy." But this primordial surge of desire—to go back, to recapture the Republic that had been—was ill-fated. Too many institutions had changed, too many venerable taboos had been broken, too many special interests had been awakened to the scent of wealth and power at the taxpayers' expense.

Robert Higgs, in his indispensable work, *Crisis and Leviathan: Critical Episodes in the Growth of American Government*, writes of the aftermath of the First World War:

> Legacies of wartime collectivism abounded: the corporatism of massive governmental collusion with organized special-interest groups; the de facto nationalization of the ocean shipping and railroad industries; the increased federal intrusion in labor markets, capital markets, communications, and agriculture; and enduring changes in constitutional doctrines regarding conscription and governmental suppression of free speech.

"Looming over everything was the ideological legacy," Higgs concludes—the change in fundamental ideas. Americans might despise him as a self-deceiving fraud, but Woodrow Wilson had changed their country permanently. When the next crises came—the Depression and another European war—Wilson's methods would be resurrected and vastly amplified by a president who had served as assistant secretary of the Navy in the Wilson administration.

Between 1898 and 1919, a certain idea of America was let go and another put in its place. The older idea was of a nation dedicated to the right to life, liberty, and the pursuit of happiness of the people who make it up. Crucial to this image of America was our traditional foreign policy: its aim and limit was to keep America strong enough to prevent attacks from abroad, or, if they occurred, to fend them off, so that the people could return to their peaceful pursuits. It was a foreign policy custom-made for the American Republic.

The new idea of America, nurtured by McKinley and Theodore Roosevelt, and brought to fruition by Woodrow Wilson, was of a nation made immensely powerful by its free institutions and dedicated to projecting its might in order to achieve freedom throughout the world. In this conception, we would be perpetually entangled everywhere on earth where we could do good. The American people would not be allowed to return to the peaceful enjoyment of their own rights until the whole world was at last free. This was—and is—the foreign policy of America as Empire, the negation of the Republic. At the end of the twentieth century, it is not clear that the American people still have the power to choose between the two.

This essay originally appeared in the February 1995 through July 1995 issues of Freedom Daily, *published by The Future of Freedom Foundation.*

9

World War I and the Great Departure

by Wesley Allen Riddle

The fiftieth anniversary of the end of World War II has provided an occasion for revisiting the momentous events from 1939 to 1945 that reshaped the world. It may well be that this commemoration will lead to rediscoveries and new appreciations—the way the Bicentennial prompted popular and academic rediscovery of American tradition dating back to the Revolution and the Constitution.

The Great War—World War I—has now faded in the collective memory of Americans. But to the extent that World War I is almost universally cited by historians to explain the origins of World War II, it is fitting—indeed *essential*—that analysis of World War II include some appreciation for American experience during the First World War. Otherwise, the appreciations may be shallow or incomplete; worse, the lessons drawn from history could be the wrong ones.

Although America's direct involvement in World War I was relatively brief, it signalled "the great departure" from American precedent at home and abroad. The Progressive Era may have been a bridge to modern times,[1] but World War I blew up the bridge and left us on the other side. It was the point of discontinuity and departure. Diplomatically, all previous American conflicts had involved threats to American security, even if some were misperceived or overstated. Even the Spanish-American War (1898) was ostensibly linked to violations of the Monroe Doctrine (1823) and to security-based concerns about hostile European governments operating in the

Western Hemisphere and quashing fledgling republican institutions in the Americas.

But Germany in World War I did not pose a security threat to the United States—not even implicitly. Furthermore, American involvement in the war marked the first explicit rejection of George Washington's and Thomas Jefferson's advice—and subsequent American foreign policy—*not* to engage in disputes that were purely European in nature. World War I is also the first American war to depend primarily upon conscripts, three million of whom filled 72 percent of wartime Army ranks. Though not bound by entangling alliances, the United States entered the war anyway to "make the world safe for democracy."

American entry into the war is all the more remarkable, since Woodrow Wilson was reelected president in November 1916 on the slogan (broken five months later) "He kept us out of war." Wilson had insisted on trading with all of the belligerents, but France and England continued to enforce a blockade of Germany. The English also mined the North Sea. All of this violated neutral rights, but the United States continued to trade—theoretically with both sides. Over time, however, it became clear that the United States traded almost solely with the Allies. Practically speaking, American neutrality had become decidedly one-sided; moreover, this fact did not ruffle Wilson's Anglophile sensibilities.[2]

While France and England put Germany in an economic stranglehold, the Allies were dependent on the merchant tonnage shipped from the United States. Germany responded by sinking American and Allied merchant vessels with her U-boats. Indeed, it was this submarine warfare, more than any other factor, that prompted United States involvement in the war: submarine warfare was "sneaky"; submarine warfare aimed at ships *suspected* of hauling cargo was indiscriminate; women and children were amongst the 1,198 passengers lost when the *Lusitania* went under. "Yellow" journalists had a field day.

World War I changed the domestic social, political, and economic environment. The administration established the Committee on Public Information (CPI), headed by progressive muckraking journalist George Creel. Because the American people were naturally averse to involvement in a European war, the CPI's purpose was to mobilize and sustain the "right" kind of public opinion—that is, the kind that would support the war. It did so by commissioning an army of 75,000 speakers to tour in support of government wartime policies. The CPI also distributed 75 million pamphlets and produced dozens of anti-German films and expositions.

Other government agencies employed similar propaganda. The Food Administration found that "meatless Mondays" and "wheatless Wednesdays," as well as other conservation measures, went over better in an atmosphere of patriotic frenzy. Likewise, the Treasury Department held mass rallies to encourage the purchase of war bonds—rallies that even Joseph Goebbels, Hitler's propaganda minister, could have appreciated.

These techniques were highly successful. The government found that overt and subtle forms of propaganda fanned the requisite passions of pride and prejudice to fight a total war in Europe. Indeed, aggressive propaganda helped to skirt constitutional and statutory limitations on war policies—policies that would never pass *rational* scrutiny in peacetime. Empirically, it proved that government propaganda aimed at arousing strong feelings of American nationalism could facilitate the exercise of extralegal and extra-constitutional government power.[3]

Sometimes the government baldly exercised that power, and sometimes the government let social pressures effect the government's design. In one instance, for example, the Wilson administration nationalized the railroads (1917). In another, a German-American was actually bound in an American flag and lynched by a St. Louis mob (1918). Civil liberties were constricted through official policy and through socially sanctioned activities—and all of this was indirectly encouraged by government propaganda.

The administration quashed leftist political opposition by seizing membership lists and arresting unpopular leaders, especially socialists and members of the Industrial Workers of the World (IWW). Leftist and conservative criticism was quelled by legislation that made "disloyal speech" illegal in wartime. The Espionage Act of June 15, 1917, and the Sedition Act of May 16, 1918, provided the legal foundation to prosecute and punish pacifists and all sorts of religious and secular groups opposed to the war. Moreover, certain alien opponents were summarily rounded up and deported in the notorious Palmer raids immediately after the war.

Meanwhile, the persecution of Germans in American society was so pronounced that Germans were forced to abandon their language and customs, at least in public. German books were burned outside numerous libraries, while Beethoven was banned from symphonic repertories. The atmosphere was such that Germans *hid* the fact they were German and changed their own names—Schmitz to Smith, and so forth. For its part, the public renamed almost every German street and landmark and even altered menus, so that *sauerkraut* became Liberty Cabbage, and so on.[4]

The War Industries Board (WIB) orchestrated American industrial production. The WIB set production schedules, allocated resources, standardized procedures, coordinated purchases, covered costs, and guaranteed profits. In tandem, the National War Labor Board (NWLB) arbitrated labor disputes, stipulated working conditions, established overtime pay, and encouraged union organization. Although the national government had assumed a great deal of power on the Union side during the Civil War, it achieved the first true command-and-control economy in America during World War I.[5]

Furthermore, the war established certain precedents for future *peacetime* emergencies. The New Deal's National Recovery Administration was patterned on the WIB; the Wagner National Labor Relations Act of the second New Deal was based on NWLB legislation.

The Selective Service Act of May 18, 1917, raised the size of the Army from 200,000 to nearly four million. Some two million men and women served overseas with the American Expeditionary Force, under the command of Gen. John "Black Jack" Pershing, and three-quarters of those were involved in direct combat.

Germans launched a massive offensive in March 1918, and American troops fought at Cantigny in May and at Château-Thierry and Belleau Wood in June to stop them. The turning point of the war came in the second battle of the Marne in July, in which 275,000 American troops were engaged. Though Pershing resisted, Americans were placed under foreign command to perform assigned roles in the Allied counteroffensive, and Americans took particularly heavy casualties in the Meuse-Argonne attack launched on September 26, ending on November 11. It was the greatest battle in which U.S. troops had ever been engaged, involving 1,200,000 men.

At some points along the line of contact, Americans took ten casualties for every German, but Allied commanders used the sheer weight of American numbers to press an exhausted German army. It was not unlike Grant's strategy of attrition during the Wilderness campaign, for which he earned the nickname "Butcher." The difference is that Wilderness occurred in an American war, and casualties resulted from the orders of American commanders appointed over men by authority of the Constitution.

The armistice was signed on the last day of the Meuse-Argonne offensive.

The war in Europe obviously interrupted the normal flow of immigrants from that continent to the United States. On the other hand, conscription and command-and-control economic policies, as well as government hiring practices, also contributed to severe labor shortages. These shortages drew hundreds of thousands of African-Americans out of the South into the industrial North. Indeed, the government sent labor-recruitment agents south to spread the message that there was economic opportunity to be had in the North. The mass movement of labor into predominantly white communities sparked interracial friction and violence.

When war ended and the huge numbers of veterans returned home again, tensions flared red-hot as blacks were displaced from their new jobs and urban unemployment and poverty rates grew.[6] Large race riots occurred in East St. Louis in July 1917 and in Chicago in July 1919; indeed, race riots occurred in nineteen other cities in 1919. Postwar labor dislocations also caused strikes to spread across the country in 1919. Acts of terrorism and violence led to antilabor hysteria, prompting the Palmer raids.

The experience of World War I shattered the Democratic Party,[7] which facilitated rival organizations to spread. The postwar recession of 1920–22 worsened social conditions. Hence, Ku Klux Klan membership increased dramatically after 1920. The upshot was that government-sponsored intolerance and hysteria, encouraged for wartime purposes, continued to grow even after the war ended. Hence political nativism crested in the early 1920s, curtailing open immigration. At the same time, segregation in the South was formalized into its most rigid legal form ever. Jim Crow literally became an American system of apartheid. Anti-Semitism also spread, with this unfortunate consequence: had immigration policies been relaxed and had public sensitivity been greater, more Jews might have been allowed to escape fascist European countries before the Holocaust.

The attitude of intolerance, combined with government power, had one more interesting political ramification, ironically related to vanishing Victorian social mores. By banning alcoholic drink, the Prohibition Amendment (1919) invaded people's privacy and freedom to choose. And it brought an explosion of organized crime during the 1920s (since tremendous illicit profits were now involved), as well as a general decline in respect for law by the middle class, which flouted the ban. The Prohibition Amendment would become the only constitutional amendment overturned by subsequent amendment.

Even America's so-called postwar isolationism was colored with the tinge of intolerance, as "America first" in international relations proved to be far less than the traditional honest friendship with everyone. The interwar diplomatic period was marked by a narrow, nationalistic approach to international finance and trade, which sometimes complicated German repayment of reparations.[8]

Finally, world historians write that World War I destroyed the old world order. The war killed a total of ten million and wounded twenty million more. Postwar starvation in Europe took the lives of millions. All told, the war swallowed a generation of Europeans, and many who survived were somehow still "lost." The Great War caused disintegration of the Austria-Hungarian and Ottoman empires.

In the United States, the most dramatic effect was a psychic and cultural disillusionment.[9] American dead numbered 112,432, due to combat and disease. The war's direct financial cost, counting interest rates and veterans' benefits, came to about $112 billion.

Everywhere, the modern age after the war was characterized by the renunciation of old values. In her book *The Romantic Manifesto*, Ayn Rand called this the "spiritual treason" of our century.[10]

In America, culture moved from the embrace of a social code based on self-restraint and virtue to one based on self-gratification; increasingly, the pursuit of self-gratification has led us to intellectual nihilism. In foreign relations, the Great War marked "the great departure," because we ceased being an exemplar and became a crusader instead. Domestically, the United States lost some of her faith in the efficacy of liberty and the potential of free men. Ever since, statist policies have predominated over the traditional American faith in free minds and free markets. Progressivism and World War I—itself the culminating event of the Progressive Era—established the rationale and justification for the modern activist state, which has since evolved into the welfare-and-nanny state.

Our reflections on both world wars, as well as the Cold War, are good. They are indispensable really, if we are to trace our departure and find our way back home.

Notes

[1] Robert Higgs, *Crisis and Leviathan: Critical Episodes in the Growth of American Government* (Oxford: Oxford University Press, 1987), chapter 6.

[2] Robert H. Ferrell, *Woodrow Wilson and World War I, 1917–1921* (New York: Harper & Row, Publishers, 1985), pp. 8–9.

[3] See David M. Kennedy, *Over Here: The First World War and American Society* (Oxford: Oxford University Press, 1980), chapter 1.

[4] Ibid.; and Wesley Allen Riddle, "War and Individual Liberty in American History," in *Leviathan at War,* ed. Edmund A. Opitz (Irvington, N.Y.: The Foundation for Economic Education, 1995), p. 141; and see Ronald Schaffer, *America in the Great War: The Rise of*

the War Welfare State (Oxford: Oxford University Press, 1991), chapters 1 and 2.

[5] See Kennedy, chapter 2; and Schaffer, chapters 3 and 4.

[6] See Daniel M. Johnson and Rex R. Campbell, *Black Migration in America: A Social Demographic History* (Durham: Duke University Press, 1981); and Alferdteen Harrison, ed., *Black Exodus: The Great Migration from the American South* (Jackson: University Press of Mississippi, 1991).

[7] Keith I. Polakoff, *Political Parties in American History* (New York: Alfred A. Knopf, 1981), pp. 298 and 302; and see p. 310.

[8] J. A. S. Grenville, *A History of the World in the Twentieth Century* (Cambridge, Mass.: Belknap Press of Harvard University Press, 1994), pp. 149–50.

[9] See Kennedy, chapter 4; and Mark A. Stoler and Marshall True, *Explorations in American History*, vol. 2 (New York: Alfred A. Knopf, 1987), pp. 96–97.

[10] Ayn Rand, *The Romantic Manifesto*, rev. ed. (New York: Signet, 1975), page vii. See Modris Eksteins, *Rites of Spring: The Great War and the Birth of the Modern Age* (New York: Doubleday, 1990).

This essay originally appeared in two parts in the August and September 1995 issues of Freedom Daily, *published by The Future of Freedom Foundation.*

10

The Roots of World War II

by Sheldon Richman

It is commonly thought that the twentieth century witnessed two world wars. It would be more accurate to say that the century had but one world war—with a 21-year intermission. To put it another way, World War II grew out of World War I; indeed, it was made virtually inevitable by it. More specifically, a case can be made that World War II was a result of American intervention in the First World War.

Counterfactual history is a risky endeavor. But the events that followed America's entry into World War I strongly suggest that had President Woodrow Wilson permanently "kept us out of war," as his 1916 presidential campaign slogan boasted, the seeds that produced World War II would not have been sown.

The Great War began in August 1914. America did not enter the war until April 1917. By that time both sides were exhausted from years of grinding warfare. There is ample reason to believe that had nothing new been added to the equation, the belligerents would have agreed to a negotiated settlement. No victors, no vindictiveness.

But it was not to be.

The messianic President Wilson could not pass up what he saw as a once-in-a-lifetime opportunity to help remake the world. As historian Arthur Ekirch writes in *The Decline of American Liberalism*, "The notion of a crusade came naturally to Wilson, the son of a Presbyterian minister, imbued with a stern Calvinist sense of determinism and devotion to duty." He was goaded by a host of Progressive intellectuals, such as John Dewey and Herbert Croley, editor of *The New Republic*, who wrote that "the American nation needs the tonic of a serious moral adventure."

On the other side, the opponents of war understood what, ironically, Wilson himself pointed out in private just before asking Congress for a declaration of war: "War required illiberalism at home to reinforce the men at the front. We couldn't fight Germany and maintain the ideals of Government that all thinking men shared."

Wilson was right. Within months, the United States had conscription, an official propaganda office, suppression of dissent, and central planning of the economy (a precedent for Franklin Roosevelt's New Deal).

While Wilson said the United States was going to war to make the world safe for democracy, he in fact entered for the less lofty principle of making it safe for American citizens to sail on the armed ships of belligerents. Regardless, what matters here is the effect U.S. intervention had on the war.

Aside from the general exhaustion of the warring nations, a major development was occurring to the east. The war had caused great hardship in Russia. Food was in short supply. Workers went on strike, and housewives marched in protest. Army regiments mutinied. In March 1917, Czar Nicholas II abdicated, and when his brother refused the throne, a provisional, social democratic government was set up in Russia. As historian E. H. Carr wrote, "The revolutionary parties played no direct part in the making of the revolution."

Despite the people's revulsion, Alexander Kerensky's provisional government stayed in the war at the insistence of the Allies and Wilson, who by then had sent American boys to Europe. When Lenin returned to Russia from Zurich, he made his Bolsheviks the one antiwar party in the country. This gave Lenin the opportunity to become the world's first communist dictator. An earlier negotiated settlement would have eased the Russians' misery and probably averted the second revolution. Lenin immediately accepted Germany's peace terms, including territorial concessions, and left the war. (Toward the end of the war, the Allies invaded the new Soviet Union, ostensibly to safeguard war materiel. The invasion created long-lasting distrust of the West.)

Thus, the first likely consequence of U.S. prolongation of the war was the Bolshevik Revolution (and the Cold War). Communism—its threat of worldwide revolution and its wholesale slaughter—was a key factor in the rise of the European despotism that sparked World War II. (Had the Bolsheviks come to power anyway and Germany had won the war, Germany would have thrown the communists out.)

Entry of fresh American power gave the advantage to the Allies, and Germany signed the armistice in November 1918. Before allowing that, Wilson, in the name of spreading democracy, demanded that the Kaiser go. The president thus was responsible for the removal of what would have likely been an important institutional obstacle to Hitler and his aggressive ambitions.

The armistice set the stage for the Paris Peace Conference and the Treaty of Versailles. Article 231 of that Treaty—the infamous war guilt clause—said:

> The Allied and Associated Governments affirm and Germany accepts the responsibility of Germany and her allies for causing all the loss and damage to which the Allied and Associated Governments and their nationals have been subjected as a consequence of the war imposed upon them by the aggression of Germany and her allies.

Germany was to become an outcast nation on the basis of its war guilt. The problem was that Germany was not uniquely guilty. World War I was the product of a complex political dynamic in which nations other than Germany—Russia and France, for example—played important roles. Nevertheless, Germany was branded as the perpetrator.

The victors imposed crushing reparations on Germany for the cost of the war. That was contrary to Wilson's original, nonpunitive program (The Fourteen Points) and to the prearmistice agreement with Germany. But at the peace conference, he acquiesced to England and France in order to achieve his dream of a League of Nations. Adding to the humiliation was the Allied occupation of the Rhineland and the tearing away of German-speaking areas in order to reconstitute Poland and create Czechoslovakia. Moreover, the treaty nullified German control in the East, which Lenin had conceded, removing what would have been a formidable barrier against Bolshevism.

Not all the hardship resulted from the treaty. During the war the Allies imposed a starvation blockade on Germany. Due to French insistence, that blockade remained in place until the treaty was signed in June 1919. The German people were made to watch their children starve for six months after the guns fell silent. The blockade killed an estimated 800,000 people.

In the 1920s, many people—Germans and others—would call for revision of the unjust treaty. But no one in a position to do anything about it heeded the call. Can one imagine ground more fertile for the growth of the poisonous vine called Nazism?

The second likely consequence, then, of U.S. prolongation of the war was the rise of Nazi Germany.

Other consequences can be speculated on. For example, Murray Rothbard has argued that the Federal Reserve System engaged in a prolonged postwar inflation of the money supply in order to help Great Britain restore its prewar gold-Pound relationship. That inflation led to the crash of 1929 and the Great Depression. Perhaps if the United States had refrained from entering the war, and if a negotiated settlement had been reached, the Fed would not have felt obliged to assist Britain in achieving its unrealistic aims.

We can now do an accounting of the likely consequences of U.S. intervention in Europe: communism in Russia (and everywhere else it later reverberated), Nazism in Germany, the Great Depression, the New Deal, and World War II (not to mention the Cold War and the growth of the American leviathan).

No one would suggest that Woodrow Wilson foresaw those consequences and intervened anyway. But the intelligent men who warned that war would lead to revolution and totalitarianism were vindicated. The war critic Randolph Bourne observed that "it is only 'liberal' naivete that is shocked at arbitrary coercion and suppression. Willing war means willing all the evils that are organically bound up with it."

And what if U.S. forbearance had not permitted a negotiated settlement and Germany had won the war? Aside from the fact that Wilson's closest advisor, Col. Edward M. House, saw no threat to the United States from a German victory, we can best answer that question with another question: Who would not trade the events of twentieth-century military and political history for the Kaiser?

This essay originally appeared in the February 1995 issue of Freedom Daily, *published by The Future of Freedom Foundation.*

11

The Causes and Consequences of World War II

by Richard M. Ebeling

When World War II ended in 1945, most of Europe lay in ruins. German cities like Dresden and Hamburg had practically been cremated from day-and-night Allied fire-bombings. Warsaw had been almost leveled to the ground by the Germans. The scorched-earth policies of both the Nazis and the Soviets had left much of European Russia, Ukraine, and the Baltic states almost totally destroyed. The Nazi death camps had consumed not only the lives of six million Jews, but an equivalent number of Poles, Gypsies, and other "undesirables."

Two Japanese cities—Hiroshima and Nagasaki—lay incinerated from atomic blasts. Eight years of war and Japanese occupation in China had uprooted millions of Chinese who had taken refuge in the wild and hostile regions of western China; and tens of thousands had died trying to make their escape.

Fifty million lives were consumed by the war.

The words of English historian Robert Mackenzie, in describing Europe at the beginning of the nineteenth century during the Napoleonic Wars, are even more apt in expressing the events of World War II:

> The interests of peace withered in the storm; the energies of all nations, the fruits of all industries were poured forth in the effort to destroy. From the utmost North to the shores of the

Mediterranean, from the confines of Asia to the Atlantic, men toiled to burn each other's cities, to waste each other's fields, to destroy each other's lives. In some lands there was heard the shout of victory, in some the wail of defeat. In all lands the ruinous waste of war had produced bitter poverty; grief and fear were in every home.

Why? For what cause, for what purpose, did men set loose the forces of destruction in this bonfire of the insanities? The answers are simple: collectivism and nationalism; utopian visions and ideological fanaticism; and the will to power.

The classical-liberal world of individual rights, private property, and civil liberty had died in World War I. Every one of the cherished and hard-won freedoms of the nineteenth century were sacrificed on the altar of winning victory in that war. And when the war was over, liberty, as it turned out, was the ultimate victim. Behind the wartime slogans of "making the world safe for democracy," "the right to national self-determination," and "a league of nations for the securing of world peace," nation-states had grown large with power. Wartime controls had replaced free enterprise; exchange controls and import-export regulations had replaced free trade; confiscatory taxation and inflation had undermined the sanctity of property and eaten up the accumulated wealth of millions. The individual and his freedom had shrunk. The state and its power were now gigantic.

And the demons had been set loose on the world. Before the war had even come to a close, Russia was swept by revolution. Tired and hungry, the Russian people wanted peace. The Czar abdicated in February 1917. But the provisional government of center-left political forces that replaced the monarchy insisted upon pursuing the war on the Allied side against Germany. This gave the Bolsheviks under Lenin the opportunity to play to the masses with the slogan, "peace, bread and land."

In November 1917, in a coup, the Bolsheviks took power. When the free elections resulted in the Bolsheviks' winning only a small number of seats to the new parliament, Lenin shut it down after only one day of being in session. Lenin and the Bolsheviks intended to bring the people to socialism—in spite of the people's own desires.

Then, the Marxian path to the paradise-to-come was traveled even further under Stalin with forced collectivization of land, central planning, mass purges of all "enemies of the people," and the Gulag.

In Italy, social unrest, communist agitation, and disillusionment with the war created the conditions for the emergence of Mussolini and his fascist movement. The "march on Rome" in 1922 brought the fascists to power. Within a few years, they were instituting their version of the collectivist utopia of the future—corporativism. All industry and trade were subordinate to the interests of the nation. The state was supreme—and the individual was the means to its end. To express this concept, Mussolini coined the term "totalitarianism."

In the 1920s, a weak, democratic government in Germany served as the background for the emergence of radical political movements. Hitler and the Nazis insisted that Germany had been victimized by the Allied powers, who had labeled Germany as the sole aggressor in World War I. And Germany was now burdened by oppressive reparations payments caused by the "betrayal" of the German people by the social democrats.

With rising unemployment and economic dislocation following the start of the Great Depression in 1929, the Nazis came to power in 1933. They promised to bring economic recovery, to purge Germany of the "alien Jewish element," and to reestablish Germany's rightful place in the world. By 1936, the Nazis had put into place their own version of the corporativist planned economy. Moreover, through state education and a vast propaganda machine, they had instituted their ideology of racism and territorial aggrandizement.

But the tide of collectivist ideology was not limited to the Soviet Union, Italy, and Germany. Except for Czechoslovakia, all of the countries of Central and Eastern Europe were controlled by authoritarian regimes—characterized by regulated economies and denial of civil liberties.

And in Western Europe, the political course of events was no different. Both the Conservative and Labor Parties in Great Britain were dedicated to the interventionist-welfare state. After 1931, Great Britain was off the gold standard, free trade was replaced by protectionism, and public-works projects were used to fight unemployment. And in France, center-left governments followed similar policies.

In Asia, China was ruled by the Nationalist (Kuomintang) Party under Chiang Kai-shek, who was attempting to introduce "modernization" through state economic intervention and fascist-type planning. At the same time, large areas of the country were controlled either by local warlords or Mao Tse-tung's communist forces. And Japan, with its own fascist-style economic order, was attempting to establish its own imperial empire in Manchuria and the rest of China.

In the United States, collectivism was triumphant as well. In the 1920s, the Republican administrations, in spite of free-enterprise rhetoric, established various government-business partnerships in the name of economic "rationalization." Federal Reserve central-banking policy was geared to managing the economy through monetary manipulation. And when the fruits of central-bank, monetary central-planning resulted in the "great crash" of October 1929, the Hoover administration responded with even greater state intervention and governmental spending. The result was the Great Depression.

With the coming of the New Deal in 1933, following the election of Franklin D. Roosevelt, America was subjected to its own brand of economic fascism, as the government imposed comprehensive controls and regulations on practically every aspect of economic life. The New Deal experience even led Mussolini to say that he greatly admired Franklin Roosevelt, because with these policies, Roosevelt had shown that he, too, was a "social fascist."

By the middle of the 1930s, collectivism was triumphant. Hardly a corner of the world was left which was not under the control of governments dedicated to a planned economy—dedicated to expanded state power. And the conditions were now in place for conflict and war.

The politicizing of economic and social life meant that every dispute—every disagreement in the world arena—was now a matter of national interest and ideological victory or defeat. Every nation-state made itself an economic fortress, surrounded with trade barriers and economic weapons of war. And matching the economic weapons of nationalist rivalry was the growth of a vast armaments race.

The political means used by all of these nation-states were similar. What separated them were the ends for which these means were being applied. For the Soviets, the goal was Marxist revolution and communism. For the fascists, it was nationalist power and imperialism. For the Nazis, it was racial supremacy and "living room" for the German people. For the British and the French, it was maintenance of their colonial empires and economic domination of world trade. For Japan, it was an economic empire in China and political domination of East Asia. For the United States, it was the consolidation of the "achievements" of the New Deal at home and, by the late 1930s, the spreading of New Deal ideology to the rest of the world.

The events of the 1930s—events that brought the world into total war—were the natural results of the emergence of the total collectivist state. With the demise of classical liberalism—and its philosophy of limited government and individual liberty—the demons of statolatry encompassed the globe. The competing collectivisms were inevitably bound to clash in the struggle for ideological supremacy. And the clashes of these competing statisms formed the backdrop for the beginning of World War II.

Part II

World War II was not a war between freedom and tyranny. Rather it was a conflict between alternative systems of collectivism. By the 1930s, there was not one major country devoted to and practicing the principles of classical liberalism—the political philosophy of individual liberty, free-market capitalism and free trade. Regardless of the particular variation on the collectivist theme, practically every government in the world had or was implementing some form of economic planning and restricting the personal and commercial freedoms of its own citizenry.

In the Soviet Union, the state owned and controlled all of the resources and means of production of the society. Production and distribution were directed by the central-planning agencies in Moscow. In fascist Italy and Nazi Germany, property and resources remained nominally in private hands, but the use and disposal of that property and those resources were controlled and directed according to the dictates of the state. In Great Britain, free trade and the gold standard had been abandoned in the early 1930s, during the depths of the Great Depression. Protectionism, interventionism, welfare-statism, and monetary manipulation were the active policy tools of the British government.

Throughout Europe and the rest of the world, the various nation-states had erected tariff barriers, regulated industry and agriculture, limited the free movement of their people, and restricted civil liberties.

The United States followed the same course. Franklin Roosevelt's New Deal was a conscious and active attempt to impose a fascist type of economic order on America. And even after much of the New Deal had been declared unconstitutional in 1935, the Roosevelt administration continued on the collectivist road with economic regulation, deficit spending, public works, welfare-statism, and monetary central planning through the Federal Reserve System.

Indeed, apart from the Soviet Union, the competing collectivisms were merely different forms of economic and political fascism. The common denominators of all of them were economic nationalism, government control of the economy, and political absolutism. And this applied to the United States as well. As John T. Flynn concisely expressed it in his 1944 book, *As We Go Marching*, the only difference is whether one thought of these policies as "the bad fascism" or "the good fascism," with the distinction being determined by whether it was some other government carrying out these policies or one's own.

The totalitarian regimes in Germany and Italy had merely taken the collectivist premise to its logical conclusion. It was for this reason that Friedrich A. Hayek entitled his 1944 book *The Road to Serfdom*, a book in which he demonstrated that the road being followed by England and the United States was the same one traveled by Germany. The only difference, Hayek observed, was that Nazi Germany was further along that road.

Economic nationalism requires that each nation-state has within its boundaries a territory sufficiently large to assure economic self-sufficiency. Hitler's drive for "living room" for the German people epitomized this doctrine. Instead of the Marxian concept of society divided into "social classes," Hitler divided the world into "racial groups," the Germans being classified by him as the superior racial group. Nationalism also means that the individual possesses neither significance nor value other than in his assigned role in serving the state, with the state being the political agent for the collective's power and destiny.

What were the British motives for resisting the Nazi quest for conquest? Speaking about the attack on Pearl Harbor on December 7, 1941, Winston Churchill rejoiced: "No American will think it wrong of me if I proclaim that to have the United States on our side was to be the greatest joy. . . . England would live; Britain would live; the Commonwealth of Nations and the Empire would live." No reference is made here to liberty or property, to the sanctity of the individual, and the limiting of government. The preservation of "the nation" and "the empire" was what mattered to him. Indeed, Churchill's political philosophy was reflected in the early 1930s, when he declared that if Britain ever found itself in the position that Italy and Germany had found themselves in after the First World War, he only hoped that Britain would find its Mussolini or Hitler to guide it.

And Churchill's disregard for the rights of other peoples and other nations was demonstrated by his advocacy of a British invasion of neutral Norway in the early spring of 1940. Of course, Hitler beat the British to that act by only a week. But only then did the invasion of a neutral country become a morally despicable act in Churchill's eyes. His disregard for other people's freedom was also reflected at a wartime conference with Stalin in Moscow, at which he offered to divide up the Balkan area of southeastern Europe between Britain and the Soviet Union. He even made up a percentage table of degrees-of-influence Britain and the USSR would have in each of the countries up for grabs.

And World War II was a godsend for Franklin Roosevelt. Having set out to give America a "New Deal," unemployment was still hovering around 15 percent by 1937 and 1938. Disillusionment was setting in among the American people as the levels of government spending and budget deficits kept getting larger and larger.

But Roosevelt now had another chance: he would give the world a "New Deal." He put on Woodrow Wilson's mantle of leadership to make the world safe for democracy. And he was surrounded by advisors who saw the world's salvation through welfare-statism and government planning.

The problem, however, was that most Americans did not want to be either the world's policeman or its global social engineer.

But Roosevelt had made up his mind about what was good for America and its citizenry. So he set out to bring America into the war. The evidence of this is so strong that both pro- and anti-Roosevelt historians admit the fact that he violated constitutional restraints and broke congressionally passed neutrality acts to create conditions inevitably leading to America's entry into the Second World War. The only dispute now is an interpretive one—was it or was it not a good thing that he did so?

And all the time, Stalin sat in the wings. By signing a non-aggression pact with Hitler—a pact that divided up Eastern Europe between Germany and the Soviet Union—he had made possible Hitler's attack on Poland in 1939. Even after the German invasion of the Soviet Union—when the Soviet Union was then the ally of Britain and the United States—Stalin was putting out feelers for a separate peace with Hitler. Hitler was just unwilling to pay Stalin's price for that peace.

At the wartime conferences at Tehran and Yalta with Roosevelt and Churchill, Stalin made sure that in the bright and better world at the end of the war, the Soviet Union would be assured domination of the European continent. In fact, at the Tehran Conference in 1943, Roosevelt even suggested that after the war, the governments of Eastern Europe should all be "friendly" to the Soviet Union. He merely asked Stalin not to make this public—1944 was an election year, and Roosevelt did not want to lose the Polish vote. The Marxist butcher who had killed tens of millions of people in the Soviet Union was thus given a free hand in half of Europe. What did Roosevelt want in return? That Stalin agreed to have the Soviet Union join the United Nations and work with the United States for world peace!

In this assortment of "allies" and "enemies," the advocate of liberty could find no champion. The "bad fascists" were busy at work in their death camps in Poland and Germany. The "good fascists" were busy at work firebombing civilian targets all over Germany and raining mass destruction on the Japanese. And the "well-intentioned" communists in the Soviet Union were busy charting their course to subjugate Eastern Europe and vast stretches of Asia, as the next steps to world Marxist victory.

For a second time in the twentieth century, the world had been plunged into a global conflict. And for a second time, surrounded by mass destruction and millions of corpses, the living believed that a better world would now rise like a phoenix from the ashes. Their hopes were to be dashed almost immediately. The Cold War was about to begin. And liberty was again about to be sacrificed on the altar of the state.

Part III

In 1945, Nazi totalitarianism was destroyed by the military might of the wartime allies. But within a few months of that victory, our comrade-in-arms, "Uncle Joe" Stalin (as he was affectionately referred to by President Franklin Roosevelt), was making it clear that the postwar period would not be an era of global peace and international harmony.

Within months of the German surrender, Stalin was tightening his grip on the Eastern European countries that had been "liberated" by the Red Army. There would be no free elections, no democratic pluralism, no market economies in the nations now in Moscow's orbit. By 1948, with the communist coup in Czechoslovakia, every one of the Eastern European countries had been turned into a socialist "People's Republic."

We now know that this was Stalin's intention from the beginning, despite the promises he gave to President Roosevelt at the Yalta Conference in February 1945. In early April 1945, less than two months after the signing of the Yalta agreements, a Yugoslav communist delegation led by Tito was in Moscow. At a late-night banquet in their honor, Stalin reflected on the postwar era. In his book *Conversations with Stalin*, Milovan Djilas recounts that Stalin at one point explained, "This war is not as in the past; whoever occupies a territory also imposes on it his own social system."

In Asia, the corrupt Nationalist (Kuomintang) government of China was soon in a fatal civil war with Mao Tse-tung's ruthless communist armies. The Soviets, after "liberating" Manchuria from the Japanese in the final days of the war, had given safe haven to Mao's forces and supplied them with military hardware captured from the Japanese. And in the United States, a vocal segment of the intellectual community tried to assure the American public that Mao and his followers were simple and honest agrarian reformers. When

China fell completely into communist hands at the end of 1949, the Chinese people soon experienced the truth, as Marxist terrorism and economic planning turned them into a nation of slaves.

The communist guerrilla movement in French Indochina under Ho Chi Minh, the communist insurgency in Greece, the Berlin blockade of 1948, and the North Korean invasion of South Korea in June 1950 all served to convince a growing number of Americans that an international threat was confronting the United States and that it required a determined and unique response on the part of the nation. Thus, America assumed the mantle of global policeman and protector of the world.

The communist threat under Soviet leadership in the postwar era was, without a doubt, unique in modern history. Here was an ideology that claimed to transcend all national boundaries and insisted that there could be no lasting peace in the world until socialism was victorious on every continent on the globe. And the carriers of this Marxist message had no moral scruples about the means and methods they used. Human life had no value to them other than as tools for the achievement of their collectivist utopia.

But in choosing political alliances and military intervention as the methods for combating this ideological evil, the United States radically transformed itself from everything it had been before the Second World War. The respected classical-liberal historian Arthur A. Ekirch, in his book *The Decline of American Liberalism*, explained the nature of this transformation:

> As a part of the struggle against communism, the American people were won over to the necessity of military preparedness on a virtual wartime basis. In America as well as in Europe, the individual citizen accordingly continued to live in a near-war atmosphere, in which his own aspirations were subordinated to the demands of the state. Tremendous expenditures, largely for military needs, mounting national debts, military conscription, a vast bureaucracy of civil servants, and the growing official nature of thought and culture were some of the evidences of the growth of statism and the decline of individualism.

The result, therefore, was that in the name of opposing the threat of aggressive socialism, the United States increasingly adopted in its domestic and foreign policy a defensive socialism. The state increasingly gained control over the lives of the American people and their property.

And why did the United States select this as the most appropriate method to fight foreign socialism? Because most people in American intellectual and political circles believed in socialism—whether or not they were willing to assign that label to their beliefs. The Great Depression had convinced them that capitalism did not work and that to a greater or lesser degree the government had a responsibility to oversee and manage the economic affairs of the citizenry. Their dispute with the Marxists, ultimately, was not over the issue of "big government," but over their abhorrence to the "undemocratic" methods employed by Marx's followers.

And in line with their socialist premises, America's political leaders attempted to use socialist methods to combat socialism in those countries on the "battleline" of the communist threat. Foreign governments were told that the only answer to preventing their own people from going over to communism was to adopt socialist policies: redistribution of wealth, a managed economy, public works, and the welfare state. Statism became the means of combating statism.

For forty-five years, the American political authorities insisted upon the implementation of such policies by "friendly" governments as a condition of receiving U.S. economic and military aid. It can only be wondered how many countries around the world have been plagued with oppressive and manipulative governments during the past four decades as a direct result of American foreign policy.

As a consequence, the United States has probably been the most successful exporter of socialist ideas in the world. Cloaked in the rhetoric of "democracy" and "free enterprise," the cumulative effect of America's example and prodding is that there is now, in fact, not one country in the entire world that actually practices the principles of limited government and an unhampered market economy.

And worst of all, the American people themselves no longer have a vision of what a free America should and can look like, nor do they even conceive of what a noninterventionist policy in foreign affairs would mean. The regulated economy at home and the interventionist state abroad have become their conception of "freedom."

The tragedy is that the foreign policy of a free society is the simplest to understand and the easiest to enforce. The government in the free society has two functions: the protection of the life and property of the citizenry from the aggression of others and the adjudication of legal disputes that arise among the citizens of that society. Beyond this, the government has no proper role to perform. In the free society, all "social problems" are matters of voluntary arrangement and mutual consent among the people themselves.

The only foreign policy in a free society is for the government to protect its citizens from foreign aggression in the form of threats to the territorial integrity of the nation. All other matters are personal and private affairs of the people. If some in the United States believe that the people of another country deserve assistance from oppression, then they as private citizens are free to volunteer to fight for freedom in that other nation. They are also free to contribute their income and wealth, by themselves or with others of like mind, to provide the requisite material assistance so that those in another country may gain their freedom through their own efforts.

But what is inconsistent with a belief in freedom is a foreign policy that taxes or conscripts some Americans so that other Americans can have their favorite foreign cause subsidized. No matter how it is labeled, this remains a forced redistribution of wealth. If it is wrong in domestic policy for Peter to be taxed or conscripted by Paul so that Luke may gain, then it is equally wrong for Peter to be taxed or conscripted by Paul to benefit some Luke who happens to live in another country.

But forty-five years of the Cold War have left Americans incapable of recapturing in their minds these most fundamental principles of freedom. And in spite of the apparent American victory over communism in the Cold War, if Americans do not regain this understanding, the Cold War will have, in fact, resulted in the defeat of liberty in America.

This essay originally appeared in the November 1991, December 1991, and January 1992 issues of Freedom Daily, *published by The Future of Freedom Foundation.*

12

The Much-Coveted
World War II

by Jacob G. Hornberger

From the first grade in their government-approved schools, Americans are taught never to question the consequences of America's participation in World War II. "We defeated Hitler. Freedom prevailed over tyranny," we are taught, "and there is nothing further to consider or discuss." The political indoctrination is so complete that the minds of many Americans will forever remain closed to more complex issues and outcomes associated with that war.

But on the eve of the fiftieth anniversary of the Japanese attack on Pearl Harbor, more and more Americans are raising questions—not only about the events leading up to Pearl Harbor, but also about the far-reaching consequences of World War II itself.

Europe, of course, has been enmeshed in conflict and war for centuries. And while there were certainly a few Americans in the 1800s who wished their government to involve itself in European disputes, by and large, Americans of that time followed the advice of their Founding Fathers (Washington and Jefferson being the notable examples): Stay out of Europe's continuous and endless conflicts.

The turning point came in World War I. President Wilson believed that the United States could put a permanent end to European wars. Seeking a congressional declaration of war against Germany, Wilson claimed that this would be the war to end all wars—the war to make the world safe for democracy. These were the aims of the war—the aims for which thousands of American men and women were sacrificed.

But despite total victory over Germany, eternal peace and universal democracy were not attained. It did not take long to see the aftermath of World War I: communism in the Soviet Union; Nazism in Germany; fascism in Italy; and imperialism in Japan.

It would be an understatement to say that after World War I, Americans were disillusioned about their participation in that noble crusade. They had learned that good intentions do not matter—that the only thing that matters is consequences. Americans had sacrificed their young in a military crusade that totally failed to achieve its political objectives.

It is not difficult to understand, then, that when war broke out in Europe only twenty years later, Americans were opposed to once again becoming involved. Up until the attack on Pearl Harbor, the position of the overwhelming majority of Americans was, "Stay out of the war—let them kill themselves, just as they have been doing for centuries. American involvement will accomplish nothing."

Did the United States, England, and France win World War II? We certainly have been taught that in our public schools. And in a strict military sense, the answer is yes—the Western powers did defeat Germany, just as they did in World War I. But as the historian William Henry Chamberlin observes in his book *America's Second Crusade*, the goals of war involve much more than just military victory over the opponent. For war is waged not as a sporting event but in order to achieve certain political ends. And in this context—the context of the political ends of World War II—the Western powers lost the war.

Why did England and France declare war on Germany in the first place? (Many Americans believe that Germany was the first to declare war.) They did so in order to free the Polish people from Hitler's dictatorship. So, what was the final result five years later? The Poles were freed from the Nazi dictatorship of Adolf Hitler, only to have to suffer under the communist dictatorship of Joseph Stalin.

Of course, we have been taught that this was a great victory—that Stalin's, rather than Hitler's, control over the Eastern Europeans was something worth dying for—and that Americans should be proud that they sacrificed hundreds of thousands of their young people in the achievement of this victory.

But how can this truly be considered a victory? After all, even though he was a friend of our rulers, Stalin—like Hitler—was not a nice man! In fact, while it is difficult to compare evil, no one disputes the fact that Stalin murdered many more millions of people than

Hitler! Moreover, although many Americans are unaware of this, Stalin's army invaded Poland at about the same time as Hitler's—pursuant to the formal partnership into which these two dictators had entered.

But what about the Jews? it is asked. Didn't World War II save them from the clutches of Adolf Hitler? No. Because by the time Germany surrendered, most of them had already been killed.

Then what about the Pacific theater? Didn't we defeat the Japanese Imperial Army? Of course, but again, that was not the political aim of those American politicians and bureaucrats who were advocating military action against Japan in the 1930s. Japan had invaded China—and many American interventionists believed that the Chinese people should be free. And so what was the aftermath of World War II? Just four years later (and continuing to this day), the Chinese people were suffering under the iron dictatorship of the communists.

What about the British and the French? Didn't victory result in their freedom? Yes—but they were free before they declared war on Germany. Of course, it could be argued that Germany ultimately would have attacked England and France, but that is entirely speculative—especially since the overwhelming evidence is that Hitler intended to move east—against the nation he considered Germany's real enemy: the Soviet Union.

What about the Americans? Didn't they win freedom? That is certainly what we have been taught. But despite all of the indoctrination to which Americans have been subjected, no documentary evidence has ever been found of a German plan to invade the Western Hemisphere. And if Hitler's forces were unable even to cross the English channel to invade Great Britain, it is very difficult to imagine how his forces could have crossed the Atlantic to invade America.

Moreover, America's "friends"—the Soviets—had openly proclaimed their aim of worldwide conquest as far back as 1917. And within just two decades, thousands of American lives were lost in Korea and Vietnam—fighting "friends" whose victory in Europe we had celebrated just a few years before.

And the terrible irony is that Americans today are much less free (or, more accurately, more enslaved) than Americans were in 1939! By that time, the New Deal—the socialist-fascist economic system foisted on Americans by President Roosevelt—was in shambles, for it had proven terribly destructive economically as well as morally. And Americans were seriously considering abandoning this way of life and returning to the principles of economic liberty on which America was founded.

But World War II put the brakes on that reversal of perspective. By the end of the war, Americans had come to accept the concept of the all-powerful government in their lives. The welfare-state, planned-economy way of life became cemented in American society. And so here was the terrible irony: American men and women being sent to die in a faraway land for freedom and, after the end of the war (and continuing to the end of the century), those remaining alive having to suffer under the socialism associated with the welfare-state, planned-economy way of life.

Furthermore, as a result of World War II, Americans of our time, unlike their ancestors, now view all foreign wars as crusades for "freedom"—especially when the "liberated" people get to live under "our" dictator, as they did after World War II. Moreover, "freedom" for modern-day Americans now means the omnipotent power of their government to sacrifice the lives and fortunes of the citizenry in the pursuit of "freedom" for foreigners.

And perhaps this is the worst consequence of World War II— that Americans have come to accept their role as mere servants— rather than as sovereigns—in American society. For how many Americans—after being forced to listen to government-approved doctrine for twelve long years in their government-approved schools to which their parents are forced to send them—question the notion that our political rulers should have omnipotent power over our lives and fortunes in both domestic and foreign affairs?

And so we have this grand and glorious legacy of World War II: brutal communism in Eastern Europe and China, thousands of American deaths and injuries in Korea and Vietnam at the hands of our "friends," the communists; the seeming permanence of the welfare and warfare state in America; perpetual foreign crusades for "freedom," along with the conscription, taxation, and control which follow in their wake, and, finally, the terrible mind-set of political subserviency which now pervades the American citizenry. If this is victory, then it is time to reexamine the role of government in American society—both domestic and foreign—and to return to the principles of individual liberty and limited government of our Founding Fathers.

This essay originally appeared in the November 1991 issue of Freedom Daily, *published by The Future of Freedom Foundation.*

13

The America First Committee

by Sheldon Richman

One of the most remarkable episodes in American history was the spontaneous and widespread opposition to Franklin Roosevelt's obvious attempts to embroil the United States in the European war that broke out in 1939. That opposition was centered in the America First Committee. In modern accounts of the war period, the committee is either ignored or maligned as a pro-fascist, anti-Semitic organization. It was nothing of the kind.

The America First Committee had its origins at Yale University Law School in 1940, where R. Douglas Stuart Jr. and other students began circulating a petition with the intention of establishing a national organization of college students opposed to intervention in the European war. (This account is based on historian Justus D. Doenecke's highly valuable book, *In Danger Undaunted: The Anti-Interventionist Movement of 1940–1941 as Revealed in the Papers of the America First Committee*, Hoover Institution, 1990.) As an undergraduate student at Princeton, Stuart had concluded that America's intervention in World War I had cost the nation dearly. He did not want the mistake repeated. In his initial organizing efforts, he was joined by Gerald R. Ford, who would become president of the United States in 1974, and Potter Stewart, who would be named to the U.S. Supreme Court in 1958. (Before long, Ford would resign from the committee for fear of losing his job as assistant football coach at Yale.)

The petition was their response to President Roosevelt's series of actions that violated America's neutrality. "We demand that Congress refrain from war, even if England is on the verge of defeat," the petition stated.

What had Roosevelt done to this point? When Hitler invaded Poland in September 1939 and Britain and France declared war, Roosevelt affirmed America's neutrality. "Within three weeks, however," writes Doenecke, "he urged Congress to remove an arms embargo that had been one of the linchpins of U.S. neutrality legislation." Congress acceded. That erosion of neutrality spurred the Yale students, who quickly sought supporters outside the ranks of college students.

Meetings with some Chicago businessmen led to plans for a large-scale organization. In July 1940, Gen. Robert E. Wood, chairman of the board of Sears, Roebuck, agreed to become acting chairman. (Wood had earlier supported the New Deal but then broke with Roosevelt. He was less anti-interventionist than others in the new committee.) In late August, the group adopted the name the America First Committee (AFC).

In its first public statement (September 4, 1940), the AFC enunciated four precepts:

1. The United States must build an impregnable defense for America;

2. No foreign powers, nor group of powers, can successfully attack a prepared America;

3. American democracy can be preserved only by keeping out of the European war;

4. "Aid short of war" weakens national defense at home and threatens to involve America in war abroad.

The statement went on to specify four objectives. First, the AFC would "bring together all Americans, regardless of possible differences on other matters, who see eye-to-eye on these principles." Parenthetically it added, "This does not include Nazis, Fascists, Communists, or members of other groups that place the interests of any other nation above those of our own." Second, the AFC would "urge Americans to keep their heads amid the rising hysteria in times of crisis." Third, it would "provide sane leadership" for the majority of Americans who were opposed to intervention. Fourth, it would "register this opinion with the President and the majority of Congress."

The Committee attracted some prestigious members or sympathizers from business, journalism, politics, publishing, and the arts. Its best-known member was aviation hero Charles Lindbergh. (He was unfairly accused of anti-Semitism as a result.) They did not all agree on every issue. Some sympathizers would decline to join or were forced to resign, apparently under pressure from interventionists. AFC member and actress Lillian Gish said she was blacklisted from film and theater and offered a $65,000 movie contract if she would resign.

It seems that government snooping and the Hollywood blacklist did not begin as anticommunist tactics—Roosevelt had the FBI investigate the AFC.

Not everyone was welcome in the AFC. Among the national committee members who were ousted were builder and American Olympic Association president Avery Brundage, who was suspected of having Nazi sympathies, and Henry Ford, who had previously espoused anti-Semitism.

One of the most important members was John T. Flynn, chairman of the New York chapter and a national committeeman. Flynn was a prominent muckraking journalist who exposed big business's connections to the New Deal. For example, he demonstrated that the Reconstruction Finance Corporation (which began under Herbert Hoover) was little more than a bailout scheme for big banks and railroads. He was a columnist for the *New Republic* until it dropped him because of his anti-interventionist position. No one was more vigilant about keeping fascists out of the AFC than Flynn. At one huge public rally in New York City, he identified a local fascist in the crowd and told him he was not welcome.

The audience expressed such hostility to the man that the police surrounded him for his own protection. Despite Flynn's efforts, some fascists and anti-Semites managed to participate in the committee. Flynn went on to write an extremely important book, *As We Go Marching*, one of the best discussions of the nature of German and Italian fascism and its similarity to the New Deal.

In its day-to-day business the AFC challenged Roosevelt's and the Congress's war-related measures (Lend-Lease, the destroyers-for-bases exchange with Britain, the occupation of Iceland, the Atlantic Charter, aid to the Soviet Union, the extension of the draft) and rebutted each argument made for direct or indirect involvement in the war. In pamphlets, radio broadcasts, and public meetings, AFC spokesmen rejected the interventionists' case that a German victory or Japan's conquests would put the United States at an economic disadvantage or lead to war later.

The AFC issued a series of talking points for its speakers bureau—short answers to common questions about America and the war. For example, to the question, "What, strictly on the basis of our own national interests, should our part [in the war] be?" AFC responded:

> It is difficult, of course, to define our national interests, but it is always safe to assume that our chief national interest is the maintenance of our democracy and the well-being of our own American people. . . . Since experience has taught us that democracy vanishes in wartime, it would seem that the surest way to keep our form of government is to avoid involvement. We should also seek an adequate national defense to make sure that we can maintain our territorial integrity in the event we are attacked by a foreign power.

To the question (often asked today), "Isn't it part of our responsibility as a world power to take a hand in settling problems that menace world peace and security?" the AFC said:

> We have no responsibilities that our people do not wish to undertake. We have no international commitments, agreed to by the people or their representatives, outside this hemisphere. Even if we did, it would not be a signal for going to war everytime [sic] there was one. Americans naturally wish security and peace for the rest of the world, but it is not entirely within their powers to bring these things about.

Other publications refuted the claims that a victorious Hitler could fight a large-scale war against the United States in the Western Hemisphere and that the United States could be strangled by foreign control of raw materials. To that still often-heard allegation (consult the recent Persian Gulf War propaganda), the AFC noted that "since we are the greatest raw material market in the world, [Hitler] would only be cutting off his nose to spite his face if he successfully withheld raw materials from us."

On December 7, 1941, after prolonged U.S. economic warfare, Japan attacked the U.S. Navy's Pacific fleet at Hawaii. On December 8, Congress declared war on Japan. On December 11, the national committee of the America First Committee voted to disband the organization. The statement issued to the public stated:

> Our principles were right. Had they been followed, war could have been avoided. No good purpose can now be served by considering what might have been, had our objectives been attained.

The national committee expressed hope that prosecution of the war would not interfere with "the fundamental rights of American citizens" and that "secret treaties committing America to imperialistic aims or vast burden in other parts of the world shall be scrupulously avoided."

Its final words urged its followers to fully support the war effort: "The time for military action is here."

This essay originally appeared in the April 1995 issue of Freedom Daily, *published by The Future of Freedom Foundation.*

14

Hard Bargain: How FDR Twisted Churchill's Arm, Evaded the Law and Changed the Role of the American Presidency

a review by Richard M. Ebeling

Hard Bargain: How FDR Twisted Churchill's Arm, Evaded the Law and Changed the Role of the American Presidency by Robert Shogan (New York: Scribner, 1995); 329 pages; $24.

Franklin Roosevelt was a master of manipulation and intrigue. His entire New Deal was presented to the American public as a scheme to save the American system of free enterprise, when it actually undermined the very principles of individual freedom and free-market capitalism upon which the country was founded. In the name of saving American democracy from radical revolution, FDR subverted the entire constitutional order upon which the United States was based.

But it was the Second World War that gave an international dimension to Roosevelt's manipulations and intrigues. Indeed, they were now raised to a fine art. This is the theme of Robert Shogan's recent book, *Hard Bargain: How FDR Twisted Churchill's Arm, Evaded the Law and Changed the Role of the American Presidency.* The focus of Mr. Shogan's story is the "destroyers-for-bases" deal that FDR made with Winston Churchill in August 1940.

In 1937, shortly after his reelection to a second term to the presidency, Franklin Roosevelt was already thinking about running for a third term. But the domestic situation in 1938 did not make his prospects for reelection promising. The American economy, still not recovered from the Great Depression years of the early 1930s, went into a new downturn. A growing number of people began talking about "the Roosevelt recession."

In 1939, the answer to Roosevelt's domestic problems emerged: the war in Europe between Nazi Germany and Great Britain and France. FDR soon convinced himself that he was the only person in America who could prepare the United States for the new emergency.

The year 1940 brought spectacular Nazi victories on the European continent. After half a year of a "phony war" on the western front, the German army and navy invaded Denmark and Norway in April 1940. This was followed in May by the German invasion of Holland, Belgium, and France. In June, the French signed an armistice that resulted in more than half of France being permanently occupied by Germany.

In the face of this military debacle, Winston Churchill replaced Neville Chamberlain as British prime minister in May. He immediately began bombarding Roosevelt with appeals for military assistance, especially for the United States to sell or give fifty destroyers to the British to help ward off a German invasion of England and to use as escorts for merchant vessels that were bringing war material to Britain. Roosevelt replied that he could not fulfill Churchill's request because he was prevented from doing so by neutrality laws passed by Congress (and signed by him) that denied him the authority to either sell or give warships to a belligerent power.

However, in late May, FDR agreed to transfer twenty torpedo boats to the British without informing Congress. When Navy Secretary Charles Edison objected, Roosevelt told him: "Forget it and do what I told you to do."

But leading noninterventionists in the Congress got wind of FDR's subterfuge, and the resulting outcry caused Roosevelt to revoke the transfer.

The president realized that any further attempts along these lines would threaten a public conflict with Congress and endanger his chances for reelection to a third term. He, therefore, turned to indirection and intrigue to accomplish his goal.

The "hard bargain" that Mr. Shogan refers to in the title of his book is the deal FDR offered to Churchill—American destroyers given to Britain in exchange for Britain's leasing property in the West Indies and Canada—for ninety-nine years—as American military bases. Churchill replied that such an agreement would be a threat to British sovereignty. But Roosevelt insisted that this was the only way that he could evade Congress and the neutrality acts. With destroyers-for-bases, he could argue, after the fact, that he was acting in the interests of national security by providing a more secure defense of the United States.

FDR and Churchill signed letters of agreement. FDR announced the destroyers-for-bases agreement during the Labor Day weekend in 1940. When reporters asked him if congressional approval was required, he replied: "It is all over; it is all done." When the reporters asked him for details about the agreement, Roosevelt answered that it involved "all kinds of things that nobody here would understand, so I won't mention them. It is a *fait accompli*; it is done this way."

An uproar resulted among the noninterventionists. Constitutional expert and political scientist Edward Corwin asked: "Why not any and all of Congress's specifically delegated powers be set aside by the President's 'executive power' and the country be put on a totalitarian basis without further ado?" Sen. Arthur Vandenberg called Roosevelt's deal "the most arbitrary and dictatorial action ever taken by any President in the history of the United States." Congressman George Tinkham said, "There is no difference between his [FDR's] action from either Hitler, Mussolini and Stalin."

In his concluding chapter, Mr. Shogan argues that Roosevelt's destroyer-for-bases deal resulted in

> a high price [being] paid in undermining the rule of law. . . . In implementing the destroyer deal, Roosevelt followed a pattern of manipulation and concealment that breached trust of the American citizenry. To avoid being held accountable, he relied whenever he could on proxies, at the cost of delay and confusion. . . . The most pertinent question about the destroyer deal and Roosevelt's other actions was the extent to which they created circumstances in which attack [upon the United States] became inevitable. And this was an issue which the President dealt with through evasion and obfuscation. . . . After expanding presidential power to forge the New Deal's domestic re-

forms, Roosevelt demonstrated how this same power could also be used to work his will abroad.

With this precedent, Mr. Shogan argues, the door was opened for every president after FDR to use the same executive power to rationalize and justify the sending of American troops to Korea, the Middle East, Vietnam, Somalia, and Haiti. After half a century of foreign intervention and over a hundred thousand slain Americans in foreign wars since 1945, the destroyer-for-bases deal of 1940 has truly turned out to be a "hard bargain."

This review originally appeared in the August 1995 issue of Freedom Daily, *published by The Future of Freedom Foundation.*

15

December 7, 1941: The Infamy of FDR

by Jacob G. Hornberger

The Japanese attack on Pearl Harbor, Hawaii—December 7, 1941—killed or injured over 4,500 Americans. It destroyed most of America's Pacific fleet. Almost 200 American aircraft were lost. Although America's defenders at Pearl Harbor fought bravely and courageously, the attack resulted in a massacre.

There is no better example of the political indoctrination that the American people receive in their government-approved schools than that relating to Franklin D. Roosevelt. From the first grade, American schoolchildren are taught to glorify and idolize the man "who saved America's free-enterprise system" and "who tried his very best to keep America out of World War II." The indoctrination is so effective and so complete that by the time Americans graduate from these government-approved schools, any thought of questioning the teachings relating to Roosevelt is virtually nonexistent.

Americans are taught that World War II—for the United States—began with the Japanese attack on Pearl Harbor. Government-approved schoolteachers pound into the heads of the students that President Roosevelt was shocked, horrified, and disappointed with the death and destruction on that fateful day.

Nothing could be further from the truth. The Japanese attack on Pearl Harbor accomplished the major objective of President Franklin D. Roosevelt: America's formal entry into World War II.

119

It is important to remember that the United States was founded on principles different from those of every nation in history. Although there were those in 1787 who wanted a ruler with omnipotent powers, the proponents of limited government prevailed. And one of the limitations on the power of the president was with respect to war: he was prohibited from waging it without a formal declaration of war from Congress.

As recently as the early part of this century, the American people clearly understood and agreed with the meaning and effect of this limitation on the power of the executive branch. That was why President Wilson went to Congress and sought a declaration before entering World War I—he knew that the United States could not legally wage war without it.

President Roosevelt understood that this higher law of the Constitution controlled his actions as well. Nevertheless, the man who did everything he could in the 1930s to destroy America's legacy of economic liberty proceeded on a fateful—and illegal—course of action: waging undeclared war on Germany and Japan in an attempt to maneuver them into "firing the first shot"—thereby justifying America's formal entry into the war.

Why didn't Roosevelt simply follow the constitutional avenue of going to Congress and asking for a declaration of war? Because he knew that the vast majority of the American people were against sacrificing their young in a second crusade in Europe and that the predominate mood of Congress was to stay out of the war.

What did the United States do to wage undeclared war? First, it violated fundamental principles of neutrality under international law by assisting and arming one of the warring sides. Through Roosevelt's Lend-Lease plan, millions of dollars of American military hardware was shipped to Great Britain—as well as to Joseph Stalin, the communist dictator of the Soviet Union—thereby encouraging a counterattack by Germany on America's ships.

But having learned its lesson in World War I—when Wilson used German submarine attacks on U.S. ships to seek a declaration of war against Germany—the Germans refused to take the bait.

So Roosevelt proceeded to go further. He began using American military convoys to ship goods to Britain—another act of war under international law. But Germany again refused to attack America's ships.

Finally, desperately trying to goad the Germans into an attack, Roosevelt ordered American ships to begin seeking out German submarines and reporting their positions to the British. One American ship that did this—the *Greer*—finally was attacked by the German submarine whose location the *Greer* was reporting to the British. Roosevelt's response: The United States has been attacked! But Congress itself refused to take Roosevelt's bait.

Thus, in 1941, Roosevelt was at his wit's end. He knew that the Germans were not going to react to his provocations with an attack on the United States—that the position of the American people, despite the evil actions of Adolf Hitler and Benito Mussolini, was: "Stay out of this war!"—that Congress was against entering the war—that both the Democratic and Republican Party platforms were against entry into another European war—and Roosevelt knew that he had falsely and deceptively promised the American people in the 1940 presidential campaign that he was doing everything he could to keep America out of the war.

Thus, Roosevelt was stymied—that is, until his focus turned to the Pacific—the area that would ultimately turn out to be his "back door to war" in Europe.

By and large, American schoolchildren are taught never to ask about the circumstances leading up to Japan's attack on Pearl Harbor. All that matters is that Japan attacked—the events leading up to the attack are considered "unimportant and irrelevant." Thus, by the time they grow up, very few Americans ever ask themselves the obvious question: Why in the world would a relatively small nation like Japan attack one of the most powerful nations in history?

Throughout the 1930s, the Japanese imperial government was waging a vicious and cruel war against China. But although Americans recoiled at Japan's aggression, there was virtually no interest in getting the United States involved in that conflict.

But by 1941, that perspective had changed—for Franklin D. Roosevelt. The decision was made to begin "squeezing" the Japanese dictators under the ostensible purpose of helping the Chinese people.

The American noose began with U.S. government military assistance to the Chinese—another violation of neutrality principles under international law. But it was tightened through two much more dangerous and fateful decisions—decisions which American schoolchildren are never taught in American history courses in their government-approved schools.

Knowing that the Japanese war machine was dependent on Western oil and other vital resources, Roosevelt, acting in conjunction with other Western powers, prohibited American citizens from furnishing any more of these items to Japan—a flagrant violation of property rights of private American citizens. Even more shocking, Roosevelt froze all Japanese assets in the United States and refused

121

to release them. And both of these actions were taken before December 7—against a nation that was not at war with the United States.

The Japanese dictators were placed in an uncomfortable situation as a result of Roosevelt's actions, for their supply of oil to continue waging war in China was soon going to be depleted. Entering into negotiations with the U.S. officials—negotiations which American students are never told about—the American officials told them: Get out of China and we will release the embargo and let you have your assets back. Unfortunately, the Japanese rulers did not permit themselves to be humbled by the American officials. If they had simply exited China in response to the noose that was now tightening around their necks, Roosevelt would again have been denied America's formal entry into the European war.

As it became more and more obvious that the negotiations were going nowhere, the Japanese prepared for their attack on Pearl Harbor. Japanese spies in Hawaii were ordered to send regular reports of ships entering and leaving the harbor. Then, the code-message indicating that war was imminent—"East Wind, Rain"—was sent to the Japanese negotiators in Washington. And this was followed by the dramatic, final response to the American demand to exit China—the response that caused Roosevelt to exclaim upon reading it, "This means war!"

And all of these messages—and more—were read by Roosevelt—before December 7, 1941! For unknown to the Japanese—and to the American people at that time—was that the U.S. government had broken the Japanese secret codes and was reading the Japanese diplomatic messages—before the attack on Pearl Harbor!

Did Roosevelt and his cronies deliver these messages to the Hawaiian commanders, Kimmel and Short, before the Japanese attack? Of course not. That would have meant that the brave and courageous men at Pearl Harbor could have prepared for the attack. Why would that have been a problem? Because if the Japanese had discovered that the Americans were prepared for the attack, the probability is that the Japanese forces would have turned back. Nothing—and certainly not Roosevelt's final bait—a few thousand American servicemen and a hundred or so American ships—could be permitted to stand in the way of Roosevelt's primary objective: America's entry into World War II.

This essay originally appeared in the December 1991 issue of Freedom Daily, *published by The Future of Freedom Foundation.*

16

Pearl Harbor:
The Controversy Continues

by Sheldon Richman

At 7:53 a.m. on Sunday, December 7, 1941, a Japanese force of 183 fighters, bombers, and torpedo planes struck the United States Pacific fleet at Pearl Harbor, Hawaii. Some 4,500 Americans were killed or wounded. As news of the surprise attack spread, William F. Friedman, an Army cryptanalyst who had helped to break the Japanese diplomatic "Purple" code, said to his wife repeatedly, "But they knew, they knew, they knew."

Meanwhile, the British double agent Dusko Popov got an incomplete account of the attack while aboard a tramp steamer. He assumed the Americans had been ready for the Japanese attack—it was he who had given the FBI the Japanese plans for the air raid. Popov would recall, "I was sure the American fleet had scored a great victory over the Japanese. I was very, very proud that I had been able to give the warning to the Americans four months in advance. What a reception the Japanese must have had!"

In Singapore the day after the attack, Royal Navy codebreaker Tommy Wisden asked incredulously, "With all the information we gave them. How could the Americans have been caught unprepared?"

Fifty years after that "day of infamy," the attack on Pearl Harbor remains a matter of the hottest controversy. Every few years, a new telling of the story stokes the fire. For example, in 1982, John Toland, a dean of American war historians, wrote in his book *Infamy: Pearl Harbor and Its Aftermath* (from which the first two anecdotes are taken), "The comedy of errors on the sixth and seventh [of December] appears incredible. It only makes sense if it was a charade, and Roosevelt and the inner circle had known about the attack. A massive cover-up followed Pearl Harbor a few days later, according to an officer close to [Gen. George C.] Marshall, when the Chief of Staff ordered a lid put on the affair. 'Gentlemen,' he [Marshall] told half a dozen officers, 'this goes to the grave with us.'"

Pearl Harbor is actually a bundle of controversial questions. In order of descending controversy, they consist of:

• whether Roosevelt and his closest aides knew there would be an attack on Pearl Harbor on December 7;

• whether they knew there would be an attack against American or British targets *somewhere* in the Pacific; and, finally,

• whether Roosevelt's policies toward the Japanese were intended to provoke the Japanese into striking at American interests, thereby providing a "back door to war" and grounds for full public support for the war effort.

The first and second questions come down to how much FDR knew and when did he know it. No one has found a document signed by FDR saying, "Pearl Harbor will be attacked on December 7." But Toland believes that Roosevelt knew that Pearl Harbor would be the target. Earlier revisionist historians were convinced that by late November, Roosevelt knew that there would be an attack on American or British possessions in the Pacific, with Pearl Harbor a likely location. (Roosevelt secretly had pledged to enter the war if Japan attacked Britain or crossed an undisclosed line in the Pacific.)

Despite differences among various historians, many of them agree on these damning points: (1) Franklin Roosevelt and his closest aides had seen Japanese messages that *should* have indicated to them (if they did not indeed do so) that Pearl Harbor would be attacked at dawn on December 7. (2) The commanders at Pearl Harbor, who were later made scapegoats, were inexcusably denied critical intelligence that would have likely caused them to take precautions that would have spoiled the Japanese surprise and probably prevented the attack.

The United States kept abreast of Japan's thinking by decoding Japanese diplomatic and military messages. The key messages included the dividing of Pearl Harbor into a grid, apparently for plotting an attack (the "bomb plot" message read on October 9); notice of an impending Japanese attack on the United States (the "winds execute" message of December 4); a scheme for signaling the movement and position of U.S. ships at Pearl Harbor (December 6); and the text and time of Japan's rejection of the U.S. ultimatum (December 6 and 7). (On reading this rejection on the evening of December 6, Roosevelt said to his chief advisor, Harry Hopkins, "This means war!")

None of these messages were relayed to the Pearl Harbor commanders—except for the last one. And it was not sent by Marshall until the last minute, and then by Western Union, rather than by faster means. By the time the telegram was received in Hawaii, the attack was under way.

The final question—about the provocations—is less controversial. Even adulators of Roosevelt now concede that he lied the nation into war. He had to, they say, because the American people were too shortsighted to support intervention. Hitler had refused to attack the United States, despite provocation. So the President had no choice but, as Secretary of War Henry L. Stimson wrote in his diary on November 25, "to maneuver them [Japan] into the position of firing the first shot."

By then there had already been much maneuvering. It consisted of the systematic strangulation of Japan. For a nation like Japan, with no natural resources and a desperate need to import its necessities, this had to lead to war.

Some American policymakers had long disliked Japan, partly because of racism, partly because of economic rivalry. Like today, some were disturbed by the presence of Japanese products on American shelves. And although the U.S.-Japanese trade was much larger than the U.S.-Chinese trade, many people thought that someday China would provide a huge market for American manufacturers, if Japan did not get there first. Thus, when Japan began hostilities against China in the 1930s, there was concern.

As early as 1938, Roosevelt quietly explored with the British the possibility of war with Japan. Japanese overtures, including an offer in 1940 to leave China and the Axis Pact, were rebuffed. In July 1940, Roosevelt began his program of economic warfare by embargoing strategic goods. In September, he prohibited exports of iron and scrap steel to Japan. In June 1941, he restricted oil shipments. About a month later, Roosevelt froze Japan's funds in the United States. This was followed by a warning that a continuation of Japan's expansionist policies would compel the United States to protect its security. Roosevelt also refused to meet with Japanese Prime Minister Konoye. Soon afterwards, the Japanese government fell, and General Tojo became prime minister.

During negotiations with Japan, Secretary of State Cordell Hull demanded that Japan withdraw from China and Indochina, leave other countries alone (including the sacrosanct colonies which the United States, Britain, and Holland had bagged though their previous imperialistic campaigns), and scrap the Greater East Asia Co-Prosperity Sphere. Japan offered concessions, but the American response suggested to the Japanese that the United States wanted no agreement. Caught in an economic vise, the Japanese began to speak of war if no settlement were reached by November. The American officials were aware of this, thanks to the breaking of the Japanese codes and the interception of diplomatic messages.

On November 20, Japan made an offer that included restoration of peace between it and China and withdrawal of troops from Indochina in return for commercial normalization. (Meanwhile, Japanese forces were moving toward American, British, and Dutch colonies, just in case the offer was refused.) Hull called the offer "utterly unacceptable." Although the U.S. military wanted additional time to prepare and Roosevelt initially wanted a six-month delay, Hull issued an ultimatum on November 26 demanding total Japanese withdrawal from China and Indochina. Recognizing that compliance would humiliate the Japanese, Hull knew that the ultimatum would not be accepted. And Hull was right—the Japanese government refused to accept the ultimatum. The next day Hull told Secretary of War Stimson, "It is now in the hands of you and [Naval Secretary] Knox—the Army and Navy." Weak, vague "war warnings" that implied a danger of sabotage were sent to Hawaii. Intercepted Japanese messages in the following days predicted a rupturing of negotiations and ordered the destruction of embassy code machines.

On the 26th, the Japanese attack force set sail from the Kurile Islands. On December 2, final approval for the attack was given, with the proviso that it could be canceled if negotiations resumed. In Washington, on the morning of December 7, Roosevelt learned that Japan would turn down the Hull ultimatum at exactly 1:00 p.m. Washington time. It would be dawn at that hour in only one place in the Pacific: Hawaii.

Was this the end result of an intentional policy or "only" monumental incompetence? Perhaps the opening of the American and British archives—still hidden from the American and British people—will someday resolve the mystery—that is, if all of the relevant documents have not been burned, shredded, or otherwise tampered with.

This essay originally appeared in the December 1991 issue of Freedom Daily, *published by The Future of Freedom Foundation.*

17

Scapegoats: A Defense of Kimmel and Short at Pearl Harbor

a review by Richard M. Ebeling

Scapegoats: A Defense of Kimmel and Short at Pearl Harbor by Edward L. Beach (Annapolis, Md.: Naval Institute Press, 1995); 212 pages; $24.95.

At 7:48 on the morning of December 7, 1941, the first Japanese planes reached the northern shore of Oahu. This first wave of attack planes had taken off from their carriers almost two hours earlier, from their positions about 200 miles north of the Hawaiian Islands. They were now only seven minutes away from the beginning of their attack run on the U.S. naval ships located at Pearl Harbor. As the Japanese planes began to prepare for their assault, Commander Mitsuo Fuchida radioed to the Japanese fleet: Tora, Tora, Tora. This indicated they had succeeded in a surprise attack. At 7:55, the Japanese torpedo bombers began diving on Battleship Row, and disaster began to rain down on the U.S. Pacific Fleet.

By the time the two waves of enemy planes finished their work at 9:45 that morning and had headed back to their carriers for the return trip to Japan, the Japanese had succeeded in sinking or damaging 18 U.S. ships (including 8 battleships), along with destroying 188 planes and damaging 159 more. Over 2,400 U.S. military servicemen were dead, and 2,000 more were wounded. Days later, smoke still billowed from the sunken *Arizona*, its smokestacks visible above the water line.

The next day—December 8—President Franklin D. Roosevelt spoke before a joint session of Congress. In perhaps the most famous presidential address in this century, FDR declared:

> Yesterday, December 7, 1941—a date which will live in infamy—the United States of America was suddenly and deliberately attacked by the naval and air forces of the Empire of Japan. The United States was at peace with that nation and . . . looking toward the maintenance of peace in the Pacific. . . . Japan has . . . undertaken a surprise offensive extending across the Pacific area. . . . I ask that the Congress declare that since the unprovoked and dastardly attack by Japan on Sunday, December 7th, a state of war has existed between the United States and the Japanese Empire.

The shock of the Pearl Harbor attack—both its apparent unprovoked nature and its destructive effect on America's military might in the Pacific Ocean—resulted in an outcry that the guilty parties be brought to justice. The defeat of Japan would see to it that the perpetrators would be made to pay for this infamous day.

But were the Japanese the only ones guilty? Why was the Pacific Fleet caught by surprise? Who was responsible for America's lack of defensive preparedness? Why hadn't anyone seen the likelihood of a Japanese attack? These questions have come up over and over again, both during the war and over the last half century since the end of the war. Edward L. Beach, a retired U.S. naval captain and noted historian and novelist (he is the author of the novel *Run Silent, Run Deep*, which was made into a movie starring Clark Gable and Burt Lancaster), has written one of the best summaries of the debate over responsibility for the Pearl Harbor fiasco. His book is entitled *Scapegoats: A Defense of Kimmel and Short at Pearl Harbor*.

Captain Beach argues that Adm. Husband Kimmel, as commander of the Pacific Fleet, and Lt. Gen. Walter Short, commander of the Hawaiian department of the U.S. Army, were made the scapegoats for the Pearl Harbor disaster. In reaching this conclusion, he undertakes three analyses: First, were Kimmel and Short derelict in their duty in not being more fully prepared for a possible Japanese attack? To answer this, Captain Beach presents an overview of the nine formal investigations of the Pearl Harbor attack by the army, navy, the executive branch, and the Congress between 1941 and 1946.

Second, Captain Beach asks, who was responsible higher up the chain of command for information about diplomatic negotiations and military dangers being sent to Kimmel and Short? And if all the relevant information was not, in fact, passed on to them, who was at fault and why?

And third, was it true that the attack on Pearl Harbor was unprovoked and unexpected? And if the attack was not completely unprovoked and unexpected, who in Washington was responsible for creating the conditions likely to create a war in the Pacific? And how much did the people in the White House and the executive branch know about the likely time and place of an attack by Japan on the United States?

The first serious inquiry was the Roberts Commission in December 1941–January 1942. The commission concluded that Kimmel and Short were guilty of having failed in their duty—a court-martial offense. FDR ordered the report released immediately. This resulted in the two Hawaiian commanders being tainted for life. But they were never court-martialed.

Except for one, all the other commissions, while saying that Kimmel and Short should have been more alert to the danger of possible hostilities with Japan, concluded that the two men had acted appropriately, given the information at their disposal. What became clear in these inquiries was that the two had not been told a lot!

During the naval inquiry in 1944, Capt. Laurence Safford, the leading cryptologist responsible for decoding intercepted Japanese messages, testified that from May 1941 on, it was clear that Japan was planning hostilities in southeast Asia. On December 1 and 4, 1941, Safford said there had been "definite information . . . that Japan would attack the United States and Britain, but would maintain peace with Russia. . . . At 9:00 p.m. (Washington time), December 6, 1941, we received positive information that Japan would declare war against the United States. . . . Finally at 10:15 a.m. (Washington time), December 7, 1941 [about 5:00 a.m. Hawaiian time], we recorded positive information . . . that the Japanese declaration of war would be presented to the Secretary of State at 1:00 p.m. (Washington time) that date."

All decoded messages, Safford explained, had gone to the president and other selected civilian and military members of the government in rapid time. Yet, both Kimmel and Short were kept in the dark about practically all these clear indications of imminent hostilities—signs that would have lead them to institute more vigilant precautions against possible attack.

133

The responsibility for failing to provide this information to the Hawaiian commanders belonged to Adm. Harold Stark, Gen. George Marshall, and Vice Adm. Richmond Turner, who were the ones higher in the chain of command who should have seen that the appropriate warnings were sent to Pearl Harbor.

Why was Pearl Harbor not warned? Captain Beach calls himself a "second-class revisionist." He does not believe that FDR knew that Pearl Harbor was going to be the site of the attack and consciously allowed the Naval forces to be destroyed to arouse the anger and indignation of the American people. Instead, he argues that it is beyond any doubt that FDR wanted war and created the conditions under which the Japanese would attack the United States somewhere:

> It is clear today that, among those responsible for the Japanese attack, first must be President Roosevelt himself. . . . The reconstruction of events confirms the supposition that Roosevelt had determined on war with Japan. . . . Second ranking in the compilation of failure and responsibility for Pearl Harbor goes to General Marshall and Admiral Stark, chiefs of the army and the navy, for . . . failure to send adequate warning to their subordinates in the field. . . . The national leadership which had the obligation of keeping our military commanders current with matters of their concern, utterly failed our commanders at Pearl Harbor and then blamed them for their own lack of alertness. . . . Giant of stature though he was, [FDR] was sometimes small enough to destroy other men to give himself protection.

Franklin Roosevelt's actions in pressuring Japan—FDR also was insistent that Japan fire the first shot, so noninterventionists could not accuse him of starting the conflict—made war almost inevitable. But the Pearl Harbor fiasco did more than just destroy the careers of Kimmel and Short; it set the United States on a course of global war that resulted in the deaths of tens of thousands of young American lives.

This review originally appeared in the October 1995 issue of Freedom Daily, *published by The Future of Freedom Foundation.*

18

Icebreaker: Who Started the Second World War?

a review by Richard M. Ebeling

Icebreaker: Who Started the Second World War? by Viktor Suvorov (London: Hamish Hamilton, 1990); 364 pages; $22.95.

In the early morning hours of September 1, 1939, the military might of Nazi Germany was set loose on Poland. As Panzer divisions crossed the Polish-German border, the German air force began its devastating rain of death on Warsaw and other Polish cities. On September 3, Britain and France declared war on Germany.

On September 17, the Soviet Red Army invaded Poland from the east and met up with the German forces at the city of Brest-Litovsk. Poland ceased to exist as an independent nation, divided between the two great totalitarian states of the European continent. World War II had begun.

But did World War II, in fact, begin in September on the plains of Poland? And was it, in fact, Nazi Germany that began the Second World War?

What made it possible for Hitler to feel secure in invading Poland to the east, and not to worry about a two-front war if Britain and France initiated hostilities in the west, was the Nazi-Soviet Non-Aggression Pact of August 23, 1939. In a secret protocol to the pact, Hitler and Stalin had agreed to divide up Eastern Europe. In the event of war, Poland would be split down the middle between Germany and the USSR, with Finland, Estonia, Latvia, Lithuania, and the Romanian province of Bessarabia assigned to the Soviet sphere of influence.

Why did Stalin enter into this fiendish pact with Hitler? After all, throughout the 1930s, the Nazi and Soviet leaders had accused each other of being the greatest evil on the face of the earth. Most historians have argued that Stalin had come to the conclusion that the Western powers could not be relied upon in case of war. Rather than face the German army on his own, it was better to sign a non-aggression pact with the Nazi devil and have the extra time to defensively prepare the Soviet Union for the attack that Stalin knew would eventually come from Nazi Germany.

Viktor Suvorov, in his book *Icebreaker: Who Started the Second World War?*, challenges this thesis concerning the rationale behind Soviet policy toward Hitler. Mr. Suvorov, a former Soviet army officer who has written extensively on the Soviet military and intelligence network, argues that the Nazi-Soviet pact was not a defensive action on Stalin's part. Instead, it was part of Stalin's Marxist strategy for revolutionary victory in Europe.

Marx and Engels believed that clashes between the capitalist nations would create avenues for the establishment of socialism. Lenin shared this belief. He saw World War I as a war among capitalist-imperialist powers, fighting over the plunder of the world. The more brutal and destructive the war, the more the power bases of the capitalist classes would be weakened. And out of this destruction would come the opportunity to transform a capitalist war into a "class war," resulting in the victory of communism.

World War I created the conditions for the Bolshevik Revolution and the triumph of socialism in Russia. Lenin believed that another world war would bring about the death of capitalism in other nations. Hence, anything that created the conditions for another world war was viewed as good from the revolutionary Marxist point of view.

Suvorov shows that Stalin shared this view. During the late 1920s and early 1930s, the Soviets assisted the Nazis in destroying the Weimar Republic in Germany. "Icebreaker" was the Soviet code name for Hitler—the man who would "break the ice," bring about another world war, and create the opportunity for the destruction of capitalism in Europe and the victory of socialism under Soviet leadership.

By signing the Nazi-Soviet pact in August 1939, Stalin deliberately produced the conditions for the world war that he wanted. Germany would fight the other two main European powers—Britain and France—and then the Soviet Union would enter the war in its final stages to come out as the ultimate victor.

Suvorov also convincingly demonstrates that Stalin was not developing defensive forces along the new Soviet border with Germany, but rather was building up a vast and powerful offensive military force. Stalin was clearly planning to enter the war by attacking Germany and then bringing socialism to Central and Western Europe on the bayonets of the Red Army. Furthermore, all the evidence suggests—and Suvorov musters a vast amount of military and political evidence—that Stalin was planning his attack on Germany for the middle of July 1941.

Hitler preempted Stalin's plan by attacking the Soviet Union on June 22, 1941. The staggering defeats suffered by the Soviet army in the early stages of the war were due to the fact that Stalin had torn down many of the Soviet defense positions and had not equipped his armies facing Germany with strategic-defense plans. All of their plans were for *offensive* operations.

The man who started World War II, therefore, was Stalin, who wanted to use Hitler as a tool for communist victory. And his plan partly succeeded. Out of the war's death and destruction, the Soviet Union was left as master of half of Europe, with Stalin as its Red Czar in the Kremlin.

This review originally appeared in the November 1991 issue of Freedom Daily, *published by The Future of Freedom Foundation.*

19

A Time for War: Franklin D. Roosevelt and the Path to Pearl Harbor

a review by Richard M. Ebeling

A Time for War: Franklin D. Roosevelt and the Path to Pearl Harbor by Robert Smith Thompson (New York: Prentice Hall Press, 1991): 449 pages; $24.95.

As the 1940 presidential campaign was approaching its conclusion, President Franklin Roosevelt—running for an unprecedented third term of office—delivered an address in Boston on October 30. He stated unequivocally his position on American participation in the war in Europe between Hitler's Germany and Churchill's England and in the conflict being fought between China and Japan: "I have said this before, but I shall say it again and again and again: Your boys are not going to be sent into any foreign wars."

And on October 23, in Philadelphia, Roosevelt had assured the American people: "There is no secret treaty, no secret obligation, no secret commitment, no secret understanding, in any shape or form, direct or indirect, with any government, or any other nation in any part of the world, to involve this nation in any war or for any other purpose."

Most Americans, having taken the president at his word, were shocked and infuriated by the Japanese attack on American military installations at Pearl Harbor on December 7, 1941. We were at peace, and, the president said, the government was doing everything possible to keep us at peace. The Japanese attack appeared unprovoked and dastardly. America was the innocent victim of naked aggression.

Historian Robert Smith Thompson, in his book *A Time for War: Franklin D. Roosevelt and the Path to Pearl Harbor,* challenges this myth with irrefutable facts—facts that demonstrate that every one of FDR's representations and promises to the American people on the war issue were lies and deceptions. Thompson shows that in the year following his election to a third term, Roosevelt followed a course of action that inevitably led to that "date which will live in infamy."

Myth: President Roosevelt did his utmost to follow a path of neutrality in the Far East, wishing only to prevent the spread of war to American soil.

Fact: Beginning in 1937, following the Japanese invasion of China, FDR instituted a series of financial arrangements to assist China in its defense against Japan. He supplied money, military materiel, and men (in the form of Chennault's "Flying Tigers") to prevent Japan from attaining any of its goals on the Asian mainland. He also instituted trade embargoes on the Japanese that threatened their economic survival unless they would surrender to U.S. demands that they withdraw from China and French Indochina.

Myth: President Roosevelt had no desire or designs for instigating a war with Japan. He used every method to find common ground with the Japanese government.

Fact: FDR entered into secret agreements with the British, Dutch, and Australian governments to form an alliance to resist Japan in East Asia. He shipped long-range bombers to China, Australia, and the Philippines that would be able to strike the Japanese home islands. And, in early 1941, under instructions from FDR, a plan was designed for initiating an aggressive war involving the firebombing of Japanese cities in 1942. In the fall of 1941, the Japanese tried to offer a variety of peace plans to the U.S. to forestall war, but the president refused to consider any of them, including an offer by the Japanese Prime Minister to meet FDR, anywhere the president chose, to find a way to prevent war.

Myth: President Roosevelt, while clearly hoping for the defeat of Hitler, tried to avoid America's entry into the European war.

Fact: In 1940, FDR promised both the King of England and Prime Minister Winston Churchill that America would not allow England to lose the war. In an attempt to create an incident, FDR instructed U.S. naval forces in the Atlantic to take on German U-boats, so that he could go before the American people and claim Hitler had started a war against the United States. And Roosevelt and Churchill had plans in the works for American combat participation in the war against Germany.

Myth: The attack on Pearl Harbor was completely unexpected and a surprise to Roosevelt and his government.

Fact: On January 27, 1941, the American ambassador to Japan warned Washington that the Japanese were planning an attack on Pearl Harbor, if negotiations broke down. Later in 1941, a Korean lobbyist, considered a reliable source of information, twice warned that an attack on Pearl Harbor was being planned. During November and the first week of December 1941, including December 6, the American code breakers had intercepted Japanese messages that clearly pointed to an imminent attack on American territories in the Pacific. These intercepted messages were seen by FDR and other cabinet members.

These are the facts behind the myths about the events leading up to the attack on Pearl Harbor. Professor Thompson quotes FDR as saying in 1942: "I am perfectly willing to mislead and tell lies if it will help win the war." It is clear that Franklin Delano Roosevelt was willing to mislead and tell lies to the American people in order to *enter* the war as well.

This review originally appeared in the July 1992 issue of Freedom Daily, *published by The Future of Freedom Foundation.*

20

Betrayal at Pearl Harbor: How Churchill Lured Roosevelt into World War II

a review by Richard M. Ebeling

Betrayal at Pearl Harbor: How Churchill Lured Roosevelt into World War II by James Rusbridger and Eric Nave (New York: Summit Books, 1991); 302 pages; $19.95.

In the early morning of December 7, 1941, Japanese bombers began their attack run over Pearl Harbor. When the Japanese had finished their bombing runs, a large portion of the U.S. Pacific fleet had been destroyed, and thousands of American servicemen had been either killed or wounded. The next day, President Franklin Roosevelt went before a joint session of Congress and asked for a declaration of war against the Empire of Japan. December 7, the president said, would be recorded in history as a "date which will live in infamy." Unprovoked and without warning, the president declared, the United States had been attacked by an enemy set on a path of world conquest.

December 7 has gone down in history as a day of infamy. But unfortunately, all of the infamous qualities of the events leading up to that day have still not been fully admitted by either the American or British governments.

Between September 1939 and December 1941, Great Britain had been fighting the armed might of Nazi Germany almost single-handedly. In the first half of 1940, Western Europe, including France, had been overrun by the Germans. In the first half of 1941, German forces, advancing through the Italian colony of Libya were threatening the British Army guarding the Suez Canal in Egypt. After June 1941, the Soviet Union was in the war against the Nazis; and by December 5, the German army was only five miles from the Kremlin in Moscow.

British Prime Minister Winston Churchill knew, from British intelligence, that Hitler had given up on his invasion plans for an amphibious assault on England. But he also knew that unless the United States came into the war, Great Britain would never be able to defeat Nazi Germany on its own. Either America came to the rescue or Britain would have to make a compromise peace with Germany. This Churchill was unwilling to do. America, Churchill had determined, had to be brought into the war.

In spite of an American population 75 to 80 percent opposed to American entry into the war, President Roosevelt was equally determined to drag the United States into the Second World War. Several attempts by Roosevelt to provoke military engagements between American and German naval vessels in the North Atlantic had failed. Hitler would not take the bait. Hitler was determined not to give Roosevelt an excuse for intervening into the war in Europe.

Both Roosevelt and Churchill turned their eyes to the Pacific, determined to use a conflict with Japan as a "back door to war." The United States made uncompromising demands upon the Japanese to withdraw Japanese occupation forces from China and French Indochina. When the Japanese refused to submit, the United States, in July 1941, froze all Japanese assets in America and persuaded the Dutch to stop selling Indonesian oil to Japan. (Indonesia at that time was a Dutch colony.) Rather than face economic strangulation, the Japanese chose to run the risk of a war with America for their national survival. And the plans for the attack on Pearl Harbor were set in motion.

Betrayal at Pearl Harbor by James Rusbridger and Eric Nave traces the history of the American and British breaking of the Japanese secret codes. They show how, from the 1920s on, both the British and Americans were able to intercept and translate most of the Japanese diplomatic and military messages. *Therefore, Britain and the United States had direct and inside information about practically all the Japanese plans and strategies leading up to the attack on Pearl Harbor.*

But the British had been able to break some codes that the Americans had not. As a result, the British may have been able to track both the departure of the Japanese fleet that had left the Kurile Islands for the attack on Pearl Harbor and its refueling point in the North Pacific halfway to Hawaii. It is possible that both the British intelligence agents reading the codes and to Winston Churchill (who received all the Japanese code information every day) knew that the Japanese were planning to attack, that the attack would be against Pearl Harbor, and that the attack would be on the weekend of December 7. *This information, if they had it, was not passed on to either Roosevelt or U.S. military intelligence.*

Passing on this information might very well have provided the time for the United States to prepare defensive measures—including a counterattack—against the Japanese. And if these defensive plans, in turn, had been discovered by the Japanese, they might have precipitated a decision by the Japanese to call off the attack. War thereby would have been prevented or delayed in the Pacific, and the "back door" to America's entering the war as Britain's ally may have been closed shut.

Thus, the British kept the information to themselves; the Japanese attacked; and Winston Churchill got what he wanted—but at the cost of thousands of American lives.

This review originally appeared in the December 1991 issue of Freedom Daily, *published by The Future of Freedom Foundation.*

21

Days of Infamy: MacArthur, Roosevelt, Churchill— The Shocking Truth Revealed

a review by Richard M. Ebeling

Days of Infamy: MacArthur, Roosevelt, Churchill—The Shocking Truth Revealed by John Costello (New York: Pocket Books, 1994); 448 pages; $24.

John Costello is a distinguished historian who has uncovered fascinating new evidence on a wide number of topics. Two of his previous works, *Mask of Treachery: Spies, Lies, Buggery & Betrayal* (1988) and *Deadly Illusions* (1993), unearthed previously unknown information about Soviet espionage in Britain and the United States. In his recent book, *Days of Infamy*, Mr. Costello turns his historian's eye to the events leading up to the disaster at Pearl Harbor.

An essential key for understanding the disaster on December 7, 1941, he argues, is the change in U.S. Pacific military strategy during that year. Before 1941, the first line of defense had been viewed as the Hawaiian Islands, with the Philippine Islands considered an indefensible military burden. But in the early fall of 1941, the secretary of war, Henry Stimson, convinced Roosevelt that the Philippines could be turned into a successful first line of attack. If the Japanese were to be stopped from any further aggression in East Asia, the United

States would have to have a deterrent that made Japan think twice before pushing on any further.

The new strategy was to send a large number of long-range B-17 and B-24 bombers for permanent stationing in the Philippines. These bombers would have the capability of firebombing Tokyo; the fear that their cities would be set ablaze if they acted in ways not wanted by Washington would keep the Japanese in line. On November 15, 1941, Army Gen. George Marshall held an "off-the-record" press conference in which he told the reporters that Japan would soon know that this was no American bluff. "Flying Fortresses will be dispatched immediately to set the paper cities of Japan on fire, in the event of war," Marshall insisted. "There won't be any hesitation about bombing civilians—it will be all-out."

But in November, the number of long-range bombers in the Philippines was still too few to create a credible threat or to hold off a Japanese attack, if one was initiated. The U.S. military needed an additional three to six months to be ready for offensive action against Japan. Peace in the Pacific was essential, therefore, for at least several months. Furthermore, the bombers could reach Japan, but could not carry enough fuel for the return flight to the Philippines; it was necessary to get permission from Stalin for American planes to land in Soviet Siberia for refueling, and Stalin seemed completely unwilling to grant this request.

From the coded Japanese diplomatic messages that U.S. military intelligence could intercept and read, the Roosevelt administration knew that the end of November was the deadline for a negotiated settlement for the Japanese. After that, Tokyo had informed its negotiators in Washington, "Things would automatically happen."

To "buy time," FDR decided to make temporary concessions to "baby the Japanese along" until the United States was ready for a fight with its offensive bomber force. But at the last minute, on November 26, the administration suddenly took a hard line, insisting that the Japanese concede everything demanded by the United States—a complete Japanese withdrawal from China and Indochina. The negotiations were over. On December 2, Admiral Yamamoto sent the fateful message to the Japanese fleet steaming across the north Pacific: "This dispatch is Top Secret. . . . Climb Niitakayama 1208, repeat 1208." The order had been given for the attack on Pearl Harbor.

What made FDR reverse his decision to "baby along" Japan with limited concessions and present the Japanese, instead, with demands that could only mean the end of negotiations? The answer lay in London. Churchill informed Roosevelt that British intelligence in Southeast Asia had clear evidence that the Japanese were poised for an attack against Thailand and perhaps British Malaya, as well. If this was true, and if the Japanese did not simultaneously attack the Philippines, bringing the United States into the war, the British would be left to fight alone. The British ambassador in Washington, Lord Halifax, was able to pin Roosevelt down after several White House meetings to promise that if Japanese transport ships were found heading for various points in Southeast Asia, "we [the United States] should obviously attack them, since they must either be going for Thailand or Malaya.... The United States will regard it as a hostile act if the Japanese invade Thailand, Malaya, Burma, or the East Indies."

Costello says that this meant that "Roosevelt therefore appears to have committed a technical breach of the Constitution by giving such clear, although unwritten, indications to the British, which he knew Churchill wanted to interpret as a guarantee of American armed support, in advance of having the approval of the U.S. legislature." To make sure that the United States was in the fight from the beginning, Roosevelt ordered that American ships be placed in harm's way in the South China Sea. "Filipino crews were to don U.S. Navy uniforms and in expendable crafts head out to specific locations that were calculated to put them in harm's way of a Japanese invasion force steaming toward Malaya," Costello explains. This was done on December 3. But the Japanese would not take the bait, and the ship returned to Philippine waters unharmed, four days later.

But the attack on the United States finally did come on December 7, saving FDR from the embarrassment of fulfilling a military commitment to the British without congressional consent. Costello devotes a large portion of his book to analyzing why Pearl Harbor was such a military disaster. And in the end he presents a convincing case that exonerates Adm. Husband Kimmel and Gen. Walter Short, the U.S. military commanders in Hawaii who were made the scapegoats for the Pearl Harbor debacle. Costello demonstrates that both Kimmel and Short were denied essential intelligence information and were given ambiguous warnings from Washington concerning the likelihood and possible location of any Japanese attack. They were, instead, the fall guys to cover up the primary responsibility for the disaster that should have fallen on the shoulders of FDR and the senior military personnel in Washington.

Costello also devotes a great deal of attention to the equal disaster that befell U.S. forces in the Philippines. Here the guilty party was Gen. Douglas MacArthur. MacArthur had exaggerated the strength and fighting capability of his ground and air forces in his dispatches to Washington. Immediately after the Japanese attack on Pearl Harbor, MacArthur was ordered to initiate offensive bombing actions against the Japanese naval and air force installations on the island of Formosa, just north of the Philippines. He did not. He even delayed permitting reconnaissance flights to determine Japanese strength on Formosa. Nor did he order the immediate dispersal of military aircraft from exposed air fields. As a result, the Japanese destroyed most of the military bomber planes that were meant to be America's first line of offense against Japan.

Why? Costello's explanation, while it at first sounds hard to believe, is that MacArthur's inaction may have been due to a bribe paid to MacArthur by the president of the Philippines, Manuel Quezon. There were some leading Philippine political figures who hoped that war might pass by their country, and that if no military actions against Japan were initiated from the Philippines, the Japanese might allow their country to remain neutral. MacArthur did not initiate any military action against the Japanese when ordered to by Washington so as not to antagonize Japan. When the Japanese did bomb and invade the Philippines shortly after the Pearl Harbor attack, there was no alternative but to fight back.

What is the evidence for MacArthur's failure to act and the reason for such failure? Costello admits that it is indirect. After MacArthur had withdrawn his command to Corregidor, Quezon authorized the transfer of $500,000 ($5 million in 1990 dollars) to a New York bank account in MacArthur's name for "distinguished service" and, at the same time, another $35,000 dollars in stock certificates at a New York bank. Shortly after this "reward" for service, MacArthur sent a message to Washington suggesting that FDR declare the Philippines "neutral" territory and surrender the country to the Japanese. Roosevelt angrily refused.

Who, therefore, is to blame for Pearl Harbor and what followed? "The chain of defeats that overwhelmed the United States in the Pacific on the days of infamy in December 1941 were the direct consequence of a major failure in military strategy and foreign policy by the Roosevelt Administration," Costello concludes. And whatever the errors and miscalculations of other military commanders of American forces in those early days of the war, "their command shortcomings pale into relative insignificance before the far more egregious dereliction of MacArthur."

This review originally appeared in the June 1995 issue of Freedom Daily, *published by The Future of Freedom Foundation.*

22

Covering the Map of the World— The Half-Century Legacy of the Yalta Conference

by Richard M. Ebeling

In the late afternoon of February 4, 1945, the "Big Three" of the Allied side in World War II—Franklin D. Roosevelt, Winston Churchill, and Joseph Stalin—took their seats around a conference table at Livadia Palace, a few miles south of Yalta on the Crimean Peninsula in the Union of Soviet Socialist Republics.

The war in Europe was rapidly reaching its end. On the western front, American, British, and other Allied forces had successfully turned back Hitler's last offensive of the war in December 1944, when the German Army had attempted to attack across Luxembourg and Belgium and cut off the British forces in southern Holland from the main body of American forces in northern France. The Western Allies, in February, were now poised to begin their assault to capture the German Rhineland and make the push into the heart of the Nazi Reich.

On the eastern front, in early February 1945, the Soviet Army was already less than fifty miles from the outskirts of Berlin. In July

1944, Moscow radio had made an appeal to the Polish resistance to take up "direct active struggle in the streets" of Warsaw to assist the Red Army, which by then had reached the east bank of the Vistula River, opposite the Polish capital.

On August 1, 35,000 members of the Polish underground Home Army rose up and attacked the German garrison in Warsaw. For sixty-three days, until October 2, they fought against the German army, at the end of which 15,000 Polish freedom fighters were dead, 200,000 other Polish civilians had also been killed, and most of Warsaw was in ruins.

During these two months, Stalin's army neither attacked the Germans nor gave artillery cover to the Polish forces who had responded to Moscow's call for armed resistance. Nor would Stalin allow British and American planes to drop supplies to the Polish forces and then land in Soviet-controlled territory for refueling.

The Polish underground Home Army had been the backbone of the anticommunist and noncommunist resistance forces. The failed uprising left them shattered. This meant that there was now no large and well-organized Polish group left to oppose the "Lublin Poles," the communist underground organization hand-picked and controlled by Stalin.

Only in December did the Red Army again take the offensive on the Polish front, and by February 1945, most of western Poland and portions of eastern Germany up to the Oder River had been "liberated" by Stalin's forces. The Red Army was now preparing for the battle to capture the capital of the Nazi Reich.

Part I—The Big Three: Winston Churchill

During this first week of February, in the former palace of Czar Nicholas II in the Crimea, the Big Three leaders were meeting to determine the fate and future of the postwar world. Chairing the opening session, on February 4, President Roosevelt proposed that "each would speak his mind frankly and freely, since he had discovered through experience that the best way to conduct business expeditiously was through frank and free speaking." FDR added that he "knew that while they were here in Yalta they would cover the map of the world."

Before the Big Three was an agenda that was truly global in its nature: the future of freedom in Eastern Europe; the fate of Germany in the postwar era; the establishment of a world-peace organization—the United Nations; the control of the colonial empires; and the strategy for victory in the Pacific War against Japan once Germany was defeated. And the horizon of their agenda stretched practically until the end of the century. At the third session, on February 6, FDR said that he "felt strongly that all the nations of the world shared a common desire to see the elimination of war for at least fifty years," and under their stewardship, he believed that this was "feasible and possible."

Who were these Big Three upon whose shoulders the fate of the world was held at this Yalta Conference? On the evening of February 8, these world leaders held a dinner for themselves at which the vodka and champagne flowed freely and forty-five toasts were made. Stalin began by proposing a toast to Winston Churchill, whom he characterized as "the bravest governmental figure in the world. . . . Due in large measure to Mr. Churchill's courage and staunchness, England, when she stood alone, had divided the might of Hitlerite Germany at a time when the rest of Europe was falling flat on its face before Hitler." Stalin "knew of few examples in history where the courage of one man had been so important to the future history of the world."

If the burden for starting the Second World War fell on the shoulders of Adolph Hitler (and, as we shall see, Joseph Stalin), the burden for its prolongation and severity belonged on the shoulders of Winston Churchill. In the late 1930s, Churchill had opposed any attempt to reach an accommodation with Hitler. After the German invasion and occupation of Poland in September 1939, Churchill had resisted any and all attempts to reach a compromise that would have limited and ended the war. As first lord of the admiralty in Neville Chamberlain's war cabinet, he was impatient with the lack of British aggressiveness. In March 1940, he persuaded the other cabinet members to violate Scandinavian neutrality and invade Norway. When German intelligence gained information about this, Hitler ordered the invasion and occupation of Denmark and Norway, beating the British by only a few days. Only then did Churchill cry out against the violation of the territorial integrity and neutrality of little countries.

In May 1940, Hitler sent his armies across the borders of Holland and Belgium, and by the middle of June, half of France was conquered by the German army; the French capitulated, and an armistice left two-thirds of France under direct German occupation. In Stockholm, Sweden, the representatives of several members of the British cabinet had meetings with German representatives about the possibility for a compromise peace.

Hitler proposed that Britain remain independent and a major sea power, neither paying Germany any war indemnities nor surrendering any portion of its empire to the Nazi Reich; Hitler spoke of offering units of the German Army to serve under British command to maintain the British Empire and preserve the mastery of the "white race" over the "inferior" peoples of the world. Hitler only wanted British acceptance of German dominance on the European continent.

Churchill, now the prime minister of the war cabinet, cut off all talks with the German government. Instead, desperately needing the help of the United States, he ordered the British air force to begin bombing cities and civilian targets in Germany, hoping to instigate a German retaliation that would shock Americans into coming to Britain's aid when photos would arrive across the Atlantic showing bombed English cities. Churchill got what he wanted—the destruction of Coventry and the London Blitz.

It is also worth keeping in mind that the mass destruction of the European Jews in the Nazi death camps did not begin in full force until 1942 and 1943. Before then, Hitler often spoke of the "final solution" as primarily involving the deportation of the Jews to somewhere out of Europe, a place like the island of Madagascar off the east coast of Africa. But with the British and Free French occupation of the island in 1942, that option was closed. In the world of "what if" history, if Churchill had not closed the door to peace talks with Hitler in 1940 and if a negotiated peace had been arranged, part of such a peace settlement could have been the deporting of the Jews of Central and Eastern Europe to Madagascar, and many, maybe most, of the six million Jews might not have had to perish in the Nazi death camps.

Throughout 1940 and 1941, Churchill did everything in his power to bring the United States into the war on Britain's side. He set up secret propaganda departments to work clandestinely in the United States and often in violation of American neutrality laws passed by Congress. He succeeded in bringing the United States into the war through the "back door" of a Pacific conflict. The British and their Australian allies had broken some of the major Japanese military codes. Churchill, in November and December 1941, was seeing day-by-day secret Japanese code material about the coming attack against the American fleet at Pearl Harbor. He failed to pass along any of this material to Washington. Better a surprise attack to arouse the indignation of the American people than any American countermove that would foil the attack before it occurred. (See the review of *Betrayal at Pearl Harbor: How Churchill Lured Roosevelt into WW II* in Chapter 20.)

This was Winston Churchill, "the bravest governmental figure of the world . . . one man . . . so important to the future history of the world," as Stalin had toasted him. But what about Stalin himself, the Red Czar of Soviet Russia? After receiving such high praise from his Soviet host, Churchill replied with a toast to Stalin. He hailed "Stalin as the mighty leader of a mighty country, which had taken the full shock of the German war machine, had broken its back and driven the tyrants from her soil." Churchill said he "knew that in peace no less in war Marshall Stalin would continue to lead his people from success to success."

Before the Bolshevik Revolution, Stalin had been a minor player in the Leninist movement, sometimes involved in bank robberies to fund revolutionary activities in the Transcaucasian area of the Russian Empire. Strong evidence suggests that he may have even played a double game, occasionally serving as an informer for the Okhrana, the Czarist secret police. After the Bolshevik Revolution and Russian Civil War, he established a powerful niche for himself as general-secretary of the Communist Party, responsible for selecting new candidates for Party membership and assigning and promoting Party members to positions of authority and power in the Soviet government. He soon had a vast and expanding network of Party members loyal to him for their personal power and privileges. By the end of the 1920s, after Lenin's death in 1924, he had defeated most of his rivals for supreme power in the Communist Party structure.

In 1929, he instituted the first five-year plan and ordered the collectivization of agriculture in the Soviet Union. When the peasants resisted the loss of their farms and private land, he waged a four-year war against the kulaks, who were private farmers whom Stalin labeled counterrevolutionaries. Planned famines, mass deportations of peasants to Siberia and central Asia, and brutal executions broke the resistance to Stalin's collective farm system. The best estimates suggest that as many as nine to twelve million peasants and private farmers died in the march towards collectivization. During this period, in 1931, Lady Astor of Great Britain was privileged with an audience with Stalin in the Kremlin. At one point she asked him point-blank, "And how long are you going on killing people?" Stalin calmly replied: "As long as it is necessary. . . . The violent death of a large number of people was necessary before the Communist State could be firmly established."

In the 1930s, Stalin destroyed all opposition to his rule and power through a series of show-trials and purges of the Communist Party, in which it is estimated that over four million people were killed. Many more millions ended up in the vast network of slave-labor camps that stretched like islands of terror and despair across the entire Soviet Union, what Aleksandr Solzhenitsyn called "The Gulag Archipelago"—with the fate of many of these being a cruel death, as well.

In 1939, Stalin began his play for Soviet domination of Europe. Years earlier, in a secret speech to the Communist Party Central Committee in January 1925, Stalin had laid out the strategy from which he never swerved in foreign policy: "But if war breaks out [in Europe] we shall not be able to sit with folded arms. We shall have to take action, but we shall be the last to do so. And we shall do so in order to throw the decisive weight into the scales, the weight that can turn the scales." Stalin's Marxist-Leninist view was that any war that broke out in Europe would be a war between the imperialist and capitalist nations. The strategy was to deflect any attack against the Soviet Union, and instead allow the capitalist nations to fight each other to exhaustion, at which point the Soviet Army would enter the war and conquer the European continent for the Communist cause.

In August 1939, Stalin put the strategy into practice by signing a nonaggression pact with Hitler, which meant that the war would be fought in the West among Germany, Britain, and France, leaving the Soviet Union safe and secure. In the meantime, the secret protocols of the Nazi-Soviet Pact gave Stalin control over eastern Poland, the Baltic republics, Bessarabia, and Finland. Stalin's plan was that in 1942, at the latest, the Soviet Army would attack Germany, now that France was finished and England was weak and isolated off the European coast. The only problem was that Hitler double-crossed Stalin first by invading the Soviet Union in June 1941. This did not stop Stalin, after the German defeat at Stalingrad in the winter of 1942–43, however, in proposing a separate peace to Hitler through intermediaries in neutral Sweden, and obviously at the expense of his British and American allies. The only thing that prevented it was the fact that Hitler was unwilling to pay Stalin's price for ending the war on the eastern front. (See the review of *Icebreaker: Who Started the Second World War?* in Chapter 18.)

This was Joseph Stalin, "the mighty leader of a mighty country," who Churchill was sure "would continue to lead his people from success to success." And what about the third figure of the Big Three, Franklin Delano Roosevelt? Stalin now proposed a toast to FDR.

Part II—The Big Three: FDR

On the evening of February 8, 1945—the fifth day of the Yalta Conference—the Big Three—Franklin D. Roosevelt, Winston Churchill, and Joseph Stalin—adjourned from the official meetings of the day and gathered for a formal dinner, hosted by Stalin, at Koreis Villa. In his account of the conference, *Roosevelt and the Russians*, Secretary of State Edward R. Stettinius recorded, "The atmosphere at the dinner was most cordial, and it proved to be the most important dinner of the Conference. Stalin was in excellent humor and even in high spirits." And Winston Churchill "manifested real hope that there could be a world of happiness, peace and security." Stalin and Churchill exchanged toasts of magniloquent mutual admiration.

Then Stalin proposed a toast to FDR. According to the notes kept by Roosevelt's translator, Charles Bohlen, and published in the Department of State's volume *The Conferences at Malta and Yalta*, Stalin said that he and Mr. Churchill had had simple decisions. Their countries were fighting for their survival against the Nazis.

> But there was a third man whose country had not been seriously threatened with invasion, but who had had perhaps a broader conception of national interest and even though his country was not directly imperiled had been the chief forger of the instruments which had led to the mobilization of the world against Hitler.

President Roosevelt replied to the generous remarks of his Soviet host and said that he "felt that the atmosphere at this dinner was that of a family, and it was in those words that he liked to characterize the relations that existed between their three countries." While "each of the leaders represented here were working in their own way for the interests of their people," Roosevelt stated that their greater "objectives here were to give every man, woman and child on this earth the possibility of security and well-being."

Franklin Delano Roosevelt had been elected the thirty-second president of the United States in 1932 as America was reaching the bottom of the nation's worst economic depression. He had run on a Democratic Party platform that called for cutting taxes, reining in the high government expenditures of the Hoover administration, eliminating excessive government regulation, and respecting the rights and responsibilities of the sovereign states.

But immediately upon taking office, FDR threw away his platform promises and began a great experiment in centralized executive power, gigantic government spending (by historical standards), and the imposition of a planned economy. In a mere 100 days, Roosevelt transformed the constitutional order of the United States. Congress passed his vast alphabet soup of programs and departments—NRA (National Recovery Administration), AAA (Agricultural Adjustment Administration), WPA (Works Progress Administration), CCC (Civilian Conservation Corps), TVA (Tennessee Valley Authority), and a legion of others. An army of bureaucratic locusts swarmed across the land—regulating, controlling, directing, ordering, and dictating. And political corruption was everywhere.

Nor was this some ad hoc, pragmatic set of emergency measures that somehow absentmindedly was stumbling America into a planned economy. No, the intellectuals who flooded Washington and filled the ocean of new government positions knew what it was they wanted. During the 1932 campaign, one of Roosevelt's supporters, Stuart Chase, published a book entitled *A New Deal*, in which he said:

> We propose then a National Planning Board [be] set up under the auspices of the Federal government . . . and manned by engineers, physical scientists, statisticians, economists, accountants and lawyers. . . . Why should Russians have all the fun of remaking a world?

James P. Warburg, who had been one of FDR's economic advisors in 1933 and who had resigned in disgust over the direction taken by the New Deal, wrote in his 1935 book, *Hell Bent for Election*:

> Mr. Roosevelt's present purpose is to give the nation a "more abundant life" by first vesting in a central federal bureaucracy headed by himself complete dictatorial powers over all the factors that affect the economic and social life of the country. . . . That is a purpose to which we cannot subscribe, because: To accomplish this purpose means to substitute for the American form of government a central "authoritarian" state, along the lines of the various European experiments in Socialism and dictatorship.

Of course, FDR did have his admirers. In a 1934 interview with *Newsweek*, Benito Mussolini said that he greatly admired the American president because, like himself, Franklin Roosevelt was a "social Fascist."

The only thing that saved America from the clutches of a permanently planned economy was the courage of the Supreme Court, which in 1935 declared several of the central New Deal programs unconstitutional. Roosevelt may have ranted against the justices as "nine old men" who wanted to keep America in the horse-and-buggy era, but David Lawrence, the founder of *U.S. News & World*

Report, was more correct when he defended the justices in his 1935 book, *Nine Honest Men*—they were men, he said, who placed a higher value on the principles of the Constitution and its protections of individual liberties and restrained federal power.

FDR was reelected in 1936, but the ideological fire that had kindled the red-hot fervor of the early New Deal days had diminished. Roosevelt needed new, virgin worlds to conquer. And with war clouds forming over Europe and Asia, Franklin Roosevelt saw his new mission: a Global New Deal. As FDR promised in point six of the Atlantic Charter that he and Churchill agreed to in August 1941, "After the final destruction of the Nazi tyranny" he would work to assure "that all the men in all the lands may live out their lives in freedom from fear or want." At what cost in tax dollars and at the risk of whose lives Roosevelt planned to assure this worldly welfare paradise for all men everywhere, he did not specify; nor did he exactly explain what "fear" or "want" meant in this context. He set himself the goal of being the world leader who took up the mantle first worn twenty years earlier by Woodrow Wilson: to make the world safe for his own conception of democracy. Once again, as FDR had entitled a collection of his speeches in 1933, we were "on our way."

Only one problem stood as a roadblock in his way: the American people. Throughout the late 1930s, up to the very attack on Pearl Harbor at the end of 1941, all the public opinion polls showed, over and over again, that Americans, in a vast majority, wanted to have nothing to do with wars in Europe and Asia. Americans were willing to generously give of their time and money to assist those harmed and hurt by the brutality of war; but they wanted no direct U.S. military involvement in foreign wars.

Franklin Roosevelt, however, decided that America should be at war and would be at war—because he concluded that the cause was just. In spite of neutrality acts passed by the United States Congress after the war had begun in Europe, he made secret military promises to the king of England and to Winston Churchill that America would assure British victory; and he sent American military vessels into hostile waters into the Atlantic and tried to instigate an incident with German naval ships to precipitate a war. When he could not get Hitler to respond, Roosevelt turned to the Pacific to find a "back door to war." And at the same time, he lied continually to the American people, assuring the citizens of the United States that he had no intention of entering into alliances with any foreign power nor of sending American boys off to fight on foreign shores.

Always anti-Japanese in his sentiments, FDR demanded that Japan completely withdraw from its recent military conquests in China. When they refused, he froze Japanese assets in the United States and embargoed all oil shipments to Japan. He entered into secret military agreements with the British, Dutch, and Australian governments for a war with Japan. The Japanese, time after time, tried to negotiate and compromise to avoid a war with America. Roosevelt refused even to respond to an offer by the Japanese prime minister to meet Roosevelt anywhere of FDR's choosing to peacefully settle their differences. Finally, in November and early December 1941, when war was clearly inevitable and the U.S. military was reading Japanese secret messages that American ciphers had decoded, the Roosevelt administration failed to inform the military commanders at Pearl Harbor to be ready for a possible attack. At the very least, FDR and the military command in Washington were guilty of gross negligence and dereliction of duty. (See the review of *A Time for War: Franklin D. Roosevelt and the Path to Pearl Harbor* in Chapter 19.)

Once America was a belligerent in the Second World War, Roosevelt set his sights on the bright and beautiful postwar Global New Deal that he wanted to give mankind. But to attain this goal, he would need a partner, and FDR decided that the perfect accomplice for this deed would be Joseph Stalin and the Soviet Union. But why Stalin? The explanation has been well summarized by Robert Nisbet in his superb book *Roosevelt and Stalin: The Failed Courtship* (1988):

> It is hard to avoid the conclusion that Roosevelt saw the Soviet Union, its record of terror and slaughter, its omnipotent dictatorship and despotism notwithstanding, as containing a greater promise of democracy and freedom than Great Britain. Somehow in Roosevelt's vision all the ugly was squeezed out and what was left was a system in Russia not extremely different from his own American New Deal. Stalin was perhaps uncouth at times, carried the blood of barbarians in his veins, but on the other hand, Roosevelt may have thought, the Soviet Union, with all warts conceded in advance, was still constitutionally pledged to its people to provide jobs, medical care and welfare very much on the order of his own New Deal; more repressive, of course, in fact too repressive, but with a level of repression not of disqualifying importance. There was also the constitutional pledge to build a classless society, which meant the kind of egalitarianism perhaps that Americans had learned from Democratic Party populists. Also the Soviet Union was

forward-looking and progressive in thrust, and the aged European imperial states were not.

When Roosevelt was preparing to meet Stalin for the first time at the Tehran Conference in November 1943, William Bullitt, former U.S. ambassador to the Soviet Union, tried to explain the true brutal nature of Stalin and the Soviet regime. Roosevelt replied:

> Bill, I don't dispute your facts. They are accurate. I don't dispute the logic of your reasoning. I just have a hunch that Stalin is not that kind of man. Harry [Hopkins, Roosevelt's confidant and personal envoy to Stalin] says he's not and that he doesn't want anything but security for his country, and I think that if I give him everything I possibly can and ask nothing from him in return, *noblesse oblige*—he won't try to annex anything and will work with me for a world of democracy and peace.

When Bullitt pressed his fears and doubts about any good outcomes from a mindless altruism towards Stalin, FDR closed the discussion by saying, "It's my responsibility and not yours; and I'm going to play my hunch."

This was the frame of mind with which Franklin Roosevelt was now negotiating with Stalin and Churchill at Yalta. It was with this good feeling towards "Uncle Joe" Stalin—Roosevelt's and Churchill's name of endearment for the mass murderer of millions—that FDR could speak that night at this Big Three banquet about an atmosphere of a "family" around that table, dedicated to the giving to "every man, woman and child on this earth the possibility of security and well-being." Never in modern history was there a darker surrealism in the use of words.

Part III—The Personal Diplomacy of the Big Three

The Yalta meeting was the culmination of the wartime conferences between Churchill, Stalin, and Roosevelt. Both Winston Churchill and Franklin Roosevelt placed a high value on personal diplomacy. Churchill believed in the "great man" theory of history. As John Charmley has recently expressed it in his biography *Churchill: The End of Glory* (1993), Churchill believed that "such men could be recognized by the mark they made on their own and subsequent ages, and knowing himself to be one, Churchill enjoyed making contact with others of the same species." He had used personal diplomacy with great effect in his relationship with FDR, first in establishing a stream of war material from America under Lend-Lease and then obtaining American participation in the war against Nazi Germany.

While deeply suspicious of communism and the Soviet Union, Churchill believed that a similar personal relationship could work with Stalin—in getting the Soviet leader to work with him in determining the political settlement that would rule the world at the end of the war. He traveled to Moscow in August 1942, wanting to establish such a relationship with the "old Bear," as Churchill called Stalin.

The first two sessions in the Kremlin went badly, with Stalin insulting the British as cowards unwilling to fight with the same aggressiveness as the Red Army. Rather than remind Stalin that the British had fought alone against Hitler for the year between the fall of France in June 1940 and the Nazi invasion of the USSR in June 1941—a year during which the Soviet Union was informally allied with Hitler under the terms of the Nazi-Soviet Non-Aggression Pact of August 1939—Churchill confided to one of his aids, "I still feel I could work with that man [Stalin] if I could only break down the language barrier." He was convinced that he and Stalin were not getting along because something was being lost in the translation. Stalin played up to Churchill at their next session, inviting the British leader to his country house outside Moscow for a late-night supper. Churchill said afterwards, "I was taken into the family, we ended friends."

Churchill again traveled to Moscow in October 1944 for a personal one-on-one meeting with Stalin. After the meeting, Churchill wrote to his wife: "I have had a very nice talk with the old Bear. I like him the more I see him." And to Clement Attlee, he wrote, "Stalin had made several expressions of personal regard which I feel were all sincere."

At the center of this meeting was a proposal of Churchill's to carve up southeastern Europe into joint British-Soviet spheres of influence. According to the British ambassador, who was present at the meeting, Churchill "produced what he called a 'Naughty document,' showing a list of Balkan countries and the proportion of interest in them of the Great Powers. He said the Americans would be shocked if they saw how crudely he put it. Marshal Stalin was a realist. He himself was not sentimental."

Churchill proposed that Romania be 90 percent under Soviet influence and 10 percent under British influence; Bulgaria would be 75 percent under Soviet influence and 25 percent under British influence; Greece would be 10 percent under Soviet influence and 90 percent under British influence; and in Yugoslavia and Hungary, the

Soviets and Britain would split their influence, fifty-fifty. Stalin changed Bulgaria to 90 percent Soviet influence and signed his approval. When Churchill suggested burning the document, Stalin told him to keep it.

Churchill, who had expressed anger and voiced condemnation over Stalin's division of Eastern Europe with Hitler in 1939, now proposed to do the same. And Churchill abided by the agreement. When, at the beginning of 1945, Stalin began forcibly deporting Germans out of Soviet-occupied Romania, Churchill said: "Why are we making a fuss about the Russian deportations in Romania of [Germans]? . . . It is understood that the Russians were to work their will in this sphere." And when members of the British Foreign Office then complained that Romanians were being sent to the Soviet Union for forced labor, Churchill said: "We must bear in mind what we promised about leaving Romania's fate to a large extent in Russia's hands. I cannot myself consider that it is wrong of the Russians to take Romanians of any origin they like to work in the Russian coal-mines." In Churchill's mind, he had gotten what he wanted: a dominant British influence in Greece and Stalin's acceptance of British naval dominance in the Mediterranean.

Churchill took the same attitude towards the fate of Poland. In September 1939, Churchill had strongly advocated Britain's going to war against Nazi Germany on behalf of Poland's independence and territorial integrity. But now in the face of Soviet designs on Poland, Churchill's tune changed. From the first meetings with British diplomatic representatives after the German invasion of the Soviet Union, Stalin had insisted that the British government accept as legitimate the Soviet conquests under the Nazi-Soviet Pact of 1939. The Soviet leader demanded the acceptance of Soviet control of Estonia, Latvia, and Lithuania, eastern Poland, the Romanian province of Bessarabia, and the border territories annexed as a result of the Soviet-Finnish War of 1939–1940.

At first, Churchill tried to resist, saying that these matters should be settled at a peace conference at the end of the war. But in the end, he conceded everything Stalin wanted. Indeed, it then became Churchill's job to serve as Stalin's diplomatic agent to get the Polish government-in-exile in London to accept the Soviet demands. Churchill told Polish Premier Stanislaw Mikolajczyk that Stalin's demands for permanent annexation of eastern Poland and a coalition Polish government with a strong contingent of communists hand-picked by Moscow were ones he agreed with "not because Soviet Russia is strong but because she is right." If the Poles resisted, Britain would just leave Poland to its fate under Stalin. After all, he said, Poland would be compensated with large portions of German territory to the west.

At his meeting with Stalin in 1944, he had told the Soviet dictator that giving Poland these areas of Germany would involve expelling millions of Germans from their homes. "The population might be moved from Silesia and east Prussia to Germany," Churchill said to Stalin. "If seven million [Germans] had been killed in the war there would be plenty of room for them." (Churchill had already made an agreement with the Czechoslovakian government-in-exile to expel over three million Germans from the Czech Sudetenland at the end of the war.)

Franklin Roosevelt also wanted a personal and what he called an "intimate understanding" with Stalin. In early 1942, FDR wrote to Churchill:

> I know you will not mind my being brutally frank when I tell you that I think I can personally handle Stalin better than either your Foreign Office or my State Department. Stalin hates the guts of all your top people. He thinks he likes me better, and I hope he will continue to do so.

And the fact that Stalin was a dictator was viewed by FDR as an advantage in cutting any deals. "What helps a lot," Roosevelt told one of his assistants, "is that Stalin is the only man I have to convince. Joe doesn't worry about a Congress or a Parliament. He's the whole works."

At their first meeting at the Tehran Conference in November 1943, Roosevelt did everything in his power to endear himself to "Uncle Joe," as FDR and Churchill affectionately called Stalin. At a private meeting without Churchill's presence, Roosevelt told Stalin that he could do anything he wanted in Poland and the Baltic republics. The transcript recounts that "jokingly" FDR said "that when the Soviet armies reoccupied [Estonia, Latvia and Lithuania], he did not intend to go to war with the Soviet Union over this point." Besides, if an election were held in these three countries, Roosevelt was "personally confident that the people would vote to join the Soviet Union." However, FDR did not press the issue of having any such free elections.

On the Polish question, Roosevelt said that he agreed with Stalin that the eastern part of Poland should be incorporated into the Soviet Union and that German territory to the west should be transferred to Poland. However, FDR explained to Stalin that the next presidential election was only a year away, and he could not make any public declarations on these issues. There were six or seven million Poles in America and "as a practical man [he] didn't want to lose their votes."

Roosevelt's cynicism on transferring peoples and lands through secret deals between himself and Stalin was complete. According to Averell Harriman, who was U.S. ambassador to the Soviet Union during part of the war, "On one occasion in May [1944] the president had told me that he didn't care whether the countries bordering Russia became communized."

To amuse Stalin and curry favor with him, FDR even sank to ridiculing Churchill in front of the Red Czar. During the Tehran meeting, Roosevelt later said:

> I began to tease Churchill about his Britishness, about John Bull, about his cigars, about his habits. It began to register with Stalin. Winston got red and scowled. . . . I kept it up until Stalin was laughing with me. . . . From that time on our relations were personal. . . . The ice was broken and we talked like men and brothers.

And what of Stalin? What did all of this personal diplomacy and "intimate understanding" among "great men" mean to him? Stalin had neither friends nor "brothers." His was a world of political intrigue and psychological manipulation. He once revealed the workings of his mind to two of his communist comrades-in-arms during a conversation in 1923. "To choose one's victim, to prepare one's plans minutely, to slake on implacable vengeance, and then to go to bed," Stalin explained. "There is nothing sweeter in the world." He slept, it is said, with a copy of Machiavelli's *The Prince* by his bed. In his Marxist mind of class conflict and capitalist encirclements, threats and enemies were everywhere. No one was above suspicion or to be trusted. If we are to believe Khrushchev, Stalin, in fact, once remarked, "I trust no one, not even myself."

How did Stalin view FDR? According to one of Stalin's translators, Valentin Berezhkov, in his book *At Stalin's Side* (1994), the Soviet dictator considered Roosevelt to be a great manipulator trying to get the best of him. When Roosevelt offered in January 1942 to send American troops to the northern Soviet port of Murmansk and the Caucasus Mountains in the southern part of the Soviet Union to free Soviet forces to fight on the battlefront, Stalin viewed this as an attempt by FDR to grab Soviet territory.

When anti-Soviet articles appeared in American and British newspapers, Stalin refused to accept the idea that the press was not under complete government control in America and Britain. He believed this was all part of a "bourgeois ploy" and a double game that FDR and Churchill were playing against him. When Roosevelt failed to immediately deliver on some of Stalin's demands because of congressional delay, Stalin said:

> Roosevelt is talking about Congress again. He thinks I will believe that he is truly afraid of Congress. . . . He does not want to do it, and he is using Congress as an excuse. It is all nonsense! He is their military leader and commander in chief. Who would dare to object to him? It is just convenient for him to hide behind Congress. But he won't take me in.

In 1944, Yugoslavian communist Milovan Djilas was in Moscow. During a late night dinner, Stalin summarized how he viewed his two wartime allies:

> Churchill is the kind who, if you don't watch him, will slip a kopeck out of your pocket. Yes, a kopeck out of your pocket. . . . And Roosevelt? Roosevelt is not like that. He dips in his hand only for bigger coins.

In his own paranoia and vision of Marxian class conspiracies, Stalin viewed Churchill's and Roosevelt's personal diplomacies as simply attempts to defeat him on the chessboard of global politics. Churchill's proposal for a percentage division of southeastern Europe into spheres of influence was, in Stalin's mind, an attempt on the part of the British prime minister to pick his pocket for a few "kopecks" in a part of Europe that Stalin planned to completely make his own. As for Roosevelt's policy of giving to Stalin everything that he could and asking for nothing in return, other than the hope that Stalin would then work with him in creating a new deal for a tired world—as exemplified in the American President's initiation of a discussion that resulted in FDR's telling Stalin that Poland and the Baltic republics were his to do with as he chose—this merely persuaded Stalin that Roosevelt was really trying to pull a fast one; Roosevelt was obviously only dipping for "bigger coins." Stalin was not going to let himself be taken in. And at Yalta, he did not.

Part IV—Remaking the Map of Eastern Europe

As we have seen, Roosevelt approached his meetings with Stalin with a determination to make friends and use the Red Czar of Soviet Russia as his partner in creating a Global New Deal. The nature of the Soviet regime and its master did not bother FDR in the least. In 1940, when Congressman Martin Dies told Roosevelt of his concerns about possible Soviet agents in prominent positions in the federal government, FDR replied: "I do not believe in Communism any more than you do, but there is nothing wrong with the Communists in this country. Several of the best friends I have are Communists." As for the Soviet Union, FDR told Congressman Dies: "I look upon Russia as our strongest ally in the years to come. . . . While I do not believe in Communism, Russia is far better off and the world is safer with Russia under Communism than under the Czars. Stalin is a great leader, and although I deplore some of his methods, it is the only way he can safeguard his government." *When FDR spoke these words in 1940, Stalin was in a tacit alliance with Hitler under the terms of the Nazi-Soviet Pact of 1939.*

In September 1943, two months before his meeting with Stalin at Teheran, FDR spent an hour and a half with Archbishop (later Cardinal) Francis Spellman. In *Summit at Teheran: The Untold Story* (1985), historian Keith Eubank explains:

> When he had talked with Cardinal Spellman on September 3, Roosevelt did not conceal his thoughts about Stalin and Eastern Europe. Stalin would receive Finland, the Baltic States, the eastern half of Poland, and Bessarabia [all the lands Stalin had coveted under his Pact with Hitler]. There was no point in opposing "these desires of Stalin, because he had the power to get them anyhow. So better give them gracefully." Moreover, the population of eastern Poland "wants to become Russian." He expected eastern Europe to come under some form of Russian protectorate.

Roosevelt thought the Russians would get about 40 percent of the capitalist economy in Europe. The job of the Europeans was to accept this and, over ten or twenty years, influence the Russians to be less barbaric.

Roosevelt also seemed to think that this civilizing process might not be too difficult because when he returned to the United States from Yalta, he told his Cabinet members that he had found in Stalin "something else in his being besides this revolutionist,

Bolshevik thing." FDR said it might have something to do with Stalin's early training for the priesthood in the Russian Orthodox Church. "I think that something entered into his nature of the way in which a Christian gentleman should behave," Roosevelt declared.

As an example of Stalin's conduct as a "Christian gentleman," in 1939 he sent the following telegram to all officials of the NKVD (the secret police later known as the KGB), as a directive for guiding the use of torture when they arrested and interrogated tens of thousands of people:

> The Central Committee [of the Communist Party] explains that from 1937 on the NKVD was given permission by the Central Committee to use physical influence. . . . The Central Committee believes that the method of physical influence must necessarily be used in the future . . . as a completely correct expedient method.

And when Stalin was informed that the use of brutal tortures was having the desired effect, he told a group of NKVD officers, "Give them the works until they come crawling to you on their bellies with confessions in their teeth." The "fix" was in, therefore, even before the Big Three sat down at that conference table in the Crimea. Writing about Yalta, George N. Crocker stated in *Roosevelt's Road to Russia* (1961):

> [The Big Three] finalized decisions so malodorous—for slave labor, forcible repatriation of refugees, the uprooting of millions of human beings from their home and lands, the breaking of pledges of the right of self-determination, and similar brutalities. . . . One is struck by the casualness—and the callousness— with which these Moguls of the twentieth century wielded the cleaver. Ancient cities [lands and peoples] were picked off like the wings of butterflies.

This is what makes the rhetoric of the "Protocol of Proceedings" issued by the United States, Great Britain, and the Soviet Union at the end of the conference so cruel, cynical, and deceptive. The section of the Protocol devoted to a "Declaration on Liberated Europe" asserted:

> the principle of all peoples to choose the form of government under which they will live—restoration of sovereign rights and

self-government to those peoples who have been forcibly deprived of them by the aggressor nations. . . . The three governments will jointly assist the people in any European liberated
state or former Axis satellite state in Europe . . . to establish
conditions of internal peace [and] . . . to form interim governmental authorities broadly representative of all democratic
elements in the population and pledged to the earliest possible
establishment through free elections of governments respon-
sive to the will of the people; and to facilitate where necessary
the holding of such elections.

Fine words, except for the fact that as Robert Nisbet observes in
Roosevelt and Stalin: The Failed Courtship (1988):

Since the time of Lenin the Soviet understanding of such
Western words as "democracy," "liberation," "freedom," and
"representation" has been a universe apart from the Western
understanding.

For communists there was always a stark contrast between
"bourgeois democracy" and "proletarian democracy." The bourgeois
variation was a "false" democracy in which the outer forms of
freedom existed—freedom of speech, freedom of the press, the right
to vote—but under which "true" freedom was denied because the
capitalists owned the means of production and thus could still
economically exploit the workers who were dependent upon them
for work and wages. Only in the socialist state, in which the means
of production were nationalized and the ruling Communist Party
planned the economy in the name of "the people," could there be
"true" democracy. To deny participation and power to "bourgeois"
political parties, therefore, was the only way to assure the triumph of
true freedom and real representation for the working masses.

This meant that in the lands "liberated" by Stalin's Red Army
in Eastern Europe—Poland, Hungary, Czechoslovakia, Romania,
Bulgaria—the only democracy that would be the permitted would be
the proletarian version in which the Communist Party, and those
other political parties subservient to it, would be allowed to come to
power in the New Deal world of the postwar period.

This was seen clearest in the section of the Yalta Protocol
dealing with Poland. Behind the Red Army, a Polish Communist
"Provisional Government"—the Lublin Poles, as they were called—
took over local political power as the Nazis were displaced in the
liberated portions of Poland. The Protocol stated:

> The Provisional Government which is now functioning in Poland should be reorganized on a broader democratic basis with the inclusion of democratic leaders from Poland itself and from Poles abroad. . . . This [broadened] Polish Government of National Unity shall be pledged to the holding of free and unfettered elections as soon as possible on the basis of universal suffrage and secret ballot. In these elections all democratic and anti-Nazi parties shall have the right to take part and to put forward candidates.

This meant that additional politicians and parties would be incorporated into the Communist provisional government on the basis of a decision about which individuals and parties were to be considered properly "democratic" and "anti-Nazi," with the communist governmental structure taken as the working political framework within which these individual politicians and parties would be permitted to participate and function.

U.S. Admiral William Leahy, who was present at the Yalta Conference, told FDR that this political arrangement was "phony" and that "this is so elastic that the Russians can stretch it all the way from Yalta to Washington without ever technically breaking it." Roosevelt replied, "I know it, but it was the best I could get." Based on his comments to Cardinal Spellman and other Americans, and from his explicit giving of a free hand to Stalin in Poland and the Baltic States at the Teheran Conference, in fact FDR really did not give a damn whether the people in these countries got anything more.

And what was Stalin's attitude? Milovan Djilas, in *Conversations with Stalin* (1962), recounts that in April 1945—only two months after the Yalta Conference and a month before the end of the war in Europe—Stalin told a delegation of Yugoslavian communists visiting Moscow:

> This war is not as in the past; whoever occupies a territory also imposes on it his own social system. Everyone imposes his own system as far as his army can reach. It cannot be otherwise.

In Stalin's Marxian mind, since the Western bourgeois democracies would impose exploitive capitalism on the working classes wherever their armies permitted, it behooved him, as the great leader of the world socialist revolution, to impose true, proletarian democracy on all those countries liberated by his Red Army.

170

Nor was there any regard, in the shifting of frontiers and the transferring of peoples from the jurisdiction of one state to another, as to whether the people whose lives were involved desired the change or not. In the portion of the Protocol on Poland, the Big Three also agreed that "the Eastern frontier of Poland should follow the Curzon line with digressions from it in some regions of five to eight kilometers in favor of Poland. They recognize that Poland must receive substantial accession of territory in the North and West." In other words, Poland, in turn, would be given large portions of German territory.

At the end of the First World War, Poland was reborn as a nation-state out of the collapsed German, Austrian, and Russian Empires. At the peace conference at Versailles, Britain and France had demarcated the eastern border of Poland, and this became known as the Curzon Line. But in 1919, a war broke out between Poland and the new Bolshevik regime in Russia. At first the Poles advanced far into Russia, but the Bolsheviks counterattacked and reached the gates of Warsaw. The Poles then mounted their own successful counteroffensive and pushed the Red Army back, far to the east of the Curzon Line. The battle line became the political frontier when a peace treaty was signed between Poland and Lenin's Bolshevik regime in March 1921.

When Stalin and Hitler divided Poland in 1939, once again erasing it from the map of Europe, the line separating Soviet and Nazi zones of occupation was partly along and partly to the west of the Curzon Line. Stalin insisted throughout his wartime meetings with Churchill and Roosevelt that the Curzon Line was to be the border between Poland and the Soviet Union, not the older frontier according to the peace treaty of 1921.

In this shifting frontier of political control between Poland and the USSR, no consideration was ever given to the preferences or desires of those living in these lands. But one thing is certain, life for those who fell under Stalin's care in eastern Poland after 1939 was far from idyllic. It is quite doubtful that Roosevelt was right when he claimed that the people in these areas wanted to be part of the Soviet Union. Peasant land was seized, with the peasants forced into collective farms. All private property was nationalized. Tens of thousands of people were executed or sent off into slave labor in the Gulag prison camps. And in a region in which most of the people were either Russian Orthodox or Roman Catholic, religion was abolished and made a punishable offense.

But if the eastern lands of prewar Poland were being carved up according to the whims of Roosevelt, Stalin, and Churchill, what they had in store for Germany was even more cruel and cynical.

Part V—Remaking the Map of Germany

When Adolf Hitler's foreign minister, Joachim von Ribbentrop, came to Moscow on August 23, 1939, to sign the Nazi-Soviet Non-Aggression Pact, Joseph Stalin hosted a late-night supper for his German guests after the signatures had been affixed to the documents. Stalin rose from his chair and gave a toast to Hitler,

a man for whom [I have] always had an extraordinary respect. . . . I know how much the German nation loves its Führer; I should therefore like to drink to his health.

In September 1940, Ribbentrop wrote to Stalin:

In the opinion of the Führer . . . it appears to be the historical mission of the Four Powers—the Soviet Union, Italy, Japan and Germany—to adopt a long-range policy and to direct the future development of their peoples in the right channels by the delimitations of their interests on a worldwide scale.

Stalin was then invited by Hitler to participate in the Axis division of the global spoils.

In October 1940, Stalin sent his foreign minister, Vyacheslav Molotov, to meet with Hitler in Berlin. At this meeting, Hitler offered his deal. The Führer was confident that England would soon be defeated. At that point, "the British Empire would be apportioned as a gigantic worldwide estate in bankruptcy," Hitler said. "All the countries which could possibly be interested in the bankrupt estate would have to stop all controversies among themselves and concern themselves exclusively with the partition of the British Empire." Germany would annex certain territories in Europe and central Africa; Italy would gain areas of Europe, and northern and northeastern Africa; Japan's territorial aspirations were to be in eastern and southern Asia; and the Soviet Union's "territorial aspirations [would] center south of the national territory of the Soviet Union in the direction of the Indian Ocean." Stalin, in other words, was being offered parts of Turkey, Iran, Afghanistan, and British India.

Molotov replied that "everything he was about to say was identical with the views of Stalin" who had "given him exact instructions" before he left Moscow. He said that he had "followed the arguments of the Führer with interest and that he was in agreement with everything that he had understood. . . . The participation of Russia in the Tripartite [Axis] Pact [between Nazi Germany, Fascist Italy, and Imperial Japan] appeared entirely acceptable in principle," Molotov said. But Stalin was interested in more than India. Soviet ambitions were closer to home in Europe and included Finland, Bulgaria, parts of Romania, and the Turkish straits leading to the Mediterranean; Stalin was also interested in the fate of Hungary and Greece. Molotov even suggested that Stalin might be interested in having Soviet military bases in Denmark, at the mouth of the Baltic Sea. Hitler's own ambitions in Europe, however, led to a heated and angry exchange between the Führer and Stalin's spokesman.

In spite of the harsh words spoken, after Molotov returned to Moscow, Stalin informed the German ambassador in November 1940 that "the Soviet Union is prepared to accept the draft of the Four Power Pact which the Reich Foreign Minister outlined . . . regarding political collaboration." But Stalin still insisted on Finland's and Bulgaria's being viewed in the Soviet sphere of influence—and that Soviet land and naval bases be established in the Turkish straits; if the Turks objected, Germany, Italy, and the Soviet Union would take "required military and diplomatic measures" to get Stalin what he wanted; and "the area south of Batum and Baku in the general direction of the Persian Gulf is recognized as the center of the aspirations of the Soviet Union."

Here was Stalin's price for formal collaboration with Hitler. But it was a price that Hitler was unwilling to pay. "Russia," Hitler said, "must be brought to her knees." The Führer ordered that the plans for Operation Barbarossa—the German invasion of the Soviet Union—be set in motion.

After Stalin signed his Non-Aggression Pact with Hitler in 1939, he told some of the Politburo members: "Of course it's all a game to see who can fool whom. I know what Hitler's up to. He thinks he's outsmarted me, but actually it's I who have tricked him." In the first months after the German invasion of the Soviet Union in June 1941, as the Nazi war machine advanced to the gates of Moscow and Leningrad, it did seem that, instead, Hitler had gotten the best of Stalin in this "game."

But now, five years later, in February 1945, as Stalin sat at the table with Roosevelt and Churchill at the Yalta Conference, deciding the partition of the "bankrupt estate" of Europe, it was clear that Stalin had won the game. Already, Stalin had acquired from Roosevelt and Churchill almost more than he had demanded from Hitler in

Europe. The Baltic States of Estonia, Latvia, and Lithuania, eastern Poland, and Romanian Bessarabia were recognized as his, outright. His "unofficial" side-deals and understandings with Churchill and Roosevelt gave him a free hand in Poland, Czechoslovakia, Hungary, Romania, and Bulgaria. Stalin made sure that the sections of the Yalta Protocols on "Liberated Europe" and "Poland," that would be published at the end of the conference, would serve as the rhetorical cover for the Sovietization of Eastern Europe. Things had not gone completely according to the long-term strategy that he had laid down in 1925 for the communization of Europe, but, nonetheless, half the continent of Europe was rapidly falling into Stalin's grip.

The issue now before the Big Three was what was to be done with Germany in the postwar period. On the second day of the conference, Stalin asked if it was their joint intention to dismember Germany. He reminded FDR and Churchill that each had presented a dismemberment plan at their meeting at Tehran in November 1943. At Tehran, on the final day of the conference, Roosevelt proposed a radical plan. Germany would be divided into five separate states. A truncated Prussia would be divided into two states, comprising north-central and northwestern Germany. The third state would be in central Germany. The fourth state would be in southern Germany, including Bavaria. And the fifth state would be carved out of western Germany. The Kiel Canal and Hamburg in the north and the Ruhr Valley and the Saarland in the west would be under permanent international control.

What Roosevelt had presented was territorially a variation of a plan put together in 1943 by Secretary of the Treasury Henry Morgenthau to permanently deindustrialize Germany. The Morgenthau Plan called for a political dismemberment of Germany, the stripping of Germany of all its industrial equipment and capabilities, and the forced "pastoralization" of the German population.

William Henry Chamberlin, in *America's Second Crusade* (1950), summarized the consequences, if the plan had been implemented:

> It is no exaggeration to say that the Morgenthau Plan, if applied in its full rigor, would have been an undiscriminating sentence of death for millions of Germans. The area in which it was proposed to forbid all heavy industries and mining is one of the most urbanized and thickly settled in Europe. It would have been impossible to turn millions of city dwellers, accustomed to earning their living in factories, offices, and shops, into self-supporting farmers, even if land had been available. . . . The

avowed purpose of the Morgenthau Plan was to turn Germany into a predominantly agricultural and pastoral country. But there was no unused reserves of land for this purpose in thickly settled, industrial Germany.

After FDR finished outlining his plan for German dismemberment at Tehran, Churchill said, "The President had said a mouthful." But he himself had no problems with the basic idea. Churchill wanted a vengeful peace. According to his private secretary, already in September 1940, Churchill had called for taking German males and "castrating the lot." He told his Cabinet that it might be a good idea to figure out a way for "segregating three or four million German males for some years" to prevent them from breeding.

At Tehran, Churchill offered his own dismemberment plan. Prussia would be cut off from the rest of Germany as a separate state. The southern provinces of Germany would be forced into a Danubian confederation. Stalin said that he much preferred Roosevelt's plan. Germany had to be permanently broken up into five or six separate states. "It was far better to break up and scatter the German tribes," he said. Furthermore, said Stalin, as part of the dismemberment of Germany, "Poland should extend [west] to the Oder [River]. . . . The Russians would help the Poles obtain a frontier on the Oder." Roosevelt agreed with Stalin; it had been far safer in the past, FDR said, when Germany had been splintered into 107 tiny principalities.

Stalin was adamant that unless the Allies dealt forcefully with Germany, in fifteen or twenty years, the Germans would start another war. Only two conditions would prevent this: the execution of 50,000 to 100,000 German officers; and the Big Three's retaining control of certain strategic points around Germany. This suddenly bothered Churchill, who said that the liquidation of 50,000 German officers would sully his honor as well as the honor of his country. "I would rather be taken out into the garden here and now and be shot myself," Churchill declared.

Roosevelt tried to calm Churchill down by suggesting that only 49,000 be executed. When Churchill finally stormed out of the room, Stalin had to go and get him; putting his arm around the prime minister, Stalin assured him it was all a joke. But the mass murder of potential enemies was nothing new for Stalin. In 1940, he had ordered the execution of 14,000 captured Polish officers in the Katyn Forest.

As for control of strategic points around Germany, Stalin said that he wanted the northern half of the German province of East

Prussia, including the ancient German city of Königsberg. "This would put Russia on the neck of Germany," Stalin assured Churchill and Roosevelt. Furthermore, besides giving the Soviet Union an ice-free port in the Baltic Sea, it would give him a piece of German territory which he believed he deserved.

At the Yalta Conference, the Big Three again endorsed the dismemberment. FDR said he "was in favor of dismemberment of Germany. . . . He added that he still thought the division of Germany into five states or seven states was a good idea." Churchill, too, stated that "the British Government was prepared to accept now the principle of dismemberment of Germany and to set up suitable machinery to determine the best method to carry it out." In the formal Protocol of Proceedings at the end of the conference, the Big Three said: "They will take such steps, including the complete disarmament, demilitarization and dismemberment of Germany as they deem requisite for future peace and security."

The other main issue at Yalta concerning the future of Germany was over reparations. Roosevelt said that, unlike after the First World War, he did not want German property in the United States to be returned to their owners. "This time," FDR said, "he would seek the necessary legislation to retain for the United States all German property for the United States." Furthermore, he endorsed any claims the Soviet Union might make for reparations, since he did not think that German standards of living should be allowed to be higher than in the Soviet Union. Also, FDR said that he supported the use of "German manpower to reconstruct the devastated regions" in the Soviet Union; in other words, Roosevelt endorsed the use of German slave labor in Stalin's Russia.

Under Stalin's insistence, therefore, the Yalta agreements contained a secret protocol on reparations. Under the protocol's terms, the Big Three agreed to:

> Removals within 2 years from the surrender of Germany . . . the national wealth of Germany located on the territory of Germany herself as well as outside her territory (equipment, machine-tools, ships, rolling stock, German investments abroad, shares of industrial, transport and other enterprises in Germany, etc.). . . . Annual deliveries of goods from current production for a period to be fixed. Use of German labor [i.e., slave labor]. . . . The total sum of the reparation . . . should be 20 billion dollars [about 150 billion 1990's dollars] and that 50% of it should go to the Union of Soviet Socialist Republics.

In August 1941, Roosevelt and Churchill had met off the coast of Newfoundland and issued the Atlantic Charter. They had stated:

> First, their countries seek no aggrandizement, territorial or other; Second, they desire to see no territorial changes that do not accord with the freely expressed wishes of the people concerned; Third, they respect the right of all peoples to choose the form of government under which they will live.

"All peoples" obviously did not include the Germans. For the sins of the Nazi regime, the German people were to be forcibly dissected and splintered into a number of weak, small states, with large territories in eastern Germany permanently transferred to Polish and Soviet control. The country was to be completely deindustrialized and weighed down with reparations to be paid out of its remaining, limited productive capacity for many years into the future. Population transfers in the millions would have to occur in the face of these territorial changes, and an unspecified number of Germans would see years of slave labor in the Soviet Gulag.

Notwithstanding such harsh punishment being planned for the German people, a further perversion was still to come—Franklin Roosevelt's betrayal of a loyal wartime ally: China. Prices were still to be paid if FDR was to obtain Stalin's intervention in the Pacific war against Japan and, more important from the president's point of view, Soviet participation in his grand dream of a new global peace organization: the United Nations.

Part VI—Remaking the Map of the Far East

In 1940, the Japanese consul general in Harbin, Manchuria, intercepted several messages sent from the Soviet foreign minister, Vyacheslav Molotov, to the Soviet ambassador in Tokyo. In one of these messages, Molotov told his ambassador: "We concluded an 'Agreement with Germany' because a war is required in Europe" between the capitalist nations, to open the door for the future communization of the European continent. Molotov went on to explain that any peace settlement that would end the war between China and Japan "might destroy our work proceeding among the suppressed peoples of Asia, and . . . it would not instigate the Japanese-American war which we desire."

If Japan turned its eyes towards conquest in Southeast Asia— including the U.S.-controlled Philippine Islands—and became embroiled in a war with America, then Moscow could feel secure that the Japanese would not invade Soviet Siberia, as well. And in the chaos that a general war in Asia would create, the breeding ground for communist revolutions would be expanded. To help seal this likelihood, Stalin signed a nonaggression pact with Japan in April 1941.

In July 1941, a month after the Nazi invasion of the Soviet Union, FDR's confidant, Harry Hopkins, was in Moscow meeting with Stalin, assuring the Soviet dictator of Roosevelt's intention of supplying the Red Army with as much war materiel as it was possible to provide, with no strings attached. On August 1, FDR told his cabinet that he wanted the aid flowing to Stalin immediately. "The only answer I want to hear is that it is under way," Roosevelt said to them. "Get the planes off with a bang next week."

At that very moment, Stalin's greatest and most successful spy in the Far East, Richard Sorge—who had warned Moscow in early June 1941 that Hitler would attack the Soviet Union during the third week of June, predicting the invasion almost to the day (even though at the time Stalin refused to believe it)—was using his agents to find out if Japan was planning to attack north at Soviet Siberia or south into a collision course with the United States. On October 4, 1941, Sorge, in his last message to Moscow before his arrest by the Japanese police, informed Stalin:

> The American issue and the question of the advance to the south are far more important [to the Japanese] than the Northern problem [the Soviet Union]. . . . There will be war with the U.S. this month or next. . . . Japan will attack the United States, then Malaya, Singapore and Sumatra.

Stalin had this information corroborated when Soviet intelligence intercepted a November 27 message from Tokyo to the Japanese ambassador in Berlin, saying that he was to "explain to Hitler that the main Japanese efforts will be concentrated in the south and that we propose to refrain from deliberate operations in the north (i.e., Siberia)."

But even as the American aid was beginning to flow into the Soviet Union to bolster the Red Army in the face of the German attack, Stalin kept this information from his most reliable spy to himself. Better not to warn Roosevelt about Japan's war intentions and better simply to watch the unfolding of the Japanese-American war that he wanted.

America had confronted Japan in the Pacific over Japanese ambitions in China. The Japanese military had occupied Manchuria in the autumn of 1931 and the neighboring province of Jehol in 1933 and had established their puppet state of Manchukuo. In July 1937, Japan initiated a new attack near Peiping (Peking), and soon the Japanese Army was advancing far into north-central China. In August 1937, Japanese forces attacked Shanghai, rapidly moved up the Yangtze River, and occupied the Nationalist Chinese capital at Nanking. Chiang Kai-shek, the head of the Chinese Nationalist government, moved his capital to the city of Chungking in western China. By 1939, even though they had occupied most of the coastal cities, the Japanese were bogged down in a seemingly unwinnable war in the vast stretches of the Chinese countryside. In 1940, in an attempt to cut off outside supplies to Chiang Kai-shek's forces, the Japanese occupied the northern part of French Indochina (Vietnam, Laos, and Cambodia). In July 1941, the Japanese occupied the southern part of the French colony.

President Roosevelt's freezing of Japanese assets in the United States and his embargo against the selling of oil to Japan in July 1941, as well as his unwillingness to negotiate any compromise with Tokyo, set the stage for the attack on Pearl Harbor. Once in the war, Roosevelt abandoned Chiang Kai-shek and the Chinese resistance against Japan. As Frederick W. Marks has explained in his study of FDR's foreign policy, *Wind Over Sand* (1988):

> In fact, Roosevelt broke virtually every important promise made to Chiang between the time of Pearl Harbor and his death in April 1945. He shipped less than 10 percent of the aid pledged. He went back on his commitment to assist Chiang's Burma campaign with an amphibious invasion. At various times, supplies ear-marked for Chungking were diverted without consultation. Scores of bombers and transports, once the entire U.S. Tenth Air Force in India, were rerouted to bypass China after the United States had given its word. Roosevelt pledged a loan of a billion dollars which was never delivered. And more than once, he promised increased tonnage to be flown from India over the Himalayan Hump. In almost every instance, such tonnage failed to eventuate.

Finally, after becoming sufficiently tired of Chiang Kai-shek's complaints about American failure to support his government, FDR ordered that a plan be prepared for the assassination of the Chinese generalissimo. In December 1943, FDR's military representative in China, Gen. Joseph Stilwell—who passionately disliked Chiang, often referring to him in public as "the Peanut"—told a subordinate, Col. Frank Dorn, that FDR was "fed up with Chiang and his tantrums, and said so. In fact, he told me in that Olympian manner of his, 'if you can't get along with Chiang, and can't replace him, get rid of him once and for all. You know what I mean, put in someone you can manage.'" Colonel Dorn prepared a plan for an airplane mishap, in which there would be engine problems and, in the process of bailing out of the plane, Chiang and his wife would be given faulty parachutes. The plan was not executed only because FDR decided not to issue final authorization.

Franklin Roosevelt's final betrayal of his Chinese ally occurred in his negotiations with Stalin over the conditions under which the Soviet Union would enter the war against Japan. In November 1943, on their way to their conference with Stalin at Tehran, FDR and Churchill met in Cairo, Egypt, with Chiang Kai-shek. At the end of the meeting, they issued the Cairo Declaration, which said that America, Britain, and China "are fighting this war to restrain and punish the aggression of Japan. They covet no gain for themselves and have no thought of territorial expansion. . . . All territories Japan has stolen from the Chinese, such as Manchuria, Formosa and the Pescadores, will be restored to the Republic of China."

A few days later, at Tehran, Stalin said that once the war was over in Europe, the Soviet Union would be prepared, after a short time, to enter the war in the Pacific against Japan. But Stalin wanted to know what could be done for him in the Far East. When Churchill asked what he had in mind, Stalin explained that, while he did not want to go into details at this time, the Soviet Union had no completely ice-free port in the Far East. FDR suggested that the port of Dairen, on the southern coast of Manchuria, could be made into a free port. When Stalin responded that the Chinese might not agree, Roosevelt said he was sure they would as long as it was under "international guarantee." Stalin replied that he thought it sounded like a good idea.

In December 1944, two months before the Yalta Conference, Stalin had a conversation with Ambassador Averell Harriman in Moscow. Stalin now laid out his terms for participation in the war against Japan. He wanted from Japan the southern half of Sakhalin Island and the Kurile Islands. In China, he wanted Soviet leases of both Dairen and Port Arthur as well as control of the Manchurian railroads running from the Soviet border to these ports in southern Manchuria. And he wanted confirmation of the status quo of Outer Mongolia as a Soviet satellite, which it had been since 1921.

On February 8, 1945, on the fifth day of the Yalta Conference, Roosevelt and Stalin held a private meeting attended by their translators (Charles Bohlen, for FDR) as well as Averell Harriman and

Vyacheslav Molotov. After discussing a number of topics, Stalin finally said that he wanted to discuss the "political conditions" under which the Soviet Union would enter the war against Japan. FDR said that he had already received a report from Harriman about their conversation in Moscow in December. Roosevelt said that he saw "no difficulty whatsoever in regard to the southern half of Sakhalin and the Kurile Islands going to Russia at the end of the war." He reminded Stalin of his suggestion at Tehran that "the Soviet Union be given the use of a warm water port" at Dairen.

Stalin replied that "there was another question and that involved the use by the Russians of the Manchurian railways." He said that the Czars had had use of the rail line running east-west across the northern half of Manchuria and the rail line running south from the city of Harbin to Dairen and Port Arthur on the Manchurian coast. Stalin said that it was "clear that if these conditions were not met it would be difficult for him and Molotov to explain to the Soviet people why Russia was entering the war against Japan." Furthermore, Stalin wanted "these conditions set forth in writing agreed to by the three powers" before leaving Yalta. In *Witness to History* (1973), Charles Bohlen admitted that Stalin's reference to the opinion of the Soviet people was nonsense. "Everybody knew that all the power in the Soviet Union resided in Stalin, but as a courtesy, no one at the Yalta Conference disputed him."

On February 11, Stalin, Roosevelt and Churchill affixed their signatures to the "top secret" protocol on Soviet entry into the Pacific war:

1. The status quo in Outer-Mongolia (The Mongolian People's Republic) shall be preserved.
2. The former rights of Russia violated by the treacherous attack of Japan in 1904 shall be restored, viz.:
   (a) the southern part of Sakhalin as well as all the islands adjacent to it shall be returned to the Soviet Union,
   (b) the commercial port of Dairen shall be internationalized, the preeminent interests of the Soviet Union in this port being safeguarded and the lease of Port Arthur as a naval base of the USSR restored,
   (c) the Chinese-Eastern Railroad and the South-Manchurian Railroad which provides an outlet to Dairen shall be jointly operated by the establishment of a joint Soviet-Chinese Company it being understood that the preeminent interests of the Soviet Union shall be safeguarded and that China shall retain full sovereignty in Manchuria;

3. The Kurile islands shall be handed over to the Soviet Union. It is understood, that the agreement concerning Outer Mongolia and the ports and railroads referred to above will require concurrence of Generalissimo Chiang Kai-shek. The President [FDR] will take measures in order to obtain this concurrence on advice from Marshall Stalin.

The Heads of the three Great Powers have agreed that these claims of the Soviet Union shall be unquestionably fulfilled after Japan has been defeated.

After the war, when this secret protocol to the Yalta agreements was finally made public, former U.S. Ambassador William C. Bullitt wrote:

> At Yalta . . . President Roosevelt broke the pledge which he had made to the Chinese government at Cairo and—secretly, behind the back of China—signed . . . an agreement by which the vital rights of China were sacrificed to Soviet imperialism. . . . In view of Roosevelt's Cairo pledge that Manchuria would be restored to China this secret agreement was entirely dishonorable.

In his book *Special Envoy to Churchill and Stalin: 1941–1946* (1975), Averell Harriman said that at Yalta he had tried to dissuade FDR from accepting the wording in the protocol. He told FDR that he did not like the U.S. endorsing the legitimacy of Soviet "preeminent interests" in Manchuria, pledging itself to seeing that these interests were "safeguarded" and committing itself to assuring that Stalin's territorial claims would be "unquestionably fulfilled" at the end of the war, regardless of Chinese agreement. Roosevelt replied that he "was not disposed to fuss about words." FDR said that "it was just language" and "he was not going to quarrel with Stalin." In clear frustration, Harriman observed: "It was my impression that as long as [FDR] could put his own interpretation on the language, he didn't much care what interpretation other people put on it."

Trading away the rights of other peoples and countries clearly never bothered Franklin Roosevelt's conscience. FDR told Harriman there were "other matters more important, the establishment of the United Nations, for example." And he wasn't going "to use up whatever trading positions he had." No, Stalin's participation in FDR's dream of a global peace organization was far more important than the national independence and personal freedom of tens of millions of people. Those were "trading positions" he was more than willing to just give away to the Soviet dictator.

Part VII—
Planning the Policing of the World: The United Nations

Franklin Roosevelt was fascinated by the communist experiment in Russia. In a conversation with Secretary of Labor Frances Perkins in 1933, FDR admitted: "I don't understand the Russians. I just don't know what makes them tick. I wish I could study them." In a later exchange, Perkins told Roosevelt about an American who had worked in the Soviet Union for a long time. Perkins had asked him what made the Russians "tick." The man answered: "The desire to do the Holy Will."

FDR excitedly replied:

> You know, there may be something in that. It would explain their almost mystical devotion to this idea which they have developed of the Communist society. They all seem really to want to do what is good for their society instead of wanting to do for themselves. We take care of ourselves and think about the welfare of society afterward.

This idea remained transfixed in Roosevelt's mind. Former Undersecretary of State Sumner Welles recounted in his book *Where Are We Heading?* (1946) that in the autumn of 1944, FDR felt confident that, in spite of the differences between the American and Soviet political systems, the Soviet and American societies were converging towards some common middle ground of welfare-state socialism. Welles wrote:

> Franklin Roosevelt saw no need to fear Communism, if an international organization existed. . . . He regarded the American form of democracy as being at the opposite pole from the original form of Soviet Communism. In the years which had elapsed since the Soviet revolution of 1917, the Soviet system had advanced materially toward a modified form of state socialism. In the same way, the American polity since that time had progressed toward the ideal of true political and social justice. . . . He felt, therefore, that even though the internal systems of the two countries could never conceivably become identical, some progress towards approximation had already been made, and that this approximation made for a better understanding between the peoples of the two nations.

He regarded this trend as making it more likely that no fundamental conflict between the two countries need ever become inevitable. . . . He felt it was indispensable that both governments should realize that in the field of world affairs their respective courses could always be parallel and need never to be antagonistic. . . . He was willing to make material concessions in order for the United Nations organization to be established. . . . It was in that spirit and with that purpose that Franklin Roosevelt attended the meeting at Yalta.

To make the world permanently safe after the defeat of the Axis powers, FDR came to believe that what was needed was a new and radically more powerful League of Nations. What began to emerge in his mind was what became the United Nations. During a visit to Washington in May 1942, Soviet Foreign Minister Vyacheslav Molotov was given an outline of what FDR had in mind. In the postwar world, FDR said, the United States, Britain, the Soviet Union, and China would have to jointly suppress any future disturbers of the world peace. Germany, Japan, and other "smaller" countries would have to be controlled and possibly disarmed. He also told Molotov that colonial possessions of "weaker nations" would have to be placed under the trusteeship of the new world organization that Roosevelt wanted to see created. Molotov replied that he thought that these ideas were quite realistic and said that Stalin would fully support them.

In March 1943, Roosevelt elaborated his ideas in a discussion with Anthony Eden, the British foreign minister. FDR said that he saw an organization with a general assembly, in which all member nations would participate. But there would also be a security council of the major powers in whose hands real authority and military power would reside. "The real decisions," said Roosevelt, "should be made by the United States, Great Britain, Russia, and China, who would be the powers for many years to come and that would have to police the world." FDR also said that these Big Four would have to permanently control strategic bases around the world.

During a conversation with William D. Hassett, a presidential aide, in April 1943, Roosevelt explained how he saw this policing of the world:

The President said the policy of policing the world [was] not insurmountable. He suggested that the United States and China would police Asia. Africa would be policed by Great Britain and Brazil, the latter because of her proximity to Africa, with other interested nations co-operating. The United States will see to the protection of the Americas, leaving the peace of Europe to Great Britain and Russia.

At the Tehran Conference in November 1943, FDR elaborated his plans for a world peace organization to Stalin. One branch of this organization would comprise only the "Four Policemen"—America, Britain, Soviet Russia, and China—who would be responsible to enforce peace around the world. If a revolution or a crisis arose in a small country, and The Four viewed this as a threat to world security, they would have the power to impose a quarantine by closing that country's borders and enforcing a trade embargo; in the face of a more serious threat, The Four Policemen would send an ultimatum which, if ignored, would lead to the defiant country's being bombed and, if necessary, invaded. Stalin found all this quite acceptable. (As George Crocker observed in *Roosevelt's Road to Russia* [1961], "There is no evidence of any discussion of the possibility that the offending aggressor might be one of The Four Policemen.")

In August and September 1944, FDR, Churchill, and Stalin sent delegations to the Dumbarton Oaks estate in Washington, D.C., to work out the organizational structure for the United Nations. During the negotiations, it soon became clear that the Big Three had differences of opinion. The Soviet delegation for a long time pushed for the idea of an international military air corps that could bomb on short notice any country labeled an "aggressor." The British delegation wanted to make sure that any questions that might undermine the integrity of the British Empire could not be brought before the United Nations for discussion. The American delegation attempted to keep alive the idea of The Four Policemen who would patrol the world. All of these positions were either diluted or modified. They were finally sorted out in a document that outlined the general structure of the United Nations.

Two major points, however, were left unresolved. Would the five permanent members of the UN Security Council—the United States, Britain, the Soviet Union, China, and now also France—each have an absolute right to veto a Security Council decision? And in the General Assembly was the Soviet Union to be given one vote or sixteen votes—one for each of the sixteen constituent republics of the USSR—as Stalin demanded? These issues were resolved at the Yalta Conference.

On February 4, 1945, the first day of the Yalta Conference, the issue of power in the United Nations came up for discussion. Stalin opened the topic by saying:

The three Great Powers which had borne the brunt of the war and had liberated from German domination the small powers should have the unanimous right to preserve the peace of the world. . . . It was ridiculous to believe that Albania would have an equal voice with the three Great Powers who had won the war and were present at this dinner.

Stalin insisted that "he would never agree to having any action of any of the Great Powers submitted to the judgment of the small powers."

Roosevelt agreed, saying that "the Great Powers bore the greater responsibility and that the peace should be written by the Three Powers represented at this table." Churchill also concurred that "there was no question of the small powers dictating to the big powers," but he suggested that the great nations should show "great respect for the rights of the smaller nations." However, Churchill told Anthony Eden and U.S. Secretary of State Edward Stettinius that he would accept Stalin's views because "everything depended on the unity of the three Great Powers."

But the final decision by Roosevelt, Churchill, and Stalin to accept the principle that the five permanent members of the Security Council would each have a veto over any decision was not merely an acceptance of Stalin's view that small powers should not control matters concerning the interests of the Great Powers, it was no less a goal of the United States. Secretary Stettinius in his record of the Yalta Conference, *Roosevelt and the Russians* (1949), insisted:

It is absolutely incorrect to state that the permanent members were granted the veto power on most questions only because of Russian insistence. The American delegation, at Dumbarton Oaks and after, favored the big-power veto on matters involving economic and military sanctions.

Roosevelt, no less than Stalin, wanted no serious interference from the "small powers" in any decisions concerning the Great Powers' policing of the world.

On February 7, the fourth day of the conference, Molotov raised the issue of how many votes the USSR would receive in the UN General Assembly. He said that the Soviet Union was withdrawing its earlier demand for sixteen votes and "would be satisfied with the admission of three or at least two of the Soviet Republics as original members." In the end, Roosevelt and Churchill accepted the inclusion of both Soviet Ukraine and Soviet Byelorussia as additional founding and voting members of the United Nations, along with the USSR itself. Roosevelt thanked Stalin for reducing his voting demand "as a great step forward which would be welcomed by all the peoples of the world," and Churchill also extended his "heartfelt thanks to Marshal Stalin and Mr. Molotov."

In his book *Franklin D. Roosevelt's World Order* (1959), historian Willard Range summarized FDR's vision and design for the postwar era:

> It is obvious that Roosevelt's conception of a collective security system under the guardianship of the Big Powers led by the United States was very paternalistic and clearly placed all the medium and small powers in the position of children in the family of nations.... His hopes for a global New Deal and a good neighbor climate of opinion had great bearing on the problem of security; and while his attitude toward smaller nations was that of a father, it was the attitude of a good father and a twentieth-century somewhat democratic and benevolent father who had the best interests of the children at heart; and if he could not quite bring himself to let the children have a vote in important family decisions, he nevertheless wanted them to express their views, be treated with decency and be made to feel important.

In his domestic policies, FDR was guided by the idea that the role and purpose of government was to use power to make a better society, even though this meant the loss of many individual freedoms of the past. Or as he expressed it in his second inaugural address in 1937, the government needed more power—"power to stop evil; power to do good." The private affairs of the American citizenry had to be brought into "their proper subordination to the public's government."

As FDR conceived it, the United Nations was meant to be an extension of this idea of political paternalism to the level of international relations. Just as FDR's National Recovery Administration (NRA) in the early days of the New Deal was meant to cartelize industry in the name of generating national prosperity, the United Nations was meant to cartelize world security in the hands of a select group of Big Powers who were to be trusted to serve the global good of all. The United States, in partnership with a handful of other Big Powers—most especially Stalin's Russia, for whose partnership FDR had been willing to give his endorsement to the enslavement of tens of millions of people—was to subordinate the affairs of the nations of the world to the benevolent supervision of the Global Policemen, who would rule them and monitor them, and if need be punish them with a military big stick, all for their own good, of course.

The consequences of this paternalistic idea, as practiced by Franklin Roosevelt during the war and at the Yalta Conference, have made up the negative legacy that has dominated American government policy at home and abroad for the last half century.

Part VIII—
FDR's Message and Legacy to the American People

On March 1, 1945, after returning to Washington from his meeting with Winston Churchill and Joseph Stalin at Yalta, President Franklin Roosevelt delivered an address before a joint session of Congress on the results of the conference. "I come from the Crimean Conference, my fellow Americans, with a firm belief that we have made a good start on the road to a world of peace," Roosevelt said.

FDR explained that the Yalta meeting had had two purposes. The first was to assure the defeat of Nazi Germany in the shortest period of time, with the least loss of life to the Allied side. The second purpose was "to continue to build the foundation for an international accord which would bring order and security after the chaos of the war, and would give some assurance of lasting peace among the nations of the world. Toward that goal," Roosevelt stated, "a tremendous stride has been made."

Germany would be under the "temporary control" of the United States, Great Britain, France, and the Soviet Union, with each of these nations having a zone of occupation. The Nazi system would be destroyed, along with all "militaristic influence in the public, private and cultural life in Germany." Germany would be disarmed and dismembered, and reparations would be imposed on the defeated nation.

The Big Three—FDR, Churchill, and Stalin—had agreed that in the countries liberated from Nazi occupation, "democratic processes" would be established for these countries to solve their own problems, with "free elections [being] held as soon as possible." As a result, Roosevelt declared: "I am sure that—under the agreements reached at Yalta—there will be a more stable political Europe then ever before."

FDR used Poland as "one outstanding example of joint action by the three major Allies in the liberated areas." The Big Three had concurred that Poland would be "a strong, independent and prosperous nation." This had been "agreed to by Russia, by Britain and *by me*. [Emphasis added.]"

Among other things, the Big Three had decided on the territorial changes concerning Poland, with the Soviet Union annexing eastern Poland and the northern half of German East Prussia, and Poland annexing the southern half of East Prussia and all German lands east of the Oder-Neisse Rivers. FDR admitted that in making these territorial adjustments, "*I didn't agree* with all of it by any means" and Churchill and Stalin did not "go as far as *I wanted* in certain areas. [Emphasis added.]"

The Big Three had also agreed on the establishment of a new international peace organization—the United Nations. FDR admitted: "I am well aware of the constitutional fact—as are all the United Nations—that [the UN] charter must be approved by two-thirds of the Senate of the United States." But "world peace is not a party question—I think that Republicans want peace just as much as Democrats—any more than is military victory." The country had united for the cause of winning the war. "The same consecration to the cause of peace will be expected by every patriotic American and by every human soul overseas."

Franklin Roosevelt told the American people that "the conference in the Crimea was a turning point in American history." In establishing the United Nations and America's new role as an active and permanent participant in political and military affairs around the world, "we shall have to take the responsibility for world collaboration, or we shall have to bear the responsibility for another world conflict."

Finally, FDR said:

> I know that the word "planning" is not looked upon with favor in some quarters. In domestic affairs, tragic mistakes have been made by reason of lack of planning; and on the other hand, many great improvements in living, and many benefits to the human race, have been accomplished as a result of adequate, intelligent planning—reclamations of desert areas, developments of whole river valleys, provision of adequate housing.
>
> The same will be true in relations between nations. . . . To meet that objective, the nations of the world will either have a plan or they will not. The groundwork of a plan has now been furnished, and has been submitted to humanity for discussion and decision.
>
> The Crimean Conference was a successful effort by the three leading nations to find a common ground for peace. . . . We propose . . . a universal organization in which all peace-loving nations will finally have a chance to join.

And I am confident that the Congress and the American people will accept the results of this Conference as the beginnings of a permanent structure of peace upon which we can begin to build, under God, that better world in which our children and grandchildren—yours and mine, the children and grandchildren of the whole world—must live.

Fifty years have passed since Franklin Roosevelt signed the Yalta Agreements and delivered his address to the American people concerning its content and its meaning for the future of the United States. The truest statement in FDR's address was: "The conference in the Crimea was a turning point in American history." United States government policy has never been the same again. It not only formalized America's new role as a political and military interventionist in global events, it also radically changed the implicit powers of the presidency in diplomatic and foreign affairs.

When Roosevelt reported back to the Congress and the American people, he was not asking for their formal approval or constitutional consent for any of the agreements he had made with Churchill and Stalin—other than the Senate's approval for U.S. membership in the United Nations. The "Protocol of Proceedings" had been signed by FDR on the basis of executive power; through his signature, he committed the United States to policies concerning Europe and Asia that affected the lives and liberties of tens of millions of people.

Roosevelt envied the fact that Stalin was a power unto himself. "What helps a lot," FDR said, "is that Stalin is the only man I have to convince. Joe doesn't worry about a Congress or a Parliament. He is the whole works." At Yalta, FDR acted with the same dictatorial style. The future of Poland had been "agreed to by Russia, by Britain and *by me*," even though in his negotiations with Russia and Britain, "*I didn't agree* with all of it," nor did the agreements "go as far as *I* wanted in certain areas. [Emphasis added.]" The personal pronouns "me" and "I" had become synonymous with the United States in Roosevelt's mind. One is reminded of the eighteenth-century French monarch who boastfully declared: "I am the State." This is what "personal diplomacy" meant, not only to the Red Czar in the Kremlin, but to the American Global New Dealer, as well.

Roosevelt could trade away the freedom of the Baltic peoples of Estonia, Latvia, and Lithuania and joke with Stalin that he certainly had no intention of going to war with Soviet Russia over them. And besides, FDR was "personally confident" that if these people, and

190

those living in eastern Poland, were given the chance to vote, they would freely opt for incorporation in the Soviet Union. Since FDR already knew in his own mind how these people would vote if they could, it was not necessary to make an issue of it and upset "Uncle Joe."

After all, FDR had his "hunch" that "if I give [Stalin] everything I possibly can and ask nothing from him in return, *noblesse oblige*—he won't try to annex anything and will work with me for a world of democracy and peace." In his own peculiar fantasy, Russian communists had an "almost mystical devotion to this idea" of really wanting "to do what is good for their society instead of wanting to do for themselves." After his meetings with Stalin at Tehran and Yalta, FDR had been convinced "that something entered into [Stalin's] nature of the way in which a Christian gentleman should behave."

Alas, as we have seen, Roosevelt's magnanimous generosity only convinced Stalin's suspicious, paranoid mind that FDR must have been laying a trap for him. "And Roosevelt? He dips in his hand only for bigger coins," Stalin had said. Years after the war, former Soviet Foreign Minister Vychaslav Molotov reflected back on his and Stalin's view of FDR during the years of the wartime alliance and said: "Roosevelt was an imperialist who would grab anyone by the throat. . . . Roosevelt believed only in dollars. . . . Roosevelt thought [we] would come groveling to [him]." Lost in the clouds of his self-made Olympian heights, FDR did not imagine that Stalin—the "Christian gentleman"—might see the world differently than himself. (Some people had understood Stalin's mind-set. Gen. John R. Deane, head of the American military mission in Moscow during the war, wrote Gen. George Marshall in December 1944: "We never make a request or a proposal to the Soviets that is not viewed with suspicion. They simply cannot understand giving without taking, and as a result even our giving is viewed with suspicion.")

In his address before Congress, FDR lied to the American people. He said, towards the end of his speech, that the agreement made at the Yalta Conference "spells the end of the system of unilateral action and exclusive alliances and spheres of influence and balances of power and all the other expedients which have been tried for centuries—and have failed."

At both the Tehran and Yalta meetings, Franklin Roosevelt practiced those very "expedients which have been tried for centuries." He gave his consent—as the president of the United States—for Stalin to view the countries and peoples of Eastern Europe as his own, to do with as he chose. He told Averell Harriman that "he didn't care whether the countries bordering on Russia became communized." He made his deals with Stalin for geographical spheres of influence—Roosevelt only asked that Stalin keep it a secret because FDR did not want to risk losing Polish votes in an election if the truth was made public.

When Harriman objected to FDR's secret protocol handing over Chinese territory to the Soviet Union, Roosevelt said that "he was not going to quarrel with Stalin" because the phrases used in the protocol were, after all, "just language." And words were meant for manipulation in the mind of the great "fireside-chat" communicator.

All of the lies, deceptions, and secret deals were justified in Roosevelt's mind because they were all for a good cause—a new world peace organization—the United Nations. Here, at least, Roosevelt was more honest in his address to the American people. He told them that what he wanted was a system of central planning for global peace. How wonderful planning had been at home! It had reclaimed the desert for cultivation; it had developed the Tennessee Valley; it had constructed public housing! Roosevelt still had a nostalgia for those early, happy New Deal days when industry was regulated through government-mandated cartels, when agriculture was managed through government price and production controls, and when Americans—from common laborers to artists and writers—were set to work making a new America—all according to Washington's central plans.

The entire world would be given its own New Deal. But central planning implies the existence of central planners. The global peace planners and enforcers were to be Big Three, with the assistance of "lesser" powers chosen by the Three Great Powers. America, Britain, and Soviet Russia had fought and won the war for the world; therefore, might as well as self-appointed "right" made it obvious who should plan and police the world's future. Each nation would have its voice in the UN General Assembly, but power and control would reside in the Security Council, where authority for the use of force against nations labeled "aggressors" would be in the monopolistic hands of Britain, France, China, Soviet Russia, and the United States.

In Roosevelt's mind, the issues of peace and war, global stability and world security would be in the hands and control of these five central-planning Great Powers. They would have the final say as to who were the guilty parties in an international dispute; they would determine the form and severity of the punishment to be borne by the country they tagged as the aggressor; they would have the power to blockade, bomb, or invade the guilty country.

True, under the UN Security Council rules, the decisions would have to be unanimous among the Big Five, since each one of them was given the power to veto Security Council resolutions. But this also meant that if The Five agreed, the country labeled the aggressor—regardless of the strength of its own argument—was faced with the potentially combined military force of the most powerful nations in the world. It also meant that if one of the Big Five were to be an aggressor, the other four would be left powerless to act within the rules of the Security Council, since the aggressor among the global central planners would surely veto any decisions deleterious to its own interests.

This was the New World Order, according to Franklin Roosevelt—his and the Yalta Conference's legacy to the postwar world. His vision and style of executive rule have been the precedents that every American president since him has followed.

Part IX—
Yalta's Postwar Legacy on American Foreign Policy

The Yalta Conference formalized the configuration of the post–World War II era for almost half a century. It codified the division of Europe into East and West. It opened Asia to communist expansion. It assured the establishment of the United Nations and the idea of the global policeman. It heralded America's permanent and prominent intervention on the world stage of international politics.

Every one of these postwar results of the Yalta Conference can be laid at the feet of Franklin Delano Roosevelt. As the practitioner of personal diplomacy through the tool of executive power, FDR either produced these results through his agreements with Stalin and Churchill or created the conditions for them to happen.

Defenders of the Yalta accords have argued that the protocol devoted to a "Declaration on Liberated Europe" said nothing about a division of Europe into spheres of influence. Technically, this is true. The agreement required free, democratic elections to be held in the countries liberated from Nazi occupation, with each of these nations having the liberty to choose the political systems it desired. But for both Roosevelt and Stalin, public statements and formal agreements were only the cover and propaganda tools for behind-the-scenes understandings.

Roosevelt had promised the American people during the 1940 presidential campaign that he had no intention of getting the U.S. into a foreign war. He also emphasized that he had not committed the United States to war through any secret agreements with England or any other belligerent power. Yet, at the very time he was publicly making these statements, he had in fact committed the United States to eventually fight on England's side against Germany. FDR used a conflict with Japan as the "back door to war," while all the time assuring the American people that he wanted to avoid a confrontation in the Pacific. Deception and lies behind public promises were part of Franklin Roosevelt's stock and trade, no less than Joseph Stalin's.

Behind the public promises at the Yalta Conference, FDR had made his private agreements with Stalin concerning the Soviet dictator's free hand to do what he wished in Eastern Europe, just as Churchill had made his own private agreements with Stalin behind Roosevelt's back about spheres of influence in the Balkans. Of course, unless the United States had been ready to go to war with the Soviet Union, Stalin was going to be able to do whatever he wanted in the countries "liberated" by the Red Army.

But what the Yalta accords gave the Red Czar was legitimacy. Using his own Marxian definitions of "democracy" and "freedom," Stalin—and later his Soviet inheritors—could claim the right to impose their own will and political order on the unfortunate people in this part of the world. Robert Nisbet correctly expressed it:

> Yalta performed a service to the Soviets that was almost as important to Stalin as the occupied areas themselves. This was the invaluable service of giving *moral legitimation* to what Stalin had acquired by sheer force. The Declaration on Liberated Europe alone accomplished that.

Roosevelt's secret deal with Stalin for Soviet entry into the war in the Pacific did the same. In the Atlantic Charter of August 1941, FDR had pledged that the United States neither wanted nor endorsed the forced transfer of people and lands. Yet, to win Stalin's promise to join in the war against Japan, FDR gave the Soviet dictator control over railroads and seaports in Manchuria—in violation of his own public promises to the Chinese government that all areas of China occupied by the Japanese would be returned. This gave Stalin the political control he wanted in the most industrialized part of China; moreover, the presence of Soviet troops in northeastern China also served as a springboard for the eventual conquest of mainland China by Mao Tse-tung's communist armies. Stalin not only allowed Mao's guerrilla forces to flood into Manchuria behind Soviet Red Army lines, but he also turned over large amounts of captured Japanese military equipment to Mao's armies.

The communist conquest of China was assured in the late 1940s when the Truman Administration imposed an arms embargo on China, following Chiang Kai-shek's refusal to form a coalition government with Mao Tse-tung. (That Chiang's Nationalist government was both authoritarian and corrupt does not change the fact that U.S. policy towards China during and after the war helped tip the scales in favor of a communist victory in that country.)

The establishment of the United Nations legitimized the idea of the right of some nations of the world to impose their conception of order, stability, and peace on the rest of the globe. Frank Chodorov introduced a special issue of *The Freeman* (March 1955) devoted to the topic of "One Worldism and the United Nations" with the following summary of the problem:

In any of its forms, One Worldism is interventionism; it is the conceit that absolute wisdom resides in some people, who are duty-bound to impose their special gift on the less enlightened. It rules out the idea that the peoples of the world might be happier if permitted to live by the particular cultures that time has evolved for them. They must be brought to conform to the perfect formula. But people do not readily give up their accustomed way of living and thinking and are resentful of interference from the outside. Hence, the very premise of One Worldism, or interventionism, leads to friction, not to peace and good will. . . . It is this conviction of "manifest destiny"—of a divine mandate to improve mankind—that makes One Worldism a threat to peace.

However, the establishment of a uniform global order, under the supervision and command of the United Nations, was going to work in the post–World War II era only if the Big Five of the Security Council were unanimous in their courses of action. But this was not the case. First Stalin and then the later dictators of the Soviet Union had a conception of a world order different from that of the political leaders of the United States. These conflicting visions of world order were the basis of the Cold War.

If Stalin would not join the United States in imposing a particular world order and instead insisted on an alternative and rival vision of One Worldism, then the United States would go it alone with its own allies on its side of the Iron Curtain. The United States took on the mantle of Global Policeman in the face of Soviet-led communist revolution in various parts of the world. America was now burdened with intervening in endless conflicts and fighting any number of wars anywhere in the world in the name of securing perpetual global peace and freedom.

When North Korea invaded South Korea in June 1950 with the support of Stalin, President Harry Truman immediately committed U.S. air, naval, and ground troops to the defense of South Korea. He neither asked for nor received a congressional declaration of war for American participation in a conflict on a far-off peninsula of the Asian mainland. With the Soviet representative absent from the Security Council, the United States pushed through a resolution in the United Nations calling for military support of the South Koreans. That became the rationale for U.S. leadership in a three-year war that cost the lives of 54,250 Americans and another 103,300 wounded.

On January 4, 1951, President Truman announced that he was sending sizable, additional U.S. ground troops to Europe. A week later, he stated that he did not need and would not request congressional approval for this expanded military commitment to NATO. "Under the President's constitutional powers as Commander in Chief of the Armed Forces," Truman said, "he has the authority to send troops anywhere in the world. . . . We will continue to send troops wherever it is necessary. . . ."

In 1962, during the first stages of the Cuban missile crisis, President John Kennedy imposed a quarantine around Cuba with no congressional approval. When Kennedy was asked at a press conference if he desired or needed congressional approval for actions that were bringing the United States to the edge of thermonuclear war, he replied: "No." But if Congress wished to put itself on record supporting his actions, "I think it would be useful, if they desired to do so, for them to express their view."

In August 1964, President Lyndon Johnson submitted the Gulf of Tonkin Resolution to the Congress. Arguing that North Vietnamese naval vessels had carried out unprovoked attacks against U.S. military ships in international waters off the Vietnamese coast, the president obtained congressional approval to take "all necessary measures to repel any armed attack against the forces of the United States and to prevent any further aggression." The resolution also declared that the United States, "as the President determines," shall "take all necessary steps, including the use of armed force," to assist Vietnam, Cambodia, and Laos in defense of their freedom.

While the resolution appeared to have been prepared in response to the North Vietnamese attack, in fact, it had been conceived in February and written up in draft form in May—three months before the incident in the Tonkin Gulf. Later investigations determined that the U.S. naval vessels were not on a "routine patrol in international waters," as Secretary of Defense Robert McNamara testified before Congress. Instead, the U.S. ships were providing support for South Vietnamese commando attacks in North Vietnam. Furthermore, the first incident—on August 2—was too minor to warrant a congressional resolution; and the second incident—on August 4—may never have occurred. Later testimony suggested that radar on the USS *Maddox* may have confused freak weather effects for supposed gunfire from North Vietnamese boats. And sonarmen aboard the *Maddox* may have misinterpreted torpedoes for what were reflections from the *Maddox*'s own evasive weaving turns.

A few weeks before the November 1964 presidential election, President Johnson assured the American people that "we are not about to send American boys 9 or 10,000 miles away from home to do what Asian boys ought to be doing for themselves." Yet, within a few years, half a million American boys were fighting and dying 10,000 miles away from home in the Vietnamese jungles. By the time U.S. participation in the war ended in the early 1970s, 58,135 Americans had died and 153,000 had been wounded.

President George Bush announced in December 1989, while Congress was out of session, that he was sending 11,000 soldiers to Panama to secure the safety of Americans in that country and to arrest Panamanian general Manuel Noriega, who was accused of being a dictator and a drug dealer. In August 1990, following the invasion of Kuwait by Iraq, President Bush began sending troops to Saudi Arabia, without congressional approval. Instead, he acted under the authority of the United Nations. In January 1991, American forces began an aerial bombardment of Iraq, which was followed by a ground invasion of Kuwait and Iraq. During the 1992 presidential campaign, President Bush said: "I didn't have to get permission from some old goat in the United States Congress to kick Saddam Hussein out of Kuwait."

With or without the United Nations, with or without the consent of Congress, every president since Franklin Roosevelt has taken up his scepter of executive power. Whether it has been sending American soldiers off to war in foreign lands or undertaking covert operations against the governments of other countries, for half a century the constitutional restraints on the warmaking and foreign-entangling tendencies of presidents have been trampled underfoot. Deceptions and distortions of facts have been the tools of the trade of presidents and their executive agents.

Whether it be in the Cold War era of Soviet-American rivalry, or the post–Cold War era of new nationalism and regional conflicts, one American administration after another has taken it for granted that the United States is to plan and police the political order of the world. Whether it has been Democratic or Republican administrations, the assumption has been that America is to socially engineer the planet for a better tomorrow.

This conception of America's role in the world is the most persistent legacy of Franklin Roosevelt's World War II policies and the Yalta agreements. It is the natural outgrowth of the interventionist and planning mentality that dominated America and the world in the 1930s. It is the mentality of the dictator—the Leader—who must guide or compel people to a better, promised land, because they are too ignorant, or too weak, or too corrupt to guide themselves to that better life. And the Leader cannot be constrained by anachronistic notions of constitutional limits on executive power to intervene into the controversies, problems, and affairs of other people.

The Berlin Wall has fallen, the Cold War division of Europe has ended, and the Soviet Empire that Stalin built is gone. These legacies of the Yalta Conference have now passed into history, along with the millions of innocent victims who were the pawns in FDR's and Stalin's personal diplomacy. But the messianic drive to plan for and lead a New World Order persists in the thinking of too many of those who guide and determine foreign policy in the United States, regardless of their political party label. As long as this remains the case, the lives, liberties, and fortunes of the American people will be at risk—as cannon fodder for global social engineering. Only when this legacy of the Yalta Conference passes into history, as well, will Americans and much of the world have a greater chance for the peace and freedom for which they have yearned for five decades.

This essay originally appeared in the February through May and the July through November 1995 issues of Freedom Daily, *published by The Future of Freedom Foundation.*

23

Repatriation—
The Dark Side of World War II

by Jacob G. Hornberger

When Hitler's forces invaded the Soviet Union in June 1941, millions of Russians welcomed and embraced the Nazi military forces. In many instances, Russian soldiers willingly surrendered to the Germans. The German invasion of the Soviet Union was the beginning of what would ultimately become one of the darkest episodes of World War II—the forcible repatriation and mass murder of millions of anticommunist, anti-Stalinist Russians.

At the center of one of the most fascinating and horrific stories of World War II was a Russian general named Andrey Vlasov. Vlasov was born in 1900 in the small village of Lomakino in the province of Nizhni Novgorod. He was one of eight children. His parents were peasants who did everything they could to see that their children received an education. Vlasov attended religious schools but finally decided to study agriculture.

During the Russian Revolution—in 1919—Vlasov was called up to serve in the Red Army. He was commissioned an officer and led men into battle against the White Army. Sven Steenberg, in his book *Vlasov*, quotes the November 21, 1940, issue of the *Red Star*: "He understood how 'to win respect, lead men, bind them to himself, and at the same time increase their self-confidence.'"

At the end of the Revolution, Vlasov decided to remain in the army, rising to the rank of colonel by the late 1930s. Then, Stalin commenced his infamous purge against the Russian officer corps. Estimates of the casualties differ, but Steenberg says:

> According to conservative estimates, about thirty thousand officers were arrested. Three of the Red Army's 5 marshals were liquidated, 13 out of 19 army commanders, more than half of the 186 division commanders. Even their families were not spared.

Vlasov survived the purge. But, as Steenberg points out, he was undoubtedly deeply affected by Stalin's murder of so many of his fellow officers and compatriots.

On June 4, 1940, Vlasov—at the age of 39—was promoted to major general. His wife, a doctor whom he had married in 1933, bore him a son. Many years before, she had had to disavow her parents because they were "kulaks"—rich peasants—traitors to communism. But Vlasov continued to secretly support them. And Vlasov also maintained another family secret—his older brother Ivan had been murdered by the communists in 1919.

In the fall of 1941, German forces were twenty-five miles from Moscow. The city was in a panic. Stalin ordered Vlasov to Moscow and appointed him commander of the Twentieth Army, whose mission was to assist in the halting of the German assault on Moscow. Vlasov took command and counterattacked the Germans, halting their advance and helping to save the city.

In January 1942, Vlasov's army took part in an offensive near the city of Leningrad. The battle went badly for the Russians, and Vlasov requested permission to retreat. Stalin refused and ordered continued attacks against the Germans. Vlasov flew to Moscow to explain the urgency of the need to retreat. Stalin again refused the request. Vlasov returned to his forces, who were now in danger of being surrounded.

At this point, Vlasov received a note from his wife that said, "Guests were here." In the midst of this crucial battle, Stalin had sent the secret police to search Vlasov's home and question his family.

The Germans surrounded Vlasov and his army. For two weeks, the general avoided capture by secreting himself in the swamps that covered the battlegrounds. And those two weeks alone in the Russian swamps caused Andrey Vlasov to do a lot of questioning and much soul-searching about the plight of Russia and her future. One day, a Russian mayor disclosed Vlasov's hiding place to German forces. Vlasov surrendered to the German army.

From the first grade in their public schools, Americans are taught the evils of Adolf Hitler and Nazi Germany. "If we had not entered World War II, Hitler would have conquered the world," Americans are taught. "There is no way that the world could have tolerated the continuation of the Nazi regime. It was necessary for tens of thousands of Americans to die to stop Hitler."

Yet, there is one uncomfortable fallacy with this reasoning. The United States and the Western world survived something even worse—the regime of Joseph Stalin and the rise and domination of the communist empire. Obviously, the world would have been better off without the evils and horrors of both Hitler and Stalin. But if we had to end up with one of them, who is to say that Stalin was better than Hitler? If we survived in a world of Stalin and communism, then why couldn't we have survived in a world of Hitler and Nazism?

Let us recall why Great Britain and France declared war on Germany in the first place (it was not Germany that declared war on them first). Hitler had invaded Czechoslovakia and Austria, obviously with the intention of ultimately moving east against the Russians. In fact, contrary to popular opinion, the evidence that Hitler ever intended to invade the West is scant. For one, Hitler considered himself a Westerner. Moreover, he had already expressed his desire for *Lebensraum*—"living space"—in Russia.

When Germany threatened to invade Poland, the British and French emphasized that they would come to Poland's aid. But this was a hollow guarantee. There was no way that England and France had sufficient military forces to enforce the guarantee. Nevertheless, once the attack on Poland took place, England and France declared war on Germany. The specific goal of British and French intervention was to liberate the people of Poland and Eastern Europe from the clutches of totalitarian dictatorship.

And so what happened at the end of World War II? What were the consequences of the most massive death and destruction that mankind has ever seen? Were the people of Poland and Eastern Europe freed from totalitarian dictatorship?

The parades and speeches in 1995, celebrating the fiftieth anniversary of the winning of World War II, have one primary focus with respect to the European part of the war: the defeat of Adolf Hitler and Nazi Germany. And there is a reason for that: If people begin reflecting on the real consequences of World War II, serious doubts will begin to form, not only about that war but about foreign wars in general—and the continued existence of the U.S. military-industrial complex.

In his campaign for reelection in 1940, Franklin Roosevelt assured Americans that he did not intend to involve the United States in the European conflict. Roosevelt was playing to public-opinion polls, since the overwhelming number of Americans did not want to intervene in the European war. Americans remembered the promises of Woodrow Wilson some twenty years before. If you will permit us to sacrifice your sons on the European battlegrounds, Wilson had told the American people, I promise you that this will be the final war—the war to end all wars—the war to make the world safe for democracy once and for all.

And so tens of thousands of Americans died so that Wilson could have his noble dream. But Wilson was wrong. Within twenty years, the warring factions were at it again. The tens of thousands of Americans who died in the First World War died in vain. They were sacrificed for nothing.

Thus, Americans overwhelmingly supported Roosevelt when he openly declared in a campaign speech on October 30, 1940: "I have said this before, but I shall say it again and again and again: Your boys are not going to be sent into any foreign wars."

Most historians now recognize that Roosevelt knowingly and deliberately lied to the American people. At the very time he was assuring them of his intentions to stay out of the European conflict, he was making secret commitments to England to help maintain the British Empire in the Far East. He was doing his best to goad German submarines into attacking American vessels. And he ultimately found the "back door" to war by goading the Japanese in the Pacific. (See Chapter 15, "December 7, 1941: The Infamy of FDR," pp. 119–23 and Chapter 16, "Pearl Harbor: The Controversy Continues," pp. 125–29.) Franklin D. Roosevelt lied his way to reelection. And the result was another American intervention into a European war.

What were the results at the end of the war? Fifty million deaths. Tens of millions uprooted. Four trillion dollars in direct costs. The most massive destruction of property that mankind has ever seen. Acts of extreme brutality. Firebombings and other terroristic attacks against noncombatants. It was the most horrific event in the history of mankind. (See Chapter 31, "The Consequences of World War II," pp. 263–67.)

But what about the Poles and the Eastern Europeans? After all, they were the specific reason that Great Britain and France had declared war on Germany. Surely, they were free at the end of the war.

Not exactly. And this is what makes American public officials—as well as the American people—so uncomfortable. Yes, it is true that the German invaders were ousted and defeated by the Allied forces. Yes, it is true that the Poles, the Czechs, and the Eastern Europeans were saved from the clutches of Adolf Hitler and Nazi Germany.

But they were delivered into the hands of Joseph Stalin and the communists.

We have been taught to believe that this was a great victory. That this brought freedom to the Eastern Europeans. That one of the great and glorious consequences of World War II was the liberation of the Eastern Europeans by Russian forces. Americans should be proud, we are told, that their sons and daughters died on the battlefield—or returned blinded or maimed—so that the Eastern Europeans could live under Stalin rather than Hitler.

But many Eastern Europeans did not live under Stalin. Instead, they died under him. For Stalin—this wonderful ally of Franklin D. Roosevelt—was one of the most brutal mass murderers in all of history. While it is difficult to compare evil, Stalin has to be considered much worse than Hitler.

Certainly, he was responsible for the deaths of many more people than Hitler. The estimates of Russian deaths under Joseph Stalin are estimated to be forty million (yes, forty million individuals!), including the approximately ten million killed as a result of Stalin's collectivization of the Russian farms in the early 1930s. Even Hitler (who killed twenty million individuals!) did not come close to matching these numbers.

Ask the Poles about the mass murder at the Katyn Forest. For decades, Russian and American government officials had scoffed at the notion that, in 1940, Russian military forces had rounded up 13,000 defenseless Polish military officers, taken them to the Katyn Forest, and shot them in cold blood. Instead, the claim was that the murder was committed by Nazi forces. Now, some forty years later, the Russians themselves have admitted that it was the communists— the great liberators of Poland and Eastern Europe—the great humanitarians—the great allies of England and the United States—who committed the murders.

Yes, the Poles were freed from the clutches of Adolf Hitler . . . so that they could live, suffer, and die at the hands of their freedom-loving liberators, Joseph Stalin and his communist comrades.

Why don't Americans have the same prejudice against Joseph Stalin that they have against Adolf Hitler? Why are brutal foreign dictators always referred to by American public officials as another Adolf Hitler rather than another Joseph Stalin?

One answer is that it is too painful to confront the reality of what happened to the Poles, the Czechs, and the Eastern Europeans at the end of the war—and for some forty years after that. Life under Nazism was not pleasant. But neither was life under communism. To confront the reality of who specifically won control of Poland and Eastern Europe is to confront the reason why so many Americans died in Europe: so that communism, not Nazism, would reign supreme in Eastern Europe.

Moreover, Franklin D. Roosevelt, who is portrayed in American history books as one of this country's greatest presidents, considered Joseph Stalin his friend. He even referred to this mass murderer as "Uncle Joe." Furthermore, since victory in World War II is always portrayed as an Allied one, Americans have a tendency to think of the three Western leaders—Churchill, Roosevelt, and Stalin—as "all the same."

In a sense, Americans are right. For all three Allied leaders had the same ideological orientation. That is, all three believed that one of the proper roles of government was to own or control the means or results of production. The labels varied according to the country— socialism, communism, the welfare state, the planned economy, the New Deal. But the principles underlying the labels were the same. When it came to economic principles, Churchill, Roosevelt, and Stalin were cut out of the same ideological cloth.

But this was not the only similarity among the three leaders of the Allied Powers. All three, as well as FDR's successor Harry S. Truman, shared another similarity with their counterpart Adolf Hitler: all five of them participated in the mass murder of millions of innocent people. And this brings us back to the issue at hand—the dark episode in history that American officials kept secret for so long—Andrey Vlasov, forcible repatriation, and the mass murder of millions of anticommunist and anti-Stalinist Russian people.

The Smolensk Declaration

Hitler, Stalin, Roosevelt, Churchill, and Truman shared two things in common—their philosophical belief on the role of government in economic activity and their participation in the mass murder of millions of innocent people.

All of them believed that government should own or control the means or results of production. Thus, each of them helped lead their respective nations down the collectivist road—to Nazism, fascism, the welfare state, the planned economy, the New Deal, and so forth.

But the misery and destitution that their economic philosophy brought to the citizenry of their countries were nothing compared to the tremendous evil associated with the holocausts in which these world leaders participated.

Hitler's holocaust, of course, is well known—six million people died in the Nazi gas chambers. Less well known is the holocaust in which two million innocent Russians were massacred through the joint participation of the United States, Great Britain, and Russia.

Americans have been taught to believe that World War II was a war of good versus evil. Unfortunately, the analysis is not that simple. For one thing, the United States and Great Britain were allied with one of the most evil political regimes in all of history—Stalinist Russia. There is nothing that Hitler and Nazi Germany did that communist Russia did not do. Hitler killed millions of innocent people. So did Stalin. Germany attacked Czechoslovakia and Austria. Russia attacked Finland. Germany invaded Poland. Russia did so at the exact same time. In fact, it is difficult to understand why Great Britain and France declared war only on Germany rather than on both Germany and Russia—both Germany and Russia had engaged in the exact same evils.

If France and Great Britain had not declared war on Germany, there is no doubt that Germany and the Soviet Union would have ultimately gone to war against each other. The Nazis hated the communists; and the communists hated the Nazis. With his move into Eastern Europe, Hitler was clearly moving eastward. And the overwhelming evidence is that Stalin was preparing to attack Germany. (See the review of *Icebreaker: Who Started the Second World War?* in Chapter 18, pp. 135–37.)

So, when Germany finally attacked Russia, the war on the eastern front became one of Nazism versus communism—not exactly a wonderful choice for either Germans or Russians. But for thousands of Russians, anything was better than the mass murderer Joseph Stalin and his communist regime. It would have been virtually impossible to find a Russian family who had not had a friend or relative killed by Stalin's forces. And political terror existed all across the nation.

Thus, thousands of Russian people had nothing but hate for— and fear of—Joseph Stalin and his communist regime. This was the reason that when Germany invaded Russia, thousands of Russians viewed the Germans as liberators rather than as conquerors.

When Andrey Vlasov was captured near Leningrad, the Germans knew that they had bagged a big prize. Vlasov was one of Stalin's most brilliant and courageous generals. The Germans removed Vlasov to a POW camp back in Germany.

There, Vlasov met many other Russian POWs. They began talking among themselves about Stalin, communism, the war, and Russia. Most of them shared two things in common—their hatred for

Stalin and communism and their love for their country. After much soul-searching, deliberation, and reflection, the Russian POWs persuaded the Germans to permit them to form a Russian army to fight Stalin's forces. And they elected Andrey Vlasov as their commanding general.

Of course, this raises questions with respect to the meaning of patriotism. Were Vlasov and his men patriots or traitors? One might argue that they were traitors because they were opposing their own government during wartime. If that is the test for patriotism, then what about German citizens, like Marlene Dietrich, who opposed Hitler—were they patriots or traitors?

Vlasov and his men believed that patriotism meant more than blindly supporting one's government. Stalin was a mass murderer, they reasoned, who had brought nothing but misery and destitution to the Russian people. Their goal was to eradicate the communist regime and establish an independent and free Russia. Here are excerpts from "The Smolensk Declaration," issued by Vlasov on December 27, 1942:

> An appeal by the Russian Committee to the men and officers of the Red Army, to the whole Russian nation, and to the other nations of the Soviet Union.

> Friends and Brothers!
> Bolshevism is the enemy of the Russian people. It has brought countless disasters to our country and finally has involved the Russian people in a bloody war waged in others' interests. This war has brought unheard-of sufferings to our Motherland. Millions of Russians have already paid with their lives for Stalin's criminal attempts to seize world-wide power to the profit of Anglo-American capitalists. Millions of Russians have been crippled and have lost their ability to work forever. Women, old people and children are dying of cold, starvation and because the work demanded of them is beyond their strength. Hundreds of Russian cities and thousands of villages have been destroyed, blown up and burned on Stalin's orders.

> Defeats such as those experienced by the Red Army have never happened before in the history of our country. In spite of the selflessness of the troops and officers and the bravery and self-sacrifice of the Russian people, battle after battle has been

206

lost. The fault lies with the rottenness of the whole of the Bolshevik system, and the incompetence of Stalin and his general staff.

At this very moment, when Bolshevism has shown itself to be incapable of organising the country's defences, Stalin and his clique make use of terror and lying propaganda to drive people to their deaths, for they want to remain in power, at least for a while, regardless of the cost in blood to the Russian people.

Stalin's allies—the British and American capitalists—have betrayed the Russian people. . . .

The Russian Committee has set itself the following aims:

a. The overthrow of Stalin and his clique, the destruction of Bolshevism.

b. The conclusion of an honourable peace with Germany.

c. The creation, in friendship with Germany and the other peoples of Europe, of a "New Russia" without Bolsheviks and Capitalists.

The Declaration then set forth thirteen specific goals, including the abolition of forced labor; the abolition of collective farms and their return to private ownership; the "re-establishment of commerce, trades and crafts" and "private initiative"; and the "complete dismantling of the regime of terror and the introduction of genuine freedom of religion, conscience, speech, assembly and the press; the guarantee of inviolability of persons and of their homes."

In March 1943, Vlasov published an open letter entitled "Why I decided to fight Bolshevism," which stated in part the following:

Inasmuch as I am calling on all Russian people to fight against Stalin and his clique, to build a "New Russia" without Bolsheviks and Capitalists, I consider it my duty to explain my actions. . . .

I am the son of a peasant, and was born in the province of Nizhni Novgorod. . . . During the Civil War, I fought with the Red Army because I believed that the Revolution would give the Russian people land, freedom and happiness. When I became a commander in the Red Army, I lived with the men and their officers—Russian workers, peasants, and members of the intelligentsia, all of them dressed in grey [army issue] overcoats. I knew their thoughts, their worries and problems. I did not lose touch with my family and my village and was familiar with the ways and means of the peasantry.

And so I realised that none of those things for which the Russian people had fought during the Civil War had been achieved by Bolshevik victory. I saw what a difficult life a Russian worker led and how the peasant was forcibly driven to join the collective farms. Millions of Russian people disappeared, having been arrested and shot without trial. I saw that everything Russian was being destroyed, that time-servers were being given positions of command in the Red Army, people to whom the interests of the Russian nation were of no importance. . . .

From 1938 to 1939 I was in China as military adviser to Chiang Kai-shek. When I returned to the USSR, I saw that during that time the command structure of the army had been destroyed for no reason whatsoever on Stalin's orders. Thousands of the best officers, including the Marshals of the Red Army, had been arrested and shot or sent to the labour camps to disappear forever. Terror was unleashed not only on the army but on the whole nation. There was no family which was not involved in some way or other. The army was weakened, the terrified nation looked to the future with horror, awaiting the war which Stalin had made inevitable. . . .

While I was in the forests and swamps [avoiding capture], I finally came to the conclusion that my duty consisted in calling on the Russian people to fight to overthrow Bolshevik power, to fight for peace for the Russian people, to fight for an end to an unnecessary war being fought for foreign interests which was spilling Russian blood, to fight for the creation of a New Russia, in which every Russian might be happy. . . .

I reached the firm conclusion that the tasks facing the Russian people can be solved in alliance and cooperation with the German people.

Of course, the logical question is, how could Vlasov cooperate with the Nazis? After all, Hitler and the Nazis were not any different from Stalin and the communists. Vlasov knew that if he was to help liberate Russia from communist rule, he had no choice but to work with the Germans. His attitude was the same as the American and British toward Stalin and the communists—politics and war sometimes make strange bedfellows. But Vlasov also believed that he could ultimately maneuver the German political leaders into guaranteeing a free and independent Russia.

Little did Vlasov and his men know that their attempt to liberate their nation from communist tyranny would ultimately result in one of the worst holocausts in history—this one provided by Roosevelt, Truman, Churchill, and Stalin.

Operation Keelhaul

Adolf Hitler did not trust Andrey Vlasov. The Russian general had served in the Russian army since the Russian Revolution. He had fought hard and valiantly in the successful defense of Moscow. It was only because of Stalin's refusal to permit Vlasov and his men to retreat during the subsequent battle at Leningrad that the German forces had defeated and captured Vlasov. It was difficult for Hitler to believe that Vlasov was now willing to lead captured Russian soldiers against Stalin and his communist regime.

So it was not until the very end of the war—January 1945—that Hitler finally relented and permitted Vlasov to lead Russian POWs into battle against the Russian army. But by this time, Germany was close to defeat. The forces under Vlasov's command—some 50,000 Russian soldiers—played a minor military role in the war.

Ironically, Vlasov's forces did have one very interesting military victory. The Czech underground sought their assistance in helping to liberate Czechoslovakia from *Nazi* control! Vlasov, who despised the Nazis as much as he hated the communists, agreed to help. *The Saturday Evening Post* later reported:

> Prague really was liberated by foreign troops, after all. Not by the Allies who did not arrive until the shooting was all over, but by 22,000 Russian outlaws wearing German uniforms. The leader of these renegades was General Vlasov, a former hero of the Red Army.

The battlefield was obviously chaotic. The Russians were approaching from the east. The Americans and British were approaching from the west. Vlasov and his forces were in the middle, and German forces were at his back. On May 7, 1945, Germany capitulated.

Vlasov knew that Stalin was not a forgiving man. After his capture, Vlasov had openly defied the communists and communism. He had tried to arouse the Russian people to revolt against their communist tyrants. Vlasov knew that capture by the communists now meant certain death for him and his men.

Andrey Vlasov chose to surrender to American forces. He did not know that Franklin D. Roosevelt, Harry S. Truman, Winston Churchill, and Joseph Stalin had already sealed his fate. He did not know that these four rulers of the Allied powers had already committed themselves to one of the worst holocausts in history. He did not know that evil pervaded not only the Nazi and communist regimes, but the American and British regimes, as well.

Part of the Yalta Agreement between the Big Three—Stalin, Roosevelt, and Churchill—involved the repatriation of Russians and Americans to their respective homelands. Keep in mind that the German POW camps contained American prisoners, British prisoners, and Russian prisoners. The Big Three agreed that as the Russians liberated Germany POW camps, American and British POWs would be turned over to the American and British forces. As the Americans and British liberated German POW camps, Russian POWs would be returned to Russia.

There was one big problem with this agreement—a problem that each of the Big Three was well aware of. American and British POWs *wanted* to return to their own forces. *Russian POWs did not want to return to Russian forces because they knew the fate that awaited them.*

Stalin wanted revenge. The Russian prisoners were traitors to communism. They deserved to die.

And Roosevelt and Churchill felt the exact same way. Russia was "our friend." Stalin was "Uncle Joe" to the American people. Any Russian who had defied Uncle Joe—any Russian who had opposed our communist friends and allies—deserved to be executed.

The revenge and ensuing holocaust had to be kept secret from the world. The American and British people had to continue maintaining their illusion that this was a war of good versus evil—that only the Nazis engaged in cold-blooded murder—that the Allies epitomized all the goodness of mankind.

Therefore, the Big Three spelled out their plans not just in the official Yalta agreement but, also, in a March 31, 1945, secret codicil to the agreement. As James Sanders, Mark Sauter, and R. Cort Kirkwood point out in their shocking book, *Soldiers of Misfortune* (1992), the codicil was kept secret from the American and British people for fifty years. The codicil outlined the secret plan by which the Russians POWs would be forcibly returned to Stalin's clutches.

American government officials called their part in the holocaust Operation Keelhaul. In his book *Operation Keelhaul* (1973), Julius Epstein described the meaning of the term:

To keelhaul is the cruelest and most dangerous of punishments and tortures ever devised for men aboard a ship. It involves trussing a man up with ropes, throwing him overboard, unable to swim, and hauling him under the boat's keel from one side to the other, or even from stem to stern. Most of those keelhauled under water are already dead when their punishment is over.

And Epstein describes his reaction to the choice of this term by American government officials to describe their part in the Allied holocaust:

That our Armed Forces should have adopted this term as its code name for deporting by brutal force to concentration camp, firing squad, or hangman's noose millions who were already in the lands of freedom, shows how little the high brass thought of their longing to be free.

The roles played by each of the conspirators was clear: Roosevelt and Churchill would force the Russian anticommunists into Stalin's hands. The communists would take over from there and do the actual killing.

How many were turned over to the Russians by American and British forces? *Two million individuals.* Yes, two million Russian people sent back to the communists where they were either immediately executed or sent to die in the Gulag.

It was not easy to "persuade" the Russian prisoners to return to the communists. Sometimes, subterfuge was used. Epstein details several examples. One took place on May 28, 1945, in Linz, Austria. British forces ordered all Cossack officials to attend an important British conference with high British officials. The Cossacks were told to leave their coats since they would be back by six in the evening. Their families were advised so that family members would not worry over their short absence. When the Cossacks appeared nervous, an English officer told them, "I assure you on my word of honor as a British officer that you are just going to a conference."

The 2,749 Cossacks—2,201 of whom were officers—were driven straight into a prison camp and were advised by British officials that Soviet authorities would soon arrive to pick them up. Epstein writes:

One Cossack officer remarked: "The NKVD or the Gestapo would have slain us with truncheons, the British did it with

211

their word of honor." The first to commit suicide by hanging was the Cossack editor Evgenij Tarruski. The second was General Silkin who shot himself. . . . The Cossacks refused to board [the trucks]. British soldiers with pistols and clubs began using their clubs, aiming at the heads of the prisoners. They first dragged the men out of the crowd and threw them into the trucks. The men jumped out. They beat them again and threw them onto the floor of the trucks. Again, they jumped out. The British then hit them with rifle butts until they lay unconscious and threw them like sacks of potatoes in the trucks.

The same scenes were repeated all along the lines—two million Russian people tricked and beaten by British and American forces so that Stalin could finish the job later on.

Some of this dirty work even took place on American soil. Epstein describes what happened to Russian POWs who were imprisoned at Fort Dix, New Jersey:

First, they refused to leave their barracks when ordered to do so. The military police then used tear gas, and, half-dazed, the prisoners were driven under heavy guard to the harbor where they were forced to board a Soviet vessel. Here the two hundred immediately started to fight. They fought with their bare hands. They started—with considerable success—to destroy the ship's engines. . . . A sergeant . . . mixed barbiturates into their coffee. Soon, all of the prisoners fell into a deep, coma-like sleep. It was in this condition that the prisoners were brought to another Soviet boat for a speedy return to Stalin's hangmen.

Andrey Vlasov—the man who hated communism—the man who hated Nazism—carefully explained his position and reasoning to the American generals. In his book *Vlasov*, Sven Steenberg describes Vlasov's conversation with one of his American captors:

He began to speak, at first slowly and dispassionately, but then with growing intensity. For one last time, he spoke of all the prospects, hopes, and disappointments of his countrymen. He summed up everything for which countless Russians had fought and suffered. It was no longer really to the American that he was addressing himself—this was rather a confession, a review of his life, a last protest against the destiny that had brought him to a wretched end. . . . [Vlasov] stated that the leaders of the ROA were ready to appear before an international court, but that it would be a monumental injustice to turn them over to the Soviets and thereby to certain death. It was not a question of volunteers who had served the Germans, but of a political organization, of a broad opposition movement which, in any event, should not be dealt with under military law.

Vlasov could not know that he was a dead man before he even surrendered to American forces. Roosevelt, Stalin, Churchill, and Truman had already decided that he needed to be executed for the "crime" of betraying his own government. There was no need to go through the time, expense, trouble, and possible embarrassment of a trial. All that needed to be done was for the Americans to turn him over to their friendly executioner, "Uncle Joe" Stalin.

American military officials delivered Andrey Vlasov to Soviet military authorities. On August 2, 1946, the Soviet press reported that Andrey Vlasov had been hanged by Soviet officials for "treason as well as active espionage and terrorist activity against the Soviet Union."

Unfortunately, all of the facts of the forcible repatriation of the Russian anticommunists have not been revealed. American and British government officials take the position that "national security" will be jeopardized if the citizenry is ever permitted to know all of the details of the Allied holocaust. Thus, fifty years after World War II, American "adults" are still not permitted by their public officials to see the government's files and records on America's involvement in the "good war" and, specifically, in the Allied holocaust.

As with most claims of "national security," the concern is not so much with the security of the nation but rather with the security of the U.S. government and, specifically, the U.S. military-industrial complex. For it is entirely possible that the American people will finally pierce through all the lies and deceptions that have clouded their minds since the first grade in the public schools to which their parents were forced to send them. It is quite possible that they will recognize the wisdom of their Founding Fathers—and see that the biggest threat to their well-being lies not with some foreign government, but rather with their own government.

Was the Allied holocaust the end of the repatriation story? Unfortunately, no. The last chapter of Stalin's, Roosevelt's, Truman's, and Churchill's horrid tale of deception, brutality, and murder involves Americans "liberated" from German POW camps by the Russians—and the role played in this chapter by the U.S. government, the same government that has always insisted that the American people "support the troops."

213

Hitler's Youth

To fully understand what happened to American soldiers who were part of the repatriation horror at the end of World War II—and why it happened—it is necessary to examine events in Germany, as well as the United States, that led up to the war.

On January 30, 1933, German President von Hindenberg appointed Adolf Hitler chancellor of Germany. Hitler's appointment at the age of forty-three was a monumental triumph for a man who, just a few years before, had been a penniless vagrant selling his artwork on the streets of Vienna.

In his biography *Adolf Hitler* (1976), John Toland sets forth Hitler's background. Adolf Hitler was born on April 20, 1889, to Alois Hitler and Klara Pölzl. Alois had been born the illegitimate child of Maria Anna Schicklgruber. Alois's father (Adolf's paternal grandfather) was unknown, but there were three possibilities: Johann Nepomuk Hiedler (the man who legitimized Alois, had his name changed, and raised him); his brother Johann Georg Hiedler; or (as Adolf himself probably suspected) a Jew named Frankenberger or Frankenreither.

Alois's marriage to Klara, Adolf's mother, was his third. During his first marriage, he had sired an illegitimate daughter. His wife later attained a legal separation when she caught him having an affair with their kitchen maid, Fanni—the result: Alois's son, Alois Jr. When the estranged wife died, Alois married Fanni. When Fanni died in 1884, Alois had already impregnated Klara, whose grandfather was the brother of Johann Nepomuk Hiedler, the man who had legitimized Alois. In 1885, Alois and Klara were married.

The Hitler home was not a pleasant place. Not only was Alois a philanderer, he was also an alcoholic—a very abusive alcoholic. Obedience was the foremost virtue in the Hitler household. Alois was a German civil servant—a customs inspector—who demanded the absolute allegiance of his children. "Do as you are told and do not ask questions" was the guiding principle of the Hitler household. Disobedience or disrespectful conduct brought immediate retribution onto the Hitler children. Toland points out that "Alois Jr. complained bitterly that his father frequently beat him unmercifully with a hippopotamus whip." When Alois Jr. was caught skipping school, his father "held him 'against a tree by the back of his neck' until he lost consciousness."

Life in the Hitler home was so bad that Alois Jr. ran away from home at the age of fourteen, never to return. Adolf then became the primary focus of his father's abuse. Adolf was continually whipped. He was also made to witness the beatings, as well, of his docile mother Klara. His sister Paula later recalled:

> [It was Adolf] who challenged my father to extreme harshness and who got his sound thrashing every day. He was a scrubby little rogue, and all attempts of his father to thrash him for his rudeness and to cause him to love the profession of an official of the state were in vain. How often on the other hand did my mother caress him and try to obtain with her kindness, where the father could not succeed with harshness!

Years later, Adolf told one of his secretaries:

> I then resolved never again to cry when my father whipped me. A few days later I had the opportunity of putting my will to the test. My mother, frightened, took refuge in front of the door. As for me, I counted silently the blows of the stick which lashed my rear end.

The abuse was not only physical, but emotional, as well. After Alois Jr. ran away, his chores were given to Adolf, who was constantly harangued by his father for failing to meet expectations. One day Adolf decided to run away from home. He had been locked in his room and was trying to escape through the window. To fit in the window, he had to take off his clothes. He heard his father coming up the stairs and covered his nakedness with a tablecloth. His father did not hit him this time but instead, in Klara's presence, teased him unmercifully with the appellation "toga boy." Adolf later confessed that it took him a long time to recover from the ridicule.

It is important to note one vitally important fact about Adolf Hitler's upbringing: The authoritarian family structure under which Adolf Hitler was raised in Austria was not an exception, but rather the rule. Millions of German children were raised under the same creed: Obey; do as you are told; do not talk back; and do not challenge the family system. Moreover, this was the family structure under which their parents, grandparents, and great-grandparents had been raised. The authoritarian patterns stretched back for centuries and had been passed on from generation to generation.

Adolf Hitler's father died on January 3, 1903. His obituary notice in the Linz *Tagespost* said:

At all times an energetic champion of law and order and universally well informed, he was able to pronounce authoritatively on any matter that came to his notice.

At the age of fourteen, Adolf became the man of the household. The authoritarian family environment was gone. Whenever someone asked him what he was going to be, Hitler responded, "A great artist." In 1905, he graduated from a *Realschule* at the age of sixteen.

The following year, Hitler's mother permitted him to visit Vienna, Europe's cultural center. Hitler was captivated by the city. He moved to Vienna in 1907, with the hope of entering the Academy of Fine Arts.

In the meantime, his mother Klara was dying of cancer. A Jewish doctor named Edward Bloch treated her with a very painful process in which the open wounds on her body were treated with a substance called iodoform. On December 21, 1907, Klara died.

Hitler returned to Vienna, where he lived a fairly carefree life of painting and attending cultural events. But he was not accepted by the Academy of Fine Arts, and life got progressively worse for him. His funds that he had inherited were depleted, and he began roaming the streets of Vienna as a vagrant, ending up in a poorhouse where he painted picture postcards for sale. It was during this time that Hitler became an avid reader of anti-Semite literature. Hitler himself wrote in *Mein Kampf* that he became vehemently anti-Semitic in Vienna upon discovering that the Jew was the "cold-hearted, shameless, and calculating director" of prostitution.

In 1913, Hitler moved to Munich, where he continued pursuing his artistic interests. His life as a struggling artist came to a sudden end in 1914. The Austrian heir, Archduke Franz Ferdinand, was assassinated by a Serb terrorist. Austria declared war on Serbia on July 28. Russia mobilized against Austria. German Kaiser Wilhelm II mobilized German forces against Russia. France and England entered the war soon thereafter.

The Austrian and German people were swept away by war fever. People roamed the streets and demanded action. German nationalists were singing: "Heil der Kaiser! Heil das Heer! We must gather all men of German tongues into one Reich and one people. An everlasting master race will then direct the progress of mankind!" As Toland points out, they could have been speaking for Adolf Hitler.

Hitler himself wrote in *Mein Kampf*:

I am not ashamed to say that, overcome with rapturous enthusiasm, I fell to my knees and thanked Heaven from an overflowing heart for granting me the good fortune of being allowed to live at this time.

Hitler, an Austrian, joined the German army and attained the rank of corporal. He served as a regimental messenger, saw combat, was seriously wounded, and ultimately was awarded the Iron Cross "for personal bravery and general merit."

As the war progressed, the European armies fought themselves to a standstill. As the troops on both sides became more and more exhausted, the probability of a negotiated settlement increased. But then the U.S. entered the war, which significantly altered the balance of power. The fresh American troops began pushing the Germans back. It became clear that Germany was going to lose the war.

As defeat loomed for the Germans, German life began to disintegrate. Marxism had already prevailed in Russia during the Bolshevik Revolution in November 1917. But the Marxists were not willing to settle for that triumph. They intended to spread their control to Germany and the rest of the world. Capitalizing on the chaos of war and the impending defeat of Germany, the Marxists began fomenting revolution in cities all across Germany. It was during this time that Hitler's deep-seated and malevolent anti-Semitism became a driving force in his life. For Hitler, like many other Germans, associated Jews with Marxism. From Hitler's perspective, the Jews and Reds were traitors to the Fatherland who, by instigating riots and insurrections on the homefront, were helping the enemy to defeat Germany.

Woodrow Wilson demanded the abdication of the Kaiser before America would agree to an armistice. Wilson's demand accelerated the disintegration of German society. Government after government across the country fell to socialist revolutionaries, many of whom were Jewish. Finally, on November 9, 1918, the Kaiser abdicated and relinquished power to the moderate socialists, led by a former saddlemaker, Frederick Ebert. As Toland points out:

> It was the end of the German Empire, begun in France on January 18, 1871, when Wilhelm I, King of Prussia and grandfather of Wilhelm II, was proclaimed the first Emperor of Germany in the Hall of Mirrors at the Versailles Palace.
>
> It was also the end of an era. Forty-eight years earlier Bismarck had achieved his dream of unifying Germany and in so doing had created a new image of Germany and Germans. Overnight the foundation on which rested the security of the Junker landowners in East Prussia and the great industrialists crumbled; and overnight the political philosophy on which the

majority of Germans had based their conservative and patriotic way of life had apparently disintegrated with the lowering of the imperial flag.

But, as Toland observes, perhaps the greatest shock for the German people was to find Ebert—a socialist and a "man of the people"—sitting as the new German chancellor, in place of a member of the Hohenzollern regime.

When Germany agreed to terms of the Allied armistice, Wilson required the German representatives to assume the responsibility for the war. Little did he know that he was handing Adolf Hitler the tool by which Hitler would later be able to claim that the socialists—the "November criminals"—had sold out Germany to the Allies.

Thus, in 1918, Adolf Hitler became one of the Western world's first anticommunists. Hitler, who himself would become leader of the National Socialist German Workers' Party (Nazi Party), would use his political philosophy of anticommunism to help propel him to the highest reaches of political power in Germany.

The Roosevelt Presidency

When Franklin Roosevelt assumed the presidency in 1933, Americans expected him to fulfill certain promises that he had made during the presidential campaign: balance the budget; lower taxes; reduce government spending; downsize government; and keep the United States out of foreign wars. Americans were in for a surprise. Roosevelt not only broke all of his promises, he also engaged in the most radical restructuring of society in American history.

For over 100 years, Americans had placed individual liberty at the top of their value scale. While there were certainly exceptions (like slavery and tariffs), the following philosophy guided our American ancestors: Individuals come into life with certain talents and abilities. They use these talents to get the food, clothing, and shelter necessary to sustain their lives. In order to improve their own well-being, they enter into trades with others—trades in which both sides mutually benefit. In this process, they begin to accumulate wealth and property. It is the inherent right of the individual to keep the fruits of his earnings and to accumulate unlimited amounts of wealth. It is the right of the individual to decide what to do with that wealth—donate it to the poor, spend it, invest it, or whatever.

Thus, the core of our ancestors' philosophy was that the individual in society—and his right to live his life the way he chooses—are sovereign and supreme. In other words, as long as an individual does not murder, rape, steal, and so forth, he has the

God-given right to be free of government control. In fact, our ancestors believed that one of government's few functions was to protect peaceful individuals as they pursued happiness in their own way.

Thus, it is not a coincidence that for over a century, our ancestors said no to: income taxation, Social Security, Medicare, Medicaid, public schooling, central banking, economic regulations, and the like.

With his New Deal, Franklin Roosevelt abandoned that philosophy. From the day he assumed the presidency, Roosevelt told the American people that what mattered was not the sovereignty of the individual, but rather the sovereignty of the nation—society—the collective. He said that whenever the freedom of the individual collided with the interests of society, as expressed through the government, the individual's interests would have to be sacrificed.

How did FDR sell this new order of things to the American people? He said that the stock market crash of 1929 proved the failure of America's free-enterprise system. What was needed, Roosevelt said, was massive government intervention into people's economic affairs in order to save free enterprise.

Of course, by 1933, the United States had an entire generation of people who had been forced to attend public (government) schools. They had been taught that good citizenship meant obedience and support of their political rulers. Thus, it did not occur to most Americans that Roosevelt was lying to them—that what had failed in 1929 was not free enterprise, but rather the socialized, central planning of the Federal Reserve Board—the agency that had been created in 1913 to stabilize the monetary system.

Immediately after his election, FDR approached Congress and asked to be given virtually unlimited powers to deal with the economic emergency. Give me the power to rule by decree, Roosevelt said, because I know the way out of this crisis.

And Congress gave him what he requested. What was Roosevelt's plan for America? Contrary to the campaign promises he had made, he embarked on a massive program of governmental borrowing; government spending; public works (including road construction); tax hikes; military spending; welfare; economic regulation; and a national youth corps. It was a way of life and a philosophy that were totally contrary to every principle on which this nation was founded.

There were two obstacles to Roosevelt's plans: the Constitution and the U.S. Supreme Court. When the New Deal legislation ultimately reached the Court, much of it was declared in violation of the Constitution and the way of life that had been established in 1787. For example, the National Recovery Act required entire industries to combine into government-protected cartels and directed them to fix wages and prices in their respective industries. If a businessman disagreed with the cartel, he was threatened with a massive protest by "Blue Eagle" demonstrators. More important, he was threatened with prosecution and punishment.

The Supreme Court said that this way of life was not constitutionally permitted in the United States. The court declared the NRA and several other New Deal programs unconstitutional.

Roosevelt was outraged. How can "nine old men" interfere with my power to do what is right for America? Roosevelt asked. He came up with a plan to pack the court with additional judges who would rule in his favor. But although FDR was changing America's economic system without a constitutional amendment, the American people refused to permit him to change the judicial system. FDR's court-packing scheme failed. However, as a result of the pressure he had put on the court, one justice changed his vote ("the switch in time that saved nine"), enabling Roosevelt to win the judicial war. From 1937 on, the court took the position that government had omnipotent powers over the wealth and economic activity of the American people.

Ironically, in 1933, another man assumed high political office, and it is instructive to review his philosophy and programs. Adolf Hitler became chancellor of Germany when that nation, too, was suffering from the Depression. The Germans actually had it worse— they were still suffering the effects of World War I. Their industrial base had been shattered; tens of thousands of young men had been killed; they were still paying reparations; their country had been split in two (the Polish Corridor separated East Prussia from the rest of Germany); and there was communist agitation.

Hitler immediately approached the Reichstag and said: Give me the power to rule by decree; I know the way out of this crisis.

The Reichstag granted Hitler his wish. And when German President von Hindenberg died, the Reichstag granted Hitler's request to combine the offices of president and chancellor into one. Hitler had secured even more power than Roosevelt to address the German economic emergency.

What did he do? He embarked on a massive program of governmental borrowing; government spending; public works (including road construction, e.g., the Autobahn); tax hikes; military spending; welfare; economic regulation; and a national youth corps. Hitler's philosophy was encapsulated in the Nazi Party platform: "The activities of the individual must not be allowed to clash with the interests of the community, but must take place within its confines and be for the good of all."

Any German who objected to Hitler's plan was immediately threatened with persecution and prosecution.

If you detect a similarity between the economic philosophy and programs of Franklin Roosevelt and Adolf Hitler, then it will not surprise you to know that Hitler sent the following letter to U.S. Ambassador Thomas Dodd on March 14, 1934:

> The Reich chancellor requests Mr. Dodd to present his greetings to President Roosevelt. He congratulates the president upon his heroic effort in the interest of the American people. The president's successful struggle against economic distress is being followed by the entire German people with interest and admiration. The Reich chancellor is in accord with the president that the virtues of sense of duty, readiness for sacrifice, and discipline must be the supreme rule of the whole nation. This moral demand, which the president is addressing to every single citizen, is only the quintessence of German philosophy of the state, expressed in the motto "The public weal before the private gain."

John Toland observes in his biography *Adolf Hitler* (1976):

> Hitler had genuine admiration for the decisive manner in which the President had taken over the reins of government. "I have sympathy for Mr. Roosevelt," he told a correspondent for the New York *Times* two months later, "because he marches straight toward his objectives over Congress, lobbies and bureaucracy." Hitler went on to note that he was the sole leader in Europe who expressed "understanding of the methods and motives of President Roosevelt."

And Hitler was not Roosevelt's only admirer. Benito Mussolini had led Italy into fascism, an economic philosophy that called for government control over economic activity, including government-business partnerships. Mussolini said that he admired FDR because he was, like Mussolini, a "social fascist."

Of course, Hitler had his admirers too. Toland points out:

> [Winston] Churchill had once paid a grudging compliment to the Führer in a letter to the *Times*: "I have always said that I hoped if Great Britain were beaten in a war we should find a Hitler who would lead us back to our rightful place among nations."

Toland points out that the American economist John Kenneth Galbraith would later write:

> Hitler also anticipated modern economic policy . . . by recognizing that a rapid approach to full employment was only possible if it was combined with wage and price controls. That a nation oppressed by economic fear would respond to Hitler as Americans did to F.D.R. is not surprising.

It was this similarity between communism, socialism, fascism, welfare statism, and New Dealism that caused Friedrich Hayek, who would later win the Nobel Memorial Prize in Economic Science, to warn the West that it was following the same collectivist, statist road as the Nazis, socialists, fascists, and communists. Hayek's famous book, *The Road to Serfdom* (1944), angered Americans—they did not like hearing what Hayek said to them.

In the late 1930s, Hitler's economic program of massive government intervention was moving toward collapse. Thus, he did what rulers have done throughout history. He moved toward war in order to distract the German people from the growing economic crisis. But the German people remembered the ravages of World War I and were overwhelmingly against another war. Even many of Hitler's generals were opposed to the invasions of Austria, Czechoslovakia, and Poland. When Chamberlain made his famous trips to Germany trying to secure peace, the German people wildly cheered him. But Hitler believed that war would be in the best interests of the nation.

As the end of the 1930s approached, Roosevelt's New Deal programs were also collapsing. There was a deep economic depression in 1937. People were figuring out that free enterprise is not saved by massive government control over people's lives and money. Roosevelt came to a firm conclusion before his reelection in 1940 that he kept secret from the voting public: Americans would have to go to war. There was a problem: the American people were even more insistent than the German people about staying out of another European war. But Roosevelt believed that war would be in the best interests of the nation.

Even though the Russian communists, the National Socialists (Nazis), the welfare statists, the fascists, and the New Dealers all had the same philosophical core, Roosevelt felt much more sympathy toward the communists. In fact, as recently opened Soviet files show, the Roosevelt administration was riddled with communist spies. Roosevelt believed that while the Nazi goals—full employment, public works, public highways, Social Security, national health care, public schooling, and so forth—were good and honorable, he did not like the notion of Aryan superiority promoted by the Nazis. He instead leaned toward what Stalin was doing, because he believed that the communists were for the little guy—the proletariat—the masses.

Hitler, on the other hand, was an ardent anticommunist. Like later American presidents, he rose to political power and justified his huge militaray buildup by pointing to the threat of communism. The goal of the communists, Hitler repeatedly said, was world conquest and domination. The West must combine to keep communism from taking over the world, he continually told Great Britain and the United States.

Franklin Roosevelt disagreed—Joseph Stalin ("Uncle Joe," he called him) was a man he could work with; the threat to world peace came from the Nazis, not the communists. Winston Churchill, on the other hand, while fighting to defeat the Nazis, fully agreed with Hitler's assessment of the communist threat to the West.

After FDR's death and the defeat of Nazi Germany, Harry Truman concluded that communism was the enemy and West Germany (even Nazis) was America's friend.

And this sets the backdrop for what happened to American soldiers who were in Nazi POW camps that were "liberated" by America's communist ally—the Soviet Union—as the war neared its end.

American POWs

The U.S. government's cry to the American people during recent wars has been: "Support the troops." A person might disagree with the war itself. Or the president may have failed to secure the constitutionally required congressional declaration of war. But, the government says, put all objections aside once the shooting starts. What matters then is that the people support the troops. The strategy is always effective in diminishing opposition to the war.

Unfortunately, however, the U.S. government has not always followed its own exhortation. Sometimes, not only has it failed to support its own troops, it has actually knowingly and deliberately abandoned them to imprisonment and death. The best example of this is what happened to American soldiers who had been captured by the Nazis and who were "liberated" by Russian forces at the end of World War II. The sordid tale of how the U.S. government failed to support its own troops is detailed in a shocking book published in 1992 entitled *Soldiers of Misfortune: Washington's Secret Betrayal of*

American POWs in the Soviet Union by James D. Sanders, Mark A. Sauter, and R. Cort Kirkwood.

On the Eastern Front, German forces had taken hundreds of thousands of Russians as prisoners. On the Western Front, they had taken Americans, British, and Commonwealth prisoners. The prisoners were incarcerated in German POW camps inside Germany.

As the Allied forces invaded Germany from the west, they liberated the German POW camps in their sector of operations. These camps included Russian, American, and British prisoners. As the Russian forces invaded from the east, they liberated camps that, again, contained Allied soldiers.

Quite naturally, the Americans and British soldiers held captive in the Russian zone wanted to return quickly to their own forces. But such was not the case with Russian prisoners. Their attitude toward returning to their homeland was exactly the opposite. Many of them hated the communist system. More important, all of them feared what Stalin and the communists would do to them for having been taken captive by the Germans.

At Yalta, Roosevelt and Churchill entered into a secret agreement with Stalin that required the United States and Great Britain to forcibly return the Russian prisoners to the clutches of Joseph Stalin. Over a million Russians were returned against their will, and most of them were either immediately killed or sent to the Gulag, where many of them later died. (See pp. 209–13.)

By the time the war ended, however, political events were shifting dramatically. Throughout the war, the U.S. government had taught the American people to hate not simply the Nazi regime but the German people, as well. Thus, for example, when thousands of defenseless women, children, and refugees were firebombed at Dresden by Allied forces, the American people, by and large, saw nothing wrong with this. Since Germany and the German people—not simply the Nazi regime—were trying to conquer the world, Americans believed, there was nothing wrong with killing them all.

Throughout the war, through his highly effective propaganda machinery, Roosevelt also taught Americans to view the Soviet communists as friends and allies of the American people.

Hitler and Churchill shared a different perspective about the communists. They both viewed Stalin and his regime as a monumental threat to world peace and security.

Why is all this important? Because it had enormous consequences that resulted in the suffering and death of millions of innocent people, including the American and British POWs "liberated" by Stalin's forces.

Roosevelt had insisted that only an "unconditional" surrender of German forces would be acceptable to the United States. The result of this unusual demand was not only that German forces fought harder, thereby prolonging the war, but also that the Soviet Union ultimately took control over Eastern Europe and East Germany.

Recall that in World War I, the Kaiser abdicated near the end of the war as a condition of peace. Suppose the same thing had happened near the end of World War II. Suppose that the United States and Great Britain had opened negotiations with Germany in 1944—before Russian forces had invaded Eastern Europe—and before millions of Jews had been killed in the Nazi gas chambers. There is at least the possibility that Hitler—whose health was failing dramatically anyway—along with Göring, Goebbels, and other leading Nazis—might have chosen to live in exile rather than continuing to fight a war they knew they were losing. If such a peace could have been negotiated, Eastern Europeans and East Germans would not have had to suffer under fifty years of Soviet domination. And millions of Jews would have been saved from the Nazi gas chambers.

But FDR's hatred of Germans and Germany—and his deep admiration and respect for Joseph Stalin and the communists—and his profound sympathy for communist goals—precluded him from exploring such a possibility. Americans would have to continue hating Germans and loving Russians until there was an unconditional surrender by Germany.

But things changed on Roosevelt's death near the end of the war. America's new president, Harry Truman, shared Churchill's (and Hitler's) perspective about the communist threat to the West. Soon after the war ended, Americans were told to immediately shift positions with respect to hatred and admiration. They were told that Germans—at least those in the western half—were not so bad after all. They had simply been misled by the Nazis. Americans were encouraged to love, admire, and assist these Germans. But those on the eastern side were still to be hated and despised, especially since they were now part of the Soviet bloc.

Americans were also told that it was necessary to begin hating the Soviet communists—the same communists who Americans had been taught were great and wonderful during the war.

All of this shifting of feelings was not lost on Joseph Stalin. Since Churchill, Roosevelt, and Truman had honored the secret agreement to return most of the Russian forces to the Soviet Union, where Stalin was able to finish off these "traitors," Stalin had honored his side of the bargain by returning most of the American and British soldiers in the Nazi camps liberated by Russian forces. But the operative word is "most."

Stalin was not a man to trust others, and he certainly did not trust Winston Churchill and Franklin Roosevelt. To ensure that Churchill and Roosevelt would live up to their side of the bargain to return the Russian soldiers to him, he retained "bargaining chips" in the form of American and British soldiers. If Churchill or Roosevelt reneged on their end of the bargain, Stalin would do the same.

As the war against the Nazis ended, the new war—the Cold War with the communists—began in earnest. The United States and Great Britain began treating the Germans (the ones in the west) more nicely and also began enlisting the active assistance of former Nazis—yes, the same Nazis that Americans had only recently been taught to hate and despise! Moreover, Churchill and Truman quietly began releasing thousands of anticommunist Russians who had still not been returned to Stalin—these Russians could be valuable friends and spies in the new "cold" war against the communists.

Stalin learned what was happening and retaliated. He permanently "retained" the American and British soldiers whom he still held as bargaining chips. What did he do with them? He carted them to the Soviet Union where they lived the rest of their lives in the Russian Gulag. How many American and British soldiers? *Over 20,000 Americans and over 30,000 British and Commonwealth soldiers!* In fact, as the authors of *Soldiers of Misfortune* point out: "Starting in 1945, the Soviet Union became the second-largest employer of American servicemen in the world."

This horrible tale is well documented in *Soldiers of Misfortune*. Much of the evidence involves the eyewitness accounts of American POWs who barely missed being "liberated" by Stalin's forces. For example, the authors detail the story of three Americans held in a German POW camp—John L. Connolly, Carmen Gomez, and Joseph Friedl. One morning in 1945, they woke to find their German captives gone. Connolly and Gomez decided to head west in search of American forces. Friedl decided to wait for Russian "liberators." Their story will chill you:

> But when the men tried to cross a bridge to the tantalizingly close American line, Red Army troops stopped them at gun point. "The Russians herded us into a bombed-out building.... When there were several hundred of us [Americans], they began to march back into Germany."

Wisely refusing to march away from their own lines, Connolly and about a dozen others ducked out of the column as it passed through town. Hours later, they ran across a team of American scout cars under the command of a brigadier general. "The Soviets are taking a column of American POWs back east," Connolly told the general. Flying into a rage, the American officer sped off to catch the column. But the POWs had vanished.

Joseph Friedl was taken back to the Soviet Union. He was one of the fortunate ones—he was released in 1946.

Another American soldier, T. Sgt. D. C. Wimberly, was straggling back to American lines and found himself in the German town of Luckenwalde. The Russians were herding back a column of German POWs to the Soviet Union, but when a few men near the end of the column saw Wimberly's American flag on his uniform, they called out: "Hey! You American? We're American. I'm from Philadelphia . . . Boston . . . Chicago. Help me!"

Americans also compared German army records of how many Americans were held in the camps. It was not difficult to see that the Soviets had failed to return all of them.

So, why has all of this been kept secret from the American people? World War II has been billed as the "good war"—the war that justifies all subsequent foreign wars. And every student in every public school across America is taught that FDR was one of our country's greatest presidents.

How could the U.S. government tell the truth about what happened to American servicemen? To tell the truth would mean exposing American complicity in the murder of over a million innocent Russian people. It would entail a closer examination of the Allied alliance with one of the most brutal political regimes in all of history. And it would expose all the scheming and machinations that resulted in the abandonment of over *50,000* Allied soldiers to our communist "friends."

What could the U.S. government have done differently as the war approached its end? It could have negotiated a peace with Germany that entailed the exile of Nazi leaders and ensured democratic regimes in all of Germany and Eastern Europe. It could have refused to participate in one of the worst holocausts in history—the forcible repatriation of Russian anticommunists—by refusing to force them to return to the Soviet Union against their will.

If Russian forces refused to return American and British POWs, one option , of course, could have been war against the Soviet Union. But if war was not a practical option at that point, then the least that the U.S. government owed its own soldiers was to let the world know what happened—so that the soldiers would never be forgotten. Imagine the loneliness those men must have felt as they were being transported to the Soviet Gulag. They had trusted their own government. They had fought and had been willing to die at the behest of their government. They had helped to win the war. Instead of coming home to their loved ones, they were being transported from a German POW camp to a Russian Gulag.

Would public pressure over the years have resulted in the release of these American and British soldiers? Possibly. But even if it did not, there was always the chance that word would leak into the Gulag—letting American and British doughboys know, before they died, that they still had not been forgotten by their fellow Americans.

Unfortunately, however, they were forgotten, because they were abandoned by their own government—the same U.S. government that starts out every new war with "Support the troops."

As the authors of *Soldiers of Misfortune* carefully document, U.S. governmental officials not only have refused to open the files on this dark and sordid episode of World War II, they have also altered and destroyed pertinent documents. Moreover, American officials still refuse to open up the files on the forcible repatriation of the Russians as well as other aspects of World War II. They claim that national security is at stake—fifty years after the end of the war.

The final questions arise: So what? Why bring all of this up now? What is the purpose? What good does it do? Why not let sleeping dogs lie? Why focus on World War II rather than simply on current episodes of governmental misconduct?

Because the lessons to be learned affect us so deeply today—fifty years after the end of World War II. And the lessons are profound indeed.

The Lessons of History

What purpose does it serve to talk about political wrongdoing of fifty years ago? What relevance does the past have to us today? So what if Roosevelt, Truman, Churchill, and Stalin cooperated in the murder of over 1,000,000 innocent Russian people? So what if FDR, Truman and succeeding presidents abandoned 20,000 American servicemen to the Soviet Gulag? Why not simply let bygones be bygones? Why bring up this dark and painful period in American history?

To confront reality is sometimes a very difficult and painful process. Human beings will often do whatever they can do to avoid the pain of facing reality. Nowhere is this more true than in how

Americans view their country. Americans simply will not accept or believe that for the past fifty years, the United States has had an economic system that is totally different from the economic system established by our Founding Fathers. Instead, they live the life of myth and delusion that they were taught in their schools—that the welfare-state and regulated-economy way of life is simply a modified form of free enterprise.

Moreover, it is easy to accept that Adolf Hitler and the Nazi forces committed war atrocities. It is much more difficult for many Americans to accept, no matter what the evidence, that two presidents they have been taught to love—Franklin Roosevelt and Harry Truman, along with American military forces—did the same.

But if we are ever going to return to a free and prosperous society, it will be essential to confront the reality of where this country has been, where it is now, and where it is going. A strong, healthy, and free society is possible only through the rejection of myth and delusion and through the acceptance of truth and reality. In his profound book *The Road Less Travelled: A New Psychology of Love, Traditional Values and Spiritual Growth* (1978), M. Scott Peck put the matter this way:

> The third tool of discipline or technique of dealing with the pain of problem-solving, which must continually be employed if our lives are to be healthy and our spirits are to grow, is dedication to the truth. Superficially, this should be obvious. For truth is reality. That which is false is unreal. The more clearly we see the reality of the world, the better equipped we are to deal with the world. The less clearly we see the reality of the world—the more our minds are befuddled by falsehood, misconceptions and illusions—the less able we will be to determine correct courses of action and make wise decisions. Our view of reality is like a map with which to negotiate the terrain of life. If the map is true and accurate, we will generally know where we are, and if we have decided where we want to go, we will generally know how to get there. If the map is false and inaccurate, we generally will be lost.

Today, Americans are living in extremely dangerous times. Our nation's economic system today is identical, in principle, to the economic system that existed in Germany in the 1930s—Social Security; Medicare; Medicaid; welfare; public schooling; central banking; and so forth. Yet, the American people insist on living their life of the lie. They continue believing that their system, unlike the

Nazi system, is "free enterprise." They refuse to face the reality of their external lives because it is simply too painful to do so. Peck writes:

> What happens when one has striven long and hard to develop a working view of the world, a seemingly useful, workable map, and then is confronted with new information suggesting that that view is wrong and the map needs to be largely redrawn? The painful effort required seems frightening, almost over-whelming. What we do more often than not, and usually unconsciously, is to ignore the new information. Often this act of ignoring is much more than passive. We may denounce the new information as false, dangerous, heretical, the work of the devil. We may actually crusade against it, and even attempt to manipulate the world so as to make it conform to our view of reality. Rather than try to change the map, an individual may try to destroy the new reality. Sadly, such a person may expend much more energy ultimately in defending an outmoded view of the world than would have been required to revise and correct it in the first place.

The result of their life with the lie is that Americans, like the Germans, continue to relinquish more and more of their lives and fortunes to public officials in order to solve the problems of "freedom."

It intrigues me that American public officials are still so obsessed with Adolf Hitler fifty years after the man's death. Notice that whenever a foreign despot becomes too tyrannical, American government officials always refer to him as another Adolf Hitler rather than as another Joseph Stalin, Pol Pot, and so on. On the conscious level, the notion is that Hitler was a political monster who comes along every few hundred years. But the obsessiveness with Hitler may very well reflect a subconscious belief that comes closer to the truth: that Adolf Hitler was not the aberrant monster who only occasionally appears in history but, instead, that Hitler was "Everyman"—every political leader who becomes corrupted with ever-increasing amounts of political power.

Alice Miller's psychological profile of Hitler in her book *For Your Own Good: Hidden Cruelty in Child Rearing and the Roots of Violence* (1983) is fascinating. As a result of the horrible physical and emotional abuse that Hitler received from his alcoholic father (see pages 214–15), Hitler was filled with repressed anger and rage. Having neither a wife nor children on which to project his feelings,

Hitler used his massive political powers to project his inner, destructive feelings on an entire race of innocent people. In the absence of the political power, Hitler would have been just another German citizen who disliked Jews.What is equally significant about Miller's work is her observation that Hitler did not accomplish his mass murders alone. The Nazi governmental system depended on the active support of thousands of German civil servants, as well as the active and passive support of millions of German people. In fact, overwhelming numbers of Germans loved and idolized Hitler in the same way that Americans loved and idolized Roosevelt. Miller says that the authoritarian society in which Germans were raised—including their families and their schools—caused the German people to view their political leaders as their daddy. Viewing themselves as dependent, adult children of the Reich, individual Germans lacked the self-esteem and inner resolve to take an independent stand against the Nazi tyranny.

Examine the situation in the United States today. Millions of Americans come from alcoholic or abusive families; in fact, it has been estimated that only 5 percent of Americans are raised in healthy families. Most Americans view their government in the same way as the German people—as their daddy who gives them an allowance (what's left after income taxation); forces them to share with their siblings (the welfare state); spanks them when they put bad things in their mouths (the war on drugs); and protects them from bad decisions (the regulated economy).

Moreover, adult children of dysfunctional families do as Hitler did—they gravitate toward political power. Is it a coincidence that the political rulers *who have absolutely no feelings of remorse for the massacres at Waco and Ruby Ridge*—Bill Clinton and Janet Reno—come from alcoholic and abusive families? Is it a coincidence that Hitler came from an abusive family? Stalin? Roosevelt?

Does this mean that the solution is to put "better" people into public office? No. Every one of us has his dark side. Political power is no different from alcohol. Drink enough liquor, and the greatest saint will become drunk. Exercise ever increasing amounts of political power, and the result is the same. Lord Acton was right—power does tend to corrupt; and absolute power corrupts absolutely.

The ultimate solution, then, is to *limit* the power that public officials have to exercise. This was the idea behind our Founding Fathers' conception of the Constitution. That document called the national government into existence but strictly limited the powers of those in office. In order to restore a free, healthy, and prosperous society, we need to continually focus on how to constitutionally prohibit public officials from exercising power in illegitimate ways.

How do we achieve this in a society composed largely of people who view government as their daddy? By continuing to focus on ourselves. The only way to improve society is to continue improving ourselves. This means improving our understanding of freedom (the external world) and improving our spiritual and mental health (the inner world). Ultimately, the healthier members of society will reach a critical mass that will lead the United States and the American people to the highest reaches of freedom ever seen by man.

This essay originally appeared in the February through May and the July through September 1995 issues of Freedom Daily, *published by The Future of Freedom Foundation.*

24

Killing Noncombatants

by Sheldon Richman

On May 11, 1940, Great Britain made a fateful decision in its approach to fighting the Second World War. On that night, eighteen Whitley bombers attacked railway installations in the placid west German province of Westphalia, far from the war front. That forgotten bombing raid, which in itself was inconsequential, has been called "the first deliberate breach of the fundamental rule of civilized warfare that hostilities must only be waged against the enemy combatant forces" (See *Advance to Barbarism* [1953] by F. J. P. Veale).

J. M. Spaight, who had been principal secretary of Britain's Air Ministry, wrote later, in his book *Bombing Vindicated* (1944), that "it was we who started the strategic [i.e., civilian] bombing offensive" with the "splendid decision" of May 11, 1940. "It was," wrote Spaight with horrifying honesty, "as heroic, as self-sacrificing, as Russia's decision to adopt her policy of 'scorched earth.'" Note that the German attack on Coventry, which is often cited as the first strategic bombing in the war between Germany and Britain, occurred six months later (on November 14, 1940). Note further that part of the British bombing strategy was apparently to provoke German attacks on England in order to stimulate support for total war against the Third Reich. As the official Air Ministry volume, *The Royal Air Force, 1939–1945: The Fight at Odds* (1953), stated:

> If the Royal Air Force raided the Ruhr, destroying oil plants with its most accurately placed bombs *and urban property with*

those that went astray, the outcry for retaliation against Britain might prove too strong for the German generals to resist. Indeed, Hitler himself would probably head the clamour. *The attack on the Ruhr, in other words, was an informal invitation to the Luftwaffe to bomb London.*

The first instance of "area" bombing, guided by a newly expanded definition of military target, occurred at Mannheim in December 1940, in which bombs were dropped on factories and the homes of factory workers. On February 14, 1942, the policy of targeting other than military sites became more explicit. With World War II now in full gear, Prime Minister Winston Churchill's British government directed the Bomber Command of the Royal Air Force to begin the destruction of German civilian morale. In other words, it was open season on cities. The decision was curious, for, as the neoconservative Paul Johnson wrote in *Modern Times* (1983):

> By the end of 1941, with both Russia and America in the war, the defeat of Hitler, as Churchill himself realized, was inevitable in the long run. The utilitarian rationale for attacks on cities had disappeared; the moral case had always been inadmissible.

The bombing policy was formalized in the Lindemann Plan in March 1942, when the Bomber Command was placed under the direction of Sir Arthur "Bomber" Harris, who inaugurated civilian bombing in the Middle East and India in the 1920s. Later that month, the city of Lubeck, an old Hanseatic port with no military significance, was targeted. In the words of the official report, it "burned like kindling." Half the city was destroyed.

By the summer of 1942, the United States was part of the air-terror campaign. On the night of July 27–28, British bombers attacked Hamburg, creating monstrous firestorms with temperatures of 800–1000 degrees centigrade over the city. The results: 40,000 people killed, 214,350 homes destroyed, 4,301 factories leveled, eight square miles burned.

On the night of February 13–14, 1945, what Johnson called "the greatest Anglo-American moral disaster of the war against Germany" occurred. Dresden, a city of indescribable beauty and no military value whatsoever, was destroyed. In two bombing waves (the second after relief efforts were underway), firestorms over eight square miles were ignited with 650,000 incendiaries. Some 135,000 people, including children in holiday carnival costumes, were killed; 4,200 acres were turned to rubble. "For the first time in the war a target had been hit so hard that not enough able-bodied survivors were left to bury the dead," wrote Johnson. "The funeral pyres were still flaming a fortnight after the raid." Why was it attacked? As Johnson put it, "The origin of the raid was the desire of Roosevelt and Churchill at the Yalta Conference to prove to Stalin that the Allies were doing their best to assist the Russian effort on the Eastern front." German civilians were barbequed for the Bolsheviks' westward offensive.

The unspeakable evil of the Dresden bombing made even Churchill pause. He wrote to the chief of the Air Staff, Sir Charles Portal, six weeks later:

> It seems to me that the moment has come when the question of bombing German cities *simply for the sake of increasing the terror, though under other pretexts*, should be reviewed. The destruction of Dresden remains a serious query against the conduct of Allied bombing. . . . I feel the need for more precise concentration upon military objectives, such as oil and communication behind the immediate battle-zone, rather than on mere acts of terror and wanton destruction, however impressive.

(The official British history of the air offensive commented that Churchill "had forgotten [his] own recent efforts to initiate and maintain the offensive.")

It was only the beginning. In the Pacific theater, the Americans applied the British strategy of targeting civilians. Sixty-six Japanese civilian centers were hit from March to July 1945, even as the U.S. authorities were receiving indications of a Japanese desire to surrender. The raids, involving 100,000 tons of incendiaries, destroyed 170,000 densely populated square miles. As night fell on March 9, three hundred B-29s laid waste to fifteen square miles of Tokyo. Eighty-three thousand were killed and 102,000 were injured in the firestorms. Up to roughly that point, the bombings in Japan had leveled two and a quarter million buildings; nine million people were homeless; 260,000 were dead; 412,000 were injured.

The climax came on August 6. After dropping more than 700,000 warning leaflets, the United States dropped a uranium bomb on Hiroshima. On that day and the days following, 200,000 died— burned, vaporized, suffocated. The deaths of some were evidenced only by the shadows they left on walls. Three days later, a second atomic bomb, this one powered by plutonium, was dropped on Nagasaki—74,800 dead. Two more cities were put on the A-bomb target list, but Japan's surrender on August 14 averted the strikes.

Thus the most destructive military conflict in human history ended. A new threshold had been crossed. The old rules of avoiding noncombatant casualties were erased. The bombing rules drafted after World War I were forgotten. The era of total war had arrived. Anyone was fair game. The murder of innocents became "collateral damage."

A sophisticated moral treatise should not be required to indict civilian bombing. Noncombatants had been ruled off-limits, because it was universally regarded as wrong to kill for the sake of sheer terror. War, though unspeakably horrific, was not to be an excuse for the dropping of all moral restraint. This made impeccable sense. The disputes between governments should not be permitted to spill onto the people forced to live under those governments. People rarely go to war. They are too busy making a living and raising their families; wars are costly. When they do go to war, they have first been whipped into a frenzy by dishonest political leaders, whose petty ambitions are often advanced by a seemingly great national purpose. The leaders rarely do the paying or the dying. They are too busy with the big picture. The details are left to the people. (See Paul Fussell's great book *Wartime* [1989].)

When Allied misconduct in World War II (or any war) is pointed out, many Americans become defensive, as though acknowledging government's moral lapses is bad manners, if not outright treason. That attitude is unbecoming to the political heirs of Jefferson and Madison, who understood the dangers intrinsic to the state and who grasped that eternal vigilance is the price of liberty. Those who wish not to dwell on Allied atrocities often respond that the enemy was engaged in such horrors as the rape of Nanking, the Bataan death march, the bombing of Rotterdam and Warsaw, the Holocaust.

So that is what it comes down to: Dresden? Tokyo? Hiroshima? Nagasaki? They were no worse than the crimes of the Japanese imperialists and the Nazis. At that point, a plea of innocence is hard to distinguish from a plea of guilty.

This essay originally appeared in the September 1995 issue of Freedom Daily, *published by The Future of Freedom Foundation.*

25

Dresden:
Time to Say We're Sorry

by Simon Jenkins

As the U.S. Fifth Army inched its way up Italy in 1944, its command constantly pondered which towns should be spared bombardment. Monte Cassino was destroyed. The centers of Rome and Florence were saved. The Pieros of Sansepulcro were reprieved at the last minute (I believe by an art-loving gunner). These decisions were taken out of respect for the civilized values that the Allies believed they were defending, even if they cost soldiers' lives. The Allies were right.

Now we are arguing about Dresden again. Yesterday its people commemorated the night, fifty years ago, that Bomber Command devastated their city, roasting at least 25,000 of its inhabitants in the notorious firestorm. They would like us to apologize. To them it was an act of pure savagery, planned at Stalin's request and aimed at civilians and refugees from the east. The war was all but over and military installations around Dresden were not targeted. The attack was a modern version of medieval "putting a city to fire and the sword."

Attitudes to the Dresden bombing have undergone many shifts over time. Immediately after the attack there was widespread revulsion. Winston Churchill, who had ordered the raid to appease Stalin, was sufficiently shocked by the reaction to question the policy of "bombing German cities simply for the sake of increasing the terror."

He referred to the bombings as "mere acts of terror and wanton destruction, however impressive." The Americans likewise distanced themselves from avowedly "terrorist" air attacks, after their own planes had gunned down people fleeing the burning city the morning after the British raid.

In the 1950s the issue was buried. Bomber Command veterans were highly sensitive about what was euphemistically called "area bombing." Their portrayal in war films was duly heroic. In the 1960s and '70s came a resurgence of doubt. This culminated in controversy after the death of the head of Bomber Command, Sir Arthur "Bomber" Harris, in 1984, and the proposed erection of a statue to him. Now on the fiftieth anniversary, right-wing revisionists defend the bombing as part of the "context" of war. It has become intellectually chic to claim Dresden was a good thing. There is little chance of Prime Minister John Major's recommending an apology.

Everything I have ever heard or read about Dresden convinces me that it was a crime against humanity—unless I adopt the morally ludicrous position that no Allied troops were capable of such a thing by definition. The Dresden raid was bitterly controversial at the time, a product of the internecine war-cabinet politics of early 1945. Harris was beyond the control of his superiors and had defied the orders of his boss, the weak Sir Charles Portal. Portal and the Americans had pleaded for the bombers to be directed against specific military and economic targets, in particular oil supplies, to speed the Allied advance across Europe. Nor could the war cabinet see any point in flattening cities and creating millions of refugees who would shortly be an Allied responsibility.

Harris was a fanatical believer in bombing cities. He was contemptuous of the oil targeting strategy. Like many commanders scenting victory, he was not interested in helping the army and longed to see his bombers carry the vanguard of victory over a flattened wilderness. Many Germans, including Albert Speer, later wrote that the one thing that could have ended the war in 1944 (and saved hundreds of thousands from the gas chambers) would have been the redirection of Allied bombing from cities to oil supplies.

There would then have been no German counteroffensive. Harris's failure to implement the Anglo-American order to attack oil supplies, as Max Hastings has shown in his book on Bomber Command, "will be remembered as one of the Allies' great missed opportunities." Harris's insubordination was the central catastrophe of the last year of the war.

Harris used incendiaries on Dresden to create a firestorm; in other cities he used high explosives. The city-center churches and palaces packed with refugees were targeted, rather than railways or barracks on the outskirts. The attack was morally identical to an infantry massacre of civilians on the ground. There was no rational argument that such terrorism would undermine Hitler. A year of saturation bombing had not brought an uprising, nor did the bombing of Berlin. As Hastings concludes, "The Wehrmacht's last stand, and the continued output from the factories until the last weeks, rendered the concept of morale bombing finally absurd."

The Thunderclap operation, as it was called, was openly "terroristic." Harris wanted to flatten "two and a half cities a month" until there were none left. He saw no distinction between the Nazis and three centuries of European culture still resplendent in the great cities of Germany. He appeared to believe that destroying what was ineffably beautiful would break the morale of a people he saw as evil. That the breaking of morale might, in ravaging Germany, be politically ineffective was too subtle a point for him. He was not above the thought that he was destroying a culture still respected by his more effete Whitehall opponents. His much quoted motto was that "bombing anything in Germany is better than bombing nothing."

The Dresden raid was part of a final destructive frenzy by an insubordinate commander, unleashed by Churchill to bring a gift to Stalin at Yalta. Even then Stalin would have been content with the bombing of supply lines and oil depots ahead of his advancing army. When he did a "Dresden" on Warsaw he at least warned the population to leave first.

Dresden was more than a distortion of the war effort or a concession to an odious ally. Dresden cannot be excused as "balancing" Auschwitz or Coventry or German punitive massacres of villages in the Balkans. That demeans the Holocaust and reduces Nazi atrocities to a level moral playing field of tit for tat. Besides, the Germans have endlessly apologized.

Harris's campaign was an aberration. It began as false strategy and became a moral obscenity. This is not hindsight. Many people, not least in the Royal Air Force and U.S. Army Air Force, opposed Harris at the time, were appalled by what he did and have been so ever since.

Saying sorry costs nothing. The Allied cause in 1945 was right and was triumphant. That rightness shows its strength when it can recognize and atone for its errors, especially when they were as awful as the destruction of Dresden.

Mr. Jenkins writes for the Times of London *and the* Spectator, *where this article originally appeared. It appeared in the February 14, 1995, issue of* The Wall Street Journal. *It was reprinted in the September 1995 issue of* Freedom Daily, *published by The Future of Freedom Foundation. Reprinted with permission of* The Wall Street Journal. *Copyright 1995, Dow Jones & Company, Inc. All rights reserved.*

26

Conserving and Destroying

by Joseph Sobran

In my thesaurus, "conserve" and "destroy" are antonyms. Why is it, then, that so many conservatives seem to relish war?

I have known conservatives who have joked pleasantly about "nuking the chinks" or flattening Tehran. Jokes are jokes, but some conservatives took an actual delight in the Gulf War; there was some loose talk of bombing, and even nuking, Baghdad. And of course many still take pride in the memory of nuking Hiroshima. We commemorate it on postage stamps.

We can and should make allowances for people who are actually in a war they didn't want and are willing to take the most extreme measures to save their sons. But I am talking about people who aren't in a war, who just like the idea of bombing in an almost esthetic sense—like art for art's sake.

Notice that it's bombing, not combat, that grabs them. Such people enjoy imagining themselves in a position of dropping tremendous explosives on cities without any reciprocal risk of being bombed themselves (which might take the fun out of it).

The terrible bombing of Dresden is also currently being commemorated, but in sorrow, not glee. Even many Americans and Englishmen feel deep regret at not only the inhumanity but the sheer crassness of the destruction of one of Europe's loveliest cities. What was destroyed was not "Nazism" but tens of thousands of innocent people, and also a city that belonged only incidentally to Hitler; for

Dresden really belonged to the entire West, which a more civilized age called Christendom. Dresden is lost to all of us. You can regret that for purely selfish reasons.

In the code of Christendom, or Christian civilization, killing civilians was regarded as incompatible with just warfare. In the modern age it has become policy. Two-thirds of those killed in World War II were civilians. Only Americans, whose homes and cities were totally spared, seem not to grasp what this means.

Southerners used to understand. They remembered the armies of Sheridan and Sherman. The Northern victors have long since awarded Abraham Lincoln a halo, but European observers of the Civil War were shocked at his ordering assaults on civilians. Even the Emancipation Proclamation was widely seen not as a humane liberation of slaves, but as a cynical attempt to incite the murders of slave-owning families. (It left slavery untouched in nonseceding states.)

But every war becomes humane in retrospect. The victors in every war feel compelled to portray themselves not only as powerful but as humanitarian. The Civil War is now primarily remembered as a war to end slavery rather than a war to prevent, and punish, secession—though freeing the Confederacy's slaves was a punitive expropriation. Despite the U.S. government's campaign of hatred against the Japanese (including the violation of the basic rights of American citizens of Japanese descent), World War II is similarly misremembered as a war against racism.

Even the nuking of Hiroshima is defended as humanitarian. It "shortened the war" and saved countless lives. Well, suppose you could shorten a war and save countless lives by slitting the throat of a single child. A utilitarian philosopher might argue that this would be morally justified. But who could bear to do it? Much easier to roast an entire city from a great height—no blood on your hands, no screams in your ears. And think of all the lives you've saved!

I wasn't born yet, but I have the distinct impression that most Americans at the time cheered the bombings of Hiroshima and Nagasaki as just what those Jap bastards deserved for Pearl Harbor and Bataan. Government propaganda films spoke of "Japs" and "Nips" with "their grinning yellow faces." It was only much later that decorum decreed that we depict the two blasts as a pair of gigantic mercy killings, saving countless lives of our Japanese friends as well as our own boys.

See how the modern state has warped our sense of right and wrong? We have become such people as would have appalled our ancestors. It's no wonder that an abortionist can be appointed to high office. The things we should have conserved have already been destroyed.

Mr. Sobran is a syndicated columnist. This essay was reprinted in the September 1995 issue of Freedom Daily, *published by The Future of Freedom Foundation. Taken from the* Joseph Sobran Column *by Joseph Sobran.* © *Universal Press Syndicate. Reprinted with permission. All rights reserved.*

27

The War Crimes of
Hiroshima and Nagasaki

by Jacob G. Hornberger

When U.S. military forces dropped atomic bombs on Japanese civilians at Hiroshima and Nagasaki, 275,000 men, women, and children were killed. Ever since, the killings have been justified by the claim that the bombings shortened the war and, therefore, saved the lives of American servicemen.

Actually, the bombings constituted war crimes for which the perpetrators should have been tried and sufficiently punished.

In war, there are standards of behavior to which civilized nations must adhere, even when fighting barbarians. Prohibited acts include: rape; pillage; torture and killing of prisoners; *and the intentional killing of noncombatants.*

Traditionally, in war, armies fight armies. To the extent possible, it is impermissible to kill civilians, especially unarmed ones.

Suppose an infantry battalion enters an enemy city. The enemy soldiers have retreated. Left behind are their wives and children. The murder of the women and children will demoralize the enemy soldiers, encouraging them to lose their will to fight. Should the infantry commander order his troops to shoot the women and children?

"But that is different," the critic says. "Dropping a bomb on women and children is not the same as shooting them in cold blood."

How is it different? Simply because the bomber, unlike the infantry-man, cannot look his victims in the eye before he kills them?

"But I would have died if we had had to invade Japan," the critic claims. And so? Everyone dies, some sooner than others. And soldiers are apt to die sooner than the rest. That is the nature of war. It is a nasty business. The soldier who wants defenseless women and children killed so that his life can be extended is certainly no hero. In fact, he is simply a coward. And a soldier with that mind-set dishonors a battlefield with his mere presence.

If rape shortens a war, is it moral for a commander to order it? Pillage? Torture, mutilation, or killing of prisoners? No. These constitute war crimes. The same holds true for the intentional killing of noncombatants. A civilized nation does not stoop to the level of its enemy, not even in war.

This essay originally appeared in the September 1995 issue of Freedom Daily, *published by The Future of Freedom Foundation.*

28

The Invasion of Japan:
Alternative to the Bomb

a review by Richard M. Ebeling

The Invasion of Japan: Alternative to the Bomb by John Ray Skates (Columbia: University of South Carolina Press, 1995); 276 pages; $27.95.

On November 1, 1945, the invasion of Japan began, under the code name Operation Olympic. Under the joint command of Gen. Douglas MacArthur and Adm. Chester Nimitz, the United States armed forces started an assault on the southernmost of the Japanese home islands—Kyushu. A force of 650,000 soldiers, 2,500 ships, and 6,000 planes attacked from three sides along the southern coast of Kyushu.

Japanese military intelligence had correctly anticipated the location of the next major American offensive after the fall of Okinawa in June 1945. They had even predicted the landing areas the American forces would select for the initial beachheads. They had fortified the coastlines and chosen a strategy of repulsing the attack on the beaches. By August, the Japanese high command had already stationed over 200,000 troops in defensive positions in Kyushu. In the first ten days of the invasion, the Japanese planned to counterattack with 6,000 kamikazes, who would perform their suicide missions against the troop-carrying ships off the coast, hoping to destroy at least 10 to 20 percent of the invasion force before they landed.

Earlier in the war, however, General MacArthur's intelligence team had broken the Japanese military codes. His code breakers had been able to read every order and instruction issued for the defense of Kyushu. The U.S. invasion planners knew almost all of the Japanese defense strategy, including troops placements and airfields where planes for the kamikaze attacks were being concentrated. As a consequence, even before the first invasion ships came in sight of land, U.S. air power had destroyed or disabled many of the suicide planes. The mountainous terrain of Kyushu made it possible for American bombers to cut the few crucial railroads and highways through which the Japanese would have been able to maintain supply lines to the defense forces facing the invaders.

Furthermore, the atomic bomb attacks on Hiroshima and Nagasaki in August had failed to bring about a Japanese surrender. By the end of October, the U.S. military had nine more atomic bombs, and they were now used tactically in three attacks to support the American invasion forces on Kyushu. Tens of thousands of Japanese were dead or dying from the atomic blasts, and resistance on the island soon weakened.

The invasion plan succeeded. Kyushu now provided the American forces with the naval and air facilities for the next and final assault on the main Japanese island of Honshu in March 1946, if the Japanese military still refused to accept unconditional surrender. But the Japanese had drained away most of their last home-island reserves in the defense of Kyushu. They had practically no kamikaze planes left, and the few they had had almost no fuel. The invasion point on the Honshu coast leading to the Kanto Plain and Tokyo was not easily defended against U.S. air and ground power. And the Soviet Union, having entered the war in August 1945, had totally overrun the famed Japanese Kwangtung Army in Manchuria. So before the invasion of Honshu had to begin, the Japanese finally surrendered.

These, of course, were the final invasions that never occurred. In his recent book, *The Invasion of Japan: Alternative to the Bomb*, John Ray Skates details the strategies and planning behind Operation Olympic and Operation Coronet— the assault on Honshu. Instead, on August 6, 1945, the United States dropped the atomic bomb on Hiroshima, followed by another atomic bomb on Nagasaki on August 9. A total of over 185,000 people were killed or injured by these atomic blasts. And hostilities ended on August 15, when the Imperial Japanese Government agreed to unconditional surrender.

But even before the dropping of the bomb, Professor Skates explains, the U.S. had rained mass death upon Japanese cities.

Giving up on precision daylight bombing, the U.S. undertook night-time incendiary attacks during the first half of 1945, burning out 174 square miles in sixty-six cities and incinerating an estimated 330,000 Japanese. The March 10, 1945, raid on Tokyo alone killed almost 85,000 people. First priority in these air raids was given to cities with high "congestion and inflammability."

In his memoirs after the war, President Truman said that an invasion of the Japanese home islands would have cost the lives of upwards of half a million American soldiers. The likelihood of such high American casualties, he argued, was the primary reason why he decided to use the atomic bomb to end the war quickly. In fact, Professor Skates tells us, no such number had ever been suggested in any of the planning estimates before the invasion of Kyushu. The estimate most generally accepted was that in the first sixty days of the assault on Kyushu, American casualties would be between 55,000 and 78,000, with the dead numbering between 14,000 and 20,000. These numbers would have been approximately equal to the losses suffered in the invasion of Luzon in the Philippines. This estimate had been given to President Truman at a meeting with the Joint Chiefs on June 18, 1945; he seemed satisfied, telling them to proceed with the plans for Operation Olympic.

Professor Skates also explains that for the Joint Chiefs in Washington, the main hurdle in constructing a military strategy that could succeed in forcing the Japanese into accepting defeat was FDR's declaration at the 1943 conference in Casablanca that the Allied goal was "unconditional surrender" by Nazi Germany, fascist Italy, and Imperial Japan. There was a strong belief among several cabinet members—especially Secretary of War Henry Stimson, Acting Secretary of State Joseph Grew, and Secretary of the Navy James Forrestal—that if the Japanese could be given assurances that surrender would not mean the elimination of the emperor and the imperial system, there was a stronger likelihood of Japan's accepting defeat. But Truman would not significantly budge.

Could both the dropping of the atomic bombs or an invasion of Japan have been prevented through a loosening of the surrender terms? Professor Skates does not discuss this in any great detail, but in July 1945, the Japanese had attempted to use both the Swedish and Soviet governments as intermediaries to end the war with the United States. Both President Truman and Secretary Stimson were aware of these Japanese feelers, but Truman still refused to approve of any private or public modification of the unconditional surrender terms. Instead, on July 25, while at the Potsdam Conference with Churchill and Stalin, Truman issued orders that the first atomic bomb was to be dropped any time after August 3. On July 26, the Potsdam Declaration was issued, stating: "We call upon the Government of Japan to proclaim unconditional surrender of all Japanese armed forces.... The alternative for Japan is prompt and utter destruction."

Thus, the last avenue to end the war before the dropping of the atomic bombs was closed. Eight months after the end of the war, U.S. intelligence officers on the army general staff undertook a "what if" study of an invasion of Japan. "They concluded," Professor Skates tells us, "that the failure of these [Japanese peace] efforts [through their embassy in Moscow] and the sudden Soviet declaration of war on 9 August would have been sufficient, even without the atomic bombs, to end the war. However, in the unlikely event that the Japanese continued in the war after the entry of the USSR, and OLYMPIC had been launched, 'The island of Kyushu would have been occupied in not over two months at a cost of 75,000 to 100,000 casualties.' In that case, concluded the analysts, the war would have ended no later than 15 February, 1946, and Coronet would not have been necessary. This author's study of the record," concludes Professor Skates, "leads to similar conclusions."

Of course, this is all "what if" history. But by not even trying to find some common language over surrender terms to bring the war to an end in July or the first week of August 1945, what we do know is what happened. Tens of thousands of innocent Japanese civilians died from atomic bomb attacks on Hiroshima and Nagasaki, with many thousands more having the consequences of radiation poisoning for the last half-century. Stalin had his opportunity to declare war on Japan on August 8 and grab the lands promised to him by Roosevelt at Yalta. And America has had the burden as the only nation in the world to have used atomic bombs and intentionally take massive number of human lives in the process.

This review originally appeared in the November 1995 issue of Freedom Daily, *published by The Future of Freedom Foundation.*

29

A Terrible Revenge: The Ethnic Cleansing of the Eastern European Germans, 1944–1950

a review by Richard M. Ebeling

A Terrible Revenge: The Ethnic Cleansing of the Eastern European Germans, 1944–1950 by Alfred-Maurice de Zayas (New York: St. Martin's Press, 1994); 179 pages;. $19.95.

Speaking to a group of German officers over dinner in September 1941, Adolf Hitler explained: "It is the eternal law of nature that gives Germany as the stronger power the right before history to subjugate these peoples of inferior race, to dominate them and to coerce them into performing useful labors" for their German masters.

In the drive for mastery over Europe, dirty work would have to be done to eliminate certain "undesirable" groups. But in the eyes of the Nazi leadership, such conduct would make German men strong. In October 1943, Heinrich Himmler told a group of SS officers:

> Among ourselves let us for once be quite frank. . . . I mean the evacuation of the Jews, the extermination of the Jewish people.

... Most of you know what it means to have a hundred corpses lying together, or five hundred, or a thousand. To live through this and at the same time ... remain decent, that made us hard. This is a noteworthy page in our history.

This is how Kurt Werner of Sonderkommando described such hard work during the massacre of over 30,000 Jews at Babi Yar in the Ukraine in September 1941:

It was not long before the first Jews were brought to us over the side of the ravine. The Jews had to lie face down on the earth by the ravine walls. . . . Each successive group of Jews had to lie down on top of the bodies of those that had already been shot. The marksman stood behind the Jews and killed them with a shot in the neck. I still recall today the complete terror of the Jews when they first caught sight of the bodies as they reached the top edge of the ravine. . . . It is impossible to imagine what nerves of steel it took to carry out that dirty work down there. . . . I had to spend the whole morning down in the ravine. For some of the time I had to shoot continuously.

In 1943, SS officer Ernst Gobel was in charge of a group of mass executions, also on the eastern front:

The victims were shot by the firing-squad with carbines, mostly with shots in the back of the head.... Meanwhile [a] Rottenführer ... shot the [small] children with a pistol.... He got hold of the children by the hair, lifted them up from the ground, shot them through the back of their heads and threw them into the grave.

In *Democide: Nazi Genocide and Mass Murder* (1992), political scientist R. J. Rummel summarized the result of Hitler's drive to create a thousand-year Reich in a new, greater Germany:

By genocide, the murder of hostages, reprisal raids, forced labor, "euthanasia," starvation, exposure, medical experiments, and terror bombings, and in the concentration and death camps, the Nazis murdered from 15,003,000 to 31,595,000 people, most likely 20,946,000 men, women, handicapped, aged, sick, prisoners of war, forced laborers, camp inmates, critics, homo-sexuals, Jews, Slavs, Serbs, Germans, Czechs, Italians, Poles, French, Ukrainians, and many others. Among them 1,000,000 were children under eighteen years of age. And none of these monstrous figures even include civilian and military combat or war-deaths.

But in 1944–1945, as the war was approaching its end with a German defeat, Hitler had no more sympathy for the German people than he had had for the Jews and Slavs, whom he despised as subhumans. In July 1944, after the attempt on his life, Hitler had declared:

> If the German nation is now defeated in this struggle, it has been too weak. That will mean it has not withstood the test of history and was destined for nothing but doom.

And in March 1945, Hitler told Albert Speer, his minister of armaments and war production:

> If the war is lost, the people will be lost also. It is not necessary to worry about what the German people will need for elemental survival. On the contrary, it is best for us to destroy even these things. For the nation has proven to be the weaker, and the future belongs solely to the stronger eastern nation [Russia]. In any case only those who are inferior will remain after this struggle, for the good have already been killed.

The German people had failed Hitler's belief in their destiny for mastery over Europe. In the Führer's eyes, they did not deserve to live. Having brought death and destruction to so many in the rest of Europe, the ravages of war now fell upon the Germans. Enemy armies were overrunning the country; day-and-night firebombings were leaving German cities nothing more than smoldering cinders. Millions of Germans were dead and wounded, and millions more were being driven from their homes with no food and only the clothes on their backs.

In his earlier book, *Nemesis at Potsdam: The Expulsion of the Germans from the East* (1977), Alfred-Maurice de Zayas chronicled the policies of the allied powers in World War II towards the defeated German nation. Now, in his new book, *A Terrible Revenge: The Ethnic Cleansing of the Eastern European Germans, 1944–1950*, Mr. de Zayas summarizes the wartime policies that resulted in the expulsion of millions of Germans from their homes in Eastern Europe and also describes the personal tragedies that befell them.

Even far more than still today, Eastern Europe before the Second World War was a patchwork quilt of different ethnic and national groups clustered together inside various nation-states. The interventionist and collectivist policies of practically all the governments in Eastern Europe meant that the state was used to benefit some ethnic groups at the expense of others. Hitler had played effectively on this situation when, in the 1930s, he argued that all German-speaking people should be unified within the same greater German Reich.

During the war, the Big Three—the United States, Britain, and the USSR—along with the Polish and Czechoslovakian governments-in-exile—determined that "the German problem" in these areas would be resolved through the forced expulsion of millions of Germans from Poland and western Czechoslovakia; for the vast majority of these Germans, this meant being forced off land and property that, in many cases, had been owned by their families for hundreds of years. The magnitude of the forced population transfers that were to be implemented was magnified by the fact that, at the Tehran and Yalta conferences, Roosevelt, Churchill, and Stalin had agreed that eastern Poland and the northern half of the German province of East Prussia would be permanently transferred to Soviet jurisdiction, while Poland would receive, as compensation, the southern part of East Prussia and all German territory east of the Oder and Neisse Rivers, including all of Silesia, most of Pomerania, and part of Brandenburg.

The result was that between 1945 and 1950, 11,730,000 Germans fled and were expelled from these eastern territories of Germany, Czechoslovakia, and other Eastern European countries; specifically, over 6.9 million from the eastern territories of Germany, more than 2.9 million Germans from Czechoslovakia, and more than 1.8 million from other parts of Eastern Europe. And besides the forced expulsion of these 11.7 million people, another 2.1 million died or "disappeared" during the expulsion process.

In thinking about the fate of these millions of Germans, Mr. de Zayas asks us not to shrug it aside as mere just retribution for the Nazi cruelties committed during the war:

> The merciless revenge that poured over the entire German civilian population of Eastern Europe . . . should also awaken compassion, for in either case the common people—farmers and industrial workers, the rich and the poor—were all victims of politics and politicians. In judging these events, the nationality of a victim should not matter; pain and suffering have no nationality. Nor does murder. Every crime is reprehen-

sible, regardless of the nationality of its victims—or of the victimizer.

In stark and gruesome detail, Mr. de Zayas presents the personal testimony of literally dozens upon dozens of these German victims during those years of expulsion. Soviet soldiers were given carte blanche to rape and plunder tens of thousands of people. In their thirst for revenge, Soviet troops gang-raped women over and over again, and some of these German women were in their sixties, seventies, and even eighties. Aleksandr Solzhenitsyn, who was a young captain with the Soviet army that entered East Prussia in January 1945, later wrote:

> Yes! For three weeks the war had been going on inside Germany and all of us knew very well that if the girls were German they could be raped and then shot. This was almost a combat distinction.

Because of his opposition to this behavior, Solzhenitsyn was arrested and sent to forced labor in the Gulag.

German male civilians were hunted down by Russians, Poles, and Czechs and brutally beaten and murdered. Homes were robbed and burned. German men, women, and children were rounded up and imprisoned, sometimes in the recently liberated concentration camps. Millions of Germans were set out on the roads and ordered to march west, with neither food nor clothing to shelter them from the elements during the long trek to western Germany.

Though the American government did not overtly endorse the brutalities that accompanied the expulsion of the Germans, support for the deportation of these millions of people was laid down as official U.S. policy while the war was still in progress. In November 1944, Franklin Roosevelt sent a letter to the Polish president-in-exile, in which FDR stated:

> If the Polish Government and people desire in connection with the new frontiers of the Polish state to bring about the transfer to and from territory of Poland of national minorities, the United States Government will raise no objection, and as far as practicable, will facilitate such transfer.

Through this endorsement and promise of assistance, therefore, Roosevelt made the United States an accomplice, before the fact, to one more of the cruel crimes that resulted from the Second World War.

This review originally appeared in the July 1995 issue of Freedom Daily, *published by The Future of Freedom Foundation.*

30

What President Clinton Should Have Said to the Japanese

by Jacob G. Hornberger

In 1993, President Clinton visited Japan. The following is a model speech that the president could have delivered to the Japanese people:

After the Japanese attack on Pearl Harbor, the U.S. government arrested American citizens of Japanese descent, placed them in American concentration camps, and confiscated their assets. There were no indictments. There were no trials. There were no convictions. These Americans were simply rounded up, taken away, and incarcerated. To our government's credit, these people were not killed, as the German government did to the Jews whom it placed in German concentration camps, but it was still wrong to jail people who had not committed—or been accused of committing—any crimes. I know that many of you had relatives who suffered this horrible tragedy. On behalf of the U.S. government, I apologize for what we did.

Unfortunately, the power to round up innocent Americans during war and place them in concentration camps is still the law of the land in the United States. Thus, upon my return to Washington, I intend to propose the following amendment to the United States Constitution: "No person, regardless of race, color, creed, or national

257

origin, shall be deprived of life, liberty, or property without due process of law, even in times of war or national emergency."

Another apology concerns the execution of Gen. Tomoyuki Yamashita, the commanding general of the Fourteenth Army Group of the Imperial Japanese Army.

Americans have been taught about the war-crimes trials that were held in Germany at the end of the war. However, our governmental schoolteachers have largely succeeded in keeping them from learning about the same type of trial that took place in the Pacific theater.

As you can imagine, there was tremendous animosity against Japan at the end of the war. There was also a thirst for retribution. It would have been considered barbaric simply to place General Yamashita against a wall and execute him in retaliation for all of the American soldiers who had been killed by Japanese forces. So our government believed that if it cloaked its killing of General Yamashita in the garb of a military trial, then people would fail to notice its act of barbarism.

At the trial, the U.S. government argued that General Yamashita was a war criminal because troops under his command had committed atrocities. Yet, it was clear that General Yamashita had ordered his troops never to engage in such conduct, had no knowledge of these atrocities, had never condoned such actions, and was unable to prevent them due to the chaos resulting from Allied bombing of Japanese command and control facilities.

Permit me to share with you the views of Mr. Justice Rutledge, who wrote a dissenting opinion when General Yamashita's case reached the U.S. Supreme Court:

> This trial is unprecedented in our history. Never before have we tried and convicted an enemy general for action taken during hostilities or otherwise in the course of military operations or duty. Much less have we condemned one for failing to take action. . . . I have not been able to find precedent for the proceeding in the system of any nation founded in the basic principles of our constitutional democracy, in the laws of war or in other internationally binding authority or usage.

Listen, also, to the words of Mr. Justice Murphy, another dissenter in the case:

> We live under the Constitution, which is the embodiment of all the high hopes and aspirations of the new world. And it is

applicable in both war and peace. We must act accordingly. Indeed, an uncurbed spirit of revenge and retribution, masked in formal legal procedure for purposes of dealing with a fallen enemy commander, can do more lasting harm than all of the atrocities giving rise to that spirit.

The military commission that presided over General Yamashita's trial consisted of five generals in the American army (the U.S. government served as prosecutor, judge, jury, and executioner), none of whom were lawyers or had any legal experience. This military tribunal found General Yamashita guilty and condemned him to death.

I confess to you—the people of Japan—that the United States government committed a grave wrong when it executed General Yamashita. We should never have attempted to quench our thirst for revenge by killing a man who had simply done his duty in the service of his country. On behalf of the United States government, I sincerely apologize for what we did to General Yamashita.

I now wish to make another apology to you regarding World War II. Prior to this century of total war, there have always been well-recognized rules of civilized warfare. For example, both sides in war usually recognize that prisoners of war will not be tortured, even if it would help to shorten the war.

World War II resulted in extreme acts of barbarism by political and military leaders on both sides of the war. We are familiar with the acts of barbarism by the Nazis, the communists, and your military leaders.

Unfortunately, those of us in the West have had a difficult time confronting the acts of barbarism in World War II committed by our respective governments.

A long-time rule of civilized warfare has been that armies fight armies and that they do not attack civilians. Fortunately, this long-time rule of civilized warfare is still recognized today, albeit not always closely followed.

Unfortunately, it was sometimes cast to the winds by Western powers during World War II. And Japanese civilians paid the price near the end of the war. I am referring to the dropping of the atomic bombs on the people of Hiroshima and Nagasaki.

This action has always been justified by our governmental officials with one argument: that the bombings shortened the war and, therefore, saved lives. But since when is this a moral argument for resorting to an act of barbarism? If torturing prisoners results in a shortening of the war, does this make the act civilized and moral?

If the Bataan death march to which your government subjected our prisoners served to shorten the war, did this justify your government's act of barbarism? If Hitler's death camps shortened the war, did this justify his acts of barbarism?

No! In war, no act of barbarism is morally justified. And civilized nations—or nations claiming to fight to preserve civilization—have a moral duty to maintain, to every extent possible, a commitment to civilized conduct, even in the course of waging the war. This means, at a minimum, the feeding and care of prisoners and the protection of civil liberties and private property for non-combatants.

It also means that armies do not indiscriminately attack civilians during wartime. War is hell, but it is made worse when nations that are claiming to represent civilization resort to the methods of the barbarians they are claiming to fight.

Even worse, three months before the dropping of the bombs, our government intercepted the following report from a German diplomat who had spoken to a ranking Japanese naval officer: "Since the situation is clearly recognized to be hopeless, large sections of the Japanese armed forces would not regard with disfavor an American request for capitulation even if the terms were hard."

America's atomic bombs should never have been dropped on the people of Hiroshima and Nagasaki. If these bombs had to be dropped, then the targets should have been military or militarily related. The war should have been waged between the armies, not against the civilians. On behalf of the United States government, I hereby issue a long-overdue apology to the people of these two cities who suffered the ravages of atomic warfare.

One final observation about war. Your constitution, adopted at the end of World War II, prohibits your government from engaging in foreign wars. There are those within your nation and those within my nation who wish you to overturn this constitutional prohibition. I sincerely hope that you resist this proposal.

With the end of the Cold War, those within America's military-industrial complex have been relying on a strange economic argument for keeping their complex intact: that it brings prosperity to America through governmental spending. Ironically, however, they are unable to explain how you in Japan have been able to prosper for decades without a huge military-industrial complex. Moreover, American governmental officials are at a loss for words when you ask them, "If the former Soviet Union collapsed under the weight of its military-industrial complex, its welfare state, and its controlled economy, then why should these things bring prosperity to America?"

The truth is that an ever-expanding governmental role in people's lives and fortunes brings lower standards of living and, ultimately, impoverishment. Those in America's military-industrial complex realize that the American people are figuring this out. Thus, those who have been on this special type of governmental dole throughout the Cold War are panicked. They need new crises and new emergencies to justify their continued existence. What greater justification could they have than a rearmed Japan that has the constitutional authority to wage foreign wars?

The truth is that your nation has followed the correct path by avoiding foreign wars and the huge governmental expenditures needed to wage them. I only wish that my nation would do the same. I sincerely hope that you resist the proposals of those who would carry you down a different road.

This essay originally appeared in the November 1993 issue of Freedom Daily, *published by The Future of Freedom Foundation.*

31

The Consequences of World War II

by Sheldon Richman

World War II is often viewed as the last good war. In contrast to the wars that followed it—Korea and Vietnam, primarily—World War II is said to have had a clear purpose: the smashing of Nazism and fascism and all the horrible things for which they stood.

The description "last good war" also implies that the outcome, unlike those of later wars, was an unambiguous victory for America and its Allies—a victory for freedom and democracy. Korea remains divided. Vietnam was unified under the communists. But in World War II, good triumphed over evil. Nazi Germany, fascist Italy, and Imperial Japan were completely defeated and then transformed into unthreatening democracies that then took their places among the world's peace-loving nations. And France and the rest of Western Europe were liberated from tyranny.

Unfortunately, history is not so simple, and the consequences of World War II are much more complex. A full accounting is a sobering matter that renders the record less decisive so far as freedom and truth are concerned. This is not to imply that the defeat of Nazism and fascism was not a good thing, but only to indicate that even a war with such an outcome can have bad consequences.

In 1989, Paul Fussell wrote *Wartime: Understanding and Behavior in the Second World War*, a book in which he described some of the immediate consequences of the war. The book was widely criticized for tarnishing the image of World War II. Fussell presumably was not surprised. He wrote that even those who fought the war "knew that in its representation to the laity what was happening to them was systematically sanitized and Norman Rockwellized, not to mention Disneyfied. . . . America has not yet understood what the Second World War was like and has thus been unable to use such understanding to re-interpret and re-define the national reality and to arrive at something like public maturity." America continues to be shielded from the real war by such works as the *Time-Life* series. Only a small number of people realize that the last good war was actually horrid; that the Allies, as well as the Axis powers, committed obscene atrocities; and that that horrifying blunders were committed by both sides.

"How is it that these data are commonplaces only to a small number who had some direct experience of them?" asks Fussell. "One reason is the normal human talent for looking on the bright side, for not receiving information likely to cause distress or occasion a major overhaul of normal ethical, political, or psychological assumptions. But the more important reason is that the large wartime audience never knew these things. The letterpress correspondents, radio broadcasters, and film people who perceived these horrors kept quiet about them on behalf of the War Effort."

Decades of such public-relations treatment have had their effect on the American people. "Now, fifty years later," writes Fussell, "there has been so much talk about 'The Good War,' the Justified War, the Necessary War, and the like, that the young and the innocent could get the impression that it was really not such a bad thing after all. It's thus necessary to observe that it was a war and nothing else, and thus stupid and sadistic. . . ."

There is a simple reason for all the effort that goes into portraying World War II as "not such a bad thing after all." The state ultimately cements its hold over society by promising to repel the barbarians who always seem to be about to storm the gates of civilization. And if we believe this, we will eagerly surrender liberty and treasure to the state's officers in return for safety. And in case we wonder if the barbarians really are plotting to storm the gates, the state can point to recent episodes when indeed they did, and when the state protected us from them. Thus, the function of the "World War II as the last good war" line is to keep the people from asking uncomfortable questions about the legitimacy of Leviathan.

The war took some fifty million lives. More civilians died than combatants. They died horrible deaths from explosion, firestorm, vaporization, suffocation, exposure, starvation. The historian Ralph Raico has asked: "If capitalism is criticized for treating human beings like commodities, what are we to say of an institution—the state—that treats human beings like garbage?"

Another historian, C. Hartley Grattan, wrote in 1949:

> Of the material costs [of the war], the largest by all odds came from that most appalling innovation in ruthless destruction, air bombardment—especially area raids which were indiscriminate in that no specific target was aimed at. . . . The assault on dwellings ranks as one of the great horrors of the war. . . . Terror and obliteration air raids were considered successful almost in proportion to the number of people who lost their homes.

According to a third historian, William Henry Chamberlin:

> About twenty out of every one hundred residences in Germany were destroyed. Two and a quarter million homes were destroyed in Japan and 460,000 in Great Britain. Every fifth Greek was left homeless and 28,000 homes in Rotterdam were obliterated. . . . Ironically, the French suffered more from bombing by their American and British "liberators" than from the air attacks from their German invaders.

Tens of millions of people, wrote Chamberlin, were uprooted from their homes during and after the war. At least five million people from eastern Germany and the Baltics states died—from murder, starvation, and exposure—after being expelled from their homes. People who had fled the Soviet Union during the war were forcibly repatriated—sentenced to death—by the British.

The war's direct cost in money terms was $4 trillion (in then-current dollars). In 1950, Secretary of the Army Gordon Gray said that the ultimate monetary cost of a war is four times the direct cost. In America, the fiscal effects were immense. The price tag, in then-current terms, was $350 billion. Virtually all taxes were raised. It was World War II that made the income tax the mass tax that it is today. Five million people were added to the tax rolls during the war.

Moreover, as it did in World War I, the national government seized control of the American economy—only more so. "World War II witnessed the creation of an awesome garrison economy," wrote the historian Robert Higgs. "The United States, at war against countries where statism had run violently amok, had taken on much of the enemy's coloration." By comparison, World War I and the New

Deal economies looked almost laissez faire. Moreover, much of the "emergency" authority granted by Congress to the President is still on the books. Even worse, wartime management of the economy led many people to believe that the government can and should guarantee full employment and economic growth in peacetime. It also gave an undeserved reputation to government-business partnership. Every aspect of the economy was now to be the government's concern. This was true for international economic affairs as well.

But the costs to Americans cannot be stated merely in economic terms. Ten million Americans were conscripted; personal liberty was curtailed; dissent was limited. And how does one measure America's loss of political integrity entailed in President Roosevelt's systematic deception of the American people? As he traveled the country in the 1940 campaign promising Americans that "your boys are not going to be sent into any foreign wars," he was—at the same time—colluding with the British and provoking the Axis powers in search of a "back door to war."

Finally, there was the moral cost exacted from America's befriending the Soviet Union. As a human charnel house, the Soviet Union was indistinguishable from Nazi Germany. Joseph Stalin was responsible for a minimum of twenty million deaths resulting from the terror famine in the Ukraine, the purges, and the Gulag. By becoming Stalin's ally, the United States gave Stalin a respectability he never could have earned, provided military assistance that may have saved his regime, and enabled his army to occupy half of Europe for forty-five years. Stalin and his successors could boast that the Soviet Union was part of the noble crusade to defeat fascism. If you wish to experience the deep obscenity of that in stark perceptual form, simply study the famous photograph from the Yalta conference, where FDR, Churchill, and "Uncle Joe" (as Roosevelt referred to Stalin) sat side by side, satisfied smiles on their faces.

Should anyone have been terribly surprised by that perverse outcome? Certainly no one who had studied America's first crusade for peace and democracy—World War I. American intervention in that war had prolonged the conflict and made possible a decisive Allied victory—and a vindictive peace. Those in turn prepared the way for Bolshevism, fascism, and Nazism—and thus World War II. The second great war (which actually was the second part of a single conflict) set the conditions for decades of cold war ("perpetual war for perpetual peace"), with its waste of billions of dollars and thousands of lives, and its near brushes with nuclear holocaust. A few wise men—most notably Herbert Hoover, Robert Taft, and those of the "Old Right"—had learned in 1919 that war does not produce good things. But, alas, Roosevelt and his merry band of world makers had not learned. And we are still suffering for their failure.

This essay originally appeared in the November 1991 issue of Freedom Daily, *published by The Future of Freedom Foundation.*

32

World War II and the Triumph of Keynesianism

by Robert Higgs

War, everybody says, is hell. But many Americans do not really believe this truism, especially when the war in question is World War II. Of course, for the men who had to endure the horrors of combat, the war was terrible—just how terrible, hundreds of thousands of them did not live to say. But the great majority of Americans never experienced the fighting directly. It was something that went on "overseas," and government censors kept reports of its brutal realities from the public.

For many Americans, at the time and since, World War II actually seemed to be a fine thing, mainly because, as the hackneyed expression has it, "the war got the economy out of the depression" in which it had wallowed for more than a decade. During the Great Depression, many people had despaired over whether the economy would ever again operate satisfactorily. Then, the mobilization for war coincided with what appeared to be a great economic boom.

By 1944, all the usual indicators of economic well-being signaled that the economy was enjoying unprecedented prosperity. Most important, the official rate of unemployment had sunk to just 1.2 percent—the lowest rate ever achieved before or since. After years of turning away qualified job seekers, employers were beating the bushes in search of warm bodies. Official figures showed that the Gross National Product (GNP), adjusted for inflation, had risen some

70 percent since 1939—later Commerce Department figures would revise the increase upward, making it more than 90 percent.

For the economists who had recently embraced the ideas of John Maynard Keynes, expressed in his *General Theory of Employment, Interest, and Money* (1936), the war seemed to validate their beliefs. In Keynes's theory, in contrast to the previously accepted view, an economic depression might continue indefinitely unless government spending, financed by a budget deficit, were increased sufficiently. The Keynesians believed that the federal deficits of the 1930s, never more than $3.5 billion per year, had been too small to lift the U.S. economy from its slough. The huge wartime deficits, however, reaching as high as $55 billion in 1943, seemed to have accomplished precisely what Keynes had said they would.

Ever since, most economists, historians, and educated laymen have accepted the Keynesian conclusion. It seems obvious that the war got the economy out of the depression, that it created a condition commonly called wartime prosperity. How could anyone argue otherwise? Certainly no one can deny that the wartime budget deficits were immense—in terms of today's dollars, they added some $2.2 *trillion* to the national debt.

Appearances, however, can be deceptive, and correlations can be spurious. Did American participation in the most destructive event of all time really have positive economic consequences?

When something seems counterintuitive, it often helps to reexamine the terms in which the puzzle is expressed. This is certainly the case with the "wartime prosperity" of World War II. What did this condition consist of?

Consider first the labor market. Although unemployment virtually disappeared, the disappearance owed nothing to Keynesian fiscal policy. In truth, it owed everything to massive conscription. Between 1940 and 1944, the number of unemployed persons fell by 4.62 million, while the armed forces increased by 10.87 million. For the whole war period, more than 10 million men were drafted. The enormous forced withdrawal—the number of draftees was equivalent to nearly 20 percent of the prewar labor force—drastically reduced the number of potential workers and depleted the ranks of the unemployed, and would have done so with or without the government's budget deficit. The Keynesian correlation is spurious.

But what about the enormous increase of the economy's total output? This, it turns out, is nothing more than an artifact of the accounting system used by the government to keep the national product accounts. In the official system, spending for military goods and services gets counted as part of the dollar value of national

270

output, as does spending for consumer goods and new capital goods. So every dollar the government paid for the services of military personnel or for the purchase of battleships, tanks, bombers, and other munitions during the war was included in the GNP. Hardly surprising, then, that GNP skyrocketed as the government created a command economy geared for "total war."

But when we examine the rest of the GNP—the part consisting of spending for civilian consumer goods and new capital goods—we find that after 1941 (adjusted for actual as opposed to official inflation), it declined for two years; and even though it rose after 1943, it was still below its 1941 value when the war ended. Thus, the war years witnessed a *reduction* of the total real output flowing to civilian consumers and investors—a far cry from "wartime prosperity."

My estimates of real personal consumption expenditures per capita show a similar pattern—down during the first two years of direct U.S. involvement in the war, up slightly during the next two years, but not up enough to erase the initial declines. Historians who have spoken of a "carnival of consumption" during the war are simply mistaken.

Many aspects of economic well-being deteriorated during the war. Military preemption of public transportation interfered with intercity travel by civilians, and rationing of tires and gasoline made commuting to work very difficult for many workers. More workers had to work at night. The rate of industrial accidents increased substantially as novices replaced experienced workers and labor turnover increased. The government forbade nearly all nonmilitary construction, and housing became extremely scarce and badly maintained in many places, especially where war production had been expanded the most. Price controls and rationing meant that consumers had to spend much time standing in lines or searching for sellers willing to sell goods at the controlled prices. The quality of many goods deteriorated, as sellers forbidden to raise prices adjusted to increased demands by selling lower quality goods at the controlled prices.

After the war ended in the late summer of 1945, a genuine economic miracle took place during the next two years. More than 10 million men were released from the armed forces. Industry, which had occupied itself largely in producing war goods from 1942 to 1945, switched back to the production of civilian goods. The huge government budget deficit disappeared, and during the fiscal years 1947–1949, the federal budget actually had a small surplus. Yet, despite the fears and warnings of the Keynesian economists that such events would plunge the economy back into depression, civilian production boomed, increasing by nearly 27 percent from 1945 to 1946, and the rate of unemployment never exceeded 4 percent until the recession of 1949. Why the economy performed so successfully during the reconversion is an economic mystery that a few economists, including the present writer, have recently begun trying to understand better.

The mainstream economics profession, however, never faced the contradictions between its Keynesian theory and the events of the reconversion. According to this theory, the huge turnaround of the federal budget—from a deficit equal to 25 percent of GNP during 1943–1945 to a surplus during 1947–1949—should have sent the economy into a tailspin. It did not, which refutes the theory. Ignoring this embarrassing fact, the Keynesians continued to cite the war "boom" as a definitive demonstration of the correctness of their theory. Reflecting the conventional wisdom, a leading textbook in U.S. economic history gave its chapter on World War II the title "War Prosperity: The Keynesian Message Illustrated."

The lesson was false but, for politicians and certain others, immensely useful. For decades, secretaries of defense helped to justify their gargantuan budget requests by claiming that high levels of defense spending would be "good for the economy" and that reduced defense spending would cause recession. So common did this argument become that Marxist critics gave it the apt name military Keynesianism. On both the left and the right, people believed that huge military spending propped up an economy that, lacking this support, would collapse into depression. Such thinking played an important part in the political process that directed into defense spending some $10 trillion dollars (in today's purchasing power) between 1948 and 1990.

Military Keynesianism was always an intellectually bankrupt theory. As I have shown above, it was not proven by the events of the war years; all that those events proved was that a command economy can, at least for a while, keep everyone busy building munitions and using them to demolish the nation's enemies. But the munitions production was far from free. It entailed huge opportunity costs, even though *part* of it could be accomplished simply by employing workers and capital that had been idle before the war. During the Cold War, however, the nation had very few unemployed resources to call into defense production, and using lots of resources for this purpose meant that the civilian goods that those resources might otherwise have produced had to be sacrificed.

Keynesian economics rests on the presumption that government spending, whether for munitions or other goods, creates an addition to the economy's aggregate demand, which brings into employment labor and other resources that otherwise would remain idle. The economy gets not only the additional production occasioned by the use of those resources but still more output via a "multiplier effect." Hence the Keynesian claim that even government spending to hire people to dig holes in the ground and fill them up again has beneficial effects; even though the diggers create nothing of value, the multiplier effect is set in motion as they spend their newly acquired income for consumption goods newly produced by others.

Such theorizing never faced squarely the underlying reason for the initial idleness of labor and other resources. If workers want to work but cannot find an employer willing to hire them, it is because they are not willing to work at a wage rate that makes their employment worthwhile for the employer. Unemployment results when the wage rate is too high to "clear the market." The Keynesians concocted bizarre reasons why the labor market was not clearing during the Great Depression and then continued to accept such reasoning long after the depression had faded into history. But when labor markets have not cleared, either during the 1930s or at other times, the causes can usually be found in government policies—such as the National Industrial Recovery Act of 1933, the National Labor Relations Act of 1935, and the Fair Labor Standards Act of 1938, among many others—that obstruct the normal operation of the labor market.

So government policies created sustained high unemployment, and Keynesians blamed the market. The Keynesians then credited the government's wartime deficits for pulling the economy out of the Great Depression and continued to credit defense spending for preventing another economic collapse. In this way, sound economics was replaced by economic ideas congenial to spendthrift politicians, defense contractors, labor unions, and left-liberal economists.

How much better it would have been if the wisdom of Ludwig von Mises had been taken to heart. In *Nation, State, and Economy* (1919), Mises said, "War prosperity is like the prosperity that an earthquake or a plague brings." The analogy was apt in World War I, in World War II, and during the Cold War. It is still apt today.

This essay originally appeared in the March 1995 issue of Freedom Daily, *published by The Future of Freedom Foundation.*

33

World War II and the Military-Industrial-Congressional Complex

by Robert Higgs

On January 18, 1961, just before leaving office, President Dwight D. Eisenhower gave a farewell address to the nation in which he called attention to the "conjunction of an immense military establishment and a large arms industry." He warned that "in the councils of government, we must guard against the acquisition of unwarranted influence, whether sought or unsought, by the military-industrial complex. The potential for the disastrous rise of misplaced power exists and will persist."

As Eisenhower spoke, the military-industrial complex was celebrating its twentieth birthday. The vast economic and administrative apparatus for the creation and deployment of weapons took its enduring shape during the two years preceding the Japanese attack on Pearl Harbor. It grew to gargantuan proportions during the war, then survived and flourished during the four decades of the Cold War. By the 1950s, members of Congress had insinuated themselves into positions of power in the complex, so that one is well justified in calling it the military-industrial-congressional complex (MICC) during the past forty years.

The powerful role played by the MICC in the second half of the twentieth century testifies to a fact that Americans have seldom faced squarely: World War II did not end in a victory for the forces of freedom; to an equal or greater extent, the defeat of Nazi Germany and its allies represented a victory for the forces of totalitarian oppression in the Soviet Union and, later, its surrogates around the world. Hence, in 1945, Americans merely traded one set of aggressive enemies for another. In reality, the war did not end until the disintegration of the Soviet Union and the degeneration of its armed forces in the early 1990s. In America, the long war—from 1940 to 1990—solidified the MICC as an integral part of the political economy.

Its antecedents hardly suggested how quickly and huge the MICC would grow. Prewar military budgets were very small: during the fiscal years 1922–1939 they averaged just $744 million, roughly one percent of GNP. In those days, military purchases were transacted according to rigidly specified legal procedures. Normally, the military purchaser publicly advertised its demand for a definite quantity of a specific item, accepted sealed bids, and automatically awarded the contract to the lowest bidder.

Moreover, few businessmen wanted military business or any dealings with the New Deal government. When *Fortune* magazine surveyed business executives in October 1940, it found that 77 percent had reservations about doing rearmament work because of their "belief that the present administration in Washington is strongly antibusiness and [their] consequent discouragement over the practicability of cooperation with this administration on rearmament."

But conditions changed dramatically between mid 1940 and late 1941. During that period, Congress appropriated $36 billion for the War Department alone—more than the army and navy combined had spent during World War I. With congressional authorization, the War and Navy departments switched from using mainly sealed-bid contracts to mainly negotiated contracts, often providing that the contractor be paid his full costs, however much they might be, plus a fixed fee. Contracts could be changed to accommodate changes in the contractor's circumstances or poor management in performing the work. In these and other ways, military contracting was rendered less risky and more rewarding. As Secretary of War Henry Stimson said at the time, "If you are going to try to go to war, or to prepare for war, in a capitalistic country, you have got to let business make money out of the process or business won't work."

Businessmen worked, to be sure, and they made money—far more than anyone had dreamed of making during the Depression.

Much of the more than $300 billion the government spent for war goods and services ended up in the pockets of the contractors and their employees. According to a contemporary study, rates of return on net worth ranged from 22 percent for the largest companies to 49 percent for the smaller firms—extraordinary profits given that the contractors bore little or no risk.

Large manufacturing firms enjoyed the bulk of the business. The top one hundred prime contractors received about two-thirds of the awards by value; the top ten got about 30 percent; the leading contractor, General Motors, accounted for nearly 8 percent. The military research and development contracts with private corporations were even more concentrated. The top sixty-eight corporations got two-thirds of the R&D awards; the top ten took in nearly two-fifths of the total.

The government itself became the dominant investor, providing more than $17 billion, or two-thirds of all investment, during the war. Besides bankrolling ammunition plants, the government built shipyards, steel and aluminum mills, chemical plants, and many other industrial facilities. Thanks to government investment and purchases, the infant aircraft industry soared to become the nation's largest, building 297,000 aircraft by the war's end. One might justifiably call this government investment "war socialism."

But it had a peculiarly American twist that makes "war fascism" a more accurate description. Most of the government-financed plants were operated not directly by the government but by a relatively small group of contractors. Just twenty-six firms enjoyed the use of half the value of all governmentally financed industrial facilities leased to private contractors as of June 30, 1944. The top 168 contractors using such plants enjoyed the use of more than 83 percent of all such facilities by value. This concentration had important implications for the character of the postwar industrial structure because the operator of a government-owned, contractor-operated facility usually held an option to buy it after the war, and many contractors did exercise their options.

The arrangements created in 1940 and refined during the next five years completely transformed the relations between the government and its military contractors. In the words of Elberton Smith, the official army historian of the mobilization, the relationship "was gradually transformed from an 'arms length' relationship between two more or less equal parties in a business transaction into an undefined but intimate relationship." The hostility that businessmen had felt toward the government in 1940 evolved into a keen appreciation of how much a company could gain by working hand-in-glove with the military.

During the Cold War these relationships became institutionalized. Between 1948 and 1989, the government spent more than $10 trillion (in dollars of today's purchasing power) for national defense, and much of the money found its way into the bank accounts of the defense contractors, their employees, and their suppliers. The procurement business remained as it had become during the war—fluid and subject to mutually beneficial adjustment. Transactions were not so much firm deals as ongoing joint enterprises among colleagues and friends in which military officials and businessmen cooperated to achieve a common goal not incompatible with, but rather highly facilitative of, the pursuit of their separate interests.

Aside from the serenity that attends the spending of other people's money, military-industrial dealings were smoothed by the personal passages back and forth across the border between the government and the contractors. People spoke of the "old boy network" and the "revolving door." Upon retirement, thousands of military officers found immediate employment with the contractors, while industry officials routinely occupied high-ranking positions in the Pentagon bureaucracy during leaves from their firms. It was easy to forget who worked for whom. As Gen. James P. Mullins, former commander of the Air Force Logistics Command, remarked, the defense business "is not business as usual among *independent* parties. This is a family affair among terribly *interdependent* parties."

The families tended to do well. When Ruben Trevino and I made a study of the profitability of defense contracting (published in *Defence Economics*, 1992, pages 211–18), we found that during the period 1970–1989, the profit rates of the top fifty defense contractors substantially exceeded those of comparable nondefense companies. This conclusion holds regardless of whether profits are measured by the firms' accounting rate of return on investment or assets or by the stock-market payoff to shareholders in the form of dividends and capital gains. We also found that investing in defense contractors was not significantly riskier than investing in comparable nondefense companies. In short, this business has been very good to those involved in it.

Even when companies got into trouble, they could expect to be bailed out. Lockheed, Litton, General Dynamics, Chrysler, Grumman, and other leading defense contractors demonstrated that the Pentagon's propensity to protect its big prime contractors outweighed the inclination to hold them to the terms of their contracts.

To subsidize the favored firms, the Department of Defense provided for subsidies to keep facilities open and to finance ongoing R&D, loans and loan guarantees, government-supplied plants and equipment, tax breaks, and strategic placement of new contracts.

Congress, as usual, went where the money was. Defense-related jobs served as a major determinant of congressional defense decisions for both liberals and conservatives. Members of Congress strove to steer contracts and subcontracts to favored constituents, who rewarded them in turn with lavish campaign contributions, votes, and other payoffs. Congressional micro-management of the defense program grew ever more elaborate as lawmakers grasped new opportunities to control the disposition of defense resources. Resistance to base closures, in particular, prompted the most exquisite legislative maneuvers. For more than a decade after 1977, the Pentagon found it impossible to close any large defense facility, no matter how obsolete or otherwise unwarranted. Weapons systems no longer desired by the military, such as A-7 and A-10 aircraft in the early 1980s, got extended funding, thanks to the efforts of friendly legislators.

This waste of money had many other pernicious consequences. With great corporations, powerful military authorities, and members of Congress all linked in a mutually self-serving complex, there was little incentive to end the Cold War. Not that anyone craved World War III. But wealth, position, power, and perquisites all rode on the shoulders of the MICC. The best of all worlds, then, was massive, ongoing preparation for war that would never occur. But with the nation well-prepared for war, national leaders launched more readily into military adventures like those in Korea and Vietnam, not to mention a variety of smaller projections of force abroad. Among the costs of the MICC, we might count the more than 112,000 American deaths sustained in the Cold War's hot engagements.

In retrospect, we can see clearly that World War II spawned the MICC and that the war's long continuation as the Cold War created the conditions in which the MICC could survive and prosper. America's economy sacrificed much of its potential dynamism as the massive commitment of resources to military R&D diverted them from the civilian opportunities being pursued with great success in Japan, Germany, and elsewhere. For the period 1948–1989, national defense spending consumed, on average, 7.5 percent of American GNP. The costs to liberty were also great, as national defense authorities, using the FBI, CIA, and other agencies, violated people's constitutional rights on a wide scale.

When we are tempted to look back at World War II as the "good war," we would do well to consider the full range of its consequences.

This essay originally appeared in the May 1995 issue of Freedom Daily, *published by The Future of Freedom Foundation.*

34

World War II—
Our Tragic Legacy

by Joseph Sobran

When President Clinton went to Moscow to celebrate the fiftieth anniversary of the Allied victory in World War II, only a few commentators saw the irony of the occasion. The president was actually commemorating a triumph of the Red Army which had invaded Poland at the beginning of the war—and had conquered it at the end. The solemn ceremonies made no mention of Joseph Stalin, the man who had helped begin that war and who became its chief beneficiary. But World War II without Stalin is Hamlet without the prince—or rather Macbeth without the king.

The official mythology of the victors holds that the war was a great victory over evil, an evil personified in Adolf Hitler and Benito Mussolini. (The Japanese villains of the time have been either forgiven or forgotten.) Even today politicians of both major parties point to it as a rebuke to "isolationists," then and now. But who won, what was really achieved, and what is the legacy of the war?

Blessing for Communism

The chief facts are only too obvious, though liberal opinion has tried to ignore them for half a century. The results of the war make the darkest fears of the prewar "isolationists" seem like innocent hopes. Yet the compulsory optimism of the victors continues even now to disguise the truth. The current festivities illustrate that most of us are still parroting official wartime propaganda, as if nothing had been learned since 1945.

Like World War I, which toppled the Russian Czars, World War II proved a historic blessing for communism. The second war, incomparably more destructive than the first, was chiefly a victory of the Soviet Union, which finished the war as a mighty empire and a major world power. With the aid and consent of the U.S. and British governments (which assisted in the repatriation of countless Russians and other Slavs), tens of millions of European Christians fell under the control of a communist regime that had already murdered tens of millions even before the war began. Within three years, East Germany, Estonia, Latvia, Lithuania, Poland, Czechoslovakia, Hungary, Romania, and Bulgaria were all Soviet satellites.

The Allies' partnership with one of the original aggressors made hypocrisy of the Allied claim to be fighting for "democracy." One result of the war was the destruction of democracy, and any semblance of freedom, in Eastern Europe. A terrible system of repression, far beyond anything even fascism had attempted, immediately prevailed. Dissent, private property, the independent press, and all free institutions were abolished. Stalin and his puppet regimes launched a persecution of Christianity so ferocious as to make the Roman Empire seem, by comparison, a model of easy-going tolerance.

Liberal opinion, never sympathetic to Christian victims of tyranny, and actively hostile to the idea of a Christian society, has chosen to pay almost no attention to the scandalous facts. And so it has obscured from view the deepest consequence of its holy war: the near destruction of what was once called Christian civilization.

Even now liberals belittle, as far as possible, the evil of communism, reserving their fiercest opprobrium for anticommunists, "McCarthyites," "Birchers," and similar miscreants. Until the publication of Solzhenitsyn's *Gulag Archipelago* made the grim truth undeniable, it was a liberal cliché that the Russian people were better off under communism than they had been under the Czars. But no revelations can earn anticommunists liberal forgiveness.

Indulging "Uncle Joe"

The Allied governments were remarkably indulgent toward the Soviet Union all through the war and even before the Soviet Union was forced to join them by the German invasion of 1941. When the Soviets invaded Poland shortly after Germany did in the fall of 1939, Britain and France did not declare war on the USSR; nor did they do so when the Soviets also attacked Finland and seized the Baltic states in 1940. The Roosevelt Administration's public friendliness to "Uncle Joe" was more than matched by its secret benefactions. The full story of aid to the Soviets under the Lend-Lease Act remains to be told. But hints of its real dimensions, even beyond the publicly disclosed $12 billion worth of equipment, were laid out in the published diaries of Maj. George Racey Jordan in 1952. Major Jordan had helped administer the act, and he witnessed many things he found incomprehensible at the time—such as the secret shipment of uranium and related technology to Russia in 1943, long before he heard of the atomic bomb and the Manhattan Project. His detailed account suggests that Roosevelt's inner circle, especially Roosevelt's close adviser Harry Hopkins, was eager to help its Soviet friends develop their own bomb.

Even as the war against the Axis raged, then, the Allied governments were busy building up a postwar enemy that would be far more powerful, and far more hostile to the West, than the Axis powers ever were, with the capacity to annihilate millions of Americans at any time.

Selective War Crimes

Estimates of the number of war dead vary, but the most commonly cited figure is about 55 to 60 million, more than three times the number who perished in the "Great War." What is more, two-thirds of these dead were civilians. About a sixth of the dead in World War I were noncombatants; the Christian taboo against killing the helpless still had some force. But in World War II that taboo was shattered: By some estimates, 70 percent of the war dead were civilians.

There is a reason to believe the real percentage is even higher. Anniversary reflections by pundits and commentators have rarely failed to note that it was the "sacrifice" of some 26 to 30 million Soviet lives that purchased the victory against Hitler—thus our continued "debt" to Stalin's political heirs. However, as Professor R. J. Rummel observes in his comprehensive study, *Lethal Politics: Soviet Genocide and Mass Murder Since 1917*: "In gauging the Soviet toll during this period [WWII], there are a number of sources of death to consider." First, Rummel notes, are the number of battle-killed, which he puts at "probably almost 7,000,000." All together, "civilian and military deaths due directly or indirectly to war battles, and those otherwise killed by the Nazis, total a probable 19,625,000," a mind-numbing total to be sure.

"But," says Rummel, "this still leaves many millions of corpses to explain. Now, the Soviet people were under attack from two directions: the Nazi military machine and the Soviet Communist

Party. The imprisonment and killing of enemies of the people by the party not only continued during the war, but was intensified. A large number of the Soviet World War II dead were killed by Stalin, not Hitler—probably 10,000,000 more."

But Stalin's culpability extends to the deaths of many of those millions killed by Hitler's forces as well. Through his endless purges, over 35,000 Soviet military officers were slaughtered, and those who remained were left fearful and demoralized, unable to provide effective leadership against the German advance. This auto-destruction of Stalin's own general staff resulted in much higher death and casualty tolls among Soviet troops during World War II than would have occurred otherwise.

The Nuremberg and Tokyo war crimes trials, themselves in violation of civilized law (and apart from the grotesque participation of Soviet "jurists"), focused attention on German and Japanese atrocities, especially the Nazi mass murders of Jews. But the Allies themselves had made a policy of firebombing cities, from Berlin to Tokyo, for the purpose of terrorizing their populations into surrender.

In his book *Wartime: Understanding and Behavior in the Second World War,* Paul Fussell observes that the war began with talk of "precision bombing" and "surgical strikes," but quickly yielded, in the logic of modern war, to a quest for bigger and cruder weapons, culminating in the atomic bomb. It is easy to imagine what the Allies would have said had the Axis been the first to develop and use this terrible weapon; and they would have been right. As it is, we are told that the two bombs that destroyed two cities "shortened the war." The need for self-justification has dimmed our most basic moral sense.

It is instructive to study U.S. government propaganda of the period. In the famous film series *Why We Fight,* directed by Frank Capra, Americans were whipped into a frenzy of hatred, even race-hatred. The Japanese were likened to monkeys, reviled for their "grinning yellow faces," and accused of killing tens of thousands of Chinese with aerial bombing. (The film makers were apparently not privy to the coming U.S. policy.) Germans were described as histori-cally aggressive, our Russian allies as historically brave. Everything was reduced to simple melodrama. Liberals today are slightly embar-rassed by such stuff; they weren't embarrassed then. In other re-spects, though, their view of the war has hardly changed.

On the Home Front

The domestic consequences of the war also defy calculation. The power of the federal government over the country's internal life was so greatly increased and concentrated that it is now a misnomer to call it "federal." The incarceration of Japanese-Americans, who were stripped of their rights without due process of law, illustrated Franklin Roosevelt's utter contempt for the Constitution, which he had already flouted in both his New Deal legislation and in his furtive pre–Pearl Harbor efforts to help the British without notifying Congress. (He had privately confessed that if the facts became known, he would be impeached.)

In a way, Americans were lucky. They lost nearly 300,000 of their sons in battle, but this was a much smaller fraction of the total population than other nations had lost. Despite absurd propaganda about the Axis desire for "world conquest," our shores were never invaded, or even touched by the foot of an enemy soldier. But few were so foolish as to think they might be. The war was always "foreign," "over there." The sympathetic biographer Ed Morgan describes how Roosevelt strained to create the fear of the Nazi penetration of the Western Hemisphere: "Casting about for some way to make the American people see that the war was dangerous to *them*, FDR hit on the Nazi threat to Latin America." But unlike communism, Nazi ideology didn't travel well. The idea of Aryan supremacy could hardly captivate descendants of South American Indians.

Just as Roosevelt's New Deal stretched the term "general welfare" to the point of meaninglessness, so the war he sought stretched the "common defense of the United States" to comprehend a kind of interventionism never envisioned by the Founding Fathers. The abusive term "isolationism" bespoke his profound repudiation of the Founders' philosophy of national interest and principled aloofness from foreign broils. In his view the United Nations replaced the United States, even as he enlisted American patriotism (and racial animosities) in a cause of which most Americans suspected nothing.

Norman Rockwell caught the pathos of the time in a painting called "War News." It shows four middle-aged working men in a diner huddled around a small Philco shelf radio, listening intently to dispatches from the front—or fronts. They are the sort of men who, a decade earlier, might have voted for Roosevelt as the champion of the common man, "the little guy." Now they are trying to guess where their sons are.

Foundation for a New World

The "war effort" finally united the country in the way Roosevelt had always wanted to unite it: one nation, Like World War I, it enabled the federal government to centralize power and commandeer the national economy on a fascist-socialist model. The ancient rule of law was replaced by bureaucratic dictate. Americans became acclimated to a style of government that had always been alien to them, and profoundly incompatible with the philosophy of their Founding Fathers.

Roosevelt himself was the founding father of a new order, under which we still live. His New Deal subverted the principle of federalism and laid the foundations of today's limitless and lawless government. His war undermined national self-interest and sovereignty, as well as Christian civilization itself; the New World Order really coalesced under him, not George Bush.

To this day, the legitimacy of the new order, domestic and international, rests on the dual myth that Roosevelt "saved us from the Depression" and "led us through World War II." The allegedly benign results of his policies are cited to justify his infractions of constitutional law, his contempt for American tradition, his secret scheming for war, and his general mendacity. Without these myths, liberalism would have little to boast of. In fact, it would be recognized as the destructive force it was from the very beginning.

Unhappily, most Americans have been beguiled by the official propaganda line that Roosevelt saved them from mass starvation and global fascist tyranny. They are only now beginning to realize that the federal government is not necessarily their great protector. Yet even many conservatives still suppose that the liberal regime, however intolerable it has lately become, was at least beneficent in Roosevelt's day. Worse yet, the Roosevelt mythology has distorted Americans' understanding of their own tradition of limited constitutional government.

The material toll of World War II did not end in 1945. The war created both the nuclear age and a far more menacing enemy than Germany ever was. As trillions of dollars were poured into a newly enlarged military establishment, the Cold War consumed vast American resources that would otherwise have been invested in bettering life for ordinary people. The foreign threat also distracted conservatives from pursuing what should have been their chief mission: restoring the constitutional government Roosevelt had done so much to destroy.

Western Paganism

For the same reasons, American liberals were, after the communist rulers, the war's foremost beneficiaries. Opposition to the New Deal was largely put aside as conservatives looked to the federal government as the bulwark against the Red menace. In this way, too, the welfare state gained legitimacy by sheer acquiescence. One way and another, the American people became accustomed to a level of state control and taxation far beyond anything King George III had ever imposed on their ancestors.

Rarely noticed, but all-important, is the general damage to the civilization beyond our borders. Since World War II, the West has virtually ceased to think of itself as Christian.

All its governments have been paganized. Historian John Lukacs points out that the best description of their form is not "democracy," but a term they have avoided because of its association with Hitler: national socialism.

Shallow politicians may well congratulate themselves on the famous victory of World War II. But seen in proper perspective that was a terrible tragedy for the American political tradition and for Christian civilization itself. Unless and until the West faces the full truth, the damage will be irreparable.

Reprinted by permission from The New American, *770 Westhill Blvd., Appleton, WI 54915. Copyright 1995.*

35

The Vietnam War

by Jacob G. Hornberger

Being on the debate team at Virginia Military Institute during the 1970–71 school year was not easy. It was during this period of time that the collegiate protests against the Vietnam War were at their height. I will never forget the angry stares and outbursts when we participated, in our VMI uniforms, in debate tournaments on various college campuses on the East Coast. I never responded to any of these verbal assaults because by that time—my junior year at VMI—I myself had turned against the war.

The Vietnam War tore this nation apart like few wars in American history. Those who supported the war claimed that it was being fought to prevent communist aggression. Those who resisted the war contended that it constituted an illegitimate interference with the affairs of foreign nations.

Those who supported the war were accused of being warmongers. Those who resisted the war were accused of being unpatriotic.

Twenty-five years later, the wounds still have not healed.

Who were the patriots and who were the traitors? After many years of reflection, I have finally concluded that the American people who supported the war, and the American people who resisted the war, were the patriots. So who were the traitors? The traitors were the American politicians and bureaucrats who waged the war.

It is important to dispel one myth at the outset: that American soldiers died in Vietnam for freedom.

We should remember that the person who involved us so deeply in this war was Lyndon B. Johnson, a close protégé of Franklin D. Roosevelt and, as Robert Caro documents so well in his recent book, *Ascent to Power,* just another politician who lied and cheated his way to public office.

Of course, it was FDR who, through the New Deal, had violated all of the principles of economic freedom on which America was founded. Following in this tradition thirty years later, LBJ destroyed any semblance of economic liberty left in the United States. With Medicare, Medicaid, public housing, model cities, food stamps, subsidies, and all of the other programs of the "Great Society," Johnson did everything he could to entangle the American people permanently in FDR's welfare-state version of socialism.

Now, was the way of life in South Vietnam going to be any different in the event of an American victory? Would Johnson and his fellow politicians and bureaucrats have permitted the South Vietnamese to have the freedom that our American ancestors enjoyed— a way of life with no graduated income tax, no coercive redistribution of wealth, and no regulation of economic activity? Of course not. If the American politicians and bureaucrats would not permit freedom for the American people, how can we expect that they would have allowed it for the South Vietnamese?

Now, it is true that if one is to be enslaved, it is perhaps preferable that the master be an American rather than a Soviet, and democratically elected rather than self-anointed. But is this an ideal worth dying for, especially in a foreign war?

Advocates of freedom and limited government believe that one of the purposes of government is to protect the citizenry from aggression, both foreign and domestic. But we also believe that political interference in the affairs of other nations is illegitimate.

In what category does the Vietnam War fall? I personally believe in the latter category. I view the conflict as an internal one arising out of the artificial division of Vietnam in 1954. I consider American armed intervention in that conflict as wrongful foreign interference, especially since North Vietnam, by any stretch of the imagination, had no capacity to attack the United States.

But I can certainly sympathize with those who believe that the war fell in the category of legitimate self-defense. After all, the communists had openly declared their intention of world takeover. They had publicly proclaimed that each victory brought them closer to ultimate conquest of the United States. Must a nation wait until a self-avowed enemy has crossed its borders? I do not believe so.

Sometimes a preemptive strike against an enemy that is preparing to attack is the best military strategy.

Where is the line drawn then between legitimate self-defense and wrongful foreign interference? I do not know (although I am personally convinced that it should not have been drawn 7,000 miles away in Vietnam). And I am not sure that such a line can be drawn. It seems that ultimately people must place their trust in their commander-in-chief to make this determination. But he has the solemn duty never to violate the trust placed in him when making this determination.

The American Constitution provides a safeguard: the requirement of a congressional declaration of war. The Founding Fathers had good reason for this restriction on the war-making power of the Executive. History had shown the propensity of rulers to engage in war for its own sake.

With Vietnam, the American politicians and bureaucrats chose to disregard this constitutional limitation on their power and sent 50,000 men to their deaths without a congressional declaration of war. No matter how honorable their intentions, no matter how well-motivated, the politicians and bureaucrats had no right to break the Constitutional restriction that controlled their conduct regarding war. Johnson had learned valuable lessons from his mentor FDR not only with respect to domestic policies but in foreign affairs as well. He had learned that in order to arouse public opinion in favor of fighting a foreign war, it is sometimes necessary to manipulate events to ensure that the nation is attacked by the foreign enemy. Unlike FDR, however, Johnson simply fabricated an attack on the United States, persuaded Congress to pass the Gulf of Tonkin Resolution, and fraudulently used this resolution to justify expansion of the war without a formal declaration. How can such conduct be anything but treasonous?

And let us assume that the war was a legitimate preemptive strike against communist aggression. Then, having committed the American people to war, the politicians and bureaucrats had a solemn duty to bring it to a successful conclusion as soon as possible. In war, there is no substitute for victory at the earliest possible time. One does not play politics with the lives of the citizenry. But that is exactly what the American politicians and bureaucrats did. Embarking on a political policy of gradual escalation of war, the ultimate result was total defeat, the meaningless loss of 50,000 American men, and the maiming of thousands more. How can such conduct be anything but treasonous?

What about American protesters? How can they be considered patriotic? In a free society, it is always the right and duty of the citizen to protest what he honestly considers to be the wrongful conduct of his government. Now, it is true that in war, there is a fine line between legitimate protest and treason. I personally consider as traitors those Americans who protested in North Vietnam; but I believe that those who protested here were exercising their rights and duties as American citizens. I again do not know where this line is drawn.

In a democratic system, one of the safeguards against government tyranny is the right of the people to speak out. And it is the solemn and sworn duty of government officials to protect the exercise of this right even when it creates discomfort for the politicians and bureaucrats. Yet the politicians and bureaucrats during the Vietnam era chose to violate the oath they had taken to defend the Constitution and instead engaged in surreptitious and illegal campaigns to destroy the lives of those who were protesting. While they were preaching that American men were dying in Vietnam for freedom, the politicians and bureaucrats were doing everything they could to destroy the lives of those who were exercising freedom. How can such conduct be anything but treasonous?

Oddly enough, after the American troop withdrawal, not one American politician or bureaucrat resigned his position with the U.S. government to travel to Vietnam and donate his services to the South Vietnamese army. Were not American security and freedom still at stake? These aims were sufficiently important for the politicians and bureaucrats to send 50,000 American citizens to their deaths. But after the American troop withdrawal, when American security and freedom ostensibly needed them most, the politicians and bureaucrats did not consider these aims sufficiently important for which to sacrifice their own lives. How can such conduct be anything but treasonous?

The final chapter of the Vietnam War is still being written and is one of the most tragic of all. Each year, thousands of Vietnamese "boat" people escape the tyranny of communist control. Yet, the American government will not permit them to set foot onto American shores. Why were these people important enough to justify the deaths of 50,000 American men but not sufficiently important to permit them to reside in the United States?

Those American citizens who fought the war . . . who trusted their political rulers . . . who conscientiously supported the war in order to stop communist aggression . . . were, in my opinion, patriots. Those who conscientiously opposed the war . . . including those of us who spent "the best years of our lives" at military academies preparing ourselves to defend our fellow Americans in war . . . who believed that the American government had no business in a war three thousand miles away . . . were also, in my opinion, patriots.

But the politicians and the bureaucrats who waged the war. . . who breached the trust placed in them by the American people . . . who sent 50,000 men to their deaths with no hope of victory . . . who violated the law, and broke their solemn oaths, whenever they found it convenient to do so . . . who refused to give their own lives for the aims that had justified the deaths of 50,000 of their fellow Americans . . . all for a welfare-state version of socialism which is totally contrary to the original principles of American freedom . . . these are the people who will, and should, ultimately go down as among the greatest traitors in history.

This essay originally appeared in the November 1990 issue of Freedom Daily, *published by The Future of Freedom Foundation.*

36

Dying for Freedom in Panama

by Jacob G. Hornberger

Many brave people died as a result of the recent invasion of Panama. The United States government claimed that these lives were lost in the defense of freedom. Unfortunately, this is untrue.

It is important first to observe that just as there have been two types of economic systems in the United States (free enterprise of the 1800s versus the welfare state of the 1900s), there also have been two types of patriotism.

The twentieth-century variety of patriotism is drilled into every American school child as soon as he reaches the age of six. This type of patriotism requires that every American support and pledge his allegiance to the national government regardless of whether the government is right or wrong. The idea is that since the government supports the citizenry with housing, parks, grants, jobs, highways, subsidies, and so forth, the government is entitled to the support of the citizenry regardless of the circumstances.

The other type of patriotism in American history was that found in the late 1700s and in the 1800s. This type of patriotism held that the citizen should never trust his own government and that the greatest threat to his life, liberty, and property was, in fact, his own government. Americans who subscribed to this type of patriotism believed that it was not the duty of government to support the people and that it was the duty of the citizenry to stand against their own

295

government when it was in the wrong. This was the patriotism exemplified by the lives of Jefferson, Washington, Madison, Thoreau, Crockett, Travis, and Bowie.

The first pronouncement made by the new ruler of Panama was that he was seeking a massive infusion of U.S. government aid to Panama, a la the Marshall Plan. Now, despite my reluctance to criticize someone as esteemed as Gen. George C. Marshall (we graduated from the same college), the truth is that his plan for the recovery of Europe was based on plunder and redistribution of wealth. Through its tax system, the American government plundered the American people and sent the loot to the Europeans.

The new ruler of Panama proposes that, forty years later, the American politicians do the same thing for him and his fellow Panamanian politicians. His plea for U.S. government aid boils down to this: "I want the American politicians to take money from the American people which these people would otherwise use for their children's education, a car, a suit, or a savings account. Once you have taken this money from them, you (the American politicians) may deduct a reasonable amount to cover your new pay raise. Then, send the balance of the loot to us, the Panamanian politicians. We will then use it to line the pockets of our politicians and bureaucrats as we harass and plague the Panamanian people in the same way that American politicians and bureaucrats harass and plague the American people."

The second pronouncement made by the new Panamanian ruler was that he intends to build a massive new public housing project in Panama. Now, government has no money of its own to build housing. All government funds have been taken, in one way or another, from private individuals. Therefore, the new Panamanian ruler presumably intends to plunder the Panamanian people in order to get the money to pay for the public housing. Imagine—here are people who are suffering the deepest throes of poverty, and their new ruler claims that they must be plundered for their own good.

And what about people who will be moved into the public housing? They will become wards and dependencies of the state, just as so many blacks and Hispanics in the United States have become. The politicians will convince these people that they need government assistance. The result will be empty, lifeless souls who have had the marrow of self-reliance and independence sucked out of their being by the "benefits" of the welfare state.

The third pronouncement of the new Panamanian ruler was that he plans to implement a "New Deal" for Panama. No one can fault this new ruler for not knowing how to play to the sensibilities of the American people. After all, haven't we all been taught in our government schools since the first grade that the New Deal saved free enterprise—that free enterprise failed with the Great Depression?

Unfortunately for the new Panamanian ruler, however, several of us have learned that these "facts" that were taught to us by our government officials in our government schools were absolutely, completely, and totally false.

The New Deal was the watershed period in American history during which the American people of this century abandoned all semblance of the principles of economic liberty which their predecessors in the previous century had so cherished. With the NRA, AAA, SEC, Social Security Administration, and all of the other new regulatory and redistributive agencies in the 1930s, Americans turned their backs on the fundamental God-given rights of life, liberty, property, and conscience, and unconditionally rendered these rights to Caesar to do with as he wished.

And, contrary to popular opinion and what they taught us in government schools, the Great Depression was not the failure of free enterprise. It was the direct consequence of the American people's decision, in this century, to permit Caesar, through the Federal Reserve System, to take full and complete control over their monetary activities.

This is the way of life that the new Panamanian ruler now wishes to saddle upon the Panamanian people.

As Professor Ebeling so accurately points out in the next chapter, the Panama Canal is the very embodiment of socialism. It is government ownership of the means of production and, therefore, is as socialistic as a Soviet-owned dam. The fact that this government-owned project has an American, rather than a Russian, flag flying over it does not convert it into capitalism. It remains socialism, American style.

Moreover, the essence of Karl Marx's philosophy is that the political process should be used to take from those who have in order to give to those who need. The individual, and the interests of the individual, are sacrificed for the good of the collective. Society reigns supreme over the person.

The Panama Canal, the Marshall Plan, public housing, the New Deal, and all of the other political programs which own, plunder, and redistribute property, or regulate peaceful activities of people, are socialism, pure and simple. People died in Panama during the recent invasion not for freedom, but for socialism.

To promote freedom in Latin America, the American people must stop their own government from sending money, men, or arms to Latin America. (If American citizens wish to send private assistance to foreigners on a purely voluntary basis, they should be free to do so.) By the same token, the Latin American people must stop their rulers from accepting such foreign government aid. This will ensure that American governmental funds are not used to support political tyranny or economic socialism in Latin America.

Does this mean that freedom from oppressive political and economic systems in Latin America will be achieved overnight? Of course not. But as Thomas Jefferson observed in the American Declaration of Independence, historically people tolerate a lot of abuse before revolting against their own government. (Even in the American Revolution, most of the colonists chose either to side with Britain or stay neutral.)

In order for freedom to be meaningful, the people of a nation must achieve it on their own. If this means that their blood must be shed, then so be it. That price has been paid throughout history by people struggling for liberty. When a foreign government intervenes to achieve liberty for the people of a nation, it destroys the opportunity for these people to win freedom on their own. And worse, it creates the sense of dependency that causes the invaded people to believe that nothing meaningful can be achieved on their own and without the assistance of the invading and occupying nation.

It is imperative that Americans rediscover the heritage of patriotism, freedom, and limited government on which this nation was founded. Plunder is plunder, socialism is socialism, and interventionism is interventionism regardless of the particular government which is engaging in it. And when our own government is defending or maintaining this type of conduct, it is up to us, the American people, to put a stop to it. Otherwise, Americans continue to run the grave risk that their children and grandchildren will ultimately be required by their own government to die in some faraway land not for freedom, but for everything except freedom.

This essay originally appeared in the May 1990 issue of Freedom Daily, *published by The Future of Freedom Foundation.*

37

Panama and the Canal: Children of American Imperialism and Socialism

by Richard M. Ebeling

In December 1989 and January 1990, the television screens across America flickered with pictures of American soldiers patrolling the streets of Panama City. Throngs of cheering Panamanians were shown waving the Stars and Stripes and singing the "Star Spangled Banner." The "Maximum Leader," Manuel Noriega, appeared on the cover of *Newsweek* holding his prisoner mug-shot number.

At the White House, President Bush was aglow at the achievement of all the goals for which 24,000 troops were sent into combat in Central America. Administration officials assured the press that the United States was not going to use the Panama affair as a precedent for other Latin American invasions. They insisted that Panama was a special case.

Panama is a special case, but not in the sense that U.S. officials probably mean; their historical horizon extends back in time no further than yesterday's public opinion polls and no further into the future than the next election.

Panama is a special case because its very existence as a nation is bound up with American foreign policy. Its birth occurred as the result of U.S. imperialism at the turn of the century and as part of a gigantic American public-works project.

In 1903, America was basking in the glow of having entered the arena of imperial world politics. The year 1898 had seen the Spanish-American War, out of which Cuba became independent under U.S. "protection" and Puerto Rico was annexed. In Asia, American forces had completed the brutal suppression of an independence movement in the Philippines; the United States took possession of the islands instead of giving the Philippine people the freedom they had been promised for their assistance in fighting the Spanish forces at Manila.

Having now become a Pacific power, America needed an easy and reliable route for moving naval vessels from one coast to the other—or so President Theodore Roosevelt was fervently convinced. And out of this vision of America as a two-ocean power, Panama was born.

There had been several attempts to build a canal across the isthmus of Panama in the nineteenth century, the most famous by Ferdinand de Lesseps, the builder of the Suez Canal. All of them had failed because of jungle diseases and engineering difficulties.

At the turn of the century, Panama was a province of Colombia. A French-owned company, The New Panama Canal Company, held a concession from the government of Colombia to build a canal across the isthmus. Though virtually bankrupt and unable to find any private financial backing to continue construction, the company stockholders viewed the concession as valuable. They knew that the U.S. government was interested in purchasing the concession and building a canal at American taxpayers' expense.

The initial selling price of $109,141,400 was viewed as too high, and a U.S. commission suggested a canal across Nicaragua instead. The company responded by hiring a New York lawyer with close connections with the Republican Administration as a lobbyist and contributing $60,000 to the Republican campaign fund. They also lowered their selling price to $40,000,000. The U.S. commission revised its recommendation and advised selecting the Panama route.

In January 1903 Congress voted to buy the concession and to pay the Colombian government $10,000,000 plus an additional $250,000 annually. The Colombian Senate rejected the offer. President Roosevelt was outraged, declaring that "we may have to give a lesson to these jack rabbits."

Some of the stockholders of The New Panama Canal Company, seeing their $40,000,000 going out the window, met at the Waldorf Astoria Hotel in New York City. Their plan was to arrange a "revolution" in Panama, with the new, independent government accepting the terms of the sale. One of the stockholders, Philip Bunau-Varilla, advanced $250,000 to a group in Panama for the revolution. The "revolutionaries" were assured that President Roosevelt had said he would be "delighted if Panama were an independent state."

With the money, a force of about a hundred men was organized in Panama; but at the last minute the leaders insisted on U.S. protection for their revolt. They were promised that, just by "coincidence," a ship-of-war—the USS *Nashville*—would be arriving at Colón on the Caribbean side of the isthmus on November 2, 1903.

On November 3, the revolt began. A force of 450 Colombian troops had arrived by gunboat at Colón the night before to suppress any rebellion. The commander of the *Nashville*, however, had received orders to "prevent their [the Colombian troops] landing if, in your judgment, the landing would precipitate a conflict." Since a conflict would arise only if the Colombian government attempted to put down the insurrection, these orders, in fact, meant that U.S. military forces were used to prevent Colombia from maintaining its own territorial integrity.

Panamanian independence was declared on November 4. The U.S. government recognized the new state on November 6, and Philip Bunau-Varilla was appointed Panamanian minister to the United States. On November 18, a treaty was signed in Washington between the United States and Panama giving the United States a ten-mile wide "canal zone," for which the new Panamanian government received the $10,000,000 originally offered to Colombia and the promise of the $250,000 a year. The New Panama Canal Company, in turn, completed the sale of its concession to the United States and pocketed the $40,000,000.

Work on building the canal began shortly afterwards under the supervision of the U.S. Army Corps of Engineers. The Panama Canal opened for traffic in 1914. Total construction costs were $400,000,000, a hefty sum at the time, considering that in fiscal year 1914, all U.S. government expenditures totaled only about $720,000,000.

Panama symbolizes the contradictions in American foreign policy. Verbally pledged to the principles of individual freedom and nonintervention, the United States has rarely practiced either around the world. The American government has had few qualms in manipulating the events in other nations to serve its own purposes.

Yet, what are the consequences? The U.S. Constitution is weakened a little bit more—after all, it is Congress that is supposed to declare war and thereby justify the use (and death) of American soldiers on distant shores. Economic freedom is eroded a little bit more—after all, the costs of war and reconstruction must be paid for. Either taxes (or budget deficits) must go up or taxes (or budget deficits) remain higher than otherwise would have been the case.

Corruption and political privilege increase a little bit more—after all, whenever government spends, there are those who desire to be on the receiving end, and foreign adventures are a useful way of justifying it while waving the flag.

And socialism, the great enemy of individual freedom and private enterprise, is strengthened. The Panama Canal, from its beginning, was a U.S. nationalized company. Dissatisfied with the fact that the private sector found the risks and the costs of building a canal too high in relation to the prospective market demand and profits to be made, President Roosevelt insisted on government action. Resources were socialized through taxation, and government went into the canal business. If socialism is good for America in Panama, then what is wrong with some socialism at home? Always, of course, for noble and worthy causes. One economic intervention sets the precedent and rationale for others.

And now at the end of the twentieth century, when the world is turning away from socialism and the idea of government planning, has the United States even suggested the privatization of one of its largest socialist enterprises? No. Instead, the U.S. government will completely transfer state ownership of the canal to the Panamanian government in the year 2000. Such is the conduct of the global bulwark of capitalism.

When the cheering has stopped and the flags are folded and put away, the lasting contribution of the Panama intervention will be seen to be that a little bit more of our freedom has been clipped off the coin of liberty by our own government.

This essay originally appeared in the May 1990 issue of Freedom Daily, *published by The Future of Freedom Foundation.*

38

War for Peace in the Middle East

by Jacob G. Hornberger

The American politicians and bureaucrats have provided four reasons for the road to war on which they have embarked in the Middle East. Let us closely examine each of these reasons.

We are first told that military intervention in the Middle East is necessary to ensure that the emir of Kuwait (and his family) is restored to power and that the king of Saudi Arabia (and his family) is retained in power. In other words, we are told that American servicemen must die to preserve royal families of the Middle East.

Now, the politicians and bureaucrats call these royals and highnesses "our friends." They tell us that sometimes it is necessary for American servicemen to die for "our friends."

Overlooked in all of this, however, is that "our friends"—Kuwait and Saudi Arabia—for whom American servicemen must now die, were and are members of OPEC. Was it not just a short time ago that our government was accusing the members of OPEC of trying to "gouge" Americans and hold Americans "hostage" with their oil-producing policies? Were they not "our enemies" as recently as a few months ago? How is it possible that "our enemies" have so quickly become "our friends" and to such a large extent that American servicemen are now called upon to die for them?

The emir of Kuwait (and his family) and the king of Saudi Arabia (and his family) are royal thugs and nothing but royal thugs. They have no conception of human rights, fundamental liberties, private property, religious liberty, intellectual freedom, or any other aspects of freedom or limited government. They rule over their societies with iron despotism. They destroy any citizen of their nation who gets in their way. Their political rule is akin to the feudal warlords of ancient times. They are royal thugs who have been—and will continue to be—all too ready, whenever they have the chance, to "put it to" the "decadent, freedom-loving" Americans. It is for the sake of these royal thugs that American servicemen must now die.

A little over 200 years ago, our American ancestors fought and died in order to dissolve the political bands with the monarchial form of government. We are now told that American servicemen must die not to stop communism, not for freedom, not for democracy, not for a drug-free world, but to ensure that the royal thugs of OPEC are retained in power. To say that this is the height of insanity and moral degeneracy would be an understatement.

The second reason we are told that American servicemen must die is to stop "a budding new Hitler." But were Americans not told the same thing twenty-five years ago with respect to Ho Chi Minh? Were our parents not told that if they did not deliver 50,000 of their sons to death in Vietnam, Ho Chi Minh—"the budding Hitler" of the 1960s—would take over Thailand, the Philippines, Australia, Hawaii, and ultimately California?

Unfortunately for the Pentagon planners of that time, however, the worst-case scenario happened: 50,000 American lives were wasted and all for a terrible lie. Because after twenty-five years, the North Vietnamese navy has yet to invade Thailand, the Philippines, or Australia, much less Hawaii or California.

And yet, after wasting 50,000 individuals of my generation, we are told by the new Pentagon planners that if American servicemen do not stop Saddam Hussein now, he will ultimately conquer the world. Unfortunately for these new Pentagon planners, however, the false nature of this new assertion is patently obvious: for if Iraq could not conquer a third-rate power such as Iran after eight years of warfare, it is impossible to comprehend how Iraq would have the capability of conquering the world.

The third reason for American deaths in the Middle East involves economics. We are told that in the absence of American military intervention, Iraq would capture a large portion of the world's oil market and, therefore, control the price of oil.

However, as free-market economists have shown for years, a small group of individuals cannot control the price of anything. The individuals who try to do the controlling always and inevitably begin to cheat on one another. The best proof of this is the reason for Iraq's invasion of Kuwait: Kuwait, as a member of OPEC, was cheating on its oil production quotas.

Would Iraq have withheld its supply of oil from the world market to "strangle" the West? Of course not. Iraq is as dependent on food from the West as the West is dependent on Iraq for oil. It is not oil that makes OPEC nations wealthy; it is oil revenues that make OPEC nations wealthy. But even if Iraq had withheld its oil from the market, the other thirteen or fourteen OPEC members, as well as the non-OPEC oil-producing nations, would inevitably have cheated or picked up the slack.

In other words, the U.S. government is sending American men and women to their deaths as a result of faulty economic reasoning.

But even more repugnant is the willingness of the American people to permit their government to send servicemen to their deaths just because the price of gasoline might increase, at least over the short term. But so what if the price of gasoline increases, let us say, to two dollars a gallon as a result of the Iraqi invasion? Yes, life might become a little more difficult for Americans. But is this any reason to sacrifice the lives of our spouses or children or the spouses or children of our friends, neighbors, and fellow citizens? Are their lives worth so little that we cannot afford instead to band together and tighten our belts somewhat—perhaps by all of us even taking one less vacation? To choose the death of our fellow citizens over a relatively small economic discomfort is an abomination.

The final reason given for the necessity of American deaths in the Middle East is that it is necessary to make the world safe. This is absolutely unbelievable! Not even to make the world safe for democracy like in World War I. This time, just to make the world safe. According to American politicians and bureaucrats, American servicemen have to die to make the world safe!

Unfortunately, the American people have never been taught in their public schools the true history surrounding World War I. Perhaps it is time that they begin learning the truth that their government officials would prefer they not know. Before World War I, the American people had been told by their politicians and bureaucrats: "This war is necessary to make the world safe for democracy. By defeating Imperial Germany, this will be the war to end all wars. If you will just deliver your sons to us to fight and die in Europe, we promise you that future generations of Americans will never again die in a foreign war."

The American people of that time trusted their politicians and bureaucrats and lost tens of thousands of their fellow Americans. But the result of World War I, of course, was the rise of Nazi Germany, Imperial Japan, and fascist Italy.

What the Americans of today also do not know, because they have never been taught it in their public schools, is that until the Japanese attack on Pearl Harbor, the overwhelming majority of the American people, despite the evil actions of Adolf Hitler, said "Never again!" to American involvement in a European war.

But having been taught in their public schools for the past fifty years that patriotism means never questioning the decisions of the Pentagon, the American people now blindly follow their politicians and bureaucrats into any foreign war, no matter how absurd or false the justification, just like lemmings being led over the cliff.

One interesting question is: Why did the American government intervene so soon in Saudi Arabia with American ground troops? The answer lies with the current chairman of the Joint Chiefs of Staff— Gen. Colin L. Powell. It was Powell's advice that American troops be sent to the Middle East immediately. Why? What was the great urgency? After all, the Iraqi troops would still be there for an attack at a later date and, in all likelihood, physically weaker due to a scarcity of supplies. And even if Iraq had invaded Saudi Arabia, which is doubtful, since it was Kuwait that was cheating on the oil production quotas, an American invasion could still have taken place through another part of the Middle East. So, why did Powell feel impelled to recommend immediately sending ground troops to Saudi Arabia?

The answer lies in the fact that General Powell has a disturbingly inadequate understanding or regard for the importance of civilian control over the military. *The New York Times* of August 17 reported that Powell acted quickly in case "a paralysis of civilian will follows." In other words, Colin Powell—not the American people— knows what is best for the American people. So, his rationale in sending in so many ground troops so quickly was to "box in" the American people so that they would have to support the war to which he had chosen to commit them. And all because General Powell knows that war in the Middle East would be in the best interests of the American people.

Not only does this attitude reflect a woeful disregard for the constitutional order of the United States, it also has resulted in tragic consequences for thousands of American citizens. If General Powell had not been so ready to "box in" the American people for their "own good," the sending in of ground forces to Saudi Arabia could have been delayed until American citizens were gradually evacuated from Iraq and Kuwait. It is incredible and unbelievable that Colin Powell would permit his distrust of the "civilian will" to jeopardize the lives of those Americans in Iraq and Kuwait whom he had to know would undoubtedly be held hostage by Saddam Hussein. Now, as a direct consequence of General Powell's precipitous action, and his unwillingness to trust the intelligence and judgment of the American people, the lives of these new American hostages—men, women, and, this time, even children—will, as a virtual certainty, end in premature death.

At General Powell's behest, a military blockade has been implemented to bring Iraq's ruler "to his knees." Not only does this ignore the fact that Saddam Hussein will be the last person in Iraq or Kuwait to starve to death, it also ignores the tremendous cost to innocent people. After all, so much concern has been shown for the emir of Kuwait (and his family), but what about the Kuwaiti people? What have they done to the United States and Colin Powell? Are they not simply victims of invasion? Why must they be starved and denied medical supplies?

The answer obviously is that while the emir (and his family) is vitally important, the lives of the Kuwaiti people are not so important; the people of Kuwait must be starved (to death, if necessary) in order to return the emir (and his family) to his royal throne.

What should the American government have done about Iraq's invasion of Kuwait? The answer is the unpopular one to the twentieth-century interventionist mind: absolutely nothing. This was nothing but a falling out among thugs and thieves. After agreeing to its "appropriate" and agreed-upon production quota as a member of OPEC—a quota that was designed to extract as much money from the West as possible—the emir of Kuwait cheated and was caught red-handed. So, Iraq "enforced the contract" by invading the land of the cheater. A pox on both their houses! And when thugs and thieves fight it out with each other, there is no reason that American lives must be lost trying to separate them.

What would have happened to the people of Kuwait? They might have continued to live their lives as they always have—only under a puppet despot rather than a self-anointed royal one. Could not the same be said of peoples in other parts of the world in which new rulers have been put into power by invading forces? And perhaps—just perhaps—the people of Kuwait would have preferred to live under a puppet despot (and possibly resist him) rather than be starved to death in a blockade or massacred in an ensuing war.

Much has been said between Saddam Hussein and George Bush about the other's being a liar. The regrettable truth is that most politicians—foreign and domestic—do not tell the truth. Three decades ago, President Lyndon B. Johnson knowingly and willfully lied to the American people about an attack at the Gulf of Tonkin. And all of us, or least the members of my generation, know the terrible results of that falsehood.

The president and the Pentagon are telling us that our forces are in the Middle East for purely defensive purposes. Only the most gullible Americans believe that they are not, once again, being lied to. Contrary to the express representations of the American government, American troops are undoubtedly being sent to the Middle East for offensive operations that will inevitably plunge this nation into one of the major wars of its history (and all of this happening without a constitutionally required congressional declaration of war).

Are not the American people entitled to the whole truth so that they, not the military planners, can decide whether this is the route they wish to take? Not according to the Pentagon planners who know better what is in the interests of the American people than the American people themselves do. The lives of the American people are merely "cogs in the Pentagon wheel" that sometimes must be sacrificed for the greater good, as the Pentagon planners define the greater good.

Unfortunately, the planners have done their job well. War is suddenly imminent; and the American people have indeed been "boxed in" to supporting, out of their sense of patriotism, the American soldier.

But there is always hope that disaster can be averted or its terrible consequences minimized. That hope lies not with the American politicians and bureaucrats. It lies with the American people and their power of public opinion. I pray to God that the people of this nation put the brakes on this madness before it is too late.

This essay was published by The Future of Freedom Foundation on August 23, 1990.

39

Down a Slippery Slope of Kuwaiti Oil

by Richard M. Ebeling

On August 6, 1990, the Security Council of the United Nations voted, thirteen to zero, to impose an economic boycott against Iraq for its invasion and occupation of Kuwait. Shortly after the council's vote, President Bush insisted, "These sanctions will be enforced no matter what it takes." Since he did not follow this statement with any request for us to read his lips, it is possible, this time, he means what he says.

The United States and all other member nations of the UN are now bound to prohibit all sales and purchases between their respective citizens and any individual, group, or organization in Iraq. This includes not only the buying and selling of oil but all other commodities, services, and financial instruments. And if voluntary cooperation for the boycott is not forthcoming, the U.S. government has declared its intention to establish a naval blockade of the various port outlets in the Persian Gulf, the Red Sea, and the Mediterranean Sea through which Iraqi and Kuwaiti oil normally flows. Three U.S. naval carrier task-force groups have been positioned to ensure against any contingency, whether it be a blockade, air strikes against Iraqi targets, or an actual ground assault to liberate Kuwait from Iraqi occupation. And tens of thousands of U.S. military ground forces are being airlifted to Saudi Arabia for an indefinite stay.

Across the political spectrum, the mass media in the United States has joined in the government's campaign. Both *The Wall Street Journal* and *The New York Times,* for example, have warned of the danger of Munich-type appeasements of aggressors, that Saddam Hussein is a modern, Middle Eastern version of Adolf Hitler who only understands—and who will only be stopped by—a show of force. Like Hitler in the 1930s, it is said, Saddam Hussein has a blueprint for conquest of the world—the world oil market, that is. And for the diplomats of the Western world, Saddam Hussein has given them the realization of their fondest dream, to relive the diplomatic strategies of the 1930s, "and to get it right this time."

Saddam Hussein is a cruel despot and he runs Iraq with an efficient and pervasive secret police. Several years ago, I had an Iraqi student in one of my classes. The young man told me how his uncle had disappeared one night, taken away by the secret police and never seen or heard from again. What was the man's crime? It seems that he had been overheard in a Baghdad coffeehouse referring to Iraq's leader as "Saddam Hussein." So what was the problem? He had failed to preface his mention of Saddam Hussein's name with the words, "The Great," and this was taken to be a negative slur against the man often referred to as "the Perfume of Iraq."

In 1980, Iraq's "Perfume" initiated a war against Iran. It went on for eight years, and it is estimated that up to a million casualties were suffered during the conflict. Also during the war, members of the Kurdish minority in northern Iraq once again rose up in rebellion against Iraqi repression. Saddam Hussein used chemical weapons on several Kurdish villages, killing hundreds, if not thousands, of residents. Over the years, since coming to power, Hussein has unceremoniously executed hundreds of people on charges of being either "spies" or "enemies of the State," with little regard for what we in the West consider due process of law. And there are reports that he has literally and personally killed messengers who have suffered the misfortune of bringing him bad news.

Evil men have done bad things for all of recorded history. Saddam Hussein is not the first and he certainly will not be the last. And he lives in a part of the world in which much of the conduct of which he is accused is, unfortunately, common practice. Despotic regimes and brutal behavior towards opponents is too often the rule rather than the exception in the Middle East. Constitutional restraints on governmental conduct are practically unknown. Nor is there any notion of a "bill of rights" which guarantee basic civil liberties. The Middle East is a part of the world in which, for many, life can be "nasty, brutish, and short."

While many of the governments of the Middle East speak of "Arab Socialism," the "Arab Nation," and the "Moslem World"—all of which have great emotional appeal for large segments of the population and which can, indeed, generate violent and revolutionary responses at various times—the fact is that Middle East politics are primarily family and tribal affairs, often linked to that brand ("denomination") of the Moslem faith to which various groups belong. Practically all of the governments in the Middle East are either monarchies or military dictatorships. And in both forms, the administration of the government is usually under the control of the close relatives of the king or "president."

In 1752, a band of nomadic tribes came out of the Arabian desert and settled in what is today known as Kuwait, presumably supplanting those who had lived there before. The al-Sabah family was chosen as the ruling house among the tribes. Until the end of the nineteenth century they ruled the area under the suzerainty of the Ottoman Empire. But in 1899, the British government cut a deal with the ruling house and made Kuwait, then a part of the Ottoman's Basra province, a British "protectorate." At the end of World War I, in spite of Woodrow Wilson's pledge of "making the world safe for democracy," the Arab areas of the Ottoman Empire were carved up and divided between Britain and France. Iraq was created out of old Mesopotamia, Kuwait was made a formally distinct entity and both were subsumed under British rule.

When Kuwait was given independence in 1961, the Iraqi government insisted that it was a part of its country. Only the stationing of British military forces prevented Kuwait's annexation at that time. After the discovery of oil in Kuwait, and the big run up of oil prices in the 1970s, the king's government set up a huge welfare state for all his countrymen. Practically no one who was a Kuwaiti citizen had to work, with the result being that imported labor became 60 percent of the entire population of Kuwait. Non-Kuwaitis had no political rights, could not take up permanent residence in the country, and were not allowed to own any real property. The country did have a parliament elected by a minority of the Kuwaiti citizenry; and the people were permitted a wide degree of free speech and a free press. But both the parliament and the free press were recently closed down, when the king's family was heavily criticized for corruption and abuse of power.

How did the present crisis arise? In 1979, Saddam Hussein expected a quick and easy victory over the Iranians. The rationale for Iraq's attack at the time was a slice of disputed territory at the mouth of the Shatt al Arab, the body of water that forms the border between

Iraq and Iran at the northern end of the Persian Gulf. Instead, the war dragged on and on. Iraq claimed to be protecting the Arab world from Iranian fundamentalism; and the Arab oil-producing countries of the Persian Gulf subsidized Iraq's war costs and home-front expenses to the tune of tens of billions of dollars, either in the form of "donations" or interest-free loans. At the end of the war in 1988, Hussein claimed "victory," but in fact Iraq was broke, heavily in debt and in desperate need of oil revenue to cover his military and reconstruction expenditures.

The problem was that the OPEC cartel was no longer what it had been in the 1970s. As with all cartels, the members found that conspiring to control production to raise the market price sets off natural market responses. New reserves and production had been forthcoming from sources outside of the cartel; and energy economizing occurred, stimulated by the higher price. And as nonmembers cut into OPEC's market share, the cartel members began to cheat on their pricing and production quota agreements to retain or capture customers. Prices had fallen dramatically from the highs of the early 1980s. Among the big cheats were Kuwait and the United Arab Emirates.

At an OPEC meeting this past July, the OPEC members, with Iraq and Iran acting as the bully boys, had agreed to set up new quotas, with Kuwait and the UAE promising to be good boys. But Iraq also demanded other things: that Kuwait "forgive" payment of its war debts and approve new "loans"; Iraq also wanted a couple of islands at the mouth of the Shatt al Arab under Kuwaiti administration to be transferred to Iraqi control. Kuwait said no. So on August 2, Saddam Hussein invaded his neighbor to take what had not been given to him. And on August 8, Kuwait was returned to the "Iraqi homeland" through formal annexation. Clearly, Hussein also hoped to be in a position to influence Saudi Arabia's oil production policy. Saddam Hussein, in other words, took upon himself the job of police enforcement agent for OPEC in a part of the Persian Gulf. Moreover, he tried to reinforce his self-proclaimed title as "leader of the Arab Nation."

What occurred, therefore, was a falling out among thieves. And, more important, it is an example of Middle East politics as usual. Saddam Hussein is merely one thug in a region densely populated with many just like him. And he has done nothing that many other governments in the area would not also like to do if they had the political and military power to get away with it. There are no "white hats" in this political desert of "black hats."

So why, then, has the United States intervened in this part of the world? Why has the Bush administration committed thousands of

American ground forces to Saudi Arabia, put in place a huge naval armada in the waters surrounding the Middle East, and declared that it intends to strangle Iraq economically and push Saddam Hussein out of Kuwait, with military force if necessary?

In his address to the nation on August 8, President Bush stated, "In the life of nations, we're called upon to define who we are and what we believe." And that "standing up for our principles is an American tradition." Yet, never once in his address, or in his subsequent news conferences, did he specify what "principles" were so at stake that the lives of thousands of American servicemen were worth putting in harm's way.

He did say, "There is no justification whatsoever for this outrageous and brutal act of aggression. . . . The acquisition of territory by force is unacceptable." If he believes so strongly that it is the duty of the United States to protect little countries from big aggressors, are we to assume that he will now ask for UN sanctions against the Soviet Union, for Gorbachev's refusal to release Estonia, Latvia, and Lithuania from Stalin's forcible annexation fifty years ago? Or will he ask for an international economic embargo against China until Peking withdraws from Tibet, a country the Chinese have forcibly occupied for forty years? It is an unfortunate fact of human history that many, if not most, international boundaries are the result of past acts of conquest in which the original residents were rarely asked their opinion concerning the change. Indeed, the entire American southwest is the result of territorial acquisition by conquest by the U.S. government during the Mexican War. Or is it only recent conquests that are open to censure?

Are the principles at stake those of individual liberty and free, representative government? President Bush said, "Kuwait's legitimate government must be restored" and "U.S. forces will work together with those of Saudi Arabia and other nations to preserve the integrity of Saudi Arabia and to deter further Iraqi aggression." If it is the vote of a free people through constitutional procedures that makes a government legitimate, then Kuwait's government was not in that category. Hereditary monarchy is a form of government that some leading Americans found less than desirable about two hundred fifteen years ago. And Saudi Arabia does not even possess the limited type of parliament that Kuwait used to have. The country is, in fact, ruled by a monarchy in which all power belongs to the royal family, in which there is no freedom of speech or the press, and in which the violation of the Moslem religious code, even in the smallest detail, can result in the cutting off of hands or feet, or public execution by severing of the head from the body. What about an independent judiciary before which a verdict may be appealed? Forget it. And free market economics? They've never heard of it. Perhaps President Bush has accepted the philosophy of cultural and ethical relativism. And perhaps he doesn't want to judge the Kuwaitis and Saudis by his own kinder and gentler values.

President Bush insisted, "The mission of our troops is wholly defensive. . . . They will not initiate hostilities but they will defend themselves, the Kingdom of Saudi Arabia and other friends in the Persian Gulf." And he said in the press conference following his address, "We're not at war." A foreign nation is told that it may not buy or sell goods and services anywhere in the world; that if it attempts to do so, American military vessels will interdict said attempt; that American military forces will encircle the nation in question and will go to any lengths to reverse a territorial occupation that that nation has made; and the president of the United States declares that the leader of that nation must go, peaceably if possible, by violent means if necessary. Yet, the president insists that this is not war. If Gorbachev in the Soviet Union had said and done such things in reference to the United States following the American invasion of Panama last December, one wonders if President Bush would have considered the same words and deeds as constituting war. But Panama was different. Yes, Panama is in our backyard and Kuwait is in Iraq's. And if it be claimed that America is not an imperialist power that tries to manipulate other country's affairs, many of the leaders and people of Latin America might beg to differ.

And this finally gets us closer to the real basis for America's military intervention in the Middle East. President Bush stated:

> My Administration, as has been the case with every President from President Roosevelt to President Reagan, is committed to the security and stability of the Persian Gulf. . . . Let me be clear, the sovereign independence of Saudi Arabia is vital to the United States.

In other words, the entire world is America's backyard, and American lives and tax dollars are to be used when it is necessary to guarantee the "security and stability" of any part of the world, as the United States government defines that security and stability.

But why the Middle East at this moment in time? President Bush explained, "Our country now imports nearly half the oil it consumes and could face a major threat to its economic independence" if an unfriendly nation were to control or dominate a large portion of the world's known oil reserves. And with Kuwait under Iraqi occupation, Saddam Hussein has control of about 20 percent of the world's known reserves.

Thus, America's intervention in the Middle East has nothing to do with human freedom, it has nothing to do with any right of peoples to national self-determination, nor with the integrity of international boundaries among nations. If tomorrow the Saudi monarchy were to be overthrown and a government "unfriendly" to the United States were to come to power, U.S. policymakers, you can be assured, would have no hesitation about violating "the sovereign independence of Saudi Arabia" in the process of replacing it with "friendlies."

The purpose behind American intervention is the price control of world oil supplies by military means. The philosophy behind this purpose, the "principle" for which the United States government is willing to risk the lives and fortunes of the American people, is eighteenth-century mercantilism. All of the rhetoric of the *economic collectivism of that era* is there: "we" must politically secure supplies of an essential resource to guarantee the nation's "economic independence"; military adventures may be required to obtain control of that resource and keep it out of the hands of others; the terms of trade (the price at which the commodity is obtained) must be shifted in our favor to maintain a "favorable balance of trade"; if "we" do not control it, "they" will, and "our" loss will be "their" gain.

The politics of the period before the economic teachings of Adam Smith and David Hume on free trade and free markets have reappeared. The life, liberty, and property of the people are once again at the disposal of the government for whatever may be defined as, "for reasons of state." Resources need to be secured in foreign lands? Then the lives of America's youth will be put up for sacrifice on faraway shores; and the wealth of multitudes who honestly work and save in the marketplace will be taxed in the billions of dollars to pay for the potential slaughter. Enemies must be isolated and economically brought down so that the officials in Washington can feel strong. Then the peaceful international commerce of all Americans will be interrupted and regulated, with the government telling the people with whom they may trade and under what conditions.

Domestically, the U.S plays the mercantilist game on behalf of producers. The government uses quotas on Japanese automobile imports, excludes high-definition televisions and South American beef, limits foreign manufactured textiles through the imposition of tariffs, and stimulates the exportation of agricultural and industrial goods with subsidies, tax breaks, and guaranteed loans for foreign purchasers.

But in the case of oil, the government views the United States as the consumer rather than the producer. As a result, the American government's goal is for a low price for Middle East oil. But Iraq's goal, as a producing nation, is for a high price. And this is an essential point: Iraq's motive in trying to control or influence Kuwaiti and Saudi oil production, along with its own, is not to deny America oil, but to limit its supply so as to obtain a better price. Zero production and thus zero sales, generates zero revenues. And too high a price through restriction of production generates a smaller revenue than if the price was lower. Thus, Iraq's motive is to sell oil to America and the rest of the industrial world, but at a production level that maximizes profits earned.

What if the United States had not intervened politically and militarily in the Middle East following the invasion of Kuwait? What might have happened? World oil prices would have risen and suffered a period of uncertainty until the political dust settled. Some amount less than the usual four million barrels of oil a day formerly sold by Iraq and Kuwait would have come on the market, as Saddam Hussein restricted supply to keep world oil prices above what they had been before the invasion.

And what would the other Arab governments have done if the United States had not intervened? What they always tend to do in these Arab rivalries: they would have bought off Saddam Hussein. They would have hailed him as "The Great" Saddam Hussein, hero of the "Arab Nation," and extended him interest-free loans and written off outstanding Iraqi debts. Bribery, blackmail, extortion, and false praise have long been the methods for solving problems in Middle East politics.

The higher price for world oil would have acted over time as the incentive for both OPEC and non-OPEC oil producers to expand the output of existing wells and to search for new reserves. The usual game would have repeated itself: cheating on production quotas, OPEC meetings in Geneva to reach new understandings, and renewed cheating as soon as the oil ministers had returned to their respective homes. Saddam Hussein might have used his military strength to put pressure on Saudi Arabia or the United Arab Emirates to cut back their output. But this merely would have magnified the usual and natural incentives for other OPEC and non-OPEC producers outside the gulf (and, therefore, outside the reach of his military intimidation) to expand production and offer lower prices to gain customers and added profits. Furthermore, the higher prices would have worked as further incentives for energy economizing and a stimulus to shift at the margin into energy substitutes. If, for political reasons, Iraq tried to destabilize oil markets by erratic fluctuations in its own production levels, buyers would soon find it to be an unreliable supplier, and Iraq would have tended to lose some of its steady customers as time went by. And erratic production would have accelerated the move towards energy alternatives.

What American intervention has created is an even more limited and unstable supply of oil. Rather than only a partial contraction of the combined Iraqi-Kuwaiti supply as Saddam Hussein attempted to push up the world price, suddenly, as a result of the UN sanctions, all four million barrels are off the market. Now other producing nations, including the United States, must replace all of it and much more rapidly than if the sanctions had not been imposed. Now there is even less certainty in the world oil market for the foreseeable future, because there is no way of knowing how long the present crisis in the Middle East will continue, nor whether it will lead to a massive military conflagration that might bring in its wake the destruction of the oil fields of Saudi Arabia, Kuwait, and Iraq.

In an economically interdependent world, Saddam Hussein's seizure of Kuwait *does* carry negative consequences for others in the international market. But that very interdependence means that political retaliation inevitably redounds negatively back at the ones instituting that retaliation. The best responses, in this situation, are the natural market responses. Interventionist responses, as Austrian economist Ludwig von Mises always pointed out, tend to create outcomes worse than the situation the intervention was meant to cure.

If what guided U.S. foreign policy was simply mercantilist fallacies and economic ignorance, then, in principle, some sound economics and judicious political reflection might rein in the interventionist spirit driving Washington policymakers. Unfortunately, mercantilism is only the economic aspect of a wider "principle" that drives the United State government. It is the same "principle" that has dominated Washington policymakers since the end of World War II: *that it is the duty and destiny of the United States to set the world straight according to the policymakers' conception of what a new and better world should be like. For over four decades, the guiding principle of American foreign policy has been the ideal of Global Social Engineering.*

It is taken for granted that any foreign dictator who is not sufficiently pro-American is a budding Hitler, who must be put in his place to prevent him from possibly disrupting Washington's conception of a well-functioning and well-designed international order. Every foreign economic policy not to the liking of Washington's social engineers is a threat to America's prosperity and economic stability. Every conflict in any part of the world carries the seed of starting World War III and, therefore, necessitates U.S. intervention. The opposite side of this coin, of course, is *the assumption that America's global social engineers know how to design, plan, and manage an international order; know how to define and supervise the maintenance of American prosperity and economic stability; and have the answers for solving or handling every regional conflict in the world, no matter how intricate and long-standing the political, cultural or ideological bases of the disputes.*

The global social engineers who gave us the Vietnam War, the failed hostage rescue mission in the Iranian desert, and the bombing of the Marine barracks in Beirut, and who lacked all predictive capacity in anticipating the collapse of communism in Eastern Europe just a year ago, now plan to design and police a new order for the Middle East. Saddam Hussein must go, they say. Good. One less tyrant in the world. But when he is gone, what happens when Iran or Syria try to fill the power vacuum, and play the same political and military games? How many tax dollars will be extracted from the American people for a permanent policing of the Middle East? And how many American servicemen will have to die so the social engineers in Washington can sleep easy?

Make no mistake, gentle reader, if the Bush administration succeeds in its present military and economic war against Iraq in the Middle East, the global social engineers in Washington will be drunk with power. They will continue to meddle, manipulate and manage until some disaster befalls us as a nation. And every act of meddling, every manipulative policy, and every political and economic management technique they implement will make us a little less free.

America has started down a potentially dangerous and slippery slope in the Middle East, and all because the social engineers have the typical planner's mentality of wanting to control the price of oil.

This essay was published by The Future of Freedom Foundation on August 15, 1990.

40

Omnipotent Government and the Persian Gulf War

by Jacob G. Hornberger

For years, many of us have been arguing that omnipotent government in foreign affairs is just as evil and dangerous, if not more so, than omnipotent government in domestic affairs. But our arguments met with indifference from some devotees of freedom and limited government, because while they could see the evils and dangers of the welfare state, the absence of war made those of the warfare state seem remote and irrelevant. With the Persian Gulf War, this is no longer the case.

No one can now deny:

(1) that the President of the United States has the unfettered and uncontrolled power to send this nation into war; and

(2) that the United States government has the unfettered and uncontrolled power to use the lives, savings, and earnings of the American people to police wrongdoing all over the world.

What does the future hold for a people whose government has omnipotent power over their lives and fortunes in both domestic and foreign affairs? What does the future hold for a people who fail to see that individual freedom and omnipotent government are mutually exclusive? What does the future hold for a people who believe that the omnipotence of their government is more important than their own individual freedom?

The aftermath of the Persian Gulf War will bring a renewed opportunity to convince our fellow Americans of the vital importance of constitutionally limiting the power of our government—not only in domestic affairs but in foreign affairs as well. While our task will certainly not be an easy one, we must not shirk from attempting it. For if we are to avert the catastrophe that inevitably awaits us at the end of this treacherous road, we must fearlessly and uncompromisingly confront both the welfare state and the warfare state. The freedom, well-being, and perhaps even the survival of the people of this nation depend on it.

This essay was published by The Future of Freedom Foundation in February 1991.

41

Players and Pawns: The Persian Gulf War

by Jacob G. Hornberger

For the greater part of this century, the U.S. government has plundered, looted, and terrorized the American people through the Internal Revenue Service. It has surreptitiously stolen people's income and savings through the Federal Reserve System. It has brutally enforced—through fines and imprisonment—rules and regulations governing people's peaceful economic activities. In a very real sense, ours is a government which has been—and is—waging a terribly immoral and destructive war against its own people.

Yet, Americans continue to delude themselves. Harkening back to their high-school civics classes, they continue to believe that America is the land of the free—that the welfare-state, planned-economy way of life was formed in 1787—and that their government is founded on moral and benevolent principles. Like the cancer patient who undergoes a denial stage upon being told of his disease, Americans refuse to face the truth: that they are not free—that they have abandoned the principles of limited government, private property, and unhampered markets on which this nation was founded—and that our government is now based on evil and immoral principles.

But many Americans who know the truth have concluded that our kakistocracy, through its liberation of Kuwait, miraculously reformed itself into a good and honorable government. Let us review the record.

Among the panoply of reasons given by the U.S. government to justify its intervention in the Middle East was its professed concern for the Kuwaiti people. But the evidence establishes that our government has even less concern for the well-being of foreign citizens than it has for its own citizens.

For many decades, our government has used money which has been plundered from the American people to give foreign aid to brutal tyrants—knowing that such money would be used to tyrannize the people who lived under such tyrants. Ours is a government which delivered millions of dollars to the shah of Iran—despite its knowledge that the money was being used to torture and kill the Iranian people . . . which actively supported Saddam Hussein despite its knowledge of his aggressive acts against Iranians and his murderous conduct against his own people . . . which embraces Mikhail Gorbachev—despite its knowledge of his aggressive acts against Lithuanians and the murderous acts of this barbaric communist against his own people . . . which willingly shakes one of the bloodiest hands in the Middle East—that of Hafez Assad of Syria—despite its knowledge of his aggression against the Lebanese and the brutal killing of thousands of his own people . . . and which feels right at home with the savage, communist tyrants of China—despite their long-time aggression against the Tibetans and their murderous conduct against their own citizenry.

And Americans have yet to confront another uncomfortable reality: that the same evil, immoral, and tyrannical government which reigns supreme in our domestic affairs also has omnipotent power over our lives and fortunes in foreign affairs. Remember—the president sent hundreds of thousands of American troops into war without seeking congressional approval. (Many Americans do not realize that a military blockade is an act of war.) By the time congressional approval was sought, the president had already—by placing American troops in harm's way—effectively cornered the Congress and the American people into supporting his unilateral decision. The subsequent debate concerned only the method by which the war was to be waged—not whether or not the war would be waged.

Moreover, the President made it abundantly clear that the congressional vote was, in any event, only window dressing—that he would order an attack on Iraq regardless of the outcome of the vote.

Why is all of this important? Because the American people must be made to realize what they have wrought for their children, and

322

their children's children, who will probably have to pay the price: a nation whose ruler has many of the same omnipotent powers over the lives and fortunes of the citizenry as those exercised by the most powerful dictators in history.

During the Persian Gulf crisis, the U.S. government preached the importance of the rule of law. But our government itself violated the rule of law by ignoring the U.S. Constitution, not only with respect to waging war without a congressional declaration of war, but also by exercising a power—policing the world—that the Constitution does not authorize.

And our government also failed to explain how the rule of law is supposed to be followed in international affairs. Was the U.S. government following the rule of law when it mined Nicaraguan harbors? If so, why did the World Court enter a monetary judgment against our government for what it adjudged to be an illegal act? And why has our government refused to comply with the World Court's judgment?

The simple truth is that there is no mechanism by which international disputes among nonconsenting, independent, sovereign nations can be adjudicated. (And the United Nations is not a judicial body designed to resolve such disputes; the Persian Gulf crisis showed that its votes are delivered in the same way as those in the U.S. Congress—to the highest bidder for cash or other consideration.) Does the lack of such a mechanism justify aggression against another nation-state—whether it be our government's invasion of Panama or Iraq's invasion of Kuwait? No. But it does show two things: that for the foreseeable future, nation-states (including the United States) will continue to resolve their disputes through military force, and, second, that the U.S. government's moralizing on the importance of following the rule of law in international affairs only evidences its own hypocrisy.

The opportunity to serve as the world's policeman is a dream come true for the military-industrial complex—that is, those who are dependent on military welfare. With the collapse of communism in Eastern Europe, the military welfare-recipients were in a state of panic. How could they now justify the tremendous tax burden associated with a huge, standing military force?

But to be able to serve as the world's policeman—especially in the Middle East—now guarantees total political and bureaucratic control over the lives and fortunes of the American people for the indefinite future. Why? Because war and the threat of war always and inevitably entail omnipotent power over the citizenry. Moreover, brutal foreign tyrants against whom such wars can be waged are never in short supply—and especially not in the Middle East! And what better place (from the standpoint of the military-industrial complex) to have the mission of establishing peace and stability than in a part of the world which has never known peace and stability?

By becoming the world's policeman whose primary beat is the Middle East, those who are on the military dole have ensured themselves perpetual existence—and perpetual control over the lives and property of the American people.

And, of course, it is the American people who are the pawns in all of this. Innocently believing that their government miraculously has become good and moral overnight, they ardently support its omnipotent power over their own lives and fortunes—the same way they have done in their government's futile and destructive wars on poverty, illiteracy, and drugs. But Americans ignore two important things: first, their role as pawns and, second, that pawns can and will be sacrificed whenever the political and bureaucratic chess players in Washington deem it necessary for the "international good."

Is there an answer to Iraq's invasion of Kuwait based on principles of individual freedom and limited government? Yes. And it is an answer which is also based on the principle of individual responsibility.

The power of our government to intervene in both domestic and foreign affairs should be strictly constrained through express constitutional limitations. In domestic affairs, this means the end of the welfare-state, planned-economy way of life. In foreign affairs, this means the end of foreign aid, the end of our government's ability to wage trade wars, and the end of its role as the world's international policeman. The power of our government should be constitutionally limited to three primary functions: protecting the American people from domestic aggressors, defending the United States from foreign attack, and resolving disputes which arise in this nation.

And the American people? They should be free to travel and trade all over the world without the permission and interference of their own governmental officials . . . and to donate their own lives and fortunes to oppose tyranny and oppression anywhere in the world. Does this mean that the American people would have to take responsibility for their beliefs and convictions? Of course—but isn't that the type of society which we desire?

Freedom for Americans is possible in our lifetime. But it will come only when they finally realize that people are not free—and can never be free—under either a welfare state or a warfare state. And when the American people finally make their own freedom their highest political end, they will discover what only a select few in history have discovered: that *true* personal pride and self-esteem come from the achievement of one's own freedom—not vicariously through the military conquests of one's government.

This essay originally appeared in the July 1991 issue of Freedom Daily, *published by The Future of Freedom Foundation.*

42

Nationalism and Classical Liberalism

by Richard M. Ebeling

For forty-five years Europe enjoyed peace. But it was a peace in the form of an "armed truce" called the Cold War. On the one side of the Iron Curtain, the Soviet Union maintained its hegemony through the threat—and occasional use—of force, as in Hungary in 1956 and Czechoslovakia in 1968. On the other side of the Iron Curtain, the nations of Western Europe set aside their age-old conflicts and animosities out of fear of the Soviet Union—with America's armed presence and political paternalism serving to "keep the peace."

Yet, Europe's peace on the basis of a divided continent was artificial. Consequently, it required rectification at some point in time. That point arrived in November 1989, when the Berlin Wall came tumbling down. In less than two years, every one of the communist regimes in Eastern Europe was gone. Every one of the republics making up the USSR declared either its independence or its sovereignty. And within the Russian Federated Republic, various regions populated by ethnic non-Russians also called for their autonomy or independence from Moscow.

But having seen the demise of communism, the political wounds across the middle of Europe have not even begun to heal. The Western Europeans seem determined to isolate themselves from the people and the commodities of Eastern Europe. Fearing a massive wave of Eastern Europeans desiring to move west for economic improvement, the Western Europeans have started to reinforce their border controls and immigration restrictions. And the appeal of the Eastern Europeans to be allowed to freely trade and exchange in the Western European market has been met with either refusal or silence.

Within Eastern Europe, the freed "captive nations" regained their political independence from the Soviets, but they are now in the process of tearing themselves apart. Yugoslavia has become the battleground of a savage civil war between the Serbians and the Croatians. Czechoslovakia may divide into separate Czech and Slovak nations. Ethnic Hungarians object to their treatment in Romania. A Turkish minority reasserts its right to its own language in Bulgaria.

In newly independent Estonia, a Russian minority feels threatened. In Lithuania, it is Polish and Russian minorities that worry about Lithuanian oppression. The Armenians and Azerbaijanis fight over Nagorno-Karabakh, a territory in Azerbaijan that is populated predominantly by Armenians. The Georgians declared their independence from Moscow, but when a people called the Ossetians, who live in a northern portion of Georgia, express their own desire for autonomy, the Georgian government responds with machine guns. The list of actual or potential disputes among these various ethnic and national groups in the former Soviet Union appears almost endless.

Having been freed from one collectivist ideology—communism—Europe is floundering under the weight of another one—political and economic nationalism.

Like modern communism, modern nationalism was also a creation of the nineteenth century. But unlike communism, nationalism was a concept espoused by a number of the classical liberals of the last century. The liberals of the nineteenth century considered human liberty to be the guiding principle in all public-policy matters. They believed that men could not be politically secure in their freedom unless the government under which they lived was freely chosen by the people. Representative government with constitutional restraints on what the political authorities could do was their ideal.

Under the old system of monarchy, political borders had nothing to do with the wishes of the people. A king conquered or traded away land and people as he saw fit. There were dozens of different peoples in Europe who spoke different languages, had different customs, traditions and cultures, and who had been separated from their cultural and linguistic kin by kings and princes who divided up Europe for their own purposes. Furthermore, these cultural and linguistic groups would often find their language and customs threatened by the domination of larger ethnic groups in a king's domain.

The classical liberal's starting premise was that *only individuals have rights. If individuals who happened to share a common language and cultural background wished to form a common political community, then that was merely an extension of their individual right of freedom of association.* Within the boundaries of these national political entities, governments would be limited to the protection of life, liberty, and property. If there were any ethnic minorities residing in these democratically created nation-states, they might remain at a linguistic and cultural disadvantage, but they would be secure in their civil and economic liberties, with the state prohibited from using its power to benefit one group at the expense of another. Or if they chose, these ethnic minorities could vote to form their own political state or to join some other state.

But instead of remaining an idea of the right of individuals in a geographical area to determine their own political fate, in the nineteenth and twentieth centuries, self-determination increasingly was transformed into a collectivist concept. National self-determination came to mean the political unification of all those speaking the same language—regardless of whether all those speaking the same language wished to belong to the same state. It came to mean the political incorporation of all lands and territories on which a particular ethnic or national group had once resided—no matter how long ago and regardless of the wishes of those presently occupying those lands and territories. It came to mean the responsibility of the state to enforce the use of a particular language and to inculcate various cultural customs and traditions through mandatory public education, propaganda, and resistance to the "invasion" of alien cultural influences—regardless of the wishes of individual citizens of that nation-state, including those who happened to make up linguistic and cultural minorities in that country.

The consequences of this collectivist notion of "national" self-determination and independence are what we are again seeing all around us. Croatians and Serbians each speak of their "historical" boundaries, and neither side is willing to let boundaries be set by the free vote of the peoples living in the disputed areas. Estonians point to the attempt at forced "Russification" under Soviet rule, but they now are trying to impose "Estonianization" on the Russian minority as a lever to get the Russians to leave the country. The Ukranian and Byelorussian governments speak about how Moscow controlled their people and their resources, while at the same time, they are setting up controls and regulations over their own people in the name of Ukranian and Byelorussian "national independence."

And the Western Europeans are no better. French farmers demonstrate against the "invasion" of "our French markets" by alien agricultural goods from Eastern Europe. Germans debate changing their very liberal refugee-status laws because Poles and Russians move in and take away "our jobs" that rightfully belong to Germans. People in Spain and Portugal fear that "our national financial capital" may soon be invested in creating jobs for Hungarians or Latvians.

To what state shall the individual belong? How may he use his property and with whom is he permitted to trade? Who is to be allowed to live in a particular geographical location? In what language will he be pressured to converse and do business? What will his children learn in school? What cultural heritage shall be subsidized and supported?

Not one of these questions is left in the hands of the individual. They are determined for him by those in political authority who define his nationality and then use the power at their disposal to make him conform to their view of national interest and independence.

The classical liberal idea of national self-determination, which was meant to serve as one of the means to the ultimate political end of individual human liberty, was sidetracked onto a collectivist path—like so many other ideas of our age. And all the nationalist tensions and conflicts that are emerging and spreading around Europe today are a result of that perversion.

Nor is there a cure for what ails Europe today other than a return to classical liberalism—with its emphasis on *individual self-determination and freedom of association.* But this is a shift in thinking for which neither Europe nor the world is ready. The collectivist bias is just too deeply embedded. And that is why we must reconcile ourselves to the fact that we shall be the unwilling witnesses to more death and destruction in the coming years.

This essay originally appeared in the March 1992 issue of Freedom Daily, *published by The Future of Freedom Foundation.*

43

Nationalism: Its Nature and Consequences

by Richard M. Ebeling

In the nineteenth century, many classical liberals believed that the ideas of "national identity" and "nationalism" were false scents that were likely to lead the world away from liberty and towards a continuation of political tyranny and international conflict. For example, William E. H. Lecky, in his study *Democracy and Liberty* (1896), argued that "the idea and passion of nationality blend quite as easily with loyalty to a dynasty as with attachment to a republican form of government, and nations that value very little internal or constitutional freedom are often passionately devoted to their national individuality and independence."

Furthermore, Lecky warned:

> The doctrine of nationalities has assumed forms and been pushed to extremes which make it a great danger to the peace of the world. It becomes the readiest weapon in the hands both of a conqueror and of a revolutionist, and, by discrediting the force of international treaties, deepen lines of division, and introducing elements of anarchy and rebellion into most great nations, it threatens the most valuable elements of our civilization.

Furthermore, while the "nationalist sentiment" seems in our century to be a natural instinct and emotion in men around the world, historians have reminded us that nationalism is a relatively new phenomenon, dating back only to the seventeenth and eighteenth centuries. Carlton J. H. Hayes explained in *The Historical Evolution of Modern Nationalism* (1931):

> We can be sure that prior to the eighteenth century A.D., it was not the general rule for civilized nationalities to strive zealously and successfully for political unity and independence. . . . The "first modern nationalists," those whose ideas and attitudes and activities have been rationalized by our philosophers and been imitated by the masses, have been in the main, men of brains and some means, belonging most often to the middle class. They are the authors and the propagandists of modern nationalism. These have provided the inspiration of nationalist theorizers and the patterns for whole nationalities.

Professor Hayes suggested three factors that made nationalism appealing for European intellectuals in the eighteenth and nineteenth centuries. First, was the idea of democracy. As intellectuals "become more democratically inclined, they discover they can best and most conveniently operate the necessary machinery of democracy within linguistic frontiers, that is, within nationalities."

Second, was the search for a secular religion. Professor Hayes argued:

> It may well be that during and since the eighteenth century the rise of skepticism concerning historic supernatural religion, especially among the intellectual and middle classes, has created an unnatural void for religious emotion and worship, a void which it has seemed preferable to supply with near-by nationalist gods and fervent nationalist cults.

And, third, was the growth of statism:

> Still another "underlying tendency" which may (and in our opinion, does most plausibly) explain the vogue of nationalism in modern times is the growth of a belief that the state, particularly the national state, can and should promote human progress.

According to Professor Hayes:

[Intellectuals] looked for fruition of their ideas not in the supernatural realm but in the realm of human reason and human effort, and hence they turned away from the church and toward the state. . . . And just as a member of any church may go to heaven beyond the skies, so every man by membership in an enlightened national state will share in the heaven on earth.

Men have been indoctrinated and educated to identify themselves—to see themselves as inseparable from—a national group. As Professor Hayes pointed out in his volume *Essays on Nationalism* (1928), "Nationalism, being a cultural phenomenon, is not 'in the blood'; it cannot be transmitted biologically from one person to another; it is an 'acquired character.'" And the European intellectuals possessing "nationalist proclivities," who desired a worldly entity to replace God for creation of a heaven on earth,

found expression [for it] in the glorification of the state and eventually . . . in the development of a kind of neo-mercantilism—a governmental favoring of national industry, national trade and national banking. This kind of mercantilism swept Germany, France, Italy, the United States, and many another national state in the last quarter of the nineteenth century.

At the same time, Professor Hayes explained, politicians discovered "that the masses when brought under [nationalism's] spell not only were less inclined to criticise their leaders but also more disposed to accept the status quo" in political and economic affairs. "On the multitudes nationalism could be made to act as sort of a laughing gas. . . . A sustained inhalation of nationalism, in a time of national election or international war" reduced the likelihood of opposition to the existing political order of things.

At the same time, nationalism tends to produce in people an increased intolerance to those who differ from themselves or who question the policies of the state to which they belong. "If nationalism, in times of international tension, encourages a whole nationality or the entire citizenry of a national state to present a united front and to evince a collective intolerance towards an alien nationality or a foreign state," Professor Hayes elaborated, "nationalism at all times actuates certain individuals and groups within a nationality to assume that they are the standard, one-hundred-percent patriots of that nationality and to adopt an appropriate degree of specialised intolerance in coping with their less endowed fellow countrymen."

Furthermore, Professor Hayes explains:

These citizens are not content with unity of national action in time of war; they must secure in time of peace unity of national word and thought and usage, and the unity at which they aim involves, of course, the adoption of their particular and peculiar brand of nationalism by all their fellow citizens. If the adoption is not voluntary, then it must be compulsory . . . all must be one as they are.

The paradox of our world today is that in spite of the twentieth century's lessons about the dangers of aggressive nationalism and mega-statism in the form of totalitarianism—in spite of the experiences of numerous ethnic conflicts and civil wars—"national conscience" is still placed above and given preeminence over individual conscience and individual freedom. The United States government insists that "the nation's" economic prosperity and well-being requires a potential trade war against Japan, regardless of the sacrifice imposed upon countless American importers and consumers of Japanese goods. Disturbed by the wide popularity and number of American films in the French movie market, the French government wants to limit the percentage of American films shown in France, in the name of preserving "national culture." Fearful that the newly independent country of Macedonia might make territorial claims on portions of northern Greece, the Greek government refuses to grant diplomatic recognition to Macedonia and prohibits the use of Greek ports by Macedonian merchants and manufacturers, with no thought to the hardship created for both Macedonian and Greek traders and consumers.

Concerned that some sectors of their national industries might not be able to compete successfully against farmers and manufacturers in a number of Eastern European countries, the governments of Western Europe restrict imports from Poland, Hungary, and the Czech Republic in the name of maintaining "national" employment and the "national heritage" of agriculture and certain traditional occupations. Determined to impose cultural and linguistic homogeneity over their territories, the governments of Romania and Slovakia prohibit the Hungarian minority in their countries from having their own schools in the Hungarian language; the Turkish minority in Bulgaria, likewise, finds itself threatened with cultural and linguistic oppression.

It might be said that in many of these cases, the cloak of nationalism is merely a cover for the state when it uses its power to benefit some selected and privileged groups in society at the expense of the rest of the citizenry.

And this may well be true. But the fact that it works demonstrates how imbedded the nationalist consciousness is in our times. But far more serious is the fact that many, if not most, people in our societies truly believe in the transcendent supremacy of "the nation" over any and every individual who happens to reside in the particular country in question.

In his study *National Consciousness* (1943), German economist Walter Sulzbach emphasized:

> National consciousness became an historic force of paramount influence, not because races or languages or cultures had changed, but because certain human groups had adopted a new attitude toward matters previously regarded with indifference. Therefore, a nation must be defined by the subjective attitude of the people concerned. . . . "Nationalism" is a certain condition of mind. . . . [A person] is nationalistic when he feels toward his nation as those citizens of Florence felt toward their city, who, according to Machiavelli, valued its greatness more than the salvation of their souls.

What needs to be changed, therefore, is the "condition of mind" of ourselves and our fellow human beings. The mythology of the transcendent "nation" must be purged from the psyche of man. Language may be the mental tool by which we think, act, and interact with other men. Culture, customs, and tradition may contain the symbols and rules by which we live and often judge our own conduct and the conduct of others. The commonality of historical experience by various peoples may be a crucial element in our personal senses of being and belonging. But nations and nationalities do not have an existence separate from the individuals who make them up, and who happen to speak a particular language, adhere to certain customs and traditions, and share a variety of common experiences and memories.

As a consequence, there is no mythical "nation" distinct from the individuals who make it up at a point in time and over time. To think otherwise is to make some members of a national group subservient to others in that group who believe they know how all in

335

the group should be made to conform and behave. In other words, it requires making some the linguistic and behavioral slaves of others who claim to have the transcendent vision of knowing how all within the group or within a geographical area should speak, believe, and act to reflect the "true national spirit."

Furthermore, the existence of others who speak different languages, practice other customs and traditions, and share alternative historical memories need not threaten any other one group of individuals with another language, set of customs, or historical memory. But for all to live together peacefully, with all their respective differences as well as similarities, and mutually benefit from each nationality's contribution to civilization as a whole, requires both tolerance and adherence to the concept of individual liberty.

The idea of tolerance means that we recognize that not all that is good belongs only to ourselves, and that only reason and experience can teach us and others which ways of life are most beneficial and desirable. And the principle of individual liberty means that we respect each man's right and responsibility to choose his own way of living, speaking, and acting, though we may not share his choices and beliefs or always agree with his forms of conduct.

Only when this radically different "condition of mind" replaces the present collectivist notions of nationality and national consciousness will national conflicts and ethnic tensions no longer disrupt and often destroy the peaceful business and personal affairs of life. Unfortunately, the vast majority of men seem unaware that it is their own collectivist habits of mind that are the cause of many of their own societal problems. So, many more nationalist wars of aggression and oppression are likely to darken our world's future.

This essay originally appeared in the June 1994 issue of Freedom Daily, *published by The Future of Freedom Foundation.*

44

National Conflicts, Market Liberalism, and Social Peace

by Richard M. Ebeling

For three years, civil war has caused massive death and destruction in the former Yugoslavia. Almost every day, the television evening news has broadcast pictures of devastating artillery bombardments, ruined towns and villages, and multitudes of killed and wounded men, women and children.

Tens of thousands of people have been turned into refugees forced to leave their homes and belongings under the terror of war and threatened mass extermination. At international conferences, the warring factions made up of Serbians, Croatians, and Bosnian Moslems have drawn lines on maps tracing out what each side views as its "legitimate" claims for control of populations and territory.

The claims to territories and populations are made on the basis of "history"; either a particular area was once part of a Serbian or Croatian state or national entity or it was a traditional homeland of one of the peoples of the former Yugoslavia.

The Kosovo region of Serb-dominated Yugoslavia is 90 percent Albanian, but the Serbs insist that Kosovo is the location of a famous battle that marks the beginning of Serbian statehood; hence, Kosovo must remain a part of the Serbian nation-state.

Alternatively, the claim is made that a region or area is populated by people who speak the Croatian or Serbian language, or who

are members of the same religious group—Catholic or Eastern Orthodox or Moslem—and thus should all be part of the same nation-state.

Finally, the claim is made that an area or territory should belong
to one nation-state or another simply because that is how far the
successes of military conquest have taken the battlelines up to this
point of the civil war; and to withdraw from any portion of this
conquered land would be an insult to those who shed their blood and
gave their lives for its "liberation."

And the divisions and conflicts that have torn Yugoslavia apart
are being repeated, or have the potential for repetition, in other parts
of Eastern Europe. Several wars, civil wars and ethnic conflicts are
already shattering the lives of thousands more in the former Soviet
Union.

In the wake of the collapse of communism in Eastern Europe,
the spirit of nationalism has gripped the minds and the actions of an
increasing number of people. And the revived nationalistic spirit has
become most troublesome in those countries of the former Soviet
Union and Soviet bloc in which a variety of ethnic and linguistic
groups live side by side. Each ethnic and linguistic group views the
others as a threat to its sense of identity and its very existence as a
distinct group. Each fears that some other group will use the powers
of the state to threaten the economic opportunities and cultural
autonomy of its members through political and legal forms of
discrimination and prohibition. Rather than seeing the government
as an agency for the equal protection of the individual rights of all,
the state is viewed as an engine for repression and annihilation of
those ethnic and national groups unlucky enough to be a minority in
the country in which they live.

And this view of government is the fundamental source of the
nationalist and ethnic conflicts that are plaguing this part of the
world. The state is considered an instrument for domination and
enforced privilege for one ethnic group at the expense of others. The
nation-state is considered the exclusive territory for a selected and
chosen group defined by historical origin, commonality of language,
or similarity of religion. Each individual within the nation-state is
defined on the basis of his possessing or not possessing one or more
of these characteristics. These determine who and what the individual is in terms of rights, privileges, and opportunities in the
country in which circumstances or accident of birth have placed
him.

The only lasting solution to the nationality problems of Eastern
Europe and the former Soviet Union lies in the consistent and
thorough application of the principles of market liberalism. Because

only market liberalism takes as its founding principle the separation of the state from all economic activity. And by liberating the market from political intervention, the state is restrained from using its powers of coercion to benefit one ethnic or national group to the detriment of another.

Under either socialism or a regulated market economy, the individual's access to employment opportunities, his ability to open or operate a business, his degree of freedom to practice his religion and educate his children in the language and customs of his choice, or even to live where he wants are all subject to the policy decisions of those who possess political power. Under socialism or a regulated market economy, the state, by definition, has been assigned the responsibility to make decisions to manage or intervene into the economic affairs of life in ways that inevitably must influence the production of goods, the distribution of income, access to resources, and the prices at which commodities may be bought and the wages that may be paid for labor.

Control over the socialist or interventionist state becomes crucial in a social environment in which the members of different ethnic, national, and linguistic groups reside side by side. One's own group must attempt to control the state if it is not to be threatened by another national or ethnic group from using the mechanisms of political power for cultural and linguistic dominance. The state can control access to land and resources to build churches and construct schools. The state can manipulate the tax structures and business licensing procedures to make it more or less difficult for members of one ethnic group or another to operate newspapers in their native language, or to enter certain trades, occupations, or professions. The state can mandate the use of a particular language and set of customs in public and private discourse and commerce. The individual's material well-being and cultural or ethnic autonomy are completely in the hands of the national socialist or interventionist state.

Under a regime of market liberalism, ethnic, linguistic, and national differences and tensions are depoliticized. When the state is separated from the economy, when all market activities are fully and completely privatized—with the government prohibited from intervening on behalf of any group or special interest—each individual is freed from the fear of coerced cultural, ethnic, or linguistic annihilation. Members of different ethnic and linguistic backgrounds can be neither forcibly segregated nor compulsorily integrated into extinction.

Each individual is free to associate predominantly with those of the same group as himself, or interact with or integrate himself into other groups, if he finds it culturally or economically advantageous to do so. Each individual is free to enter the market and privately acquire resources, open businesses, and practice the trade, profession, or occupation he chooses.

Each individual is free to send his children to the private school of his choice, in which the curriculum reflects the values he cherishes and the traditions he wishes passed on to his progeny. He may earn his living and raise his children in blissful cultural isolation, or he may become a cosmopolitan—a citizen of the world—speaking many languages and sharing in the customs and cultural contributions of a variety of the national heritages represented in his own country and those beyond the borders of his own state.

But besides reducing, if not eliminating, many of the causes for ethnic conflicts in society, the liberal market order, in which a number of different national groups peacefully and tolerantly live and interact on the basis of voluntary association and mutual respect, also improves the quality and character of the general civil society in which such a diversity of people reside. Indeed, some liberal thinkers have even argued that the existence of a variety of different national groups within one political state is the healthiest of social orders. This was the view, for example, of Lord Acton in his essay "Nationality" (1862):

> The combination of different nations in one State is as necessary a condition of civilized life as the combination of men in society. Inferior races are raised by living in political union with races intellectually superior. Exhausted and decaying nations are revived by the contact of a younger vitality. Nations in which the elements of organization and capacity for government have been lost, either through the demoralising influence of despotism, or the disintegrating action of democracy, are restored and educated anew under the discipline of a stronger and less corrupt race. This fertilising and regenerating process can only be obtained by living under one government. . . . The fusion takes place by which the vigour, the knowledge, and the capacity of one portion of mankind may be communicated to another. Where political and national boundaries coincide, society ceases to advance, and nations relapse into a condition corresponding to that of men who renounce intercourse with their fellow-men.

For this reason, classical liberals like Lord Acton rejected the dogma and militarism of those who aggressively attempted to impose the ethnically homogeneous nation-state on a geographical area. Nationalism of this sort, Lord Acton argued,

> does not aim either at liberty or prosperity, both of which it sacrifices to the imperative necessity of making the nation the mould and measure of the State. Its course will be marked with material as well as moral ruin, in order that a new invention may prevail over the works of God and the interests of mankind.

Rather than being the cause of conflict and war, the multi-ethnic character of many Eastern European countries could be the strength for their rebirth now that the heavy weight of communism has been lifted off them. But this will be the case only if the ideal of market liberalism and a fully depoliticized economic order completely replaces the collectivist institutions and thinking of the past.

This essay originally appeared in the May 1994 issue of Freedom Daily, *published by The Future of Freedom Foundation.*

45

Social Conflict,
Self-Determination, and
the Boundaries of the State

by Richard M. Ebeling

For the advocate of classical or market liberalism, the depoliticization of economic life is considered the primary avenue for the diminishment of social and cultural tensions in society. The removal of the state from all involvement in market activities, other than as protector of life and property and legal arbiter of interpersonal disputes, means that political power may not be used to benefit any in the society at the expense of others.

In the free-market society, all human relationships are based on voluntary agreement and mutual benefit. Individuals can be neither compelled to trade nor prohibited from trading with any others in the society. Every citizen in the classical-liberal society may freely compete in any line of endeavor in which he chooses to try his hand; his success or failure will depend upon whether those to whom he offers his product or service view what he has for sale as being more attractive than what they might acquire from his rivals. The free man in a classical-liberal world may live wherever he desires, restrained by neither emigration prohibitions nor immigration barriers; all he need do is to pay the price demanded on the market to those offering transportation services to the desired destination, and then to purchase or rent accommodations from those who own property in the location in which he wants to take up either temporary or permanent residence.

In the community of free men, no man may be forced to speak a particular language, practice any specific customs or traditions, or contribute to any cause or charity that he does not personally wish to assist with either his time or money. But at the same time, he cannot force any others to speak his language, practice his customs or traditions, or contribute to the causes and charities that he considers worthy of support. Out of either conviction, preference, or practical convenience, every man in the free society chooses to speak one or more languages, adheres to one or several sets of customs or traditions, and participates, to one extent or another, in the cultural and social activities of the subgroups of the wider community he voluntarily decides to be a part of.

The free society spontaneously generates various integrated and segregated social relationships. For some, it will not matter with whom they rub shoulders when they patronize a restaurant for a meal or a drink. For others, it will be "intolerable" to have to sit next to people of a particular social or racial background if one is to enjoy an evening out. In the free society, some people will thrive on cultural diversity, while others may want to predominantly interact only with "their own kind." But even these distinctions will be blurred to various degrees, because even the most tolerant of human souls will have discriminatory standards and preferences for some personal relationships, while even the most bigoted individual will find it useful to go beyond his own narrow circle for certain transactions and associations for his individual betterment.

But regardless of how depoliticized and open the free society, the fact remains that in any given country, there will sometimes be one or more minorities that feel put upon by the majority. This may occur not because the state has or uses its power to coercively discriminate against a particular group, but simply because some larger group uses another language, practices other customs and traditions, and shares a different historical memory. The signs in the stores and the laws passed by the legislature are in a different language than that of those in the minority. The customs and holidays observed by the majority are different from theirs. Even in the freest and most tolerant country, a minority speaking a different language and having different traditions and cultural mores may feel excluded. The minority feels separate and apart.

In the world as it is today, these inevitable feelings of apartness that a member of a linguistic or ethnic minority may experience are amplified precisely because the state has and uses its political authority to discriminate against and persecute various groups in numerous ways in countries around the globe. One of the answers to this problem that was developed in the nineteenth and twentieth centuries is the idea of the right of secession, or the right to self-determination through the method of a plebiscite.

What such a policy of self-determination should mean from a classical-liberal perspective has been explained by the Austrian economist Ludwig von Mises in his book *Liberalism* (1927):

> The right of self-determination in regard to the question of membership in a state thus means: whenever the inhabitants of a particular territory, whether it be a single village, a whole district, or a series of adjacent districts, make it known, by a freely conducted plebiscite, that they no longer wish to remain united to the state to which they belong at the time, but wish either to form an independent state or to attach themselves to some other state, their wishes are to be respected and complied with. This is the only feasible and effective way of preventing revolutions and civil and international wars. . . .
>
> The right of self-determination of which we speak is not the right of self-determination of nations, but rather the right of self-determination of the inhabitants of every territory large enough to form an independent administrative unit. If it were in any way possible to grant this right of self-determination to every individual person, it would have to be done. This is impracticable only because of compelling technical considerations, which make it necessary that a region be governed as a single administrative unit and that the right of self-determination be restricted to the will of the majority of the inhabitants of areas large enough to count as territorial units in the administration of the country.

For more than two years, tensions have been growing between Russia and Ukraine over a number of political and economic issues, but one of the most heated has been the political status of the Crimean Peninsula along the Black Sea. Famous as the site of the Yalta Conference during World War II, Crimea has a population of 2.7 million people, of which about 70 percent are ethnic Russians. Another 20 percent are Ukrainian (though most of them speak Russian), with an additional 200,000 people being Crimean Tartars. The Crimea was conquered by Imperial Russia from the Turkish

Empire in the eighteenth century, and was the site of "The Charge of the Light Brigade," made famous in Lord Tennyson's poem about the Crimean War between Russia, and Britain and France in the middle of the nineteenth century. Under Soviet rule, the Crimea was a part of the Russian Soviet Federated Socialist Republic. In 1944, Stalin deported practically the entire indigenous Tartar population to Soviet Central Asia, accusing them of having collaborated with the Nazis during the war. In 1954, Nikita Khrushchev gave the Crimea to the Ukrainian Soviet Socialist Republic as a "gift."

After the Soviet Union collapsed in 1991, the Crimean peninsula remained a part of independent Ukraine. In February and March of 1994, elections were held for a president and for deputies of the regional Crimean parliament. Russians voted overwhelmingly for candidates advocating either greater autonomy or independence for the Crimea, or its reunification with Russia. The Tartar minority predominantly voted for candidates supporting Ukrainian control, since many of them were fearful of renewed persecution if they came under Russian authority.

In May 1994, the Crimean parliament voted to establish the Crimea as an autonomous political entity relatively free of Ukrainian control. The Ukrainian government in Kiev responded that this threatened the territorial integrity of the Ukrainian state and would not be tolerated. Russian President Boris Yeltsin warned Kiev: "No forcible actions against Crimea should be undertaken. Crimea is an independent republic within Ukraine. It has the right to its own political stand, to make its own decisions." The Russian military daily newspaper *Red Star* stated that "if a conflict flares up, it will eclipse in its scale everything we have encountered before." And Russian Foreign Minister Andrei Kozyrev said: "The Yugoslav drama should not be repeated in Crimea. There the [war] started with demands of sovereignty and ultimatums to back up state integrity."

How should the matter be settled? The classical-liberal solution, as outlined by Professor Mises, would suggest that each village and town in the Crimea should have a plebiscite, in which the residents would decide between independence, reunification with Russia, or continuing political ties with Ukraine. Portions of the Crimea, on a new political map, might look like a colored checkerboard, with some villages where the majority of the occupants are Tartar being the same color as Ukraine. Other portions of the Crimea, perhaps most of the peninsula, would be the same color as Russia on the map. And possibly some areas would be a color different from either Ukraine or Russia, being those districts or towns in which the majority had opted to form a separate Crimean government.

Would this prevent the continuing discomfort of some ethnic or linguistic minorities who might still find themselves surrounded by a majority of people who speak a different language or practice different customs in the village or town in which they reside, or would it prevent political discrimination and favoritism against them by the majority if state power was used in this way? Unfortunately, no. But it would tend to minimize the number of people who might find themselves in the situation of being an ethnic or linguistic minority within a political entity.

And equally unfortunate, this in no way assures that the political entities created and reshaped by means of political self-determination through the mechanism of the plebiscite will follow classical-liberal policies within their new borders. Indeed, in the present ideological environment that envelops the world today, it is highly unlikely. Faith in the state as the great god who cares for all of man's needs is still too strong an element in people's minds. But while a policy of political self-determination would not guarantee domestic liberty in the political entities created through means of local plebiscites, it would minimize one of the causes of civil war and international conflict.

State borders and political frontiers would no longer be determined by blood and conquest, but by the local choices of the people themselves who reside in each and every corner of the world. And they could be open to revision and change periodically as demographics and people's preferences changed. A plebiscite might be held once every ten years, as a formality. Or it could be held whenever, for example, two-thirds of the population in an area petitioned for the holding of a plebiscite. Such a system for the defining of the boundaries of political entities does not necessarily imply an exclusionist nationalism. The people of some regions, towns, and districts might wish to form separate states that are consciously multiethnic, multilinguistic, and culturally diverse precisely because of the societal advantages of such pluralistic communities (see "National Conflicts, Market Liberalism, and Social Peace," Chapter 44).

While the principle of political self-determination neither establishes nor guarantees a regime of liberty within the states created through the method of local plebiscites, it does offer a classical-liberal alternative to the linguistic, ethnic, and racial wars of the type that have been pulling apart the former Yugoslavia, South Africa, Rwanda, Armenia, and Azerbaijan, and which threaten a growing number of other countries around the world. And by reducing international tensions and domestic civil conflicts, political self-determination might help foster a social climate more conducive to the establishment of the self-determination of individual liberty within nations over time, as well.

This essay originally appeared in the September 1994 issue of Freedom Daily, *published by The Future of Freedom Foundation.*

46

Practicing the Principle of Freedom—At Home and Abroad

by Richard M. Ebeling

As an advocate of individual freedom, I consider all forms of government interference in people's lives, other than those minimally essential for the protection of life, liberty, and property, to be morally wrong, politically harmful, and economically counterproductive. As part of that political philosophy, I believe that the government of the United States should no more intervene into the internal affairs of other countries than in the personal, peaceful, and voluntary affairs of its own citizens at home.

Many of my fellow countrymen follow courses of action in their own lives that I consider stupid, immoral, and harmful. But I also feel strongly that it would be morally wrong and pragmatically counterproductive to force my fellow countrymen to follow the courses of action I consider to be wiser and richer for them.

Either every man must be respected and protected as a free agent in his own affairs, or we run the risk of degenerating into a society of coercing meddlers, each with his own banner of "right living," each trying to use the political power of the state to make his fellow citizens bend to his vision of the good, proper, and virtuous life. Society becomes a war of all against all, as individuals sharing similar conceptions of that "right living" form coalitions for strength in the struggle for votes, influence, and control of the state's authority to use force.

But men being what they are, even when they begin as pure-at-heart "true believers," wishing only to use the state for the good of others (as they conceive that good), soon are taken over by the "dark side of the force." The welding of power over others becomes an aphrodisiac, a "high" stronger than any narcotic; and, besides, having political power also has its use for material gain, both for oneself and for those with whom one is in coalitions for power. Few have been able to resist these temptations over the ages. Even when the first generation of coercing meddlers coming to power remained fairly uncorrupted by the opportunities for personal gain, their heirs in acquiring the reins of political authority have tended to have fewer inhibitions for resisting these temptations.

Furthermore, coercion can never, ultimately, be a means for making men good or virtuous. Force can control men's behavior—it can prohibit them from doing certain things and command them to do others—under the threat and use of various physical or psychological punishments. But this does not make those actions moral or virtuous. An act is moral or virtuous only by virtue of it being the free choice of a human being who, in principle, could have done the opposite. Morality and virtue are in the minds and hearts of men, not in the control of their external conduct.

Imposed conformity is not morality; it is the denial of morality. By narrowing or abrogating the field in which a man in his actions must make up his own mind as to what is "the right thing to do," the state removes the necessity to more conscientiously think and decide about what he should do as a self-responsible human being. By denying him the freedom to choose in various corners of his life, the state frees the individual from being more fully responsible for his actions. When men are freed from responsibility for their actions, the conditions are created for the growth of a climate of amorality: "It's not my responsibility; I paid my taxes" or "I'm not accountable; I just obeyed orders."

In the free society, the only appropriate means for trying to change other people's conduct is through reason, persuasion, and example. The coerced man often harbors resentment and anger in his heart, both against the coercer and at himself because he had not the courage to resist being made to do what he did not want. The free man, when he changes the things he does due to the persuasion or example of others, feels gratitude and joy for having been shown a better purpose in life or how to more successfully pursue his ends. When other men freely choose to change their behavior due to our arguments or example, it is more likely, therefore, to represent an actual change of heart or of mind. And that is how the world is, ultimately, really changed—one person at a time, for good or evil.

Men and governments in other countries, in this century and those in the past, have done many evil things. They have killed, brutalized, tortured, and destroyed; and especially in this century, it has been done on a scale that goes beyond our mind's ability to fully comprehend. They have shocked our conscience and made us doubt the existence of any humanity in the human being. In a world of such conduct by others in other lands, it has been natural that many in America have wanted to "do something"—to come to the aid of those victimized by evil and to stop evil from doing it anymore.

But similar to the pattern too often at home, people disturbed by the immoral acts of others abroad have turned to the state to right the wrongs occurring in foreign lands. They have wanted their government to intervene in the affairs of people in other countries, to oppose bad governments and evil men and, in their place, foster good government and support better men. Rarely has this been successful in achieving the end desired; and even when the result in the short run has seemed better than what had been before, the intervention has often had longer-run, usually unintended, consequences that have made new outcomes often similar to the ones the intervention was meant to cure.

Even when people oppressed by a tyrant have been liberated from their torment, the people freed frequently turn against their liberators. It begins to play on their pride that they were not able to free themselves. Also, the liberating government is often not satisfied with merely eliminating the evil government; to justify the sacrifice made by its own people, in lives and money, to free those who had been living under foreign oppression, the liberating government tries to establish a "new order" of good government and honest politics in that foreign land.

But, alas, good government and honest politics often have different meanings for the people in that foreign country. Customs, traditions, and other societal practices call for political structures and methods of authority frequently quite different from what the liberating government's "advisors" view as the good or the better. Irritated and angry at the appearance of being told by the liberators how to live their lives and run their affairs in their own country, the people in that foreign land soon start wishing that the meddling Yankee (or the Limey Brit, or the French Frog, or the Russian Bear) would go home. And too often, the emotional reaction of being dictated to by the foreign power (who only yesterday was hailed as the great liberator), plays into the hands of the demagogue and would-be new tyrant hoping to ride to power on the wave of antiforeign sentiment. The military forces and civilian advisors of the liberating government soon find themselves the new targeted enemy of the very people whom they wanted to free from the evils and injustices of the past.

At home, the interventionist government often finds itself— sooner or later—governing a "house divided" over the justification for the intervention and its continuance. Sometimes there is no consensus from the start that the foreign intervention is justified. People in the society, to the extent they take any interest in international events, take different sides concerning who is in the right and who has been wronged in that foreign country—who is the oppressor and who needs to be freed. If the foreign intervention is undertaken, then from the start, there will be many in the country who oppose and resent their wealth being taxed and the lives of their loved ones in the military being put in harm's way to fight for "the wrong side." If the foreign intervention has broad support among many in the society, then dissent is muted at first.

But if the intervention is not short and clearly successful, then second thoughts begin to emerge among a growing number of people: Was the intervention the right thing to do from the start? Are we becoming the enemy of the very people we wished to befriend? Are we making the situation in that country worse than it was before? Is it worth the sacrifice in men and money—ours and theirs—to continue the intervention?

Even if the foreign intervention seems to have been successful—with the goals appearing to have been achieved quickly, with minimal sacrifice in lives and money, and with "our boys" already having come home—the intervening government often leaves behind a situation in that foreign country that soon becomes not much different from what existed before. Why? Because merely overthrowing the existing political order and imposing a new political order does not change the ideas, beliefs, customs, and traditions of the people. Such impositions may temporarily affect the external behavior of those people, but it does not transform what guides their sense of right and wrong, good and bad, just or unjust; these are matters of their hearts and minds, and these cannot be coerced into change. The only alternative is for the intervening government to stay on in that foreign country as a permanent, coercing meddler, and that usually only leads to more problems, not solutions.

What, then, is to be done in the face of evil in other lands? For the advocate of freedom, the answer is the depoliticization, the privatization of foreign intervention. In our private life, we have many friends, neighbors, and family members whom we care about and desire to help; we desire to help them in getting through times of trouble and hardship, and we want to help them in trying to find better principles to guide their lives, so many of the problems that have been caused by their past choices do not happen again.

Sometimes these tasks are more than we, ourselves, can try to solve, so we form voluntary associations, organizations, and clubs to pool our efforts with those who share the same desire to help and see value in the same peaceful methods for attaining the end. Others "go it alone" in their endeavors to assist their fellow men, and still others form different associations because, though they believe in the same end, they think there are better means to achieve it than the ones we decide to try. And others in the society choose not to participate at all in these types of tasks, because they place a higher value on other things, in terms of an expenditure of their time, money, and efforts. No one is compelled to care or to help, nor is any one forced to accept one way of doing things as the only correct method. Such voluntary associations and institutions are among the essential foundation stones of civil society. They are also the free society's private solutions to what are called "social problems."

The depoliticization or privatization of foreign intervention means an approach analogous to the private institutions of voluntary association for the handling of domestic "social problems." Those who see distress and hardship among peoples in other lands, and who desire to assist them, should not be restricted in forming associations and charities to pool their resources to supply such help. But neither should others who do not share that same concern, or who consider there to be other answers to solve those foreign problems, be compelled to provide assistance if they choose not to.

If oppression reigns in a foreign land—if a peaceful people in another country is threatened or aggressed against by another state— any citizen in a free society should have the liberty to volunteer his help. This help can include financial contributions or personal service. He can offer to fight alongside the "freedom fighters" resisting their own government's tyranny, or he can offer his services in the military of that foreign country to help repel the aggressor nation. He can choose to do so for free or for pay. He can form associations and societies to pool his own resources with those of others to buy military equipment, medical supplies, or emergency food and clothing. He can try to persuade others in his own country to see the rightness in the cause and join him in fighting the good fight to win freedom for others in those other lands.

But what would be inconsistent with any person's crusade in the cause of freedom in other lands would be to abrogate the freedom of his own fellow citizens in the pursuit of that cause. It is easy to say that all that is asked for is a small violation of the liberty of his fellow citizens in the good cause of the freedom of so many others. But is this any different from the appeal often heard, that it is only small violations of people's liberty that are being asked for to feed the hungry, to house the homeless, to assist the poor, to support the handicapped, to . . .?

Once the principle of liberty is breached, no matter how deserving the cause may sound, all other such abridgments soon become matters of pragmatic judgment. Well, if it seemed reasonable or meritorious to abridge some people's liberties for this cause, then surely to extend that abridgment just a little longer, or a little more, for this other good cause cannot be objected to, can it? If we sacrificed some people's liberty to intervene in country X for a good cause, then surely to do it again or more forcefully for the noble endeavor of helping these other unfortunate people in country Y cannot be objected to, can it? Where does it stop? And whose judgment shall prevail in making this decision?

The fundamental duty of the state is the protection of the life, liberty, and property of the citizenry within its own territorial jurisdiction. If the state goes beyond this, it can do so only by taking the wealth, income, and resources of some to improve the circumstances of others, i.e., by means of coercive meddling. Either we have the protection of equal individual rights for all before the law or we have unequal privileges for some at the expense of others. This is the choice concerning the role of the state, whether in domestic or foreign affairs. There is no third alternative.

This essay originally appeared in the December 1995 issue of Freedom Daily, *published by the Future of Freedom Foundation.*

47

The Most Dreaded Enemy
of Liberty

by James Madison

O f all the enemies to public liberty war is, perhaps the most to be dreaded, because it comprises and develops the germ of every other. War is the parent of armies; from these proceed debts and taxes; and armies, and debts, and taxes are the known instruments for bringing the many under the domination of the few. In war, too, the discretionary power of the Executive is extended; its influence in dealing out offices, honors, and emoluments is multiplied; and all the means of seducing the minds are added to those of subduing the force, of the people. . . . [There is also an] inequality of fortunes, and the opportunities of fraud, growing out of a state of war, and . . . degeneracy of manners and of morals. . . . No nation could preserve its freedom in the midst of continual warfare. . . .

[It should be well understood] that the powers proposed to be surrendered [by the Third Congress] to the Executive were those which the Constitution has most jealously appropriated to the Legislature. . . . The Constitution expressly and exclusively vests in the Legislature the power of declaring a state of war . . . the power of raising armies . . . the power of creating offices. . . . A delegation of such powers [to the President] would have struck, not only at the fabric of our Constitution, but at the foundation of all well organized and well checked governments. The separation of the power of declaring war from that of conducting it, is wisely contrived to exclude the danger of its being declared for the sake of its being conducted. The separation of the power of raising armies from the power of commanding them, is intended to prevent the raising of armies for the sake of commanding them.

James Madison was the fourth president of the United States. This essay is from Letters and Other Writings of James Madison.

About the Authors

Doug Bandow is a senior fellow at the Cato Institute, a public policy research organization based in Washington, D.C. He is a nationally syndicated columnist with Copley News Service and the former editor of *Inquiry* magazine. Before that he served as a special assistant to President Reagan and as a senior policy analyst in the office of the president-elect and the Reagan for President campaign.

Bandow has written and edited several books, including: *The Politics of Envy: Statism as Theology* (Transaction); *Perpetuating Poverty: The World Bank, the IMF, and the Developing World* (Cato Institute); *The Politics of Plunder: Misgovernment in Washington* (Transaction); *Beyond Good Intentions: A Biblical View of Politics* (Crossway); *Human Resources and Defense Manpower* (National Defense University); and *The U.S.-South Korean Alliance: Time for a Change* (Transaction). He has also been widely published in such periodicals as *Foreign Policy, Harper's, National Interest, National Review, The New Republic,* and *Orbis,* as well as leading newspapers including *The New York Times, The Wall Street Journal,* and *The Washington Post,* and has appeared on numerous radio and television programs, most notably ABC Nightly News, American Interests, CBS Evening News, CNN Crossfire, CNN Larry King Live, Good Morning America, Nightline, and the Oprah Winfrey Show.

Mr. Bandow received his B.S. in economics from Florida State University in 1976 and his J.D. from Stanford University in 1979.

Richard M. Ebeling is the Ludwig von Mises Professor of Economics at Hillsdale College, Hillsdale, Michigan, and serves as vice president of academic affairs for The Future of Freedom Foundation. Born in New York City in 1950, he received his B.A. in economics from California State University, Sacramento, and his M.A. in economics from Rutgers University. Professor Ebeling has been a lecturer in economics at the National University of Ireland at Cork and assistant professor of economics at the University of Dallas. He has been at Hillsdale College since 1988.

Among his most recent writings are: "World Peace, International Order Classical Liberalism," *International Journal of World Peace* (Dec. 1995); "The Political Myths and Economic Realities of the Welfare State," in *American Perestroika: The Demise of the Welfare State* (Hillsdale College Press, 1995); "Austrian Subjectivism and Phenomenological Foundations," *Advances in Austrian Economics*, Vol. 2 (1995); "Expectations and Expectations Formation in Mises's Theory of the Market Process" in *The Market Process: Essays in Contemporary Austrian Economics* (Edward Elgar, 1994); "How Economics Became the Dismal Science," in *Economic Education: What Should We Learn About the Free Market?* (Hillsdale College Press, 1994); "Liberalism and Collectivism in the 20th Century" in *The End of 'Isms'? Reflections on the Fate of Ideological Politics After Communism's Collapse (Basil Blackwell, 1994);* Economic Calculation Under Socialism: Ludwig von Mises and his Predecessors," in *The Meaning of Ludwig von Mises* (Kluwer Academic Press, 1993). His articles have also been published in Brazil, England, Poland, Lithuania, and Russia. He has edited several books that contain articles by him, including *Disaster in Red: The Failure and Collapse of Socialism; Money, Method, and the Market Process: Essays by Ludwig von Mises; Austrian Economics: A Reader; Austrian Economics: Retrospects on the Past and Prospects for the Future; The Global Collapse of Socialism; Global Free Trade: Rhetoric or Reality?*; and *Can Capitalism Cope? Free Market Reform in the Post-Communist World.* Professor Ebeling is also the co-editor of two books published by The Future of Freedom Foundation: *The Dangers of Socialized Medicine* and *The Case for Free Trade and Open Immigration.*

In 1991, Professor Ebeling made six trips to the former Soviet Union, consulting with the government of Lithuania and with members of the Russian Parliament in Moscow on free-market reform and privatization of the socialist economy. He was in Vilnius, Lithuania, in January 1991 and witnessed the Soviet military crackdown in which thirteen Lithuanians were killed. He was in Moscow in August 1991 during the failed coup attempt and was at the barricades with the defenders of freedom at the Russian Parliament. He again traveled to Lithuania in August 1993 for consultations on market reforms and privatization.

Robert Higgs is research director for The Independent Institute in Oakland, California, and editor of its new book, *Hazardous to our Health? FDA Regulation of Health Care Products.* He received his Ph.D. in economics from Johns Hopkins University, and he has taught at the University of Washington, Lafayette College, and Seattle University. He has been a visiting scholar at Oxford University and Stanford

University, and a fellow for the Hoover Institution and the National Science Foundation. Dr. Higgs is the editor of The Independent Institute book, *Arms, Politics and the Economy*, and the volume, *Emergence of the Modern Political Economy*. His authored books include *The Transformation of the American Economy 1865–1914*, *Competition and Coercion*, and *Crisis and Leviathan: Critical Episodes in the Growth of American Government*. A contributor to numerous scholarly volumes, he is the author of over 100 articles and reviews in academic journals, as well as many articles in such publications as *The Wall Street Journal* and *The New York Times*.

Jacob G. Hornberger is founder and president of The Future of Freedom Foundation, an educational foundation whose mission is to present an uncompromising moral, philosophical, and economic case for individual freedom, private property, and limited government.

Mr. Hornberger was born and raised in Laredo, Texas, and received his B.A. in economics from Virginia Military Institute and his law degree from the University of Texas. He was a trial attorney for twelve years in Texas. He also was an adjunct professor at the University of Dallas, where he taught law and economics. In 1987, Mr. Hornberger left the practice of law to become director of programs at The Foundation for Economic Education in Irvington-on-Hudson, New York, publisher of *The Freeman*.

In 1989, Mr. Hornberger founded The Future of Freedom Foundation. He is a regular writer for The Foundation's publication, *Freedom Daily*. He also has spoken to groups all over the United States, as well as England, Eastern Europe, and South America. He is the co-editor of two books published by the Foundation: *The Dangers of Socialized Medicine* and *The Case for Free Trade and Open Immigration*.

Simon Jenkins writes for *The Times of London* and *The Spectator*.

Ralph Raico is professor of European history at the State University of New York College at Buffalo. He received his Ph.D. degree from the University of Chicago, Committee on Social Thought, where the head of his dissertation committee was F. A. Hayek. Among Dr. Raico's recent articles and essays are: "Rethinking Churchill," in *The Costs of War*, John V. Denson, ed.; "Austrian Economics and Classical Liberalism," in *Advances in Austrian Economics*, vol. II; "The Theory of Economic Development and the 'European Miracle,'" in *The Collapse of Economic Planning*, Peter J. Boettke, ed.; "Classical Liberal Roots of the Marxist Doctrine of Classes," in *Requiem for Marx*, Yuri N. Maltsev, ed.; and *Classical Liberalism in the*

Twentieth Century. Dr. Raico has also contributed to *The Review of Austrian Economics*, the *Zeitschrift für Wirtschaftspolitik*, the *Cato Journal*, and other scholarly journals. He is the translator of Ludwig von Mises's *Liberalism* and of essays by F. A. Hayek contained in Hayek's *Collected Works*.

Dr. Raico's book on the history of German liberalism is scheduled to be published in Germany in 1996. He is currently at work on a history of European liberalism.

Dr. Raico was editor of *New Individualist Review*, and senior editor of *Inquiry*. He has lectured widely in Europe, the United States, and Canada, and is Fellow in Social Thought of the Cato Institute, Washington, D.C.

Sheldon Richman is vice president of policy affairs at The Future of Freedom Foundation. He is the author of *Separating School & State: How to Liberate America's Families*, published by the Foundation.

Mr. Richman's articles on population, federal disaster assistance, international trade, education, the environment, American history, foreign policy, privacy, computers, and the Middle East have appeared in *The Washington Post*, *The Wall Street Journal*, *American Scholar*, *Chicago Tribune*, *USA Today*, *Washington Times*, *Insight*, *Cato Policy Report*, *Journal of Economic Development*, *The Freeman*, *The World & I*, *Reason*, *Washington Report on Middle East Affairs*, *Middle East Policy*, *Liberty* magazine, and other publications. He is a contributor to the *Fortune Encyclopedia of Economics*.

A former newspaper reporter, senior editor at the Cato Institute, associate editor of *Inquiry* magazine, and senior editor at the Institute for Humane Studies at George Mason University, Mr. Richman is a graduate of Temple University in Philadelphia.

Wesley Allen Riddle is a native of Houston, Texas. He served as youth advisor for the state of Texas to Ronald Reagan and Citizens for the Republic from 1978 to 1979. In 1979 he was appointed to the United States Military Academy at West Point, New York, where he graduated cum laude in 1983.

As an Army officer with the Air Defense Artillery branch, he served in a number of stateside and overseas assignments, including combat duty as a Patriot Missile battery commander in the Gulf War. Following the war, he pursued his master of philosophy degree in modern history (M.Phil.) at Oxford University, graduating with Distinction in 1993 and earning the university's Sara Norton Prize for original thesis. Since then, Mr. Riddle has been a faculty member at

West Point in the department of history, where he is assistant professor and teaches American Political Tradition and Advanced History of the United States. The Heritage Foundation recently named him Salvatori Fellow for the 1996–97 term.

Mr. Riddle has published numerous essays and book reviews in scholarly journals and public-opinion magazines here and in England and is a Distinguished Member of the International Society of Poets. He is a member of Phi Kappa Phi and Phi Alpha Theta honor societies. His military decorations include the Bronze Star Medal and the Army Parachutist badge.

Joseph Sobran began a 21-year term of employment with *National Review* in 1972. He has been a syndicated newspaper columnist since 1979 and was a weekly commentator on CBS Radio's "Spectrum" from 1979 to 1991. He has written for many publications. In addition to his newspaper column, he writes regular columns for *The Wanderer* and *The Rothbard-Rockwell Report*.

He is the author of two books, *Single Issues* and the recently completed *Outing Shakespeare*, which attempts to prove that Edward de Vere, seventeenth Earl of Oxford, was the real author of the works we call Shakespeare's. He is currently working on a book about the U.S. Constitution, to be called *Post-Constitutional America*. In 1995, he launched his own monthly newsletter, SOBRAN'S.

About the Publisher

The Future of Freedom Foundation

Founded in 1989 and based in Fairfax, Virginia, The Future of Freedom Foundation is a 501 (c)(3), tax-exempt, educational foundation. Its mission is to advance liberty and the libertarian philosophy by presenting an uncompromising moral, philosophical, and economic case for individual freedom and limited government. FFF's publication, *Freedom Daily* ($18 per year), is a monthly journal of libertarian essays.

FFF's uncompromising tradition is carried forward in its books and tapes. The books are: FFF's award-winning *Separating School & State: How to Liberate America's Families* by Sheldon Richman; and three books edited by Jacob G. Hornberger and Richard M. Ebeling: *The Dangers of Socialized Medicine; The Case for Free Trade and Open Immigration;* and *The Failure of America's Foreign Wars.*

The Foundation neither solicits nor accepts government grants. Operations of The Foundation are primarily funded through subscriptions and donations.

The Future of Freedom Foundation
11350 Random Hills Road, Suite 800
Fairfax, VA 22030
(703) 934-6101
fax (703) 352-8678
75200.1523@compuserve.com

Selected Bibliography

Acton, Lord (John Emerich Edward Dalberg-Acton). "Nationality," in *Essays in the History of Liberty*. Indianapolis, Ind.: Liberty Classics, 1985.

Ambrose, Stephen E. *Rise to Globalism: American Foreign Policy, 1938–1976*. New York: Peguin Books, 1976.

Abgell, Norman. *The Fruits of Victory*. New York: The Century Co., 1921.

———. *The Great Illusion* [1911]. New York: G. P. Putnam's Sons, 1933.

———. *This Have and Have-Not Business: Political Fantasy and Economic Fact*. London: Hamish Hamilton, Publisher, 1936.

Armstrong, Anne. *Unconditional Surrender*. New Brunswick, N.J.: Rutgers University Press, 1961.

Balabkins, Nicholas. *Germany Under Direct Controls: Economic Aspects of Industrial Disarmament, 1945–1948*. New Brunswick, N.J.: Rutgers University Press, 1964.

Barnes, Harry Elmer. *The Genesis of the World War*. New York: Alfred Knopf Co., 1929.

———. *In Quest of Truth and Justice: De-Bunking the War-Guilt Myth* [1928]. Colorado Springs, Colo.: Ralph Myles Publisher, Inc., 1972.

———. "Pearl Harbor After a Quarter of a Century," *Left and Right: A Journal of Libertarian Thought*, Vol. IV (1968).

———. *Revisionism: A Key to Peace and Other Essays*. San Francisco: The Cato Institute, 1980.

———. *Selected Revisionist Papers*. New York: Arno Press & The New York Times, 1972.

———, ed., *Perpetual War for Perpetual Peace: A Critical Examination of the Foreign Policy of Franklin Delano Roosevelt and Its Aftermath*. Caldwell, Idaho: The Caxton Printers, Ltd., 1953.

Bartlett, Bruce R. *Cover-Up: The Politics of Pearl Harbor, 1941–1946*. New Rochelle, N.Y.: Arlington House, Publishers, 1978.

Baudin, Louis. *Free Trade and Peace*. Paris: International Institute of Intellectual Co-operation, 1939.

Beach, Edward L. *Scapegoats: A Defense of Kimmel and Short at Pearl Harbor.* Annapolis, Md.: Naval Institute Press, 1995.

Beard, Charles A. *American Foreign Policy in the Making, 1932–1940: A Study in Responsibilities.* New Haven, Conn.: Yale University Press, 1946.

———. *The Devil Theory of War: An Inquiry into the Nature of History and the Possibility of Keeping Out of War.* New York: The Vanguard Press, 1936.

———. *Giddy Minds and Foreign Quarrels: An Estimate of American Foreign Policy.* New York: Macmillan Co., 1939.

———. *President Roosevelt and the Coming of the War 1941: A Study in Appearances and Realities.* New Haven, Conn.: Yale University Press, 1948.

Beisner, Robert L. *Twelve Against Empire: The Anti-Imperialists, 1898–1900.* New York: McGraw-Hill Book Co., 1968.

Belgion, Montgomery. *Victor's Justice.* Chicago: Henry Regnery Co., 1949.

Bethell, Nicholas. *The Last Secret.* New York: Basic Books, 1974.

Brown, Elizabeth Churchill. *The Enemy at His Back.* New York: The Bookmailer, 1956.

Bruce, Stewart E. *The War Guilt and the Peace Crimes of the Entente Allies.* New York: F. L. Searl & Co., 1920.

Burns, C. Delisle. *A Short History of International Intercourse.* New York: Oxford University Press, 1924.

Carpenter, Ted Galen, ed. *America Entangled: The Persian Gulf Crisis and Its Consequences.* Washington, D.C.: The Cato Institute, 1991.

———. *A Search for Enemies: America's Alliances after the Cold War.* Washington, D.C.: The Cato Institute, 1992.

Carter, Boake, and Thomas H. Healy. *Why Meddle in the Orient? Facts, Figures, Fictions, and Follies.* New York: Dodge Publishing Co., 1938.

Castle, Eugene W. *Billions, Blunders and Baloney: The Fantastic Story of How Uncle Sam Squanders Your Money Overseas.* New York: Devin-Adair Co., 1955.

———. *The Great Giveaway: The Realities of Foreign Aid.* Chicago: Henry Regnery Co., 1957.

Chamberlin, William Henry. *America's Second Crusade.* Chicago: Henry Regnery Co., 1950

———. "From Appeasement to Containment," in *Beyond Containment.* Chicago: Henry Regnery Co., 1953.

———. "What Became of Isolationism?" in *The Evolution of a Conservative.* Chicago: Henry Regnery Co., 1959.

Charmley, John. *Churchill: The End to Glory.* London: Hodder & Stoughton, 1993.

Cohen, Warren I. *The American Revisionists: The Lessons of Intervention in World War I.* Chicago: University of Chicago Press, 1967.

Colby, Benjamin. *'Twas a Famous Victory: Deception and Propaganda in the War with Germany.* New Rochelle, N.Y.: Arlington House, Publishers, 1974.

Cole, Wayne S. *America First: The Battle Against Intervention, 1940–1941.* Madison: University of Wisconsin Press, 1953.

————. *Charles A. Lindbergh and the Battle Against American Intervention in World War II.* New York: Harcourt, Brace Jovanovich, 1974.

————. *Roosevelt & and the Isolationists, 1932–45.* Lincoln: University of Nebraska Press, 1983.

Costello, John. *Days of Infamy: MacArthur, Roosevelt, Churchill—The Shocking Truth Revealed.* New York: Pocket Books, 1994.

————. *The Pacific War, 1941–1945.* New York: Rawson Wade Publishers, Inc., 1981.

Cowen, Tyler. "The Marshall Plan: Myths and Realities," in *U. S. Aid to the Developing World: A Free Market Agenda,* Doug Bandow, ed. Washington, D.C.: The Heritage Foundation, 1985.

Crocker, George N. *Roosevelt's Road to Russia.* Chicago: Henry Regnery Co., 1961.

Deane, John R. *The Strange Alliance: The Story of Our Efforts at Wartime Co-Operation with Russia.* New York: The Viking Press, 1946.

Delaisi, Francis. *Political Myths and Economic Realities.* London: Noel Douglas, 1925.

Dickinson, G. L. *The International Anarchy, 1904–1914.* New York: The Century Co., 1926.

Doenecke, Justus D. *In Danger Undaunted: The Anti-Interventionist Movement of 1940–1941 as Revealed in the Papers of the America First Committee.* Stanford, Calif.: Hoover Institution, 1990.

————. *The Literature of Isolationism: A Guide to Non-Interventionist Scholarship, 1930–1972.* Colorado Springs, Colo.: Ralph Myles Publisher, Inc., 1972.

————. *Not to the Swift: The Old Isolationists in the Cold War Era.* East Brunswick, N.J.: Associated University Press, 1979.

Eberstadt, Nicholas. *Foreign Aid and American Purpose.* Washington, D.C., American Enterprise Institute, 1988.

Edoin, Hoito. *The Night Tokyo Burned: The Incendiary Campaign Against Japan, March–August, 1945.* New York: St. Martin's Press, 1987.

Ekirch, Arthur A., Jr. *The Civilian and the Military.* New York: Oxford University Press, 1956.

————. *The Decline of American Liberalism.* New York: Longmans, Green and Co., 1955.

Eksteins, Modris. *Rites of Spring: The Great War and the Birth of the Modern Age.* New York: Doubleday, 1990.

Elliott, Mark R. *Pawns of Yalta: Soviet Refugees and America's Role in Their Repatriation.* Urbana: University of Illinois Press, 1982.

Epstein, Julius. *Operation Keelhaul.* New York: Devin-Adair, 1973.

Farr, Finis. *FDR.* New Rochelle, N.Y.: Arlington House, Publishers, 1972.

Fay, S. B. *The Origins of the World War,* 2 Vols. New York: Macmillan Co., 1930.

Fenno, Richard F., Jr., ed. *The Yalta Conference.* Boston: D. C. Heath & Co., 1955.

Ferrell, Robert H. *Woodrow Wilson and World War I, 1917–1921.* New York: Harper & Row, Publishers, 1985.

Ferrero, Guglielmo. "Forms of War and International Anarchy," in *The World Crisis,* William E. Rappard, ed. [1938]. Freeport, N.Y.: Books for Libraries Press, 1969.

———. *Militarism* [1902]. New York: Benjamin Blom, Inc., 1971.

———. *Peace and War* [1933]. Freeport, N.Y.: Books for Libraries Press, 1969.

———. *The Unity of the World.* New York: Albert & Charles Boni, 1930.

Fish, Hamilton. *FDR, The Other Side of the Coin: How We Were Tricked into World War II.* New York: Vantage Books, 1976.

Flynn, John T. *As We Go Marching.* Garden City, N.Y.: Doubleday, Doran, 1944.

———. *The Decline of the American Republic.* New York: The Devin-Adair Co., 1955.

———. *The Roosevelt Myth.* New York: The Devin-Adair Co., 1948; rev. ed., 1956.

———. *The Truth About Pearl Harbor.* New York: John T. Flynn, 1944.

———. *While You Slept: Our Tragedy in Asia and Who Made It.* New York: The Devin-Adair Co., 1951.

Fussell, Paul. *Wartime: Understanding and Behavior in the Second World War.* New York: Oxford University Press, 1989.

Garrett, Garret. *The American Story.* Chicago: Henry Regnery Co., 1955.

———. "Rise of Empire" in *The People's Pottage.* Caldwell, Idaho: The Caxton Printers, Ltd., 1953.

Grattan, C. Hartley. *The Deadly Parallel.* New York: Stackpole Sons, 1939.

———. *Why We Fought.* New York: Vanguard Press, 1929.

Grenfell, Russell. *Unconditional Hatred: German War Guilt and the Future of Europe.* Old Greenwich, Conn.: The Devin-Adair Co., 1953.

Grenville, J. A. S. *A History of the World in the Twentieth Century.* Cambridge, Mass.: Belknap Press of Harvard University Press, 1994.

Hamlin, C. H. *The War Myth in United States History.* New York: Vanguard Press, 1927.

Harper, F. A. "In Search of Peace," [1951] in *The Writings of F. A. Harper,* Vol. 2. Menlo Park, Calif.: Institute for Humane Studies, 1979.

Harrison, Alferdteen, ed. *Black Exodus: The Great Migration from the American South*. Jackson: University Press of Mississippi, 1991.

Hayes, Carlton J. H. *Essays on Nationalism*. New York: The Macmillan Co., 1926.

———. *The Historical Evolution of Modern Nationalism*. New York: Richard R. Smith, Inc., 1931.

Hazlitt, Henry. "Can We Buy Off Communism?" (The Marshall Plan), *Newsweek* December 15, 1947).

———. "Collectivism on Relief," (The Marshall Plan) *Newsweek* (July 19, 1948).

———. "Communism and the Marshall Plan," *Newsweek* (March 8, 1948).

———. "Dangers of Dollar Diplomacy," (The Marshall Plan) *Newsweek* (July 12, 1948).

———. "The Future of Foreign Aid," (The Marshall Plan) *Newsweek* (January 16, 1950).

———. "Future of the Marshall Plan," *Newsweek* (February 27, 1950).

———. *Illusions of Point Four*. Irvington-on-Hudson, N.Y.: The Foundation for Economic Education, 1950.

———. "The Marshall Plan: We Cannot Buy Off the Russians," *Newsweek* (January 26, 1948).

———. "Sense Instead of Dollars," (The Marshall Plan) *Newsweek* (March 28, 1949).

———. "Subsidizing Planned Chaos" (The Marshall Plan), *Newsweek* (June 23, 1947).

———. "The Uncalculated Risk," (The Marshall Plan) *Newsweek* (January 5, 1948).

———. "What Are We Trying To Do," (The Marshall Plan) *Newsweek* (February 28, 1949).

———. *Will Dollars Save the World?* New York: D. Appleton-Century Co., Inc., 1947.

Higgs, Robert. *Crisis and Leviathan: Critical Episodes in the Growth of American Government*. New York: Oxford University Press, 1987.

Hobson, J. A. *Richard Cobden: The International Man*. London: Ernest Benn, Ltd. 1968.

Huxley-Blythe, Peter. *The East Came West*. Caldwell, Idaho: The Caxton Printers, 1964.

Hyde, Montgomery. *Room 3603*. New York: Farrar & Straus, 1964.

Irving, David. *Churchill's War*. New York: Avon Books, 1991.

———. *The Destruction of Dresden*. London: William Kimber & Co., Ltd., 1963.

———. *Hitler's War*, 2 Vols. New York: Avon Books, 1990.

Johnson, Daniel M., and Rex R. Campbell. *Black Migration in America: A Social Demographic History*. Durham: Duke University Press, 1981.

Karp, Walter. *The Politics of War: The Story of Two Wars Which Altered Forever the Political Life of the American Republic, 1890–1920*. New York: Harper & Row Publishers, 1979.

Kennedy, David M. *Over Here: The First World War and American Society*. Oxford: Oxford University Press, 1980.

Kimball, Warren F. *Swords or Plowshares? The Morgenthau Plan for Defeated Nazi Germany, 1943–1946*. New York: Lippincott & Co., 1976.

Kimmel, Husband E. *Admiral Kimmel's Story*. Chicago: Henry Regnery Co., 1965.

Kubek, Anthony. *How the Far East Was Lost: American Policy and the Creation of Communist China, 1941–1949*. Chicago: Henry Regnery Co., 1963.

Layton, Edward T. *"And I Was There": Pearl Harbor and Midway—Breaking the Secrets*. New York: William Morrow and Co., 1985.

Liggio, Leonard. *Why the Futile Crusade?* [1965] New York: Center for Libertarian Studies, 1978.

——— and James J. Martin, ed. *Watershed of Empire: Essays on New Deal Foreign Diplomacy*. Colorado Springs, Colo.: Ralph Myles Publisher, Inc., 1976.

Manly, Chesley. *The Twenty-Year Revolution, from Roosevelt to Eisenhower*. Chicago: Henry Regnery Co., 1954.

Marks, Frederick W., III. *Wind Over Sand: The Diplomacy of Franklin Roosevelt*. Athens: The University of Georgia Press, 1988.

Marshall, Jonathan. *To Have and Have Not: Southeast Asian Raw Materials and the Origins of the Pacific War*. Berkeley: University of California Press, 1995.

Martin, James J. *American Liberalism and World Politics, 1931–1941: Liberalism's Press and Spokesmen on the Road Back to War Between Mukden and Pearl Harbor*, 2 Vols. New York: The Devin-Adair Co., 1964.

———. *Beyond Pearl Harbor: Essays on Some Historical Consequences of the Crisis in the Pacific in 1941*. Little Current, Ontario: Plowshare Press, 1981.

———. *Revisionist Viewpoints: Essays in a Dissident Historical Tradition*. Colorado Springs, Colo.: Ralph Myles Publisher, Inc., 1971.

———. *The Saga of Hog Island and Other Essays in Inconvenient History*. Colorado Springs, Colo.: Ralph Myles Publisher, Inc., 1977.

Miller, Stuart Creighton. *"Benevolent Assimilation": The American Conquest of the Philippines, 1899–1903*. New Haven, Conn.: Yale University Press

Millis, Walter. *The Martial Spirit*. Cambridge, Mass.: Literary Guild of America 1931.

———. *Road to War: America, 1914–1917.* New York: Houghton Mifflin, 1935.

Milsche, F. O. *Unconditional Surrender.* London: Faber and Faber, Ltd., 1952.

Mises, Ludwig von. *Liberalism, in the Classical Tradition* [1927]. Irvington-on-Hudson, N.Y.: The Foundation for Economic Education, 1985.

———. *Nation, State, and Economy: Contributions to the Politics and History of Our Time* [1919]. New York: New York University Press, 1983.

———. *Omnipotent Government: The Rise of the Total State and Total War.* New Haven, Conn.: Yale University Press, 1944.

———. *Socialism, An Economic and Sociological Analysis* [1922; rev. 3rd ed., 1951]. Indianapolis, Ind.: Liberty Classics, 1981.

Morgenstern, George. *Pearl Harbor: The Story of the Secret War.* New York: The Devin-Adair Co., 1947.

Morley, Felix. "Democracy and Empire," in *Freedom and Federalism* [1959]. Indianapolis, Ind.: Liberty Press, 1981.

Neumann, William L. *After Victory: Churchill, Roosevelt, Stalin and the Making of the Peace.* New York: Harper & Row, Publishers, 1967.

———. *America Encounters Japan: From Perry to MacArthur.* Baltimore: The Johns Hopkins Press, 1963.

———. *Making the Peace.* Chicago, Henry Regnery Co., 1948.

Nisbet, Robert. *The Present Age: Progress and Anarchy in Modern America.* New York: Harper & Row, 1988.

———. *Roosevelt and Stalin: The Failed Courtship.* Washington, D.C.: Regnery Gateway, 1988.

Nock, Albert Jay. *The Myth of a Guilty Nation.* New York: B. W. Huebsch, Inc., 1922.

Peterson, H. C. *Propaganda for War.* Oklahoma City: University of Oklahoma Press, 1939.

Polakoff, Keith I. *Political Parties in American History.* New York: Alfred A. Knopf, 1981.

Ponting, Clive. *Churchill.* London: Sinclair-Stevenson, 1994.

Radosh, Ronald. *Prophets on the Right: Conservative Critics of American Globalism.* New York: Simon & Schuster, 1975.

Raimondo, Justin. *Reclaiming the American Right: The Lost Legacy of the Conservative Movement.* Burlingame, Calif.: The Center for Libertarian Studies, 1993.

Rand, Ayn. *The Romantic Manifesto,* rev. ed. New York: Signet, 1975.

———. "The Roots of War," in *Capitalism: The Unknown Ideal.* New York: The New American Library, Inc., 1967.

Ravenal, Earl C. *Never Again: Learning from America's Foreign Policy Failures.* Philadelphia: Temple University Press, 1975.

Regnery, Henry. "Revisionism—World War II," in *Memoirs of a Dissident Publisher.* Chicago: Regnery Books, 1985.

Reiners, Ludwig. *The Lights Went Out in Europe.* New York: Pantheon Books, 1956.

Riddle, Wesley Allen. "War and Individual Liberty in American History," in *Leviathan at War*, ed. Edmund A. Opitz. Irvington, N.Y.: The Foundation for Economic Education, 1995.

Robbins, Lionel. *The Economic Causes of War* [1939]. New York: Howard Fertig, 1968.

Rothbard, Murray N. "The Foreign Policy of the Old Right," *Journal of Libertarian Studies* (Winter 1978).

———. "War, Peace and the State," in *Egalitarianism as a Revolt Against Nature and Other Essays.* Washington, D.C.: Libertarian Review Press, 1974.

Rummel, R. J. *Death by Government.* New Brunswick, N.J.: Transaction Books, 1994.

Rusbridger, James, and Eric Nave. *Betrayal at Pearl Harbor: How Churchill Lured Roosevelt into World War II.* New York: Summit Books, 1991.

Russett, Bruce M. *No Clear and Present Danger: A Skeptical View of the United States Entry into World War II.* New York: Harper Torchbooks, 1972.

Sanborn, Frederic R. *Design for War: A Study of Secret Power Politics, 1937–1941.* New York: The Devin-Adair Co., 1951.

Sanders, James D., Mark A. Sauter, and R. Cort Kirkwood. *Soldiers of Misfortune: Washington's Secret Betrayal of American POW's in the Soviet Union.* Washington, D.C.: National Press Books, 1992.

Schaffer, Ronald. *America in the Great War: The Rise of the War Welfare State.* Oxford: Oxford University Press, 1991.

Shogan, Robert. *Hard Bargain: How FDR Twisted Churchill's Arm, Evaded the Law and Changed the Role of the American Presidency.* New York: Scribner, 1995.

Silberner, Edmund. *The Problem of War in Nineteenth Century Economic Thought* [1946]. New York: Garland Publishing, Inc., 1972.

Skates, John Ray. *The Invasion of Japan: Alternative to the Bomb.* Columbia: University of South Carolina Press, 1995.

Spencer, Herbert. *Facts and Comments* [1902]. Freeport, N.Y.: Books for Libraries Press, 1970.

Staley, Eugene. *Foreign Investment and War.* Chicago: University of Chicago Press, 1935.

———. *War and the Private Investor* [1935]. New York: Howard Fertig, 1967.

Standley, William H., and Arthur A. Ageton. *Admiral Ambassador to Russia.* Chicago: Henry Regnery Co., 1955.

Stenehjem, Michele Flynn. *An American First: John T. Flynn and the America First Committee.* New Rochelle, N.Y.: Arlington House, Publishers, 1976.

Stoler, Mark A., and Marshall True. *Explorations in American History,* Vol. 2. New York: Alfred A. Knopf, 1987.

Sulzbach, Walter. *"Capitalistic Warmongers": A Modern Superstition.* Chicago: University of Chicago Press, 1942.

————. *National Consciousness.* Washington, D.C.: American Council of Public Affairs, 1943.

Sumner, William Graham. *War and Other Essays* [1911]. Freeport, N.Y.: Books for Libraries Press, 1970.

Suvorov, Viktor. *Icebreaker: Who Started the Second World War?* London: Hamish Hamilton, 1990.

Swanwick, H. M. *Collective Insecurity.* London: Jonathan Cape, Ltd., 1937.

Tansill, Charles Callan. *America Goes to War.* New York: Little, Brown and Co., 1938.

————. *Back Door to War: The Roosevelt Foreign Policy, 1933–1941.* Chicago: Henry Regnery Co., 1952.

Taylor, A. J. P. *The Origins of the Second World War.* New York: Atheneum, 1961.

Theobald, Robert A. *The Final Secret of Pearl Harbor: The Washington Contribution to the Japanese Attack.* Old Greenwich, Conn.: The Devin-Adair Co., 1954.

Thomas, Hugh. *Armed Truce: The Beginnings of the Cold War, 1945–1946.* New York: Atheneum, 1987.

Thompson, Robert Smith. *A Time for War: Franklin D. Roosevelt and the Path to Pearl Harbor.* New York: Prentice Hall Press, 1991.

Toland, John. *Adolf Hitler,* 2 Vols. Garden City, N.Y.: Doubleday & Co., Inc., 1976.

————. *Infamy: Pearl Harbor and Its Aftermath.* Garden City, N.Y.: Doubleday & Co., Inc., 1982.

————. *The Last 100 Days.* New York: Random House, 1965.

————. *The Rising Sun: The Decline and Fall of the Japanese Empire, 1936–1945.* New York: Random House, 1970.

Tolly, Kemp. *Cruise of the Lanikai: To Provoke the Pacific War* [1973]. Dallas, Tex.: Admiral Nimitz Foundation, 1994.

Tolstoy, Nikolai. *The Secret Betrayal.* New York: Charles Scribner, 1978.

Topitsch, Ernst. *Stalin's War: A Radical New Theory of the Origins of the Second World War.* New York: St. Martin's Press, 1987.

Utley, Freda. *The China Story.* Chicago: Henry Regnery Co., 1951.

————. *The High Cost of Vengeance.* Chicago: Henry Regnery Co., 1949.

Vagts, Alfred. *A History of Militarism, Civilian and Military.* London: Hollis and Carter, 1969.

373

Veale, F. J. P. *Advance to Barbarism: The Development of Total Warfare*. New York: The Devin-Adair Co., 1968.

———. *Crimes Discreetly Veiled*. New York: The Devin-Adair Co., 1959.

Waller, George M., ed. *Pearl Harbor: Roosevelt and the Coming of the War*. Boston: D. C. Heath & Co., 1953.

Wedemeyer, Albert C. *Wedemeyer Reports!* New York: Henry Holt & Co., 1958.

Wittmer, Felix. *The Yalta Betrayal*. Caldwell, Idaho: The Caxton Printers, Ltd., 1953.

Wormser, Rene. *Conservatively Speaking*. Mendham, N.J.: Wayne E. Dorland Co., 1979.

———. *The Myth of the Good and Bad Nations*. Chicago: Henry Regnery Co., 1954.

Zayas, Alfred-Maurice de. *Nemesis at Potsdam: The Expulsion of the Germans from the East*. Lincoln: University of Nebraska Press, 1989.

———. *A Terrible Revenge: The Ethnic Cleansing of the Eastern European Germans, 1944–1950*. New York: St. Martin's Press, 1994.

Index